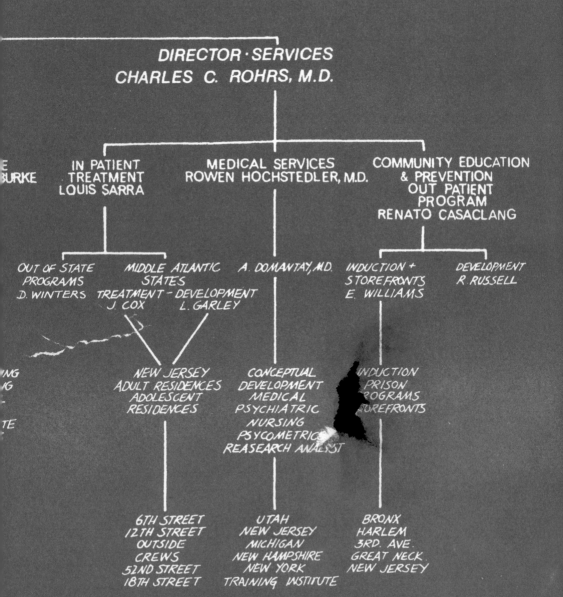

CTORS
LEVIN, ESQ.

CTOR
EN·GERBER

DIRECTOR·SERVICES
CHARLES C. ROHRS, M.D.

IN PATIENT TREATMENT LOUIS SARRA	MEDICAL SERVICES ROWEN HOCHSTEDLER, M.D.	COMMUNITY EDUCATION & PREVENTION OUT PATIENT PROGRAM RENATO CASACLANG

BURKE

OUT OF STATE PROGRAMS D. WINTERS	MIDDLE ATLANTIC STATES TREATMENT – DEVELOPMENT J. COX L. GARLEY	A. DOMANTAY, M.D.	INDUCTION + STOREFRONTS E. WILLIAMS	DEVELOPMENT R. RUSSELL

NG
G

TE

NEW JERSEY
ADULT RESIDENCES
ADOLESCENT
RESIDENCES

CONCEPTUAL
DEVELOPMENT
MEDICAL
PSYCHIATRIC
NURSING
PSYCOMETRICS
REASEARCH ANALYST

INDUCTION
PRISON
PROGRAMS
STOREFRONTS

6TH STREET
12TH STREET
OUTSIDE
CREWS
52ND STREET
18TH STREET

UTAH
NEW JERSEY
MICHIGAN
NEW HAMPSHIRE
NEW YORK
TRAINING INSTITUTE

BRONX
HARLEM
3RD. AVE.
GREAT NECK
NEW JERSEY

BY JUDIANNE DENSEN-GERBER, J.D., M.D.

DRUGS, SEX, PARENTS AND YOU (with her daughter, Trissa Austin Baden)
WE MAINLINE DREAMS The Odyssey House Story

We Mainline Dreams

JUDIANNE DENSEN-GERBER, J.D., M.D.

We Mainline Dreams

THE ODYSSEY HOUSE STORY

DOUBLEDAY & COMPANY, INC.

GARDEN CITY, NEW YORK

1973

Book design by M. F. Gazze
Library of Congress Catalog Card Number 72–89302
ISBN: 0-385-00371-4
Copyright © 1973 by Judianne Densen-Gerber, J.D., M.D.
All Rights Reserved
Printed in the United States of America
First Edition

74-11461

Grateful acknowledgment is made to the following for permission to reprint their material:

"New York City's Drug Death Rise in Year of the Ostrich" by Jean Dietz, July 5, 1970, issue of the Boston *Globe*. Reprinted through the courtesy of the Boston *Globe*.

"The Inquiring Fotographers," May 4, 1972, Copyright © 1972 by the New York *News;* "Odyssey House Offers to Aid Children," August 2, 1970; "Lease on Hope for Addicts," March 1970; Photograph "He's On Dope to Be One of the Boys," February 27, 1970, copyright © 1970 by the New York *News;* photograph "City Drug Scene Rated a Shocker by U. S. Aides," July 4, 1971, copyright © 1971 by the New York *News*. Articles and photographs appeared in various issues of the New York *News*. Reprinted by permission of the Chicago Tribune-New York News Syndicate, Inc.

Photograph by Jack Robinson from *Vogue*, Copyright © 1970 by The Condé Nast Publications, Inc. Reproduced by permission of the publisher.

"President's Drug Plan Assailed," June 24, 1971, issue of Lawrence *Eagle-Tribune*. Reprinted by permission of the publisher.

"Here a Place That Makes You Want to Come Back," by Victoria Pellegrino, August 1970 issue of *Pageant*. Reprinted by permission of Pageant Magazine, © 1970.

"Who Cares About Drug Abuse?" February 2, 1970 (Editorial); "Odyssey House Director Favors Compulsory Curing of Addicts," January 11, 1972; "Care Center Chief Sees 100,000 Child Addicts Here by Summer," January 25, 1970; "Metropolitan Briefs: 'City Starts New Drug Drive,'" March 29, 1972; and photograph of Odyssey House Choir. Articles and photograph appeared in the New York *Times*. Copyright © 1970/1972 by The New York Times Company. Reprinted by permission of the publisher.

Memorandum dated June 22, 1967, from Oliver Pilat. Reprinted by permission.

"A Process Leading to Solutions," April 21, 1971, Rocky Mountain News. Reprinted by permission.

Portions of Jack Anderson's column, December 1, 1971, New York *Post*. Reprinted through the courtesy of United Feature Syndicate.

The following are credits for the photos appearing on the indicated pages:

Bradford Bachrach—frontis, 402
Michael Baden—pp. 349(top), 351, 352, 353, 387
Judianne Densen-Gerber—p. 349(bottom)
Copyright © 1968 by Pat Goggins—p. 95
Bernard Goldsmith—pp. 76, 115, 205, 223, 224, 258, 289, 291, 309
Neil Kitagawa—pp. 4, 28, 32, 43, 63, 89, 135, 143, 158, 159, 237, 311, 325
Manchester (N.H.) *Union-Leader*—p. 269
Fred Marcus—pp. 395, 385(bottom)
New York *Times*—p. 18
Courtesy Odyssey House, New York—pp. 196, 240, 293, 306, 318, 385(top)
Courtesy Odyssey House, Utah—p. 287(top)
Courtesy Governor Nelson Rockefeller's Office—p. 27
Deborah Stevens—p. 141
Courtesy of the Suffolk County Police Department—p. 155
U. S. Department of Defense—p. 272
From *Vogue* (photo by Jack Robinson)—p. 398
Rocky Walton—p. 7
Margaret Williams—p. 317
John Warren Wright Studio—p. 264

To all our enemies—

for without the constant struggle,

we would not have grown

and

To all our friends—

because they are part of the odyssey

Contents

Acknowledgments

First to June Callwood who for a period of a year traveled the Odyssey with us not as an observer but as an active participant and contributor. She ably sifted through a myriad of tapes, articles, notes and thoughts to give me the framework upon which to build this book.

Second to Lisa Drew, the Editor from Doubleday who stimulated us to do this book, who spent tireless uncomplaining hours helping to correct the manuscript and choosing the pertinent items from years of squirreled memorabilia. She quickly moved from the status of stranger to friend.

Third to Michael Baden and Carol Sarra a little bit for the creative time they devoted to this book but mostly for just being themselves, always giving endless support and comfort to whatever task is at hand.

Fourth to all of the Odyssey House Staff who have struggled along with me to build the agency and who have laughed and cried over, criticized and approved the pages of this book.

Fifth to Frederick Cohen, John Cox, James Murphy, Charles Rohrs and Louis Sarra who were willing to openly and honestly share with me and all the readers their personal odysseys.

And lastly to the readers for their interest in us and for their comments which we hope will be sent to us at Odyssey House 208–210 East 18th Street, New York, New York 10003.

I welcome letters for it is my firm belief that to grow and develop one must dialogue with life and other people—our Odyssey commitment is that "we see ourselves best in the eyes of our brothers."

Welcome.

Judianne Densen-Gerber, J.D., M.D.

June 1972

Introduction

Odyssey House headquarters is a double building on East Sixth Street in New York City around the corner from the seedy Fillmore East Theater and in the heart of an area where young people dressed like hippies shoot heroin in their veins and carry knives.

Odyssey House is also a 1920s tourist lodge in the graceful town of Hampton, New Hampshire, where green lawns roll under old trees and sidewalk slabs are tilted from the root growth underneath.

Odyssey House is also a 125-year-old Landmark townhouse on West 12th Street in Manhattan that once was owned by General Winfield Scott, a hero of the Mexican War; and it's a store on a Harlem street where the stench of vomit and urine and garbage is choking; and it's a remodeled apartment house in Salt Lake City, Utah, a mansion in the dying heart of Newark, New Jersey, and an average American home in Flint, Michigan.

In all of these locations—thirty-three of them spread over six states —one of the country's best drug addiction programs is flourishing. It's a tough-minded, structured psychiatric therapeutic community that works for more than 80 per cent of the addict patients who remain past the first six weeks. It is most effective with addicts who *don't want* treatment but must stay in Odyssey because the courts have sent them there, thereby putting an end to the myth that an addict must seek treatment himself in order for it to be successful.

Odyssey believes in accountability. The three or four hundred residents in treatment at any one time in the Odyssey facilities are held responsible for their actions. It is considered a betrayal of their potential to do otherwise. Accountability is part of getting addicts well. The fundamental cause of most addiction is an inability to think in terms of consequences.

The agency itself is zealously accountable. The finances are reviewed twice a year by an outside audit, the residents are required to give up urine daily for examination by an independent laboratory for the presence of drugs, and the statistics gathering and case files are mountainous.

Odyssey doesn't consider drug addiction the whole problem. Its goal is more than the cure of addiction: It aims to treat the underlying emotional problem of the addict, which usually is dependency and a sense of futility. Unlike many other drug-treatment programs, it seeks to return its residents to the community. Most do return, and many of them now are businessmen, military heroes, secretaries, executives.

Most of this is the work of an unusual woman, Judianne Densen-Gerber Baden, winner of multiple Women of the Year awards, who by the time she was thirty-three had a degree in medicine, specializing in psychiatry, and another in law. She was married to Dr. Michael Baden, Deputy Chief Medical Examiner of New York City, had four children—out of six pregnancies—one of whom had died. She had started Odyssey House with seventeen addicts and a bankroll of $3.82. She was the scourge of all administrators and politicians who didn't respond effectively and quickly to a demonstrated need, particularly if those in need were children.

It is inadequate to say that she *cares* about children; her feeling is closer to reverence.

It was Judianne Densen-Gerber who took a children's choir composed entirely of former drug users to Washington to sing for the Congress. It was Judianne Densen-Gerber who went to court to defend herself against a charge that she had committed the crime of treating *too many* children. It was Judianne Densen-Gerber who put a slum-stunted, twelve-year-old, former heroin-addicted boy on her lap to testify before a state Legislative hearing on the problems of youth and drugs. This action moved New York State to pass a bill appropriating $65 million to treat child addicts.

Early in 1971 Doubleday undertook to explore the possibility that some of the zest and agony and outrage and splendor of Judi and Odyssey could be captured in a book. The editors visited one of the regular Tuesday executive staff meetings and came away dazed by the tumult of cheers, curses, orations, tears, interruptions, irrelevancies, incisiveness, humor and *eating* that accompanies dedicated problem-solving at Odyssey.

Dr. Densen-Gerber was agreeable to do a book, providing it was existential. She didn't want a chronicle of Odyssey's five-year history; that was over. She didn't want a book about herself; that was

xvi

nonsense. Waving her hand inclusively at the room full of lounging, amused staff, she said, "It should be about *all of us!*"

This book attempts to meet that extraordinary condition. It is stuffed with Odyssey House memorabilia: clippings, posters, memos, directives, snapshots, correspondence. The chapters are distilled from more than a hundred hours of tapes taken during meetings, marathons and group therapy sessions that lasted four or five hundred hours. It's untidy but real.

There are six principle figures in the book: Judi herself; James Murphy, second-in-command to Judi, and now Director of Odyssey, a former heroin addict who in 1970 was asked by Washington to chair the drug committee of the White House Conference on Youth; Dr. Charles Rohrs, the other Director, a laborer's son who re-thought some of his views about the welfare state after he joined Odyssey's staff; Frederick Cohen, a brilliant college dropout facing a possible thirty years in prison for drug trafficking when he came to Odyssey, who, twenty-three months later, as Associate Director of Expansion, was in the office of the Secretary of Defense presenting a military addiction treatment program; Louis Sarra, formerly of the Mafia, with fifteen years of heroin addiction behind him, who became Associate Director and head of the treatment of several hundred residents; John Cox, who mugged people in Harlem to get money for heroin and two years later was Assistant Director of Odyssey and administrator of two and a half million dollars worth of Odyssey property.

The book on Odyssey was not so much written as shuffled, and reshuffled by June Callwood. In the end, it was edited by her and the six Odyssey people directly concerned, along with Lisa Drew, a Doubleday editor, proving that an animal designed by a committee does not invariably have the head of a donkey, the legs of an ostrich, the body of a tiger and the tail of a crocodile.

June 1972   June Callwood
                                                        Toronto

ON ODYSSEY

Once in the life time of man, comes the return of reality, for there is no escape, there is no seclusion, and there are no unanswerable questions.

There is, however, the confounding attempt which makes the difficult seem impossible, and the impossible, fantasy.

In Odyssey House, the time has come for the search of inner self. It is now realized that man must openly confront his past in order to grow and face the future. He must realize that the shadow of the past is just that. Then, and only then, can the future be no longer a wish. And Reality is no longer feared. And, that there is no shame in error, as long as it is understood that in error comes knowledge, and in knowledge, the beginning step of man.

—TOMMY MOTT
Ex-addict, former resident
of Odyssey House

We Mainline Dreams

The Trial

The trial of the City of New York versus Dr. Judianne Densen-Gerber, me, the Executive Director of Odyssey House, finally took place on April 15, 1971, about a year and a half after I had been charged with an offense arising out of treating too many heroin-addicted children in overcrowded conditions.

The summons said I had violated the City Building Code, which certainly was true. The building in question, located in the most blighted and lawless part of the Bronx, had been approved as a residence for nine nuns. At the time of the summons, the building inspector counted thirty-two children living there. If he had come by a little later, he would have found sixty-four.

I had a lawyer who insisted that I plead not guilty. He intended to cite a century-old provision in the law which declares that in some situations an illegal act is justified.

The Thoreau-like ancestor who wrote that one into the books must have anticipated a case such as mine. I was looking forward to explaining on the witness stand that the reason the children were crowded into the building was because there was no place else for them to find help in the entire state of New York. Just about the time I was being served with the summons, the New York State Narcotics Addiction Control Commission was assuring the public that it knew of only twenty-eight cases of heroin-addicted children. It was a strange pronouncement at that time: 224 teen-agers died of heroin overdose in New York City in 1969.

Odyssey House has several imperatives concerning man's responsibility to his fellow man. One of them is that we never turn away anyone who wants help: We *had* to treat the children addicts. More was on the line than the possibility I would be fined heavily or sent to jail, leaving my three young children without their mother. Not only was I, as a psychiatrist and lawyer, risking censure from two stern professional organizations, but Odyssey's future was put in jeopardy by our treating children without official permission. All of our facilities could be closed down.

But faced with a city full of addicted and dying children with no one to help them, I had no choice. In the autumn of 1966 Odyssey House began with just that kind of moral decision. Seventeen hard-core heroin addicts told me, a green and decidedly naïve psychiatric resident, that they wanted to get well. They meant completely well: no maintenance on some socially accepted substitute drug like metha-done or cyclazocine, no lifelong dependence on a community of ex-addicts, no crutches of any kind. They meant the real thing: independent, full-functioning human beings, cured of addiction.

Working in the drug field wasn't at all what I planned to do with my life. I had intended to be a sedate professor of Forensic Medicine at some safe status university. As with many career women who are concerned about keeping a good marriage and raising happy children, I was seeking a job option that would allow ample time for my family. In addition, I am a member of The Establishment. Part of my background is rich, lifelong Republican and more than slightly right wing.

Yet I agreed, reluctantly, to link my future with seventeen junkies because I had promised them that if they truly wanted to get well, I, as their doctor, would help them. I couldn't break my word.

In part, I had made that reckless promise because I found that I related personally to the loneliness and isolation of the addict. In my early thirties I was learning some things about myself through identification with them. In a sense, we were all—the seventeen addicts and I—on a journey together through changes, an odyssey; hence the name Odyssey House.

Eventually, we proved that drug addiction is curable; cure had been said to be impossible. Odyssey has treated thousands of addicts. It has spread into six states. We use many techniques, some of them borrowed and some invented, to develop a psychiatric therapeutic community.

As Odyssey grew, we necessarily came into contact with all levels of government. Meeting our politicians has been a profoundly desolating experience. Too few, but these give us hope, are responsible people. The best I can say about most of them is that they are incompetent on all levels except game playing. Unfortunately, many are corrupt and ruthless and a few are thoroughly nasty individuals. They and we who vote for them are destroying this wonderful country.

It was this kind of powerful city politician who attacked me, placing conformity to a building code above the lives of children. The summons was designed to shut me up. I had become an embarrassment to the Lindsay Administration.

The so-called crime in question took place in the Hunt's Point section of the Bronx, also known as "Little Calcutta." It is believed by many to be the worst urban slum in the United States. You shouldn't miss it when touring New York City, Fun City, if you want to get the strong, juicy flavor of Mayor John V. Lindsay's Administration. Along with Harlem, Hunt's Point has the highest rate of homicide and narcotics use in the City. Eighty-five per cent of all deaths in one section of Hunt's Point are from unnatural causes.

It isn't safe to walk down Fox or Tiffany streets in the daylight. Police will not foot-patrol there. The schools are wrecked and some classrooms have no teachers because they are too afraid of the students. Children have died right in the classrooms from drug overdose.

If you roll up the car windows and lock the doors, you can drive through the streets. While sight-seeing, look at the secondhand stores where almost all the stock is stolen goods. Many of the men and women slumped in the rubbish on the sidewalks are alcoholics and/or heroin addicts, nodding after a fix. Eighty per cent of the adult population is one or the other, or both.

You'll note that most of the windows in the tenements are broken. The buildings have the appearance of being bombed out and abandoned, yet people live in them at a density of three thousand per block. Almost all are either Puerto Rican or Black. Seventy-five per cent are on welfare, half of them move from one place to another within this jungle every year.

Most poignant of all, exuberant, doomed children spill laughing through the rotted doorways and play catch joyfully in the street. Children make up 67 per cent of the population.

Through archways you can see the central courtyards behind the buildings, where raw garbage is piled fourteen feet deep. Everywhere there are fat rats. There is a simple way of getting rid of garbage in Hunt's Point. It is thrown out of windows: "air mail."

People whose apartments border on this neighborhood have triple locks and long metal bars on their doors. Their halls are guarded by killer dogs trained to go for the jugular. Without such protection, addicts would strip the rooms to the bare walls and beyond. They even take the plumbing pipes.

This is the gracious locale where in October 1969 Odyssey opened a treatment facility in an empty church building, only to be served, a few months later, with a summons, which in that neighborhood is

ludicrous. It's doubtful that the Building Department had ever issued a summons there in its entire history. Certainly there were no proper forms at hand; the summons was written on a parking ticket and issued to the house mother of the unit. Later I was to be substituted as the defendant.

When the press reported the issuing of the summons, All Souls Unitarian Universalist Church, our family's church where my Husband is a member of the Board of Trustees, asked the distinguished Arthur Goldberg, a former United States Supreme Court Justice, to defend me. He agreed. Mr. Justice Goldberg later turned the case over to Theodore Sorensen and Edward Costikyan, two members of his law firm, Paul Weiss, Goldberg, Rifkind, Wharton and Garrison. Mr. Costikyan actually did most of the preparation of the case and acted at my trial. He is an influential figure in New York State's Democratic Party and one of the nation's greatest trial lawyers, a man of winning mildness and courtesy with a tough, brilliant, stalking mind.

The fee to me, if his firm had charged one, which it didn't, would have been over $20,000.

On that April day of the trial, we had a bizarre situation: The awesome Edward Costikyan appearing in a case involving a Building Code violation in a nondescript Bronx courthouse. In addition to this improbability, there were also two startling witnesses waiting to testify on my behalf, the District Attorney for Queens, Thomas Mackell, and Dr. Beny Primm, the Director of one of New York City's major methadone-maintenance programs. The press was also there, from the New York *Times* to the *Village Voice*. Television camera crews waited outside.

We *all* waited, while the court went about its normal business of

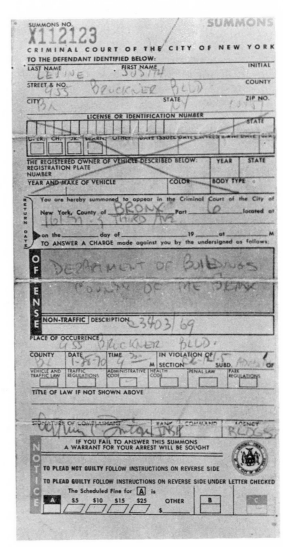

hearing small domestic disputes, neighbors fighting over the placement of garbage cans, a wife annoyed by surveillance from a separated husband, insults—"You know what she call me? A crazy! And she is a stool pigeon for the landlord!" The Judge, Jerome Kidder, urbane and relaxed, handed out poor-man fines; one dollar, two dollars.

This continued through the drowsy morning and past the recess. The courthouse was located in a tired, tacky neighborhood of disconsolate bars and shoe stores displaying bargains in bushel baskets. Our courtroom was on the second floor, a large plain room unadorned except for the flag and a plaque, IN GOD WE TRUST. Tall narrow windows were open to counteract the stuffiness, letting in a soft spring breeze and an assault of trucks, sirens and horns. Much of the testimony was inaudible beyond the first few rows.

Nevertheless, the benches were filled. Odyssey House was out in force. Many of the staff were there, the assured ex-addicts and professionals indistinguishable from one another. The Odyssey House Choir arrived by bus, all of them dressed in glee club crested navy blazers or jumpers, pale blue shirts or blouses, well-pressed trousers or skirts. Residents of the South Bronx building arrived next, the younger girls wearing bobbysocks.

They filed in quietly, found places to sit without confusion and watched, attentive and composed, regardless of whether they could hear or not. They resembled well-behaved students from a good school who had come on a field trip designed to give them a brushing knowledge of the seamier side of life. However, one of the girls had been a prostitute at the age of twelve and one of the boys had been a killer before he was eighteen. Most of the Odyssey residents were former drug addicts.

I turned to look at them with pride, and those who caught my eye beamed back assuringly at me. Most of them had been in court themselves and had been found guilty. I was aware that they were identifying with me, standing before a Judge, and knew how frightened I felt.

My case came up shortly after the morning recess. Costikyan, a precise, unremarkable-looking man, advanced his argument. "It is a little unusual that we are relying on a section of the criminal code that is rarely, if ever, invoked," he began in his mild voice. The defense conceded, he said, that there were more people in residence at 955 Bruckner Boulevard in the Bronx than were permitted by the Certificate of Occupancy, but it would demonstrate that there was justification.

The Judge leisurely read the section that had been cited and appeared unimpressed. He pointed out that "imminent private in-

Child who used drugs five years
before coming to Odyssey House at the age of sixteen.

jury" or "imminent public injury" must be proven in order to enter a claim of justification. Costikyan replied that he would do so: There was public injury because people were endangered by untreated addicts who spread their addiction, and there was private injury because individual children were dying of drugs. The Judge was skeptical. The overcrowded building, he said, presented both health and fire hazards, which perhaps were an even greater risk to children.

"If the alternative were to keep these children on the street, which it was," said Costikyan crisply, "then the risk of fire is the lesser one."

The Judge shook his head. "If a philanthropic and well-meaning group of citizens wished to find a place for these narcotic addicts," he said, "I'm sure they could find more suitable premises."

"There was no place in New York City," replied Costikyan firmly. "The Church ripped open the doors and said, 'Take this building.' There was *no other place*." The Judge sighed and said he would have to hear the circumstances before coming to a decision.

The only witness for the prosecution was the Department of Buildings inspector who had counted the inhabitants at Bruckner Boulevard. A beefy man whose face was marbled with burst blood vessels, he kept referring to his notebook while testifying. His tone was ponderous and righteous, a man just doing his job. Which he was.

He described the building as a three-story, non-fireproof structure with seven bedrooms, certified for an occupancy of nine members of a religious order. When he inspected the premises, he counted thirty-two persons living there. The sleeping arrangements were triple-tiered bunk beds, under which additional mattresses or pallets were stored, to be pulled out into the floor space at night.

This completed the case for the prosecution. Mr. Milton F. Tingling, from the office of New York City Corporation Counsel, sat down and awaited developments.

The defense first called Thomas J. Mackell, handsome, white-haired, tanned, his eyes humorous under dramatic black brows. He identified himself as District Attorney for Queens County in New York State since 1967 and previously a State Senator for twelve years. The Judge smiled warmly at him. They had greeted one another and chatted during the recess.

Mackell's witness-box style reminded me of William Jennings Bryan. As I listened, I felt comforted. Resonantly and with great concern, he described the spread of addiction among adolescents in 1969 and 1970. He declared that statistics alone can't reveal the number of youngsters who won't reach adulthood, the men and women crippled for life, the sorrow of the parents. He testified that Dr.

Stanley Yolles of the National Institute of Mental Health had reported that there were eighteen thousand addicts in a forty-block area of Central Harlem. These addicts represented almost half the total resident population. One third of them were between the ages of sixteen and twenty-one, two thousand addicts were younger than sixteen. He added that there was a direct relationship between crime and addiction.

"What facilities were available in the City of New York in January 1970 to treat those children?" asked Costikyan.

"None," replied Mackell promptly. "Except those provided by Odyssey House."

The Judge was amazed. "What did you do when they came into your court?" he asked.

Mackell explained that the family courts, which hear cases involving juveniles, could refer those who wished to be treated nowhere except Odyssey House.

"Do you know of other places than Odyssey House?" the Judge persisted.

"I know of none on a residential basis."

In the hush that followed, Costikyan asked if addicted children created a risk of public injury.

"Serious and grave," nodded Mackell.

The Judge tried another tack. "Forty people at Odyssey House doesn't make much of a dent in the problem, does it? A drop in the bucket, am I right?"

Mackell replied with dignity that it was worth it if one life was saved.

"If five thousand are not inoculated against the disease and you inoculate twenty, you do not make much inroad . . ." the Judge began.

"Confucius says that the longest journey begins with a single step," Mackell told him imperturbably.

"Nobody quarrels with the fact that Odyssey House is doing a very worthy thing," said the Judge, getting up, stretching, walking around his raised platform for a few steps and then resuming his seat. "But the statute reads 'imminent public injury or imminent private injury.'"

Mackell's reply was an explanation of the high risk to the individual and to the public from untreated addicts on the streets. He spoke warmly of Odyssey's treatment method.

The Judge was still questioning. "Do you argue that the desirability of having treatment is so great that it justifies using a building that is a fire trap?"

"Yes," said the Queens District Attorney without hestitation.

During the lunch adjournment that followed, reporters clustered around Mackell. They asked him to enlarge on his testimony concerning the government's lack of response to drug problems. He did so with fluent ease. He was on depressingly familiar ground.

Odyssey House residents waited quietly while someone located a pizza restaurant nearby where they could be fed cheaply. On their way out one of the television crews asked them to line up on the steps of the courthouse and pose with Tom Mackell in the front row. They did so, delighted and grinning in the thin April sunshine.

I ate veal and peppers, I remember. I felt grateful that the facts of the drug situation in New York City were being aired at last. But I had just learned that there would be a serious omission in establishing the record of the government's neglect because Dr. Primm would not be available to testify. Apologizing with genuine distress, he said he was required elsewhere that afternoon. As Director of a drug-treatment program very different from Odyssey's and a respected Black physician, his appearance on our behalf to expertly assess the extent of addiction among children was a vital part of our presentation. His departure depressed me.

When we returned to the courthouse, Father Louis Gigante of St. Athanasius Roman Catholic Church took the stand. He testified that he had rented Odyssey the former nuns' residence on Bruckner Boulevard for a token dollar a year. The building was empty, he explained, and this was intolerable to him because there were an estimated forty-eight thousand drug addicts in that part of the South Bronx with no residential-treatment facilities whatsoever.

"So I broke the door down and turned it over," he said. It was literally true. On the day we took possession Father Gigante hadn't been able to find his keys, so he picked up a hammer and smashed the locks.

Father Gigante is a robust man with silvering dark hair, black-rimmed glasses that give him a scholarly look, a burly body and enormous gusto and impatience. His testimony was delivered in a voice that bounced off the rear walls. He needed little prodding from Costikyan.

He told of a survey of grades five to eight in a small parochial school, the children being between eleven and fourteen years of age. About twenty of them were found to be using drugs, some of them injecting heroin. He was shocked, particularly since this was a highly disciplined school. He could only imagine what must be happening elsewhere. He felt the obligation to do something, so he turned to Odyssey.

10

"Was the addiction of children a risk to the public?" asked Costikyan, his mind on the terms of the statute.

"Certainly," the priest replied. A teen-ager under the influence of drugs had killed someone in his district, a photographer had been killed on the street, two teen-agers had died of drug overdose. He added, "I have no qualms about housing forty, fifty, *sixty* in that building if they are comfortable enough. It was a necessity."

"Was there no place else?" asked the Judge pointedly.

"As far as I know there is still no place for adolescents in the South Bronx. No one was taking care of the kids in the streets. They were just walking around, and an epidemic was beginning to arise because kids were infecting other kids."

The Judge observed mildly that there probably wasn't much point in treating heroin addicts anyway. Father Gigante declared with flashing eyes, "If we save five, or four, or three, or *one,* it's worth it. With Odyssey House, kids have a chance to be better citizens and a possibility of being responsible human beings in the future."

He was a great witness, his clericals a billboard of his piety and self-denial, his manner earnest, outraged, convincing. As the Judge continued to demur about the likelihood of heroin addiction being cured, the priest lost his restraint. He turned abruptly to the rows of spectators in the court and shouted, "Matty, stand up! How long did you use drugs?"

Matthew Ancona jumped instantly to his feet. He's a small, dapper man with a narrow black mustache, shiny black hair that lies flat on his head. A former television cameraman and barbiturate addict who had been sent to Odyssey by Tom Mackell, he had become one of the agency's top executives. He yelled, "I used drugs for seven years and I've been clean for four!"

Before the Judge could recover, Father Gigante roared, "Louie!" and Louis Sarra, sitting some distance from Matty, stood up and shouted back, "I used drugs for fifteen years and I've been clean for five!" Louie has sandy-gray shoulder-length hair, guileless blue eyes, a cracked, high-pitched voice. When he was a teen-ager he carried a loaded gun to school every day; he's now head of treatment at Odyssey House. Father Gigante was scheduled to officiate at Louie's wedding in a few months.

Others were getting to their feet all over the courtroom as the Judge called for order on pain of contempt. Calm was restored quickly. It had been a moment of real splendor. There were no more references from the bench about the hopelessness of heroin addiction.

Our next witness was Bruce Levy, a young architect on the staff of Odyssey House. Bruce did his required field work with us and then stayed on, excited by what we were doing. He crisply described the fire drills held regularly at our Bruckner Boulevard address, the placement of fire extinguishers according to safety regulations, and the public address system available on all floors for fire warnings. There were at least two people on duty and awake all night to make periodic fire runs throughout the building.

Wearing granny glasses and shaggy hair in contrast to his neat business suit, Bruce delivered this information in a decisive, no-nonsense manner and was impressively self-possessed.

As my name was called to testify, my Husband, Dr. Michael Baden, squeezed my hand reassuringly. It is necessary for me to know that whenever I am in difficulty he will be with me. I swore to tell the truth, the whole truth, and nothing but the truth with a feeling of relief that after eighteen months of strain it was almost over. At last, I had an opportunity to explain myself.

I described my professional credentials for the record, my graduation from Columbia University Law School in 1959 and from New York University School of Medicine in 1963. I said I also was a married woman with three children, which is another kind of credential.

There followed a grim recital of the statistics on drug abuse. I used the now-famous Baden formula, developed by my Husband, to estimate the number of people affected. Prior to and including 1968, I told the court, no one under the age of sixteen had died in New York City of drug overdose, and the presumption properly could be made that there were very few child addicts. In 1969, however, there were fifty-five children sixteen and under dead from drugs. Using the Baden formula this mortality figure indicated that there were at least 5,500 to 11,000 living heroin-addicted children.

The New York City Board of Education made a survey of its public schools in 1970 and found that 7 per cent of children in grades nine to twelve were involved in serious drugs. That works out to 35,000 drug-using children in New York City high schools alone.

THE NEW YORK TIMES, SUNDAY, JANUARY 25, 1970

Care-Center Chief Sees 100,000 Child Addicts Here by Summer

By THOMAS F. BRADY

The clinical director of Odyssey House, a therapeutic organization for drug addicts, predicted yesterday that juvenile heroin addition in New York City would rise to 100,000 children by summer.

The director, Dr. Judienne Densen-Gerber, spoke at a seminar for city school teachers at Queens College organized by the Institute for the Advancement of Criminal Justice and financed by the International Telephone and Telegraph Company.

Dr. Densen-Gerber, a lawyer and a psychiatrist, said 224 teen-age deaths from heroin had been reported last year, with 55 of the victims under 16 years of age. The rate this year, she went on, has already risen to one a day.

The "epidemic" began in August and coincided with Operation Intercept, a Federal campaign against marijuana smuggling that drove the price of the relatively harmless drug up to that of heroin and in consequence led many youngsters to try the "main line" narcotic, she said.

Erwin Tobin, director of health and physical education for the city's schools, denounced as "irresponsible" those who advocate the lifting of bans on marijuana, he said also that since September the school system had dropped the age for beginning antinarcotics education from the eighth grade to the fourth grade. He said juvenile drug use was increasing but he gave no figures.

Dr. Densen-Gerber said her estimate was based in part on the known ratio between registered adult narcotics addicts and adult narcotic deaths. She said that in 1968 a total of 60,000 addicts were registered in the city and 600 drug deaths were reported but that only 300 of those who died were among the 60,000 listed.

The deaths, she said, were 1 per cent of those registered, which would mean that there were at least 22,400 juvenile addicts last year for 224 deaths, if the proportion is the same. However, since only 300 of the adults who died were under registry, it would probably be safe to change the ratio to one-half of 1 per cent, she said, which would increase the estimate of juvenile drug addicts to about 45,000 last year. Addiction is increasing, she added, and the juvenile drug death rate is probably lower than that among adult addicts. In consequence, she said, she feared the number of young addicts might reach 100,000 by midyear.

Last week, a private Bronx treatment center for adolescent addicts run by Odyssey House, was ordered vacated because it was in violation of the new Building Code. The center, a former convent in the narcotics-ridden Hunts Point section, has housed as many as 39 child addicts but has a legal occupancy for 9 persons only.

Governor Rockefeller offered Odyssey House 70 beds in the children's center at Creedmoor State Hospital in Queens Village as a substitute, but Odyssey officials turned down the offer.

There are three Odyssey Houses in New York City—one in the Bronx, one in Harlem, and one on the Lower East Side.

Two years later:

Metropolitan Briefs

City Starts New Drug Drive

An intensive antinarcotics campaign aimed at vulnerable "young kids who are not hooked" was disclosed yesterday at City Hall by Mayor Lindsay.

Posters, radio and television spots prepared by Young and Rubicam, the advertising agency, at no cost to the city, were described as "probably the toughest you have ever seen."

The theme, "Don't Join the Living Dead," is carried through in scripts prepared for radio and television, depicting the evils of drugs such as the inexorable drive toward violence, crimes against the person and the heartbreak of a family coping with the addict.

"Prevention," the Mayor said, "is a vital part of the city's war against drug abuse. We have chosen to concentrate in this campaign on the young predrug user — specifically the vulnerable youths from ages 8 to 15."

The Mayor said that it has been estimated that at least 70 per cent of high school students have experimented with drugs; 8 per cent, or 22,000 high school teen-agers, use heroin, and 32,000 use barbiturates and 42,000 use amphetamines.

This appalling ratio was duplicated in the eighteen-year-olds reporting for induction physicals in New York City. The United States Army reported that 7 per cent of them had to be disqualified from service because of intravenous use of drugs.

Some in the courtroom were looking horrified as I unfolded the extent of the problem. Only the Odyssey House residents were unmoved. It was not news to them that thousands of children were addicted to heroin. They are those children.

One medical definition of epidemic is that it can be used whenever 1 per cent of a target population is afflicted by a disease. Therefore, with 7 per cent of school children addicted to drugs, it is appropriate to call addiction an epidemic.

"I saw no addiction in the age group under sixteen from the year 1966, when I began in the drug-addiction field, until the middle of 1969," I informed the court. In June 1969 I saw my first addicted child, and after that date, addiction exploded among children. In the period before the trial, I, personally, had seen between 2,000 and 2,500 addicted children, the youngest of whom was twelve.

Odyssey House was not licensed to treat anyone under the age of sixteen. When distraught parents came to Odyssey for help, we had to turn them away. We also had to advise them that there was no residential treatment available anywhere. The New York State Department of Social Services was paroling child addicts to the streets, some to die of overdoses shortly thereafter.

At the time the summons was served on me, "Albany said the children do not exist," I told the Judge. A spokesman for the New York State Narcotics Addiction Control Commission told the press that the Commission saw no need to start a rehabilitation center for adolescent addicts—the problem didn't warrant it. Yet, I was telling the press that there were about 25,000 child addicts in Harlem, the Bronx and the East Village alone.

In August 1969 my Husband took matters into his own hands, a not-unusual move on his part whenever I am blocked and confused about what I should do. The medical librarian in his office went to Michael and told him brokenheartedly that his fifteen-year-old son was in Youth House, under arrest for possession of narcotics. He learned that the boy was mainlining heroin. He asked Michael if he could persuade me to treat the child. Michael worked out a plan.

They waited until I was out of town visiting our daughter at her summer camp. Michael then telephoned Ellis Williams, the head of Odyssey's induction department, and told him that he was referring a fifteen-year-old boy for admission. Ellis assumed incorrectly that the decision to accept the child and break the law must have come from me. The boy was inducted.

I returned home to find that Odyssey was treating a child, something we had no license for, no funding for, no staff for. But once I saw the child there was no way that the law would force us to put him on the street, as Michael knew so well before he called Ellis. So Odyssey opened its doors. We figured that if we were going to hang for one, we'd hang for them all. Within a month, we admitted forty more children.

In the beginning they slept on bedrolls on the floor of the auditorium in our Mother House, while we mounted a frantic campaign with the City and State to obtain funds and a suitable building for them. As time passed and our appeals all had been rejected, we moved the children into the Bruckner Boulevard residence and supported them with what private donations we could muster.

"How long do you intend to house those children there?" asked the Judge.

"Only as long as there is no other facility," I assured him.

The Judge still didn't accept that the children couldn't be housed elsewhere. Had I really tried to find more suitable quarters?

I reeled off a numbing list of people we had contacted, starting with President Nixon, Governor Rockefeller and Mayor Lindsay, fol-

DAILY ✠ NEWS
NEW YORK'S PICTURE NEWSPAPER ®

NEWS photo by Jack Smith

Deputy Mayor Robert Morgenthau and Dr. Judianne Densen-Gerber are joined by youngsters at Odyssey House press conference.

Lease on Hope for Addicts

By EDWARD BENES

A temporary lease on life for 300 adolescent addicts was assured yesterday when Deputy Mayor Robert Morgenthau announced that the city would lease the Evangelical Deaconess Hospital in Brooklyn to Odyssey House for a period "of at least six months" for use as rehabilitation center.

Morgenthau, chairman of the city's newly created Narcotic Control Council, said the "city is going to make every effort to help Odyssey House, a pioneer in the field of combating adolescent narcotic addiction, to find other quarters at the end of that period of time."

Option Picked Up

Morgenthau, who said he has only become involved in the problem of drug addiction among children since his council was formed 10 days ago, said the city recently picked up an option to buy the abandoned hospital for about $135,000.

"However, this building at 629 Chauncey St. had previously been promised to the Bushwick community by the city to be used as a child day care center, therefore the short lease," he said.

Dr. Judianne Dense-Gerber, executive director of Odyssey House, accepted the city offer "as a beginning, at least a roof over the heads of the adolescents who need help." Odyssey House will pay $1 a year for the building, but must raise funds for all other costs, maintenance, food and staff.

Dr. Denser-Gerber agreed to move out, with 30 days notice, when the city is ready to take over the building for the day care center.

Late yesterday, however, it appeared as though Odyssey House would have difficulty in occupying its new home.

When staff members and six resident addicts of the Odyssey House accompanied Dr. Densen-Gerber to the Brooklyn address, they were barred from entering by more than 50 members of the Bushwick Community Association.

A spokesman for the community group said its members had nothing against a rehabilitation center for young addicts, but argued that they had been promised a day care center for four years by Mayor Lindsay.

"Lindsay let us down, now he is trying to pit our community against Odyssey House and we're not going to let him do it," the spokesman said. "These facilities must be used for what was promised to us."

Odyssey House has been searching for facilities since August 1969 from either the state or city. Recently, an Odyssey House residence, at 955 Bruckner Blvd. was cited by the city for overcrowding. The case is pending.

The day Evangelical Deaconess Hospital was leased to Odyssey House by New York City. The next day the City took it back.

lowed by every relevant agency in the City and State and then a number of individuals with clout. It resulted in nothing.

"The City gave me a lease for the Brooklyn Deaconess Hospital one day in front of a press conference and took it away the next," I told the Judge, keeping my face expressionless and my tone neutral.

He was surprised. "Was the lease signed?"

"Yes," I nodded. "They took it back because they said it was promised to other people, but it was vacant for a long time afterward. Then the State offered us a wing of Creedmore Hospital, which we found was a series of cells full of fecal material with bars on the windows and obscenities on the walls. It was totally unsuitable as a therapeutic environment for children."

I could have mentioned a good deal more frustration. Odyssey had submitted an annual budget of $324,516 to treat the children to every level of government and to many private foundations, again without success. In order to establish a legal basis for treating children, Odyssey had applied to the State Department of Social Services for a license, and it was rejected. The grounds were that the Bruckner Boulevard building did not meet the requirements; it was too crowded. We weren't going to be permitted to treat children under sixteen purely because we were treating too many children under sixteen.

I expected the arrival of the Red Queen at any moment.

Meanwhile it was December of 1969, and two hundred and ten teen-agers already had died of heroin overdose in New York City. I was making bitter statements to the press and on television. "There is plenty of money appropriated in this state—fifty-four million this year—but it is not being used by the Narcotics Addiction Control Commission to cure, to rehabilitate, to educate," I said at one point. "It is used instead to propagandize the idea that narcotics addiction has been eliminated. To go to Albany on the backs of two hundred and ten children is a national and moral disgrace."

And again, "The morgue allotment is about six and a half feet of space, which a child doesn't take up. For a living child, the regulations say you need sixty feet. And so the children who need sixty feet when alive need only six and a half feet if you don't care for them."

At Bruckner Boulevard, we didn't even have six and a half feet per child. They were sleeping as many as twenty in a bedroom with the overflow on bedrolls in the halls. We survived on private donations. One church raised fifteen thousand dollars. Someone brought in a huge quantity of corn flakes. When cyclamate drinks could no longer be sold in grocery stores, the manufacturers gave Odyssey 43,200 cans of soft drinks for the tax write-off. We were wryly grateful.

Christmas was approaching. Combining sentiment and strategy we decided it was appropriate to have our ex-addict children sing carols to their elected leaders. We notified a selected group of politicians that we would visit them. The New York *Times* covered the event and understood our message:

"Outside Gracie Mansion in the crystalline twilight, the choir from Odyssey House last night sang 'Silent Night' in memory of the 210 teen-agers who killed themselves with overdoses of heroin in New York City so far this year.

"A voluntary shoe-string operation, Odyssey House, financed without state or city money, spent the day yesterday singing outside the homes of public officials in memory of the 210 who will not see this Christmas and also to protest inactivity in dealing with child addiction . . ." And more.

When the choir sang for United States Senator Jacob Javits he said he was moved to tears. Mayor John Lindsay arrived at Gracie Mansion from a tennis game while the choir was singing. Wearing a trench coat and sneakers, he thanked the children cordially. New York's Governor Nelson Rockefeller advised Odyssey House that he wouldn't be at home when the choir called, and he wasn't.

Seymour Domaclang, an ex-addict on the staff of Odyssey House, drew a special Christmas card for Lawrence E. Pierce, Chairman of

Odyssey House Children's Choir

the Narcotics Addiction Control Commission in New York State. Chairman Pierce had refused to fund our Adolescent Treatment Unit because, in his opinion, it wasn't necessary. The press was informed by the Commission that there were only twenty-eight addicts under the age of sixteen in the entire state. At that time Odyssey had sixty-six at Bruckner Boulevard.

We worked ceaselessly to move the government. Parents of our addicted children organized themselves and bombarded the Mayor, the Governor and legislators with letters pleading for help for Odyssey. They often enclosed snapshots of their child.

The parents formed a picket line in front of the Governor's elegant apartment house, pushing shopping carts and carrying placards asking for table leavings. Mrs. Happy Rockefeller sent down a case of tomato soup. The picket line started on a twenty-four hour basis then changed its tactic and became a "hiccup" strike—turning up at irregular and unpredictable hours around the clock.

After about six months of this, Governor Rockefeller paused one day and asked one of the women pickets how long she intended to continue. She replied, "Governor, if you knew your son was alive in the jungle, how long would you look for him?" The Governor, at the point of tears, hastily got into his car.

We held a press conference at the Bruckner Boulevard house and introduced the children to the media. The net result of that was more children. We had thirty-five children at the time of the press conference, and by nightfall the next day we had sixty-one.

I remember one day when we gave six separate press interviews. For about three months we worked an average of eighteen hours a day, writing and submitting budgets, going to City Hall, to Albany, to Washington, appearing on radio and television shows, taking the children to sing in the state legislature, attending yet another funeral of a child dead from heroin overdose.

We began to wonder if anyone cared about children at all. We did some research and discovered that at the turn of the century there was a Society for the Prevention of Cruelty to Animals long before there was a Society for the Prevention of Cruelty to Children. In the early 1870s a child who was chained to a plow by her father was protected by the courts only by the Judge ruling that she was an animal and therefore entitled to consideration under the animal protection laws.

Our fight was not to get funds for Odyssey House, which we made clear again and again. We wanted someone to be funded to treat children, but we didn't care who. When the State negotiated with us tentatively one time to fund a seventy-bed treatment unit, we said, "Fine, but what do we do with the seventy-first child?" And the State said, in effect, "How many beds do you insist on?"

Our reply was, "We don't know. What we want from you is a commitment to treat every sick child. *All the children who need help.*" The State negotiators demanded that we limit our patients intake, and when we refused they lost interest. They could not understand the concept of a commitment to treat *every* sick child.

In December 1969 the world was shocked by the death of Walter Vandermeer, who was a few days past his twelfth birthday when his body was found in a Harlem communal bathroom with his syringe beside him. He was the youngest known drug fatality in New York City's history.

Joseph Lelyveld wrote a sensitive story of that child's pain for the New York *Times.* He called it, "Obituary of Walter Vandermeer, a Heroin User Who Lived to Be Thirty in Twelve Years."

He described what so many of us know about the lives of ghetto children—that as many as a dozen social agencies will be aware of the child who is falling to pieces and all will have case histories about him, but none has the time, the funds or the facilities to stop the process. The child is shunted from one to another until he disappears, unnoticed, between the cracks.

Lelyveld named some of the agencies who were aware of Walter Vandermeer and gave the dates they stopped caring. "Only his file continued to move," he wrote. "For his last fourteen months he was left to himself, with no consistent supervision of any kind

. . . His diet was made up of Yankee Doodle cupcakes, Coca Cola and, when he had the change, fish and chips.

"It was a life of frightening emptiness and real dangers. The only regular thing about it was the daily struggle for survival."

My Husband was the Medical Examiner who was called when the child was found, some eighteen hours after he died. He said Walter weighed only eighty pounds. When he returned from the tenement bathroom where Walter died, Michael came into the kitchen where I was working. He showed me the child's size eight Snoopy sweatshirt, which said, "I wish I could bite somebody. I need a release from my inner tensions."

Michael put the shirt on the table and, very moved, said, "This is smaller than our Daughter wears and just a little too large for our Son."

Michael told me how he found Walter. "He was in a bathroom shared by five or six families, sitting on the edge of the tub with his head resting on the sink. His works were on the sink: the needle, syringe, glassine bag and cooker, and there was a paper bag in the tub with another cooker in it. He was wearing the sweatshirt and sneakers; he looked like a typical kid. Except he was dead from heroin." Michael performed the autopsy.

Afterwards, Walter Vandermeer's partner came to Odyssey House. A frail fourteen-year-old, his name was Marvin Fortnoy. We dubbed society's wailing over the dead Walter while being indifferent to the needs of the live Marvin, "Fortnoy's Complaint."

Child addicts astounded us with accounts of how they obtained money to purchase heroin by holding up taxicabs. The combined weight of two of them often didn't equal that of an adult. We began to see our first mini-muggers.

The newspapers dwelt on the pitiful details of Walter Vandermeer's life and death for days, to my despair. The press and public were fascinated by a dead child but not interested in living children. Fortnoy promised to bring us two others from his gang, one of whom was only eleven. Though Bruckner Boulevard was bulging, I couldn't discourage his recruitment. Odyssey redoubled its efforts to raise funds for children and find a larger building.

We encountered refusal to help in an unexpected place. When we asked the New York City Board of Education for teachers for our children, I was shocked to be turned down. We assumed there would be no difficulty since children who are ill are entitled to a visiting teacher under home-bound regulations. We were told that Bruckner Boulevard did not have a sufficient number of bathrooms and, besides, the doors did not open outward.

20

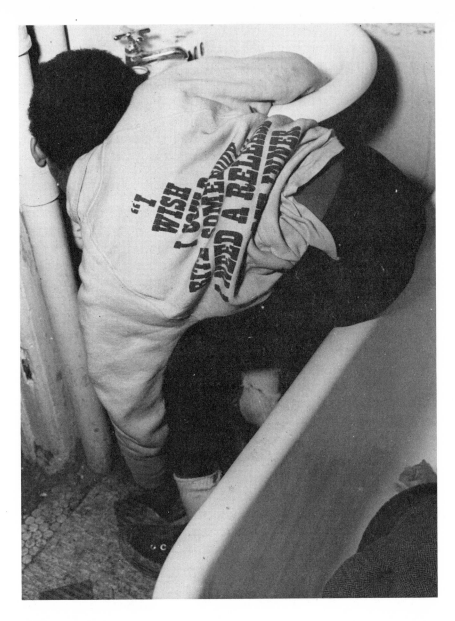

Walter Vandermeer as he was found.

I raged on a television program. "Years ago in America we learned in log cabins, we learned in barns, we learned wherever there were people who were willing to teach. In New York City you learn only if there are adequate separate bathrooms for the teachers. That is a disgrace."

Shortly after Christmas, New York police arrested a heroin peddler who was eleven years old. He was making fifty dollars a day selling to his age group.

That same week the twelve-year-old daughter of Dr. Guillermo Salazar, a prominent East Side psychiatrist, was found in a stupor after a three-day drug binge. She told reporters that she took little blue, orange, green, pink and icy white pills, as often as she could, day or night. She used hash, pot, LSD, heroin, speed—anything she could get.

Politicians were beginning to pay some attention: their own children were involved. The son of the Governor of New Jersey was arrested on drug charges; the son of the Governor of Oregon was addicted to heroin; the son of a former Undersecretary of Commerce was arrested, as was the son of a City Manager of Hartford, Connecticut, on drug charges. Children of politicians from all over the country were getting into trouble with drugs.

Still Odyssey had no support for treatment of children. It remained the only facility in the country that was addressing the crisis. We were treating children from twenty-six states, one third of them sentenced and sent to Odyssey by the courts in their home towns.

By the end of 1969 there were 224 teen-agers dead of heroin overdose in New York City, but we continued to be told that addiction didn't exist among children. As a psychiatrist I could see that this Kafka-esque situation arose because the City administration rather than problem-solve, used the mechanism of denial, a primitive defense adopted in times of stress to protect against a threatening situation one cannot face. I understood what was happening but couldn't change it through traditional channels. I felt trapped. The bad, counterproductive decisions did not result because the decision makers received faulty information—rather, the decisions were based on political expediency of the moment without regard for facts readily available.

During the fight, I was under intense pressure because my Husband worked for the City of New York and I was directing much of my outrage at City Hall. As it happened, a long overdue promotion for him remained pending throughout that time. There were many nights when I cried myself to sleep because I felt, on a symbolic level, I was being asked to choose between my Husband's career and dying children.

Finally, there was some response from the authorities to the noise I was making. They served me with a summons for violating the Building Code at 955 Bruckner Boulevard.

The *Congressional Record* of the United States Senate for January 27, 1970, reads:

"WILLIAMS (Dem.-New Jersey): Mr. President, it is with great dismay that I have learned of the arrest of Dr. Judianne Densen-Gerber on the charges of violating New York City's Building Code by running an overcrowded facility. To many of our nation's youngsters, particularly those afflicted with the dread disease of drug addiction, this arrest must come as a cruel and shocking blow. . . .

"It will be pitiful indeed if Dr. Densen-Gerber is convicted for running an overcrowded facility. One must ask, who is the criminal? . . .

"At a time when the drug problem among the very young is reaching critical proportions, New York City's police have incredibly demanded the closing of the one facility devoted solely to the rehabilitation of teen-aged drug users. . . .

"The City could have offered alternative facilities. It has several that in any case ought to be turned into centers for the treatment of drug addiction. . . .

"The State has other facilities it could have offered, including a recently refurbished but still unused hospital."

Senator Williams is one of the politicians in this country who gives us hope.

The New York *Daily News* reported a few days later, "Mayor Lindsay acknowledged yesterday that he was 'not satisfied with the present efforts to defeat the narcotics problem' but he sidestepped questions as to whether a critically needed treatment center for teen-aged addicts was planned or whether the city would free money for drug programs."

Not long after this, Odyssey received a letter from the City's Addiction Services Agency stating that treatment centers indeed were needed. The problem was that they would be too expensive to run because the Health Code demanded more space for children than for adults.

It is ironic that many of these early laws protecting children were written by my Mother, Beatrice Densen. She had not intended the law ever to work against the interests of children.

The New York Association of Voluntary Agencies on Narcotics Treatment, known as AVANT, a long-established coalition of eleven agencies in the drug field which includes Odyssey House, sent a letter to the Speaker of the New York State Assembly, documenting the need for treatment units for drug-addicted children. AVANT begged the State to turn over a summer camp to Odyssey and two other agencies, to be operated jointly as an adolescent treatment facility.

23

The letter had no effect.

Odyssey was admitting between four and six children every day. I appeared on David Susskind's television show with five formerly addicted boys and girls who were in treatment at Odyssey House. Susskind was shocked when one of the teen-agers made casual reference to the fact that he bought heroin from his high school teacher and other school employees. Odyssey had discovered that this was not an uncommon situation.

"Children catch addiction," I explained on that show. "They get it from the child to the right or to the left of them, rather than seeking it out as an adult addict does." It is different than adult addiction, and the children's chances of rehabilitation are better. The treatment period is likely to be much shorter than with adults.

"Despite the difficulties in the facility, which is severely over-crowded, the children have a most encouraging attitude and spirit," I commented. "They're idealistic. I wish the adults in treatment were even halfway as positive as the children."

At the end of the show, Susskind broke a rule. He was so touched that he asked viewers to send Odyssey donations. In the days that followed, Odyssey received $45,000 from the public. We needed every penny just to stay open. We still depend greatly on private donations.

Because of the entrenched apathy and the futility of every effort we had made, I did something that still depresses me. I had been asked in February to testify at a State legislative hearing on drugs, a joint Committee on the Protection of Children and Youth and Committee on Youthful Drug Abuse. I talked about it to James Murphy, my righthand man.

"Jimmy, I have to go to my twenty-sixth legislative hearing to testify about child addiction," I told him despondently. "I don't imagine it will do any more good than any of the other times."

"You're going to have to do something different," Jimmy suggested. "Maybe you should take some of the children and let them answer the committee's questions. Better still, let *them* ask the committee what the hell they're doing."

Initially, I decided against the idea but woke up the next morning resolved to do it. I would take with me one child, Ralph de Jesus, who had just come to Odyssey. He was twelve but he looked more like an eight-year-old. I selected him with a heavy heart because I was aware that the publicity he was about to receive might confuse him. I knew, as his doctor, that it was almost too much to expect that after the excitement died down Ralphie would remain in treatment. For the sake of thousands of addicted children, including

Ralphie, I would have to take the chance. It was the only way treatment for children such as Ralphie would ever become available.

Ralphie was so small that he had to sit on my lap while he testified. Perched there in his jeans and sneakers, he told the legislators that he had been using drugs for about a year.

"I started sniffing heroin, then skin-popping, then mainlining. I learned how to do it in the street in my neighborhood. I used to see my friends doing it, and I didn't want to be left out."

Assemblyman Chester Hart asked in a parental tone if Ralph had any information about heroin; was he aware of what he was doing? Ralphie replied in a matter-of-fact voice, "All I knew about heroin was that it could kill me."

His last fix, Ralphie related, had been eight days before. He was also a pusher, he added. He peddled heroin at his school for two dollars a bag and had "a lot of customers." He was, I think, in the sixth grade.

Assemblyman Manuel Ramos asked the child where he lived. Ralphie replied that he came from the South Bronx, which is Ramos' district. Ramos fled the room in tears.

A picture of Ralphie on my lap was on more than four hundred newspaper front pages the next day and even appeared the following year in the *Encyclopedia Americana*. We believe that it was the single factor that broke the dam of denial and apathy. A few months later Governor Rockefeller, man enough to admit he had misjudged

---

DAILY NEWS, FRIDAY, FEBRUARY 27, 1970   ☆   3

12, He's on Dope to Be 1 of the Boys

By EDWARD BENES

The joint legislative committee investigating teenage drug abuse sat in shocked silence yesterday as a 12-year-old addict openly related his involvement with narcotics in the Hunts Point section of the Bronx.

NEWS photo by John Pedin
Ralphie, 12, tells Odyssey House narcotics probers how he began.

The boy, who is called Ralphie, a skinny, 60-pound, barely 4-foot resident of Odyssey House, admitted he had taken a shot only "about eight days ago."

"Nobody taught me, nobody forced me, but I didn't want to be left out when I saw my friends use drugs," he said. "I started by sniffing glue and cleaning fluids, then I smoked pot, snorted heroin, skin-popped and mainlined," the soft-spoken youngster said.

Ralphie said he was the baby of his family and that none of his six older brothers or sisters are addicted "but most of my friends use drugs now and I wanted to be one of them."

Under the gentle prodding of State Assemblymen Manuel Ramos, in whose district the boy lives, and Vincent Riccio of Brooklyn. Ralphie said he learned about drugs in the streets around Bruckner Blvd. He has already survived a siege of hepatitis caused by his drug habit.

Also Sold Narcotics

The boy said he mainlined heroin for six months before his family took him to Odyssey House at 955 Bruckner Blvd. last Friday. He testified while sitting on the lap of Dr. Judianne Densen-Gerber, executive director of the private rehabilitation and therapeutic center.

Ralphie said he sold drugs to other youngsters around his school, PS 60 at 888 Stebbins Ave. The drugs, he said, were given to him by some adults and some bigger kids for sale. "I had a lot of customers," he told the committee.

The youth said he supported his habit at first by stealing pocketbooks and by breaking into apartments and taking "anything I could find."

"I even mugged some people," he told his startled audience. When pressed how such a little fellow could mug anyone, Ralphie explained: "I did it with some of my older friends and one of them even had a gun."

In his role as a pusher, the boy said he sold mostly $2 bags of heroin to schoolmates, but the code of silence of the streets prevailed and he refused to give details about his supplier.

The boy's testimony brought tears to the eyes of Assemblyman Ramos, and the assemblyman left the hearing room for a short time.

When he returned, Ramos, in a fiery shouting speech declared: "Let's call a spade a spade. The economic level for addiction is within the reach of 8-year-olds now."

"When one of my kids asks me for a quarter, I hesitate to give it to them, not because I am a stinker or I'm cheap, but because I'm afraid, I'm scared about what they are going to buy with that quarter," Ramos admitted.

He begged the chairman of the committee, Assemblyman Chester R. Hardt (R-Erie), and the other members to take a message back to Albany calling for mandatory urine testing of all students to discover whether they are using narcotics.

"Any conscientious parent will not object," he said, "and if any teachers do, throw them out of the school system, they are not worthy of being called a teacher."

Reaction to Rocky's Plan

The program of "total war" announced Tuesday by Gov. Rockefeller to combat drug addiction of adolescents was generally praised by other witnesses as "a step in the right direction," but fears and doubts were expressed as to its effectiveness under the present structure.

City Councilman Carter Burden doubted if the program will ever get off the ground because $200 million must be raised through a special bond issue in a time of tight money.

the situation, pushed through an adolescent drug treatment bill allocating $65 million for addicted teen-agers. Odyssey received about a half million dollars from the allotment.

No one had responded to the death statistics, to the letters, to the press editorials, to picket lines, to the children singing in the cold. But they couldn't escape tiny Ralph de Jesus talking about his last fix.

Ralphie left Odyssey soon after the hearing, rattled by the deluge of attention he received. He returned to the streets where, because of television exposure, he is known as "Channel Two." I have been told that no one will sell drugs to him because of the notoriety, and therefore he is clean. It means a great deal to me that he didn't become re-addicted.

Many people were wondering why cheap heroin was suddenly flooding the schools. In February *TIME* magazine published an article that contained part of the explanation. The spread of heroin, it stated, "is related to the success of Operation Intercept, the ad-

Odyssey accepts our share of state Adolescent Addiction monies.

ministration's recent attempt to stem the tide of marijuana flowing across the Mexican border. As the supply of pot dwindled and the price rose, heroin pushers dropped their prices to within reach of even modest preteen allowances." One of the experts consulted by *TIME* was my Husband, Dr. Michael Baden.

Michael was sitting a few feet from me, projecting encouragement, as I finished my testimony in the Bronx courtroom, a full year and a half after my long battle to get funding and facilities for adolescents had started. The Judge seemed tired. His line of questioning now concerned the source of Odyssey's residents. He was openly surprised when I told him that more than half our residents are sent to us by the courts.

"Are agencies still referring children to you, even though they know you are violating the building standard?"

"Yes."

"What are they doing about this situation?" asked Judge Kidder.

"They are helping us fund-raise to find another space," I told him levelly.

He sighed and murmured kindly, "You are immensely qualified in all areas."

Then he delivered his decision: "There is reasonable doubt as to the guilt of the defendant," he declared. "I find *not guilty*, but this is not to be used as a precedent. . . ."

The courtroom erupted as Odyssey residents and staff leaped to their feet, pounded one another on the back, hugged and cheered. My first reaction as they crowded around me, some of them crying, was one of exhaustion. I hadn't realized how tense I had been.

A twisted man in a wheel chair edged his way through the mob and congratulated me. His son is an ex-addict in the Odyssey House program, doing well.

Michael and I went home to pack. We were leaving the next morning for Fairbanks and Anchorage, where we had been asked to lecture and consult on ways of controlling the drug epidemic in Alaska.

First Odyssey adolescent graduate.

In my moment of depression, I think of you, and my commitment.

I think of the times we spent together. My crying, and you just listening, talking to me in a soft voice that no one else had ever spoken.

Trust us Moni, we're not going to hurt you.

Hours and hours passed and I was amazed, amazed, that someone so special was really interested in me.

Its hard to believe, me, Monique LaVoie has someone who really cares about her.

You're beautiful and I love you.

I wondered from that moment on hoping that maybe again some day you would again be there.

I waited and waited until it happened, once again I was alone, I needed someone but didn't know who to turn to. All I wanted was a hand to hold, or a soft voice to once again listen to.

I didn't know how to go about finding you, so instead I ran the other way.

The way that led me further away from you and took me away from everyone.

I couldn't stand the guilt, the loneliness, the distorted voices of criticism being said about you. I had to find you.

Once again, I thought of you, and my commitment, the times of crying, and you listening, the feeling of someone caring. I had to come back. I returned, like Little Red Riding Hood getting lost in the woods, and then finding Grandma's house.

Come here, I'm glad to see you made it. What, didn't you think that you meant anything to us. A feeling of warmth and love as you bent over to kiss me and say hello.

Why, why did you run Moni. Do you know how people felt?

Moments of silence as I mumbled yes, because of closeness, and caring, I hurt others. Yes, but how do you think they feel about you? Once again silence, not knowing what to say, but taking a chance in saying "they love me?" Yes, so what do you say when you hurt people who love you? I love you, and you hurt me, so what do you say?

As tears fell I loved you. I knew what to say, "I'm sorry," come here, running across the room I felt you even though we were a distance apart. I ran but only this time in the right direction.

Once again silence of just me crying and you holding me and talking to me in the soft voice of long ago. I was at ease, secure, and knew you wouldn't hurt me.

I had made it, finally after struggling all through the woods I found Grandma's house, and never ever again was I going to get lost.

I know the path now, thanks to you.

I Love You, Judi.

* Written by a sixteen-year-old resident from the Odyssey House Female Adolescent program.

QUARTERLY REPORT
ADOLESCENT TREATMENT UNIT
JUNE 15, 1971

Name:	A.B.	Level I
Age:	12	
Race:	Puerto Rican	
Date Admitted:	3/31/71	
Years Using:	1 month	
What Used:	Heroin	

Physical Disabilities: None
Diagnostic Impression of Mental Status: None
Personal Evaluation:

A.B. is doing fair. He is a manipulative child who will go to extremes to try and get what he wants. Apparently this has succeeded in the past. His aunt allowed him considerable latitude and set few guidelines. His parents are separated and there appears to be little relationship between him and his father. I do not know whether or not he will stay since he has often tried to split. He changes his mind after a group and some confrontation but continues to play the game. I don't perceive any severe psychological malfunction just a behavior problem. He is appropriately aggressive and is able to use his hands. Time will tell what his course of treatment will be. At this time manipulation is the big problem that we are working through.

Submitted by: Carl F. Lazzaro

QUARTERLY REPORT
18TH STREET A.T.U.
JUNE 15, 1971

Name: C.D.   Level 1
Age: 14
Race: Black
Date of Admission: 12/22/71
Years Using: 3 years
What Used: Glue, Marijuana, Pills
Physical Disabilities: None
Mental Status: 1. Stutters slightly and appears to have
                            difficulty concentrating and organizing
                            his thoughts.
                         2. Admits to having hallucinations.
                         3. Childhood schizophrenia.
                         4. Multiple drug abuse.
Personal Evaluation:

C.D. has been in the program for over six months and he has just made Level 1. It has taken him a long time to accept help. Prior to passing his probe, he would hide in a closet or under a bed. He still has no friends in the house. The only feelings he has shown is to the dog whom he feeds, washes and takes care of.

Submitted by: Herbert Goldberg

He is moving very slowly, but we have taken steps to give him very specific direction and guidance.

Carl F. Lazzaro

QUARTERLY REPORT
GRAMERCY PARK A.T.U.
JUNE 15, 1971

Name: A.M.   Level II
Age: 16
Race: White
Date: Admitted 11/12/70
Years Using: 2 years
What Used: Marijuana, Barbiturates, Amphetamines,
    LSD, Cocaine, Hash, Heroin
Physical Disabilities: None
Diagnostic Impression of Mental Status:
            1. Drug Abuse: Heroin
            2. Personality Disorder: Tension discharge
               type—depressive underlay undoubtedly due
               to deprivation.

Personal Evaluation:

A.M. is rather non-verbal in group settings and activities, but seems to have a lot of insight into what's going on. He doesn't give too much to his groups unless he feels threatened. Also tends to swing along with the crowd if everyone is moving in the same direction. When things are not going in one direction in his group, he'll go to the outside and look in. He has no feelings for other people or things other than himself. At this point he really doesn't see anything wrong with himself. He knows enough to just slide by and doesn't feel threatened by his peers or anyone around him. Pressure has to be applied across and down before he can start to do anything. A.M. will need a lot of pressure in order to complete the program. He is, at this point, the least likely to complete Odyssey House in his peer group.

Submitted by: Harold Robinson

He was just made Level II Ramrod, and this should give him the additional involvement that will make or break him. I feel that he will make it.

Carl F. Lazzaro

Metropolitan Hospital.

It Started
with Seventeen Addicts

It actually started in 1965 with one addict, Alfred Enriquez, called Tony, who at thirty-seven had been admitted to Metropolitan Hospital for his fourteenth detoxification for heroin addiction. He had been an addict for ten years. He was one of seventeen thousand admissions to that hospital in a period of six years, out of which there were eight known cures. It was a revolving door, at a cost to the taxpayers of $104 a day per patient.

Tony was the first heroin addict I ever had as a patient. It was early in 1965 and I was thirty years old, married, pregnant for the sixth time, with my third child, and a graduate in law and medicine. I was starting my residency in psychiatry at Metropolitan as part of what was called the Mothers Program. At that time Metropolitan had the only program in the country that permitted women physicians with families to have most evenings and weekends free during their training.

Tony was sent to me for private therapy because he wanted long-term treatment. There was no form of psychiatric therapy for addicts at that time except the traditional Freudian one-to-one. My mentor was a Freudian psychiatrist who advised me that addicts did not respond to analysis. He told me if I took Tony as a patient, I would be wasting my time. He said most of them had an inability to love because their childhoods were so damaged.

In the years since, Odyssey has demonstrated that addicts can be cured. There are more than a thousand who have passed through Odyssey and now are living drug-free lives. Tony Enriquez has been drug-free since 1966. He is now a member of the command at Phoenix House, New York City's multi-million-dollar endowed drug-addiction program. In 1967 he led an attempted coup against me within Odyssey, but curiously enough, even afterwards he continued to keep his private-therapy appointments with me. He was a complicated man. I was naïve in that for a little while I continued to treat him.

When we first met, however, I had a sense of recognition. I was working on *Who am I?* and was in a particularly desolate stage of self-examination, wondering if it was going to be possible for me to continue as both a mother and career woman. It was something no one could help me with, not even my Husband. Tony and I talked about feelings of extreme loneliness, feelings of being different, feelings of great pain, feelings of not being understood.

I met addicts other than Tony because I asked the Chairman of the Department of Psychiatry at Metropolitan Hospital for maternity leave. He said leave wasn't necessary as he would give me an easy assignment instead. I could work on the drug-addict ward. In those days most of the medical profession believed that addicts couldn't get well no matter what treatment was attempted. Therefore, I could sign in for an hour or two every day, showing token interest, and it would be sufficient to qualify for my residency.

He sent me to the hospital's Drug Research unit where cyclazocine, a substitute for heroin, was being tested for the Federal Government. The ward had the traditional hospital setting with the patients lounging around all day in their pajamas watching television and gambling. The only therapy they received was a daily dose of the cyclazocine maintenance medicine. Occasionally, they sniffed glue in Arts and Crafts. Louie Sarra was among them.

The attending physician, Dr. A. Ronald Sorvino, was becoming more and more disillusioned with substitute-drug maintenance. He felt psychotherapy had to play a role; addicts could be sent back to society only after a change in their antisocial attitudes. He asked me to begin a program of long-term group psychotherapy.

Because of the similarity of emotional tone that I had found with addicts through my sessions with Tony Enriquez, I had become interested in their problems and therefore agreed to start the program. I think it's how most people do things. They are attracted because they identify with someone or with the situation itself. They're caught, as I was, because it represents a piece of themselves.

I couldn't imagine, being an idealistic, enthusiastic young resident, why this group of patients should be different from any other patients and not respond to therapy. Many of them were very charming. They were young, they were intelligent, they were gifted, they were sensitive—as well as being scheming, manipulative and difficult. I felt they could be turned around. If these people were salvaged, it would be gratifying.

One of the best-known doctors then working in the field of addiction was Dr. Efren Ramirez, who was head of an addiction-treatment unit in Rio Pedras, Puerto Rico.* Michael and I combined a visit to Ramirez with a much-needed and deserved post-partum rest for me. Our Son Lindsey had just been born.

He was emphatic that the negative manipulative skills of the addict could be redirected to a positive channel that would result in self-growth. He encouraged me to begin such therapy at Metropolitan. He promised that when he came to New York we would work together.

I had much to learn when I began. I met with failure after failure. Louie Sarra and I often tease one another about those days, recalling how they used drugs on the ward, how they fooled me, how they played many other games while I thought I was accomplishing great things.

I tried everything the books advise: token economy, aversion therapy, heroin challenges, shock and maintenance. We attempted everything I'm watching others do now and discarded almost everything. They are really games, psychiatric games, statistics-gathering games. Indeed, I often observe that we professionals, like the addicts, do not learn from experience, particularly the experience of others.

Meanwhile, I was not making myself popular with the hospital authorities. One of the first conflicts occurred when I demanded that women addicts be treated. For six years there had been fifty hospital beds for male addicts and not one for females. I was appalled by this fact. As with present-day prison reform, there was little concern about the women whom society has defined as wayward and therefore punishes as fallen women. Society carries such concepts about female wickedness even to the point of punishing their children as well. At my insistence, the hospital provided five beds for female addicts.

One day I was asked by some medical authorities in the hospital

---

* Later Ramirez was to come to New York City to become the City's first Co-ordinator of Narcotics Programs and then the first Commissioner of the Addiction Services Agency. Michael and I joined Ramirez, in his early days in New York, as members of the founding core group which designed the city's drug programs.

Ramirez, ex-Governor Munoz Marin's son-in-law, used group-therapy methods. He was claiming a 90 per cent success rate. He insisted, "There is no such thing as physiological addiction. The addict's problem stems from a fundamental but treatable character disorder."

to persuade my patients to submit to a liver biopsy, for which they would be paid five dollars apiece—which could be used when they went out on passes. The research doctors needed tissue from normal livers as controls on their newest project. There is a 1 per cent morbidity rate from liver biopsies. They insisted that I ask the patients, since they would do anything for me—"even jump off a bridge"—and the doctors wanted their livers. I refused to co-operate. There should be informed consent when healthy people are asked to submit to tests that are for research purposes and that have nothing to do with their own well-being.

I went to the office of Arnold Fraiman, Commissioner of Investigations for New York City, and complained about what I was being asked to do. In addition to the request for liver biopsies, I had been instructed to write orders for the nurses to give heroin to patients so their brain-wave reactions could be studied. Several patients became re-addicted after these tests. Some of my patients had begged the authorities not to give them heroin and asked me to help them, but we were told that they could not remain in the hospital if they refused the heroin challenges.

After my complaint to the Commissioner's office, all pressure on me suddenly stopped. Things were becoming complex and confused, however. Nothing on the ward seemed to be going right, and then I discovered that private therapy had failed because Tony Enriquez was using heroin again.

"Private therapy won't do it," I told him. "You have to enter the community." I hoped his presence on the ward would provide the necessary strength and turn the group around. I said to him, "Will you come into Met Hospital as a patient and police the ward from within? You could set a positive dynamic for the rest of the group, and you could all get well together. You've got nothing to lose by entering. At least you'll detoxify and lower your habit." He was using over $100 a day of heroin.

Tony agreed and entered the hospital in August 1966. He made no promises to me, except that he would assess the situation and tell me what could be done. He didn't believe that a group of junkies could be turned around, and he had no intention of adding another failure to his record.

Three weeks of debate, arguments and shouting followed. Tony told me to go on my summer vacation and leave it to him. When I returned they were still in turmoil. I continued to induct into the group anyway, and one of the first inductees, David Algarin, told me that he had given a urine specimen in place of Louie Sarra because Louie was using drugs.

I decided that was it. I confronted the group and said I was ready to walk out. Louie said that I should stay—he would be the one to leave. He did. Fifteen months passed before I saw him again.

The remaining patients split into two groups, one composed of those who believed the program should be real and those who preferred that it remain casual as it was. We held the first of Odyssey's walk-the-walks. We have a saying that it isn't enough to talk-the-talk, you have to walk-the-walk. Those of us who wanted the group to move in a positive way sat on one side of the room and the others, one at a time, were interrogated about their motives and either walked across to join us or left the room. At the end, fourteen had walked-the-walk.

Tony was voted president, and the group met without me. The next day Tony informed me that those who were in the cyclazocine-testing program had decided, as part of their newly found firmness of purpose, to break away from the maintenance drug. The concept of maintenance meant to them that they were crippled and different from other people—"once an addict, always an addict." The concept of psychotherapy meant they could change their lives and be cured normal people. They wanted to be drug free while they worked on becoming well. The hospital authorities refused the request. It was explained that there was funding for a drug-maintenance project, not for a drug-free treatment project. It appeared that the hospital was funded to test drugs, not cure patients.

We continued anyway, and it was the beginning of Odyssey. We used group-therapy techniques borrowed from everywhere, from Synanon, from Daytop, from Maxwell Jones, from whatever we could find on the subject. The fourteen expanded to seventeen, and we spent all our waking time together. We would stay in a room for sixteen, eighteen, twenty hours at a time, examining and re-examining and examining again where we were all at.

We reached the point where we could almost finish each other's sentences. We knew each other's idiosyncrasies, we knew what to expect from one another, the peculiarities that make each of us unique —some of which are positive, some of which are not so pleasant, some of which are downright pathological. But at least we traveled beyond surprise.

We were a core group. Ever since then Odyssey has used a core group whenever we expand to a new facility. We move as a team.

I needed to examine myself, to determine where I was going. My residency would be finished in a year and I would have to decide what would be my lifework. Whatever I chose would determine the rest of my life, to a large degree. That year, 1966, I used to evaluate me: my own worth, who I was, where I was going, my identity as a female, my relationship with my Husband, my relationship with my children, whom I love so intensely that I'm still terrified I will overwhelm them if I'm not careful.

I used the community. I lived in that community of seventeen addicts almost in the same way they did. I was learning during those exhausting hours a great deal about personal development. I was learning how to make decisions, how not to be frightened, how to go against authority figures on issues of integrity if I truly believed they were wrong. I was learning to stand up, learning to identify with other people's pain, learning to admit my own pain, which is very difficult.

I had to tear away a large amount of denial that had insulated and protected me, but also had kept me from seeing what was real. It was hard work. We were all engaged in extremely hard work. Disputing authority was particularly unchartered for me—I had been raised in a home that required unquestioning obedience to authority figures.

A battle was coming with the doctors who opposed the request to stop the cyclazocine. Those of the seventeen who were still on it were becoming more and more indignant. They felt they were developing abilities to function without drug dependency during our therapy sessions, and they wanted to stop the drug. The authorities continued to refuse. They were funded for a drug-research program, they repeated, not a drug-abstinence program. Their goal was to monitor drug maintenance, not cure addiction.

Dr. Sorvino and I met. We decided that the patients had a right not to take research medication if they so wished. In September 1966 we began to detoxify them. The other doctors retaliated. I was barred from the ward and moved to the emergency room, which was comparable to putting a police lieutenant back on the beat. It was hinted that my certificate of having successfully completed my residency would be denied. Eventually, however, I received it. Dr. Sorvino, who had encouraged me to stop the cyclazocine, decided it was in his best interests to resign from the hospital. The nurse on the ward, who believed in the therapeutic community, was brought up on charges, accused of being too close to the patients. Like myself, the nurse and some attending physicians sympathetic to us were not permitted on the ward. The patients were left without a therapist.

To the amazement of the authorities involved, this did not end the program. None of the patients left. Rather they made notes of everything that transpired in their group sessions and read them on the telephone to me for supervision. My comments then were relayed back to the group.

The doctors opposed to the program feared that my Husband would tell his fellow Commissioners what was happening, so a doctor carrying the name Maximillian Fink angrily ordered Michael not to talk to me. Our sex life developed added spice because every time we were in bed there was Maximillian Fink and his ban against verbal communication.

A few weeks later the hospital, exasperated, discharged those patients who were participating in the therapeutic community. The group had no name at that time and called itself "Just Us." "Just Us" came to me with $3.82, all they had among them, and asked if I would continue to work with them. I had made a promise some time back that as long as they kept the commitment to work to get well, I would never abandon them, so I couldn't refuse.

I hadn't intended any of it. I was reluctant every step of the way. I was a status-oriented person who had gone to law and medical schools because I believed that the documents would give me a sense of worth and an unshakable place in the community. I wanted to use them to overcome the feelings of inadequacy I had as the only child of an overpowering Mother. Even after I finished my lengthy education I still had a great need for outside approval and for a secure road, which certainly appeared jeopardized if I cast my lot with a bunch of junkies.

Being a renegade isn't my emotional style. In Odyssey, we insist on respect for authority. But when it is a question of integrity, I do what has to be done. I saw it in simple terms. Seventeen people want to get well. I am their doctor. I can help them. Therefore, I must. There was nothing else to be done.

The seventeen stayed first at Daytop Village, a drug rehabilitation center on Staten Island, while Dr. Ramirez attempted to find other quarters. After he failed, he told me that circumstances were against it and I should forget them. It was too soon—the City authorities weren't ready for such a concept. I couldn't accept his advice. Some of the patients, one of them a female in her eighth month of pregnancy, came and camped on the floor of my luxury apartment on the East Side. They spent their days house hunting while the others waited in a borrowed log cabin near Bridgewater, Connecticut.

We had our name, Odyssey. A friend of the group, the famous Alfred Winslow Jones, cocreator of the Dow Jones average, observed to me and Tony over lunch that we were rootless and moving from place to place. We appeared to be on an odyssey, he said. We seized

Fifteen of the original seventeen addicts.

upon the name at once. The group was going through its own changes, or Odyssey, as was each of its individual members. The whole is more than a reflection of its parts.

The first Odyssey House was hard to take. It was a seven-room clapboard building on East 109th Street that had been abandoned to winos for months. It rented for seventeen dollars a month. All the windows were broken, the plumbing and furnace didn't function, and the roof leaked badly. Nevertheless, the seventeen cleaned it up and moved in, helped by donations of materials and money from intrigued businessmen and merchants. A nearby Italian bakery, Ragona's, sent over bread every day.

After the group was settled the ex-addicts visited the 23rd Police Precinct in order to explain the program and invite the officers to come over for a cup of coffee. Eventually, the police donated a new coffee maker. One of them, Sergeant Ray Hart, was interviewed on television's "Today" show. Odyssey, he said, was "an oasis in the desert."

Odyssey appeals to the police: It is based on law and order. We believe that strict enforcement of the law increases the possibility of getting people well. It is the first step to treatment. Only with law enforcement and medicine working together can addiction be conquered.

There is no question of behavior being free in Odyssey; it definitely isn't. Each resident knows firmly where he belongs and what is expected of him. Raw addicts start at the bottom with no privileges and few rights. If, during what we call a probe, he is accepted into the treatment phase from the motivational one, he can rise with diligence from Level I to Level IV, earning privileges and responsibilities along the way. Finally, if the resident's proposal outlining his future plans for himself is approved, he becomes a candidate-out and is ready to return to the mainstream of society. It takes from ten months to three years.

Behavior should be structured. We can't act out whenever we like, or do whatever we want, particularly in inter-personal relationships. It is a paradox that often when you structure behavior you free attitudes.

We should be able to think of everything and then do just those things that are not destructive. We should allow our imaginations to play, we should allow ourselves to dream, we should allow ourselves to fantasize—so long as we can come back to reality and enrich reality with those elements of fantasy that make life more stimulating, more delightful.

What we're seeing with young people today is behavior totally free, so that, in defense, attitudes must become rigid. It should be the other way around: behavior circumscribed and attitudes, consequently, freed. If you have stimulation for your mind, you can be free within a rigid system. As Byron wrote, "Stone walls do not a prison make."

Odyssey has had a symmetrical structure from the beginning. Symmetry is easier for people to learn and relate to. It puts order in their chaotic lives. There are three phases of the therapeutic community—motivation, treatment and re-socialization. Each of these phases has three steps. You enter Odyssey the same way you leave. For instance, you enter as a candidate-in through an inquiry-in and leave as a candidate-out through an inquiry-out.

From the beginning there were three other significant dynamics. One was inadvertent but fortuitous: the original seventeen addicts, men and women, were of all races and ethnic groups—White, Black, Puerto Rican, Catholic, Protestant and Jewish. Odyssey has remained fully integrated ever since—at the top administrative level as well as the resident one. From both Black and White elements of the community-at-large, there has been pressure to separate the program on racial lines, but because of our history, we are firmly committed to the concept of militant integration as a solution to the country's racial problems. Unless there is communication, there will be no progress.

The second dynamic introduced early at Odyssey was daily urine testing, done by an independent laboratory. It became our

4

3

109th Street facility.

practice as a result of Louie Sarra's gaming. We realized we needed carefully supervised daily urine testing in order to be sure that the patients and staff were clean of drugs. If traces of illicit drugs are found in the urine, the resident is discharged with the right to begin the program again; the staff member is fired but he may become a resident in treatment. There is always a witness when urine is collected so there is no possibility of switching samples.

Few other drug-rehabilitation programs require their residents and staff to give up urine. The omission makes a farce of the programs. If you don't check whether or not they're taking drugs, you can't claim to be rehabilitating addicts, and you must be positive that the staff members are good role models.

The third dynamic came from the original seventeen. They confronted the professionals with the fact that no one should be turned away—a deaf mute heroin addict had applied for admission, and the professionals, highly verbal people, felt they couldn't cope with him as a patient. The medical staff was about to reject him when, in order to help, the addicts offered to learn sign language. Odyssey since has had a credo that *no* sick person can be turned away without being offered a chance. There is no waiting list. At one time, indeed, we had a community of seven deaf mutes including a pregnant girl. One of them, when asked to describe his concept of Odyssey, handed me an unopened rose.

While the group was settling into that shambles of a house in East Harlem I was in contact with them a minimum of twenty hours a week.

I was taking care of administration, fund-raising and setting up a Board of Directors. I was running groups, finishing my residency and meeting the responsibilities at home of a demanding Husband and three small children.

The press came calling, and one of the best accounts of those early days was written by Don McNeill of the *Village Voice*. "The quarters are cramped in the small house," he wrote. "Upstairs men are jammed into two rooms, sleeping in triple-deck bunks they built themselves. The three women in the group share a room behind the tiny living room on the first floor.

"There is no privacy and this is intentional. No secrets are tolerated. Nothing is considered too personal to be discussed. It's up to each individual to challenge others and get them to move."

The core group came from widely varied backgrounds, he noted. "Some attended college, some never attended high school. They range in age from nineteen to forty, their addiction ranges from two to twenty-three years, they have twenty-five children.

"They computed that in one year they had used $400,000 worth of drugs, or at least $1,200,000 in stolen property, or roughly $90,000 apiece."

Along with saving the lives of the addicts, obviously Odyssey, by removing these people from the streets, was providing a substantial financial benefit to the community. Yet, ironically, we were existing on a total budget of ten dollars a day.

In March 1967 Odyssey House was incorporated as a not-for-profit charitable corporation, licensed by the New York State Department of Social Welfare. We obtained our charter after for the first time experiencing the vicious circle of bureaucratic reasoning. When we applied for the license, we were informed that it couldn't be granted because we were treating patients in an inadequate building. However, because we didn't have a license and could not, therefore, receive status as a charity under Federal Income Tax Regulations, no one would donate to us because we weren't tax deductible and therefore we didn't have the money to buy or rent adequate quarters. We were told that if there weren't patients in treatment getting well but only a proposal on paper, there would be no problem about obtaining the charter. The whole world is Kafka.

We overcame the block when a group of friends applied for personal loans from a bank. When Dr. Ramirez obtained an eight thousand dollar grant for us from the Dreyfus Funds, we purchased a building on Sixth Street in the East Village. It had been operated by Temple Emmanual Brotherhood as a settlement house for immigrant Jews beginning their American odysseys.

It could house seventy people comfortably. For the first time it gave us room to grow. It had some faults, however. There were no adequate kitchen or bathroom facilities. Six years later, we are still without them because we can't obtain a permit to renovate. Our architects have applied repeatedly but the authorities tell us they can't grant one because they are unable to decide what category of building we are. Until they determine whether we are a nursing home, halfway house, hospital or something else, the residents, as they have for the past six years, must carry the food from the second floor kitchen to the basement dining room.

We moved into the building in May 1966, and a month later, on June 23, we received our first public funds, a six-month operational grant from the Community Mental Health Board of the City of New York. In August I finished my residency at last and moved into my office with the orange walls; I love orange—it is so alive. I was openly taking charge of the agency. The future looked marvelous.

In October all the patients walked out. Every one. It is known in

Odyssey history as the "Great Split." It is one of the most painful experiences of my life. I was on one side and Jimmy Murphy was on the other. He had been one of the original seventeen. He was the last one admitted to "Just Us" before its members were discharged from Metropolitan Hospital. When he came on the ward I don't think he weighed a hundred and forty pounds, and he's over six feet tall. He was emaciated. His skin was impossible, covered with sores, his arms were both so swollen with edema that he could barely lift them. He rarely spoke, and when he did he stammered so severely he could barely be understood. He was almost silent for the first six months.

My first impression of him was, *here's Casper Milquetoast.* I figured he would be the one we would always have to protect. I felt he was terribly inadequate, terribly insecure. My first acquaintance with Jimmy was with a physical and emotional wreck. That was James Murphy.

Jimmy Murphy 1

When I came into Metropolitan Hospital in September 1966, it was my third detoxification for heroin. I weighed about a hundred and forty, and I'm six foot one. When you're out on the street, you don't take care of yourself and your diet can consist of nothing but Pepsi-Cola for days. Both my arms were so swollen from using bad stuff, from missing the veins, from neglecting infections, that when the doctors wanted some blood for testing they had to take it out of my wrist. I also had a case of hepatitis, untreated for the past three months, and pronounced acne.

I wasn't certain if I were alive or dead. I didn't much care either way.

I didn't talk to anyone. I thought it was a waste of time. I reasoned that everybody was full of shit, everybody had his own game, his own self-interest at heart. I didn't see anything to believe in, or anyone. When you get right down to the nitty gritty, I thought it was better to be by yourself. At least, you would be dealing with a known enemy, yourself, rather than something unknown; namely, the rest of the world.

I didn't notice Judi very much. She was leaving the program. Having been punished by the Department of Psychiatry, she was banished to the Emergency Room. Her patients were giving a party for her. I wasn't invited, not being a member of the therapeutic community she had started, and anyway I was sick from heroin withdrawal.

I watched them from my end of the ward. For the first time in the three days that I had been in the hospital, I saw someone high on drugs. Two men and a girl weren't just high, they were stoned.

The rules were that no one was allowed drugs, and I waited to see what would happen.

They suspected from the start that I had supplied the drugs. I insisted that I hadn't, explaining that I had come into the hospital to kick, and I would not bring in drugs under that circumstance. I followed a kind of logic, sick as I was: If you were kicking, you kicked; you didn't mess it up by having a stash of drugs. It's an important ethic with me to keep my word. I'm rigid and proud about promises. In the street I'd steal from you without a thought, but if ever I promised not to rob you, everything you owned would be safe from or with me.

The therapeutic community patients called me into their group and demanded that I tell them where I had hidden my drugs. I continued to deny that I had any until finally they believed me. Then they asked if I thought the girl was high. I said I couldn't tell, since she was sitting at the other end of the room. They said, "Come over and take a look at her."

I did and it was even more obvious that she was stoned, but I said I couldn't tell. One of the first things you learn in the drug world is not to squeal on anyone; this reinforces the "code of the streets." While they discussed it, I sat there with them. Judi was guiding the dispute, but I wasn't very aware of her. What amazed me was that everyone seemed so upset about the three who were high. They were all junkies, dope fiends, what did they care about somebody getting high? Their attitude was contrary to one of the first rules on the street: *Don't get involved.*

Even though I was uncomfortable because of withdrawal, I sat there for four hours. I wanted to see if they really would discharge the people who had used drugs. If they didn't, it would reinforce my belief that everybody was full of shit. If they did, then they really believed in something—which was incredible to me. I waited and they threw them out. Their obvious commitment appealed to me.

So I became part of the program. I would show them that I could do what they were doing. I didn't tell them what I had in mind since I didn't care to communicate. I set about becoming a full-functioning robot, which was no problem. I didn't speak, but my bed was made perfectly every day, the work I was given was done well. It's the way I had been taught to live—that it doesn't matter what you're feeling inside so long as you perform according to the expectations of those around you.

I learned that at home. It was reinforced in the Roman Catholic schools I attended. My family was lower middle class Irish Catholic. I was born in 1946 and we lived in Washington Heights in New York

City. My father had a blue-collar job with a railroad company.

There are early memories of my parents having many fights, mostly about my father's drinking. By the time I was five I was staying away from the house as much as possible. I lived in the streets, looking for something there. I didn't know what it was, but I knew that what I wanted wasn't at home.

It's strange that I can remember every detail of the house where we lived when I was small, and can draw it accurately today, but I can't remember *me*. I have no recollection of whether I was afraid in those days or depressed or what. I still have difficulty describing my feelings.

I became part of the street gangs that were around in the fifties. I tried to emulate the leaders, the guys who were good fighters and had the most nerve. We stole sodas from soft-drink trucks, smoked cigarettes, dropped balloons of water on people from the trees in the park.

My mother is a long-suffering kind of woman, very responsible and dedicated. When I was small she remained at home, and I think she felt threatened by having a son. Most of the males in her family had been heavy drinkers and she dreaded the responsibility of raising me. I suspect that she was sure she would fail and I would become an alcoholic. She didn't know how to cope with me and I played on that.

I started to get into trouble around the sixth grade. I hated homework and wouldn't do it. The teacher asked every morning if I had done it and I would answer no.

I had been taught to be truthful. It was important in our family to tell the truth. When I told the teacher the truth, he would call me up to the front of the room and hit me. The Brother who did it was about two hundred and fifty pounds and six foot four. He would hit extremely hard. He used a ruler and gave me a choice of which hand I wanted to hold out, and then he'd hit it three times.

It happened every morning. I felt that not doing my homework was worth the price of being hit three times a day. Nobody was going to tell what to do. My family had little to say about my refusal to do homework because my marks were always in the nineties. Even when I went to high school and continued to reject homework assignments, I still got marks of eighty or eighty-five in all subjects.

As I got older, the gang fights got rougher. They were using axes, guns, rifles. It wasn't my thing at all and I would stay out of it, but the neighborhood was getting scared. Some people were badly hurt. Once I was present when about twenty kids caught a rival gang member who had a wooden leg. They tore off the leg so he couldn't run and then threatened to kill him with a rifle. Someone stopped it in time.

When I was thirteen I began smoking marijuana with the gang. Two years later my father found some in my pocket and told my mother about it. I protested that it wasn't marijuana, that someone at school had given it to me, and everything else I could devise. She believed me, not him.

It was the first time I had lied and betrayed my father. I felt bad about it, playing one parent against the other that way. My father got a little bit drunker that night.

As my drug use progressed to pills, before going home I would disguise my drug high by drinking a little liquor so my breath would smell of alcohol. My mother would yell at me for drinking, and I'd go to sleep and that would be that.

However, I hated alcohol. I had seen what it did to every male in my family and it repulsed me. Most of all, I hated the aggression and violence the drunkard showed. Consequently, one of the attractions of heroin was that it produced passivity. I liked the quiet of drugs rather than the noise and anger of alcohol.

At fifteen, I was staying out until one or two in the morning. My amphetamine use began during the summer I was sixteen. I heard that "ups" weren't addicting, which is far from the truth. Amphetamines are the worst of all the drugs of abuse, including heroin.

At seventeen, I graduated from high school and started to work as a trainee in the Bank of New York. In addition I was taking courses related to the subject of banking. However, when it came time to turn in a term paper, it represented homework again, and I refused to do it. So I dropped out of school.

I was smoking pot every day and taking pills on the weekends. Gradually I began to take pills during the week as well. I moved to another bank on Wall Street, the Bank of Montreal. About a year and a half later, I was promoted to junior officer in a loan department, responsible for about thirty million dollars' worth of negotiable securities.

I smoked marijuana during my lunch break. I was eating alone down by the docks. I was trying something new, "Cibas," which is the street name for Doriden. I rationalized that one pill is the same as another. I washed the pill down with two ounces of cough medicine, the kind with codeine in it. It was nuts, but it gave me a mild drowsiness. Friends told me it resembled a heroin high.

I had snorted heroin once when I was fourteen. It didn't do much for me. I used LSD seven or eight times and lost interest, although one time on acid there was a space of about twenty seconds when I was sitting on a rock in the park and thought that I had the whole world in my hands. I can't remember what it looked like, but I'll never forget the feeling.

That was seven years ago. I'm still waiting for my nirvana.

One weekend I was invited to a party with a friend, Micky, who used drugs with me and had a light heroin habit. A few days before, he said we needed some cocaine because the party was going to last the whole weekend. We had pot, pills and cough medicine but we wanted to add a spoon of cocaine as well. We tried to find it for two days but it was impossible. There was some kind of panic on.

When we asked a dealer for cocaine, he said he could get us a bag of heroin instead. Micky said okay but I was disappointed. I wanted coke. He said, "Listen, I'm going to get a bag." I said, "Okay, get two."

We went to the party at a girl's house in Brewster, New York. It is a quiet, upstate community. Her parents were away for the weekend. We told her we wanted to smoke pot, and she told us to use the attic because some of the people at the party were squares.

In the attic, I asked Micky if he planned to snort the heroin. He said no, because he had brought some works. "How much do you want?" he asked. I said a quarter bag. Thinking I would only skin pop, he gave me more. I decided to mainline. It surprised him and he asked why. I said, "Why not? Why waste time snorting and skin popping? If you're going to use heroin, you might as well mainline." I was seventeen at the time.

So I mainlined and I never felt anything like it. The room seemed to spin and I actually grabbed for the rafters in the attic. Then what happened is what usually happens the first time you shoot heroin: I was sick.

From that moment on, I felt special; I was one of the few people in my neighborhood who had a heroin connection, a dependable supplier. I had something that other people didn't have. It gave me prestige.

Once I started, I continued to mainline heroin. I was becoming more and more depressed. I looked around at the people in the bank. It upset me that their desk or their cigar or their position reflected how they felt about themselves and how they felt about everyone else. I felt trapped. Forty years from now, that would be me. My Catholic upbringing had emphasized that it was irrelevant to have feeling about what you're doing. What matters is going through the motions properly. I was beginning to realize that that was a lot of bullshit, and I didn't want any part of it.

Along with being a junior executive in the bank, responsible for millions in negotiable securities, I was dealing drugs. It gave me a good feeling to sell drugs because people wanted me. I was still living at home, being dependent to that extent, and the dependency of addicts on me, their supplier, offset that feeling. It also provided me with a way of relating to people; I was a benefactor.

One day I resigned from the bank. They were getting ready to bust me anyway because I was taking pills right in the office. I'd swallow two or three pills with a paper cup of water. I shot heroin every day except Wednesday. It gave me an illusion that I was in control of my habit to miss a day. Eventually the Wednesday abstinence went too. I wasn't worried: it was a light habit, I figured, only a bag a day and two bags on weekends.

A month after my resignation, I got a terrific headache that lasted for three days. It was so bad, my mother called the doctor. He took my blood pressure and saw the needle tracks on my arm. He told her that I was an addict.

To give you an idea of the distorted way I was thinking, I regarded him as totally unethical for telling my mother even though I was living in her house and she was paying his bill.

She was so upset by my addiction that I told her I was sick because I had quit. How could I still be taking heroin when I had been in the house for three days? I asked her. She believed me.

The doctor left me some codeine, enough for me to get high for the next three days. Later that same doctor wrote prescriptions for me, knowing I didn't need the narcotic medication except to feed my habit.

I financed my continuing habit in the traditional way: stealing. I started by breaking into cars, but that didn't provide much money and it was hard on the feet. I switched to stealing large roasts of beef from supermarkets. It's called *cattle rustling*. You work with a partner and then sell the roasts in housing projects or some middle-class neighborhood. You ended up with about thirty dollars for fifteen minutes' work. I observed cynically that nearly everyone, even if they know it, will buy stolen goods if they are a bargain, and in this way they help make addiction possible.

Micky and I reached the point where we were burglarizing apartments. We stuck to the lower floors so there would be easy access and exit. We had very little trouble. Many people leave their front doors open. If they don't, most locks are easily broken.

My habit no longer could be described as light, even by me. I was using between fifteen and thirty dollars' worth of heroin a day.

At that time a Black girl I was intimate with became pregnant.

She was addicted too. Given the reality of our addiction, the attitude of society toward interracial marriages and the difficulties a child of mixed parents would encounter, I made the decision there should be an abortion. She found the abortionist and it was done.

For the first time, I personally realized the conflicts around blackness and whiteness in this society. The baby was a person who had not been allowed to exist partly because of racial attitudes. I felt cynicism, anger and apathy. I went out and got high.

I was detoxified three times on methadone. It's much worse than quitting heroin cold. When I first arrived at Metropolitan Hospital in September of 1966, I began methadone detoxification again. After three days I asked them to stop the drug, insisting that I was all right. I would rather face kicking heroin cold than methadone withdrawal. It was an awful time. I couldn't sleep because of the pains in my arms and legs. I tried soaking in a hot bath, but it didn't help.

So I went to the nurse's cage and asked for medication. The nurse was Mrs. Devlin, a little old Irish lady in her seventies, who had become a legend among the drug addicts at Metropolitan. She told me she didn't have any medication for me. She told me to wait a minute and then she gave me a red lollypop instead. It was either hit her or laugh, so I laughed.

I had chosen to go to Met because Micky, my partner in drugs and crime, was there. He used to telephone me at home, raving about how good the program was. I went mostly to detoxify and to lower my habit and be healthy enough to go back on the street and shoot drugs again. In the back of my mind I knew I had to choose among several alternatives: one, support my habit by selling drugs heavily; two, move to a country where heroin was legal; three, take one last fix and commit suicide; and four, stop drugs.

There must have been something working on the subconscious level in favor of choice *three,* because after I arranged to be admitted to Met, I overdosed twice. I had never taken any overdoses before. The second one knocked me to my knees, but I remained conscious. The first one put me out cold for two hours.

When I came to and saw the expression on my mother's face, I realized that she had thought I had died. I wonder if my heart actually had stopped while I was unconscious, and if so, for how long.

I had just joined the therapeutic community at Met, which then had no name, when the message came that we were going to be thrown out of the hospital. Judi was in the Emergency Room as punishment, our nurse had been sent to the blood bank and there were other harrassments. For instance, the lights would go on and off at crazy times. There were a lot of meatball things like that.

The purpose of it all was to convince the patients who had been part of the cyclazocine research experiment to go back on the drug. They were refusing, insisting that they were finished with drug dependency, and so the hospital was applying pressure.

The hospital doctors did some incredible things on that ward. There was the day when they asked Judi to persuade her patients to submit to liver biopsies, and another day they tried to shake her confidence in her work by means of a forgery. They showed Judi a letter that said that twenty-six out of twenty-eight urines on the ward had come back positive, demonstrating that the therapeutic community was obviously a failure, because the patients were using drugs.

The letter purported to be from the Office of the New York City Medical Examiner. The hospital obviously didn't know that Judi's Husband, Michael Baden, was the Associate Medical Examiner and was in charge of the city's laboratory to screen urine for drugs. Later, Judi told me that she called him at his office very upset and told Michael that the least he could have done was tell her directly that the program was no good. That's how she discovered that the letter was a fake. Michael told her no such urine report had ever been sent out by his office, and that the thirteen urines which his office had analyzed were free of drugs.

My decision to stay with this beleaguered program was no decision. I wasn't really there. At every group when asked how I felt I would say, "I feel much more a part of the group." That was my one-liner, and it seemed to satisfy them.

There was a grain of truth in it. For the first time in my life, I was beginning to feel a part of something. I wasn't aware of it at the time. I thought I was going through the motions and fooling them. But at least I had been clean of drugs for three weeks. This was the longest period without them in the seven years since I began. Something was happening.

Eventually Met Hospital threw us out. Dr. Efren Ramirez, City Narcotics Coordinator, made an arrangement for us all to be transferred to a ward at Manhattan General Hospital. We went there and were told that the males could be admitted but not the three females. There was some rule about it.

We explained that we were trying to build a meaningful program based on people believing in something. We couldn't drop three people because they happened to be the wrong sex. The hospital wouldn't accept us any other way, so we left.

Dr. Ramirez arranged for us to stay at Daytop Village for one week. There we were to have a vacation, think things over and make plans. It was nothing like a vacation. We seventeen did the laundry, the cooking and the cleaning normally done by eighty residents. On the day before our departure, we were offered a log cabin in Bridgewater, Connecticut, by a former Met Hospital vocational therapist, Ken Dupré.

Eleven of us went there. The others who were in charge of the program slept in Judi's and Michael's apartment on the floor of their living room. That's how we put together Odyssey's first Board of Directors. Some of the people in their co-operative apartment house were indignant at having ex-addicts coming and going while others thought it was the most inspiring thing that had ever happened. We formed the Board from the latter group.

The log cabin was an experience. There were holes between the logs and, since it was November, it was excruciatingly cold. I made the discovery that newspapers between blankets make good insulation.

The water wasn't connected when we arrived so we worked all the first night under the cabin hooking it up. In the morning when we went to shower we found that we had connected the hot water to the toilet, so we had to do it over again.

I stayed with the group at that point because I thought if they were so crazy as to put up with such conditions, maybe I had found a home. People in Bridgewater were very warm to us. They invited us to speak at a church and have dinner in their homes. They had nothing to gain by it—that made an impression on me.

When the others who remained in New York succeeded in renting a house on 109th Street, we left Connecticut. The first thing that greeted me there was a paint brush. I was told to paint the office. I was cold and hungry because I had been driving for two hours, but the group stressed obedience and I did it.

Those were unbelievable times. Once somebody gave me a piece of gum. Gum was a luxury then because we were penniless. Five minutes later he asked to have the gum back. I said, "I already have it in my mouth." He said to give it to him. He used it to plug a hole in a water pipe in the kitchen. Every morning after that when I came down to the kitchen I expected to see it full of bubbles from the bubble gum.

It may not seem so hilarious now, but it struck me as very funny then. We were seventeen people sleeping in three rooms, and humor was the way we maintained our morale.

I remember one group vividly, in which a fellow resident named Ernie told us gravely that he had something to cop to. Odyssey uses "cop" to mean "confess." He looked as though he was about to cry and we were sitting on the edge of the chairs. He said he had stolen a can of sardines from our larder and thrown the empty can in the neighbor's garbage. He felt so guilty that he had to tell us about it. We were all starving, and I think everyone was thinking the same thing: "Shit, I wish I'd got the can first."

The work was divided according to our skills. Someone was a cook, someone was a painter, someone else was a businessman, someone else was an auto mechanic. Because of my bank experience, I was assigned the books. There wasn't much to do. We were living on ten dollars a day for all seventeen of us.

Whenever she could get away from her duties at Met Hospital, Judi joined our groups. She had made the commitment to us that if we wanted to start a program she would help us, and she never failed. She didn't have to stick with us. We had nothing to lose, but we knew she was risking a lot. The reason that Odyssey is unique is that Judi never deserted us—it's one of the few programs anywhere run by professionals and ex-addicts co-operatively and not by a majority of one or the other.

It amazed us that Judi, with so many other professional options to choose from, would help us, seventeen unpromising ex-addicts in an unfunded derelict of a house.

Previously, all of us had been very hostile to professionals. In and out of hospitals as much as we had been, we saw professionals as people who prevent the patients from getting contraband, if they can; people from so different life experiences that there was no way of relating. Addicts on the street maintain a certain attitude, a certain stance, to avoid being killed. It's not possible to explain that and other things to someone sitting there with a pad and pencil jotting it down. And furthermore, they seem unreal, hiding behind their titles.

Judi was different. She struck us as being a person. She knew what she was doing and was for real. At that time one of the phrases used commonly in the program was "being for real." It meant dropping what you had been on the street and what you usually pretend to be—getting rid of your image. Just being you, good and bad. Judi was for real.

She constantly drew analogies between herself and the patients. She said she could be just as devious and just as dishonest as we were, but she chose not to. Why had we chosen such a life style? What did we have to show for it?

We had nothing. We came in the program with nothing—nothing in our pockets, no friends, no family. Not even a soul left.

I would sit back in those groups and watch Judi. The first observation I made was that she was able to think on about five different levels at the same time. There was order in her thinking, no matter how random it might sound. She was able to plan ahead and spring things on us. It was fascinating to listen to her.

I should have known that she would not allow me to continue as a dutiful robot forever. I had been in the program about six months when we held a marathon which concentrated on me for about seven hours. The group wanted me to admit how fucked up I was, and for seven hours I kept assuring them I was fine.

I couldn't figure out what they wanted. As the hours passed, I concluded that I should reveal everything in my past that I had kept hidden. I trotted out the skeletons, the terrible things I had done, but they kept saying, "What else can you come up with?" It was so much a part of me to talk only of factual superficialities, rather than real feelings, that it never dawned on me that what they wanted was an expression of what I was feeling. I became increasingly frustrated. I wanted to please them, to meet their expectations. I didn't know what to *do*, and it never dawned on me that they wanted me to *feel*, not do.

So I left the group and went upstairs to pack. I had a record player and I planned to sell it and buy enough heroin to overdose. Shooting dope again would be the same as commiting suicide and I was thinking, *Why not go all the way?*

I was changing my clothes when Judi and Tony Enriquez, our ex-addict Director, came in. They asked me where I was going. I began to cry, something very rare for me. I said, I'm tired of being here. I don't like being this close to people and feeling that I can't be close to people without hurting them or getting hurt. I want to go out and forget it.

I'm going to kill myself, I told them. I will never be able to have real feelings.

Judi pointed out that I was having real feelings right then. Still crying hard, I denied it. She assured me that I was feeling more deeply all the time, that I was making great improvement.

I don't remember exactly what else she said, but I became calmer. The essence of my first marathon experience took place in that room with only two other people. I decided to stay and went through the usual nonsense of being embarrassed. After that I loosened up and became a little more verbal with the whole group.

My feeling for individuals in the program didn't improve much at first, but I began to realize that I had developed a strong feeling for the group as a whole.

I had no money and no close friends; I had nothing tangible from my half a year in Odyssey. But it came to me suddenly that I had gained more from the program than the program had gained from me. The one who benefited the most was Jimmy Murphy. Around that time, I reached the conclusion that I was going to stick it through, no matter what.

After making my decision, I noticed the beginning of closeness with some individuals. I was closer in a real sense, rather than pretending to be close in order to use them, to set them up to do things for me. Best of all, the closeness didn't terrify me; it was all right. I could handle it.

A few months later, we moved into the Mother House on East Sixth Street. Judi asked me to draft the budget for potential government funding. On June 23, 1967, we were funded for $243,000 with the budget I wrote. Judi wrote the accompanying program narrative and checked the figures, but the reality was that I had done the fiscal section myself.

Judi kept saying, "Look what you did, Jimmy. You've got us all this money!" It was kind of her, since it was a joint effort. Still I took pride in it. I had accomplished something for my group with another person after a lifetime of being an island unto myself.

The building on Sixth Street was a depressing sight. There were fourteen tons of ashes in the boiler room and no way to get them out of the basement except by pulley and relay, a pailful at a time. We filled up two garbage trucks on the same day that we presented the budget. I worked on it all night. In the morning, Judi, Tony and I delivered it to Ramirez's office and answered some questions. When I came back to the house, I helped to carry out the ashes. Everybody was working.

While we were loading the ashes, a neighbor passed by, stopped and said, "Hey, I hear this building is going to be used by drug addicts. When are they moving in?" There was a silence and someone answered, "We are the people who are moving in." The neighbor said, "Oh" and walked away quickly.

He came back about three weeks later and apologized. He'd had some misconceptions of what an addiction treatment program would be like, he said, and when he saw how hard we were working he felt he had been rude. He still drops in to say hello.

The building hadn't been used in eight months. Cats had moved in through a window left open and the smell was terrible. It took us three weeks of constantly washing the walls, floors and ceilings with the special soap used in morgues before we were rid of the stench.

It was crazy. At that point, there were eleven people in the program. We had all the work in front of us and no one to help us do it. Still it had to be done.

Of the original seventeen, only nine were left. Mel Williams had

5

been the first splittee, leaving in January. More splits, Dickie Aubert and Shirley Levine, left in March; they said they were in love.

Dickie was one of four sons, all of them heroin addicts. His brothers were triplets. He used to tease me and Micky, calling us his sons. We felt that he was looking out for us and we missed him when he left. Dickie was a very humorous guy, always joking; very sensitive, very intelligent. Thin and toothless, he looked like a Black Mahatma Gandhi.

He used to thrive on the fact that he could eat corn on the cob even though he had no teeth; very strong gums. He went into detail about his sexual exploits and the advantage of being toothless.

In September, about six months after he left, Judi's Husband called to say that the morgue had been notified that Dickie was dead of an overdose. He was in a rooming house on 74th Street. Judi, Tony and I went there. He had a sheet covering him and all I could see was his foot. His girl, Shirley, very pregnant and in acute congestive heart failure, from rheumatic heart disease, was high on barbiturates and hysterical—there was no talking to her. We took her to Bellevue. They released her and she died about a year later in a cheap rooming house. The maggots were eating her because she wasn't found for a week. Their son was now an orphan.

We learned that Dickie had taken drugs only once or twice since leaving Odyssey. He'd been keeping in touch with us, telling us that he was clean and feeling good. He was working full time at a stationer's, but she had returned to drugs. He couldn't cope.

That night after we arrived back in the Mother House, someone walked down the street with a transistor radio playing "A Song for My Father." It made my skin prickle, since Dickie had often called himself my father.

Dickie's death came after I had begun to have a relationship with my real father for the first time in our lives. The program had helped me to be able to approach him and establish a bond. Ironically, by the time I was able to reach out to him he had undergone surgery with the removal of his larynx for cancer, which prevented him from ever speaking again.

We had to communicate now by writing notes, by facial expression, by body language and by empathy—which Judi and Odyssey House had taught me. The tragedy of Dickie's death for me was that he hadn't allowed the program to help him in the same way as it had helped me.

A month after Dickie's death, all the residents left the program. I should have seen it coming, but I didn't appreciate the signs until much later. Judi was working at Odyssey full time, having just completed her residency, and Tony, the ex-addict Director, began to complain about working with a professional staff. He kept saying things like, "I can't do anything with these fucking professionals. They don't understand us addicts."

In some respects he was right—some of the professionals were difficult—but he used to act like a lunatic. He would yell and scream, and there were about ten groups in which Tony got up and banged on the tables, almost throwing chairs. Judi would cry.

We should have looked at this interchange in the light of what Tony was trying to do, and eventually did do. But we put it down to a personality clash and dismissed it.

According to the lines of authority, Judi was at the top of the agency as Clinical Director. Since she hadn't been able to be with us constantly, as Tony had, the attachment we had for him and his own charisma made it hard for us to see Judi's points or detect where Tony was coming from. In addition, most of us needed a strong father figure, which we had not had, and we had had too much mother.

It began to be clear that there were two groups forming—the ex-addicts on one side and the professionals on the other. I felt closer to the professionals, especially Judi, in many respects, but I had made an emotional commitment to the ex-addict group. My loyalty wasn't to the concepts embodied in Odyssey House, as it should have been, but to the people in the group.

One night I was on duty from midnight to eight, when I was called into the office with the rest of the senior residents and told by Tony that we were finally going to get rid of the professionals. Then the ex-addicts would run their own program. He asked what we all thought of the idea. As it went around the room everyone seemed to be in agreement. When it was my turn, I said I didn't see how it could work. If it happened, I added, I would leave the program.

The next day was vicious. We were all instructed to write out our complaints against Judi which would be submitted to the Board of Directors to obtain their support. Judi arrived and asked innocently, "What's going on?"

When she found out, she was distraught. Everyone was upset; I was upset. The others were pressuring me to join them in the rebellion. We'd been together thirteen or fourteen months, and I didn't want to fight with them. Just before the Board meeting they asked me, "Are you going to stay with the group or go with Judi?" I said neither, I was going to leave.

Tony suggested, "Why don't you stay with Judi if that's what you really want?" He couldn't have said anything better, from his point of view. I always took my mother's side at home against my father and I was nursing deep regrets, feeling guilty about it. It was irrational of me, but I decided abruptly to be loyal to the male-led group.

When the Board meeting ended, the ex-addicts had lost. Our proposal to get rid of professional controls was rejected. We were told that Judi hadn't been attacked personally during the meeting, which was not true. We were told a number of lies which we believed. Many of the group don't know the truth today; some died, some returned to drugs.

We left, supposedly to start another program, and lived in a borrowed facility in Peekskill, New York. I couldn't figure out what was happening, but there seemed to be something wrong. Tony and the others leading us conferred a good deal.

Four of us, three men and a girl, were given a hundred dollars and sent to New York to find funding and a building for the new program. We used a three-room apartment as headquarters and nearly went nuts because it was so cramped. When all of us sat in the living room our knees touched; we decided it gave us only slightly more space than we would have had in the morgue.

We stayed away from Judi and Odyssey. She had promised me a copy of the minutes of the Board meeting. When they didn't arrive, I concluded that she didn't want me to see them. I reasoned falsely that probably they didn't show the professional point of view to any advantage.

Less than five weeks after the split had occurred, we reported back to Tony that we had succeeded in obtaining co-operation from a church. It would provide an umbrella for our fund-raising and house-hunting. He said never mind, he had a new plan. Instead of starting our own program, he had arranged for us all to go to Phoenix House, a new drug rehabilitation program that New York City was running. Tony had been offered an executive position there at what he said was a small salary. I later learned he made almost $20,000 the first year. Others were hired as well. They wanted me to persuade the group to follow their orders.

A few refused. One had been drug-free for two years and felt he was ready to be on his own. The senior female said she had been planning to leave anyway. When it came to me, I said I would give it a try.

A week after I arrived at Phoenix I was made head of the business office. My initial impression of Phoenix was that it was only another ex-addict sub-culture, the kind that residents never leave. The final straw came when I was punished for choosing the words *Intellectual Enthusiasm* as part of the "Thought of the Day." I was chided because the words had too many syllables, making them difficult for the residents to understand. I saw no point in staying longer. I left.

I was confident that I would never shoot heroin again. I knew it was stupid. There were better ways to handle one's problems.

I went home. The next day I visited a friend, James Slater, who ran a community center. Jim wanted to talk about Judi, but I didn't want to hear it. I was puzzled about Tony's actions, I told him. He was supposed to lead us all out of the wilderness, but halfway through he couldn't handle it. It's hard to be a follower when the leader quits. Jim persisted, "Talk to Judi. You haven't been getting the correct information."

I told him no. He asked why I was acting so threatened. My ego got in the way again, but for a change it worked to my advantage. I promised to see her.

All the way over to the Mother House I rehearsed my explanation about loyalty to the group. My first shock came when I arrived there and learned that Tony had just left. He had been seeing Judi for his regular private therapy sessions at the same time that he was telling us she didn't know how to treat or relate to addicts and ex-addicts. I was shaken by that and surprised to see that several of our group had returned already.

Then Judi gave me the minutes of the Board meeting. She explained that copies cost eight hundred dollars apiece, so she wanted me to read them on the premises. She had advised my mother that I could read them there, but when I got the message I had thought it was a game.

After that there was only the obstacle of apologizing to her. That took about three hours.

> I can't hear and I can't see,
> Please God let them pity me.
> God in heaven take my heart,
> I don't want this world which sets me apart
>
> I bring a rose which has no odor
> And yet the rose I do relate
> This is my feeling of love and hate
>
> Where am I at I ask the world
> The smell of a man makes me shiver
> For my handicap I really quiver
>
> Shed the petals, but harden the stem
> Than you really can begin.

—TOMMY MOTT

James P. Murphy.

'So much to do in so little time' at youth conference

'A process leading to solutions

Judy Kooker
Foreign relations

ROCKY MOUNTAIN NEWS PHOTOS
BY JOHN GORDON

James P. Murphy
Drugs

By JOAN McCOY
Rocky Mountain News Writer

ESTES PARK — Obtaining an interview with a task force co-chairman at the White House Conference on Youth is no easy task, as reporters have been discovering at the YMCA of the Rockies near here, where nearly 1,500 young people and adults have gathered for this three-day national meeting.

Publicized a great deal for its problems, due to lots of now and a few dissenting factions, the conference has most participants all wrapped up in meetings held everywhere from the corner of the dining hall to the backstairs of one of the numerous buildings on the 00-acre site.

Confronted briefly in a hallway was James P. Murphy, youth co-chairman of the drugs task force, who sees the conference "not so much a final answer will be found as the beginning of a meaningful process which will

eventually lead to solutions.

A FORMER DRUG addict, Murphy currently is director of the Odyssey House drug rehabilitation program. He believes "there are many answers to the problems brought about by an advanced technological society" and that "a conference such as this is needed because individuals have become alienated by society as a whole."

Brought together to discuss and improve upon recommendations in their task force's report to the conference, delegates after the first day of sessions were, in Murphy's words, slipping a lot . . . they realize they have so much to do and there is so little time." (The final scheduled meeting is at 3 p.m. Wednesday.)

The 25-year-old co-chairman feels drug usage today is "almost a fad. Students use them because everyone else does. It's like alcohol and sex were at one time. Now is the time to attack the underlying problems and to offer kids alternative directions.

"There is a need for immediacy. The kids here are very dedicated and interested in

the problem. They have worked hard and are committed to keep on working hard long after this conference ends. Much of what they have done has involved research in their own communities."

MURPHY SEES three basic steps to attacking the drug problems in this country: "One, openly confront the problem. Two, establish a process whereby dialogue takes place. Addicts have a lot in common, but for each one there is a different reason why three, motivate the community to solve its own problems."

The director of Odyssey House, which has 26 facilities in four states, also sees his type of program being established on college campuses and in ghetto neighborhoods.

In regard to addicts helping other addicts, Murphy commented: "Addicts are like other people. Some are secure, some are insecure; some are stable, some are not; some are mature, some are immature. It simply depends on the person.

"Someone who has used drugs can relate better, but this doesn't mean he can find the solution. If I have had open heart surgery, this does not mean I have had training to perform such an operation."

Murphy feels the news media has done an adequate job in reporting the drug story, "especially on impact . . . getting across the real amount of those on drugs." But, he dislikes personal experience stories that have been published because "they often give certain impressions that could get kids started on

drugs rather than frighten them away."

BETWEEN MEETINGS, Judy Kooker, youth co-chairman for the task force on foreign relations, said she found a great deal of anti-government feeling among the people she talked with in the eight months of researching for her segment of the conference.

"We walked into cities total strangers and were surprised with how well we were accepted. But, first we had to make it clear we were not representing the government," explained the second year master's degree student at the Johns University School for A d v a n c e d International Studies.

"We found people pretty candid about discussing their problems, but many were more interested in the major concerns of their community than in foreign relations, so we tried to relate through what they were immediately involved in. We found, more

than anything else, the people had definite feelings of hopelessness about having any impact on what any level of government does."

Official task force visits were made to New York, Chicago, Baton Rouge and Tampa, but Judy pointed out "individual trips went as far as Sydney, Australia, to get opinions from U.S. servicemen."

Judy said discussions showed "the gap in foreign policy assumptions between youth and adults is wider than we had thought, but the willingness of adults to discuss this with youth is greater than we had thought."

The Great Split

At some point in the history of most drug-addiction therapeutic communities, usually when they are between eight months and two years old, there is a palace revolution. Addicts are accustomed to the jungle fighting of the streets, and thus these battles for control are often vicious. At Odyssey the struggle was between the professional staff who had been in charge of the agency and the ex-addicts who had been in treatment from the beginning. The latter felt they were well enough to take over from the doctors. Our battle, in addition, had the other dynamic of ex-addicts trying to shake off their therapists as children shake off parents when they reach that omnipotent age between immaturity and maturity.

Daytop Village has had such internal wars several times. Synanon had one early in its history. Quaker Rehabilitation went through the same destructive process, as did Challenge House in Massachusetts. Odyssey's travail began on Thursday, October 26, 1967, when Tony Enriquez, leading the residents, notified me that I was being kicked upstairs to be fund raiser and Clinical Director Emeritus; I would not be permitted to treat the patients or run the agency any longer.

I went through tremendous pain and self-evaluation in the weeks that followed. The issue of whether he or I would be in charge went to the Odyssey Board of Directors; the majority supported me instead of Tony. When he was fired, he left and all but one of the patients followed him. Eight of those who deserted me were among the original seventeen addicts I had grown so close to in Metropolitan Hospital. Betrayal from those you trust causes the deepest kind of hurt. I was even more wounded later when I learned that the power play had been motivated by greed. There are many people on all levels throughout the United States even today who see the addiction epidemic and consequent community panic reaction and desperation to do something as a way to get rich quick. In our instance, these people wanted the building, the charter and the tax exemption that Odyssey had.

On reflection I also see it as an attitudinal conflict. The professionals at Odyssey were all brain, and the fascinating physical fact about the brain is that it can't feel its own pain. For itself, it has no pain receptors. The professional represented an intellectualized, anesthetized head, while the addict was the emotional, raging gut.

The gut can feel only pain. Thought is unable to control its impulses. Like the addict, it is an explosive entity, constantly seeking gratification, and cannot be moderated by the head.

The one area of the body that has the best of both worlds is the heart. It can either be controlled by the head or can operate independently.

I use the head, the heart and the gut as symbols of the factions in Odyssey. The professionals and their overintellectualized defenses contend with the addicts and their acting-out seeking of gratification; what arbitrates is the heart, which therapeutic communities describe as love and concern.

Odyssey has the heart, combining both thought and feeling. We're run by professionals *and* ex-addicts. It's a combination of organization and discipline. As more and more experiences are shared, we become indistinguishable from each other. We even forget who came from what world, for we now travel together as a new breed.

In the professional world, the code is respect. It is constantly concerned with established status. There is vast preoccupation with such matters as being invited to the right party and the amount of floor space in one's office. Such rumination on the pecking order necessitates maintaining distance between self and others. Distance, by definition, is threatened by the experience of love.

Respect is irrelevent to the addict. First of all, he knows he isn't worthy of respect. He hasn't lived a life that would make anyone want to look up to him, yet he still needs a coin of human exchange so he constantly demands love, concern and understanding. There's really nothing particularly lovable about him. I often say to the addict, "What are you talking about? What have you done to earn love? Maybe you're unloved because you're a miserable horrible creature that nobody should love, not even a mother."

Many of them are hard to love. Why should we love them? Often they beat their own children—recently, one addict's child was bitten and beaten to death by her mother's boy friend. Some addicts prostitute their own daughters; some of them put their wives on the street;

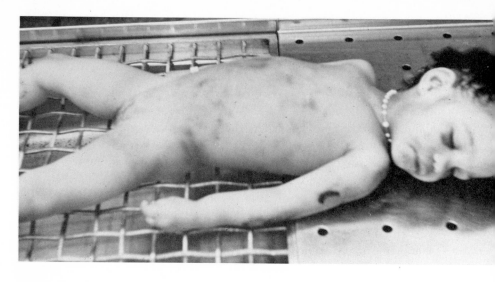

Nine-month-old child bitten and beaten to death
by boy friend of addict mother.

some steal from their mothers. Who could love such people?

When I encounter staff members who intellectualize universal Christian love for everything human I want to say, *Fuck you*. I don't know what the hell they're talking about.

Since love and respect cannot be a common medium of exchange between professional and ex-addict, we have a concept of trust instead at Odyssey. It's more than a semantic game to say that trust differs from love. Trust begins with trusting that your sense of self will not permit you to do anything against another human being. The other human being has the same trust and knows you are committed to not destroying him or using him for your needs at the expense of his. You can count on it: It won't happen; you won't be stabbed in the back.

Relationships at Odyssey are built on a foundation of trust. Raw addicts have to feel that Odyssey does nothing that isn't in their best interests. We are not out to cut or hurt. When the patients accept that, they begin to get well. They begin by trusting the concern and perception of their peer group, move on to trust the staff and eventually trust themselves to behave responsibly. That's when they graduate.

Love is somewhere beyond trust. It's an earned feeling based on a long period of mutual commitment or mutual accomplishment during which there has been growing together a partnership. Many

66

people claim to love others, but they don't trust. I doubt the depth of the relationship. Love can come out of trust, but not the other way around.

Trust was a key word during the power struggle of 1967, which Odyssey usually calls the "Great Split." Tony Enriquez had graduated from the program and become Executive Director. My title was Clinical Director, which carried slightly more authority. Tony joined in a plot to displace me.

It was very confusing. A strange element in the pain and chaos of the events that followed was that Tony continued to see me once a week as my private patient. The only change was that he refused to lie down on the couch as he had before but sat facing me while I continued to try to help him with his insight. Even after the fight was out in the open and he had led the exodus from Odyssey, he came back promptly for his appointments. Because I thought my professional ethics demanded it, I permitted this curious situation to continue for about six weeks. I thought it would be improper to terminate a patient, even one who had hurt me so deeply.

Shortly after we bought the building on East Sixth Street in May of 1967, the battle for control began. Tony informed me that I shouldn't speak to the residents. I should channel everything through him. He would be the one to deal directly with them. Also, he would be the only one permitted to enter my office. I was still finishing my residency at Metropolitan Hospital so that I had limited time for the patients, but he wanted a total separation. It was an odd restriction to put on a Clinical Director. I could not accept it.

I was inexperienced and naïve to treachery then. Dick Davison was on the scene. He and his wife Grace had arrived out of nowhere in December 1966 bearing Christmas gifts for the residents. Tony and some of the others asked that Dick be made a member of the Board of Directors. I agreed. We were desperate for friends at that time. The Davisons, however, always related directly to the patients, even those who had only been in the program a brief time, inviting them out to dinner and on excursions without consulting me.

We started to have strange meetings. Dick Davison, Tony, me and a press agent of a certain Greek multi-millionaire. We met once in the wealthy man's office, and they wined and dined me. I didn't understand what it was all about. I knew they were getting me ripe for something, but I couldn't figure what was going on.

At the time, we were planning a movie about Odyssey House and negotiating with a large New York City bank for a $30,000 grant to do it. One Tuesday, Dick arrived in my office with a contract for the production of a film, which he told me to sign at once. I told him I couldn't because I first had to obtain approval of the Board of Directors, since under the contract Odyssey was to relinquish rights to the film.

He turned to Tony and said, "Tony, tell her to sign it." Tony told me, "Sign it." I refused. Dick informed me that the bank wouldn't give Odyssey the grant unless the contract was written that way. He said the bank had insisted on it. I still refused and repeated that I had to get consent from the Board of Directors.

Later I called the bank and found that it knew nothing about the contract.

Dick took me out to lunch some days later to The Blue Sea restaurant and said that I shouldn't be naïve about the matter; I should take care of the therapy and let businessmen take care of the financial end of the agency. He suggested that addiction was the commodity of the decade, and we shouldn't miss the boat. Many people would benefit from the money that would be poured into treatment programs.

He was a founding member and is now on the Board of Directors of the Phoenix House Foundation. The New York *Times* ran five editorials on drug abuse in May 1970 questioning the massive amounts of public funds that disappear into Phoenix House and are not accounted for. It noted, for instance, that Phoenix House residents that year received a half million dollars in welfare payments, which were turned over to the Phoenix House Foundation, "a private group that owns the Phoenix facilities and leases them to the city's Addiction Services Agency. This is a shadowy arrangement deserving councilmanic investigation."

But there wasn't an investigation, and the following year Mayor Lindsay put even more money into Phoenix. According to a report prepared by the Office of the Controller of the City of New York (Abraham Beame) examining the operation and activities during the period 1968–70 of the Phoenix House Foundation, Inc., six buildings rented by Phoenix House were owned by companies of which Dick Davison was the sole stockholder. During the course of the investigation, effective July 31, 1969, Dick Davison transferred his stock to the Foundation, the Beame report noted.

The day of our private luncheon I told Dick that for me to become involved in anything shady was unthinkable. I said, "First of all, I don't need the money. I don't need to risk my law license or my medical license. I don't need to lose my self-respect. How could I live with myself? And how could the patients get well if we do the same things they've done? On one hand, the patients want something to believe in, and on the other, they're always looking for the loophole. They will be lost if we have no integrity."

Another situation was developing at the same time. I should have put two and two together. Many of the doctors involved in therapeutic communities in the New York City area had been meeting on a regular basis to share and solve their problems together. Often the meetings lasted through the night until breakfast. The work was hard and often discouraging. We were a source of comfort and support to one another.

Around February or March of 1967 Dr. Mitchell Rosenthal arrived from California. He had been hired by Dr. Ramirez as a Deputy Commissioner in the Addiction Services Agency. He joined our group of doctors, and he said that we should turn over all our agencies to the ex-addicts.

After one meeting in which he said this, he took me aside and said that the doctor who ran Bronx State Hospital, a member of our group, would be easy to remove. The doctor was a respected psychiatrist, a good friend of mine and a member of the Odyssey Board. Mitch said if I would work with him, we could dump this doctor and he would see to it that the City would give me Bronx State to run as well as Odyssey.

I said, "Mitch, we're supposed to help each other, not take each other over, not undercut each other. This is a hard enough disease to treat without fighting among ourselves. The principles we live by in therapeutic communities necessitate that we who run them should help one another. Let us not say one thing and do another."

I left him, feeling sadness, went home and couldn't sleep. The next day I asked my good friend Ramirez to come and see me. It was the first week of October. I told him what had transpired and warned him that Mitch was an extremely ambitious young man. Efren replied that he was aware of it, but that times were such that he needed someone tough to clean up the mess that the drug programs were in. He said he thought he would be able to handle Mitch when the time came.

My omnipotence was ridiculous. There I was warning Efren without the slightest suspicion that Odyssey's safe bastion would soon be the target and would almost be destroyed.

Two years later at a Christmas party at his home Ramirez told me that I had been right about the Addiction Services Agency. A year before he had caught members of his staff acting improperly and he attempted to fire them. The Mayor, John V. Lindsay, had sent for him immediately, Efren related, and told him that he couldn't tolerate another scandal in his Administration—he was just recovering from the one with James Marcus who had been City Water Commissioner—and instead he insisted that the staff members remain. Ramirez resigned.

Two weeks after my fruitless warning to Ramirez about Rosenthal, I received a telephone call from Mel Williams, one of the original seventeen, who had been probated to Odyssey by the courts for five years. Mel told me that Tony had just thrown him out. I told Mel that I couldn't take his side, or any side, until I made some other inquiries. I said he was to meet me in my office in the morning. I called Tony and asked him what had happened. Tony angrily retorted that I didn't have a right to know. I answered, outraged, "What do you mean, I don't have a right to know! I'm the Psychiatric Director and I have a right to know why patients are discharged from my care. Besides that, Mel is probated to me. He's in my custody." The conversation continued but seemed to be going nowhere, so I told Tony I would see him in the morning.

On October 26 I walked into the house and found that all the patients—*all*, those who had been there one day and those who had begun with me at Met Hospital—had been up all night discussing the situation. They had a new job for me. I was to be head of Odyssey House *Emeritus*. Tony said I didn't understand the patients and therefore I had no right to treat them. He had the patients list the instances of my "lack of understanding," in order to justify his action. The worst infraction, it appeared, was that I sometimes was too pre-occupied to say "good morning." However, I was good at fund-raising, so my future role would be to aid Odyssey in that capacity. He said he would see to it that they—the Board—would continue to pay me at the same salary. It was obvious the Board would have to decide be-tween us.

In the weeks that followed, further accusations against me came from dissident members of the Board and some City officials. They were vicious. They said I had struck one of the patients, that my Hus-band had threatened another with violence. It was even hinted that I was having an affair with Tony. Those were beautiful times.

I didn't know what to do. I just leaned on Michael, and cried. I had to make some sense of it, so I chose to interpret the upheaval as normal progress in Tony's therapy. Often a patient must turn against his therapist in order to become independent. The rest of the com-munity, I reasoned, had been caught in the transference. Still I considered myself responsible for what was happening. I felt I should have foreseen it as a possibility. It was all too involved being friend, boss, therapist, mother and colleague. I was becoming more Freudian—I realized that those roles can't be mixed.

I told Tony I didn't want the patients involved, that it should be between him and me. Our relationship within the agency clearly could not continue. We would ask the Board of Directors to choose between us.

One of the people on the Board was Henry J. Foster, Jr., of New York University Law School. Foster acted as if he were judge of the situation, claiming to be impartial. However, as the minutes of the Board of Directors meeting illustrate, his attitude was distinctly prejudiced. He questioned whether it was possible for a woman psychiatrist to work with addicts. He called me "a smothering mother." He said about me that "she had set out to destroy them [the addicts] and herself [me] by her course of conduct." He summed it up by declaring that a woman psychiatrist could not help addicts achieve independence because she wouldn't be able to let them go.

Foster met with Ramirez and Mitch Rosenthal before the Board meeting, and it was proposed that the Addiction Services Agency take over Odyssey for a six-month period to investigate the dispute. That meant Mitch would have the agency.

I discovered later that Odyssey had some advantages that others wanted, which would be obtained in a take-over. We had an Internal Revenue Tax exemption and a Department of Social Services charter. Interestingly, Phoenix House as an arm of the Addiction Services Agency had neither of these. Later, the Phoenix House Foundation, Inc. was established, with Dick Davison and Mitch Rosenthal becoming members of the Board of Directors. And also we had the building on East Sixth Street, which Ramirez liked.

"The day I have to turn the agency over to you under these circumstances is the day I blow up the building," I told them.

I later discovered a letter to Tony from Mitch, dated before the coup, asking him as Director of Odyssey for his budget requirements for the coming year.

The by-laws of the Odyssey Board of Directors require five days' notice before an emergency meeting of the Board can be held, so for the five days we all waited. The residents lived in the auditorium, having a party. Dick and Grace Davison treated them to pizzas and Chinese food. I didn't interfere. The pain was so great I did what I always do at such moments, I withdrew. I stayed in my office and cried. I couldn't go home. I had to think it through. Michael came to me and held me. He was endlessly strong and he didn't then, doesn't ever, feel that problems are complicated. His attitude was "You're confronted, you move ahead. You do not give up!" I was contemplating doing the latter.

The professional staff gave me courage. They were loyal to me, every one. They said they would continue to work with me at Odyssey even if I had no funds to pay them. They would survive by taking second jobs, so they could stay. The lack of funds was soon to be a reality.

The Board met finally on the night of October 30. Grace Davison arrived to wait it out with the residents with a flower painted around her eye, the stem trailing down her cheek. I asked what it was, this odd make-up. She said, "This is for your coffin. I'll throw it on it."

It went on for hours. They listened to Tony, they listened to me, they argued and shouted. Then they voted. There were eighteen on the Board at that time: twelve were for me and six opposed. Odyssey and I are deeply grateful to David Beiles, Renée Belfer, George Congram, Nicholas Coolidge, George Daniels, Beatrice Densen, Arthur Friedenheit, Robert Leibowits, Blaise Levai, Helen Lubell, and Elliot Taikeff. These eleven, along with my vote, saved Odyssey.

The Board removed Tony as Executive Director. He and Dick Davison promptly resigned from the Board. I was given a week to reorganize the agency and report back. The following day the patients followed Tony. They had been told that I manipulated the votes of the Board. Dick Davison arranged for them to stay at Parish Acres in Upstate New York, and they waited there for me to fall. They had been promised it would not take long, and they would be returning to Sixth Street soon. The church people were given to understand that these homeless addicts had been mistreated by the Board and myself.

The impartial Henry Foster loaned them his car and remained in constant communication with them.

Two days after the Board meeting, Commissioner Ramirez ordered the Board by telegram to appear in his office. Only a few responded. Others were indignant and felt that they had put their faith in me and the matter was ended. Foster and others who voted against me attended, sitting in the front row with Tony. Davison found a seat in the rear.

Ramirez announced that he was freezing Odyssey's funds and taking over the agency. He had no legal right to do so. My Husband was there. He clearly stated that he would openly and vigorously oppose such illegal and unethical conduct. Ramirez pulled back from the take-over, but said he wouldn't release any funds.

A few hours later I called him, my old friend and teacher, and asked what was happening. He replied, "Handle it yourself." He asked me to report to him, and we arranged a meeting the following week. My attitude was still that of a respectful student, and I took his instruction to mean that I should prove myself, show him that I was capable of handling the agency and weathering this crisis without requiring his intervention. I interpreted that he was testing me.

I met with him as we had arranged, I with a fully developed psychoanalytic analysis of the underlying dynamics that led to the rejection of the therapist. I was still convinced that the root of the difficulty was the transference and countertransference that had arisen out of the fact that Tony was my private patient.

Ramirez received me in his office. With him was Mitch Rosenthal. I started to describe my theory to Ramirez, and Mitch interrupted. He said, as I recall, "I told you, Efren, she's full of this psychiatric shit. She's not capable of running an agency. She doesn't understand what it's all about."

Mitch presented me with their plan. I could remain as titular head of Odyssey, but I would have to accept Mitch Rosenthal as my supervisor and his ex-addicts would run the agency. I said, emphatically, *"Certainly not."*

When I informed them of the Commissioner's demand, the Board was outraged. There was another stormy meeting on November 7. Henry Foster said we should accept the Commissioner's decision for the sake of the patients.

He said, "I don't want to kill this whole House. I think it is dead right now. I don't think this House will have a single drug addict or ex-drug addict in it a week or two weeks from now.

"I think it is all through, that you can convert this into apartments. I don't think any court in New York City, I don't think any probation department, I don't think Dr. Ramirez, I don't think anybody else in a responsible position will entrust, let alone finance, anybody at this place.

"I think the only solution for Odyssey House at this moment is for the immediate retirement of the Medical Director. I would fight to have her retained as a consultant under the supervision of a competent medical director. I would fight for that. I think that that is the only possibility of survival of this as that kind of institution.

"Otherwise, and I want you to know what you are voting for, you are all through in my judgment. This is not a threat. This is stated as the facts as I see them."

There was a motion to remove Henry Foster from the Board for cause. He continued to make provocative statements: He had called other members of the Board "psychopaths." A colleague turned to him sorrowfully. "Before, I was going to abstain with anguish. Now, in view of this latest outburst of Mr. Foster, I vote enthusiastically for his expulsion."

Professor Foster was expelled, and the matter was laid to rest. We began to rebuild Odyssey.

Apparently, when Davison and the others realized that they could not force me out, they abandoned the pretext of "building a new program" with the former Odyssey residents. At the end of

November they parceled them out, a few to prison and the rest to Phoenix. A number of the latter split rather than go to Phoenix.

Jimmy Murphy was waiting for the minutes of the Board of Directors meeting that I had promised to send him. Because they cost eight hundred dollars a copy, I notified his mother that they would be made available for him to read in my office instead. He didn't come, and so had no way of checking what Tony was telling him. He was one of those who went to Phoenix, but he left a week later.

He went to visit Jim Slater, a mutual friend. Jim said, "Go and see Judi. You don't know the truth." Jimmy came to Odyssey and discovered that Tony had just left after having a therapy session with me. It was his last one. I had put a stop to them. I said to Tony, "What's the sense of this? If I'm too incompetent a therapist to treat ex-addicts, what are you doing here every week?"

Tony later appeared before the Addiction Services Agency certification board, on which Michael was sitting. Michael reported to me that Tony talked in glowing terms of me. He said that he owes his life to me. I subsequently learned that at the time of the split he rejected all efforts made to persuade him to testify that I had been immoral in any way. He said he didn't object to attacking me on the basis of my professional skill with ex-addicts, but he would not lie to attack me personally. On some level, he must have responded affirmatively to therapy. He didn't sink as far as others did.

The final straw was my discovery some months later that the night before it all began, Mitch Rosenthal sat in my office with his feet on my desk, smoking a cigar and trying out my chair for size.

The New York *Times* in May 1970 reported that in the three years between 1967 and 1970, when Mitch Rosenthal ran Phoenix House with the help of Dick Davison, Phoenix had received thirty-four million from the City and treated about eleven hundred patients. This compares with Odyssey's budget in the same three-year period of $1,174,166 during which time we treated 400 patients. Phoenix is the City's official program, fully funded and then some, yet the residents accost people on the streets of New York begging for money. I doubt if the residents know what is going on.

The office of New York City's Controller Abraham Beame reports that in one two-month period in 1971, Phoenix collected two hundred thousand dollars in street donations. In 1969 Phoenix ran a raffle at Hart's Island. Beame's office says that approximately one hundred and twelve thousand dollars was collected, none of which appears in the Phoenix books.

Phoenix doesn't require residents to give up urine for the presence of drugs. Dr. Rosenthal and his staff have announced that they do not believe in urine testing for the presence of illicit drugs because it makes the residents feel they aren't trusted. As far as I'm concerned, Phoenix isn't even running a rehabilitation program if it doesn't test urines. I wish someone would discover where the money is going.

Though the "Great Split" was very painful for me, it was a maturing experience. In Odyssey terms, it was my re-entry, my graduation. I was no longer in treatment myself, I was no longer Efren Ramirez's pupil. I was alone and I had to sink or swim.

I had been problem solving on levels similar to the patients, resolving my feelings of inadequacy and dependence along with them. But after the split I had no doubts that I could lead and survive.

There was only one experience more painful in all my life. I suffered in similar ways when my defective child was born, soon to die. One has the feeling that everything one has worked for, everything one has built, everything one has dreamed, has come to naught. It represents the vulnerability of the human condition in which, no matter how prepared we believe ourselves to be, there is no safety. We are all waiting for Godot.

And so we re-evaluate. The only way we can bear such realization is to keep busy, and earnest re-evaluation meets the need to be preoccupied. I spent a month in retreat considering what had been good about Odyssey and should be retained and what should be changed. During the process, the grief I carried eased.

Jimmy Murphy was with me and Louie Sarra joined us, a sheepish returnee.

POSTSCRIPT FROM JUDI
ABOUT LOUIS SARRA

Louie missed the "Great Split" because he had left Metropolitan Hospital before the original seventeen found their positive direction. He's a key figure in Odyssey history because he was the first. His own odyssey began in 1965—before mine—when he entered the cyclazocine research unit. I met him a few months later, in January of 1966, just after I had had my baby and had returned to the ward to work with the allegedly hopeless addicts.

I was wearing a fluffy white Mongolian lamb coat with matching boots and hat. Louie came into my office to be interviewed by me. He was wearing the mandatory blue hospital pajamas, which are so de-humanizing because the patients are always futilely trying to hold them closed and there's no underwear underneath. There are never sufficient buttons.

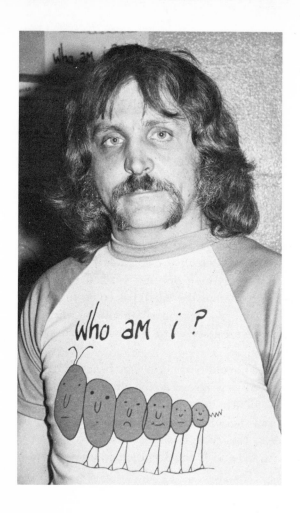

Louie sat down, nervous and trembling. I had a thirty-page questionaire to fill in about each cyclazocine patient. I looked at him sitting there, this frightened man with a high voice. I don't know why I did it, but on an impulse I tossed out all their questions and asked my own. I said, "Who are you?"

He didn't know who the hell he was. He answered he was Louie Sarra. I said I didn't mean that. I meant, what did he want out of life? Where was he going? Where had he been? He was thirty and had fifteen years of addiction behind him. He couldn't answer.

I also remember that it was Louie who wasted three hundred dollars of the best vocational and rehabilitational testing Metropolitan Hospital could buy. It was designed to reveal Louie's aptitudes. It reported that Louie had none. He would never be interested in work. Nothing interested Louie. He had no talents. He had no gifts, nothing. That was who Louie Sarra was.

Louie Sarra 1

The first time I saw Judi was at Metropolitan Hospital. At that time she was pregnant, she was big. She called me to her office a few months later. She had on a white furry Abominable Snowman coat with white furry boots and a white furry hat. She was sitting there when I walked in. She asked, "Who are you?"

I told her my name. She said, "No. I want to know who you are, what motivates you." She really threw me off. To me *Who are you?* means *What's your name?* I thought, "Is this woman crazy? I tell her my name and she keeps asking who I am." My first impression was that she was off-the-wall.

She came into the ward every day, checking on the four of us who were the cyclazocine guinea pigs. It was one of the first cyclazocine experiments in the nation. Cyclazocine blocks heroin—if you're on cyclazocine you can't get high. Addicts don't like it as well as methadone, however, because cyclazocine has no sensation, while methadone gives you a good high.

Soon after she arrived, Judi started a therapeutic community on the ward. She formed it from patients who had come to the hospital for detoxification, but it didn't include the four of us testing cyclazocine. We four had a comfortable arrangement with the hospital. We were permitted to leave the ward every morning at nine, returning at five. We explained that we wanted to look for jobs.

What we did all day was cop drugs. Cyclazocine had no effect on drugs other than opiates, so we smoked pot and shot speed.

Judi worried about us. She felt that we weren't getting any therapy because we were left out of her group. Then one day Louis Cascio and I were arrested with drugs. The police called Judi at Met Hospital and the next day she came down to the jail and made a deal with us. If we gave up pass privileges and joined her therapy program, she would ask the court to probate us back to the hospital. We would have to start at the bottom.

It was better than jail, so that's how I got into the therapeutic community. She blackmailed us. One day I told her so, and she said, "You're right. It *is* blackmail."

It was also the first time that I had been asked to make that kind of choice, meeting someone's demands on me.

My opinion of her was changing. I sat back in the therapy groups and saw that she was really trying. We could express feelings to her, angry, nice, or whatever. It was very surprising. We could talk to her, and she's a psychiatrist.

I felt sorry for her. We were a wild gang of junkies not long off the street. The language was terrible, and she'd accept a lot of verbal abuse—threats even—people standing on her desk yelling at her. One guy beat his chest and screamed at her because he lost his pass. When we were escorted on a walk through Central Park, for instance, we'd manage to cop soft drugs somewhere along the way. If they took us to the museum, we'd duck into a liquor store and get a bottle of gin. We all kept works—hypodermic syringes and cookers—hidden on the ward, about five sets of works per patient. Every now and then Judi would say that she wanted the ward clean. To make her feel good, we'd give her one or two sets. Even though we were blocked from heroin, there were plenty of other drugs to use. We were stoned practically every night.

She took away passes for whatever infractions she discovered, and once she made a decision she never weakened, but no one was thrown out of the program. She seemed to have made a commitment to us, a big one.

I worked my way up in the program by being slick. We had levels then, rough versions of the levels we later developed for Odyssey House. There were beginner, intermediate, and an advanced group. As you moved up your privileges increased and you could have longer passes. Your responsibilities increased along with it. There was a supervisor of the snack kitchen, a supervisor of cleaning, a supervisor of laundry, little things like that. In a hospital setting, there is little opportunity to take care of one's own needs.

I became supervisor of the supervisors. My title was President of the Ward. Because I appeared to be doing so well I had the longest pass. I could leave on Friday evenings and come back Monday mornings. Over the weekend I shot speed.

I was obliged to renew my pass on Sundays, and unexpectedly one Sunday Judi was on the ward and asked me to give up urine. I was high on speed, so I asked a friend, Richard Alves, to urinate in the bottle for me. He hadn't used any drugs so his urine would pass the test.

Later Rick was sore at me because I voted against him having a pass—the group used to make those decisions—so he ratted on me. During his admission interview, Judi asked him if he had anything he wanted to tell her before he become a member of the community. He said, "Yeah. I gave up urine for Louie."

I was busted down to the beginner group.

Rick is doing well now, running a chain of dry-cleaning establishments, married with four kids. He was one of the original seventeen who started Odyssey.

I wasn't among them. After I was busted I left the hospital. Part of the reason was that I was sore about it, but mostly it was because I really hated one or two people in the program. If I stayed, I figured I might break their legs. I had a great deal of respect for Judi by that time and what she was trying to do, and I didn't want to cause her any trouble.

I quit the program and went home, where I got re-addicted on heroin.

Home is an Italian neighborhood in Brooklyn where I was born in 1936. My parents were Italian, my mother still speaks with a heavy accent. I was the youngest of five children, a change-of-life baby. My mother was about forty-four when I was born, but I think she was glad about me. Both parents were very proud of me and spoiled me. They had high hopes that I would be a doctor or something impressive like that.

One of my brothers was retarded, the result of having meningitis when he was six months old. He lived at home. I remember him when I was about six and he was in his twenties. He used to beat me around the head. I don't think he was mean, maybe I teased him. When he got mad one time he put his hand through a glass window. He would throw things and have fits. He was toilet trained but sometimes he would urinate out the window. I don't know his real name; we called him Sonny.

My mother told the doctor about him hitting me. The doctor said that someday he might hurt the baby, meaning me, and suggested that my mother put him away. My parents were frightened for me and sent Sonny to an institution. The family would visit him there, sneaking me in despite the rules against small children because Sonny always asked for me. It bothered me that we didn't bring him home with us. I'd ask my mother or father why Sonny couldn't come home and they would answer that it wasn't allowed.

Sonny died in the institution about seven years later. By that time I knew that they had put him away because of me, and I felt very guilty about it. I thought that if they hadn't sent him away maybe he wouldn't have died.

One time when Judi and I were alone in her office I told her about that brother. She started to cry. She told me that she had given birth to a retarded child who died. My pain about my brother reminded her of the pain she felt about her own child. Later I learned there was more to it. I represented to her, her Daughter, Trissa, who had been born before the retarded child. She felt that Trissa might have been affected in the same way I was if the retarded child had lived.

At the time I felt I was responsible for making her feel so bad. I reached out and held her hand while she cried. It was the first time that I felt friendship with her beyond a doctor-patient relationship. It was a turning point for me. From that time on I had a commitment to Judi as a person. I didn't feel any commitment to the program she was trying to start, but Judi meant a lot to me.

She helped me understand my feelings about my father and his death. My father was a hard-working man, a college graduate in engineering. It was the Depression, and while we had no luxuries, there was always enough to eat. I never owned a bicycle, but we weren't in the slums. He would get up around five every morning because it took two hours to travel to work. He would come home around seven, have dinner with us, turn on Gabriel Heatter, take a bath and then read the newspaper until he fell asleep.

To give you an idea of what kind of man he was, he never bought eclairs, which he loved, unless he could buy enough for the whole family. My mother would say, "Get yourself an eclair. Who will know?" But he never did.

He was meticulous about the family budget and kept an account book with some money in a locked drawer. I helped him with the ledger and he kept track of every cent he spent. I was nine or ten when I started breaking into the desk and stealing the money. I would take a ten dollar bill and change the figures in the ledger to correspond.

That was my first stealing. It was a big deal to be nine years old and have a ten dollar bill in my pocket.

My father was incapable of believing anyone in the family would steal, particularly from one another. He never suspected even though he often had less money in the drawer than he thought was there. I felt guilty about it as I grew older.

My father took me to movies on Saturdays. We were a very close family. My parents never went out, they lived just for the kids. My mother was soft. When I played hookey, she'd get mad and tell my father. He'd get out the strap and he'd whack me one or two times. She'd jump up and say, "That's enough!" and he'd stop. Neither of them had it in them to be disciplinarians.

One Saturday my father asked me to go with him to Manhattan. He had to see someone on business. I played ball a lot when I was a kid and I told him that I had a game. He wasn't the type to say, "You've got to go with me." So he went alone to the train station, where he got sick and fainted. While he was unconscious, someone stole his wallet.

He managed to get back home and when I heard what happened I felt guilty that I didn't go with him. If I had been there, maybe it wouldn't have happened; at least his money would not have been stolen.

His fainting had been a heart attack. He died two days later. I was eleven at the time. A year after that my brother died. It was heavy.

I wasn't smart as a whip in school as my parents had hoped. After my father died, I started to be wild. I remember a teacher or psychologist saying that if I couldn't be the brightest kid in the class I must have made up my mind to be the wildest.

I did what wild kids do—smoking, fighting, being a truant, stealing all over the neighborhood. When I went to high school, I was away more days than I attended. Whenever I did go to school I just sat there.

I was really wild. I started carrying a gun after I left grammar school. I bought it from someone to make me feel big, and I kept it loaded. I was a nut. I carried it most of the time in a jacket pocket or stuck in my belt. I had a holster for it. Once a friend said that I wouldn't dare use it, so I shot him in the leg.

It's almost ludicrous to say it, but the gun had something to do with me being shy. I was an uneasy insecure kid and the gun represented safety and strength. It quickly gave me the reputation of being a dangerous person and people treated me with fearful respect, which I liked.

I grew up in a neighborhood where there was a well-known Mafia Family. I started hanging out with them when I was fourteen, doing little favors like running errands. A few of us kids attached ourselves to them and they took an interest in us. It was like having a friendly big brother.

There were no men left at home and my mother had no control over me. She was in her sixties then and in very poor health. I was able to come home when I pleased and do what I wanted.

I admired racketeers. They were my idols, fast guys who had

money. I knew some who were big names. I respected and followed their adventures. What attracted me was their power. The police had no control over them. Because of my association with them I could go to movies in the neighborhood for nothing and pick up free cigarettes in the candy stores. We had the whole neighborhood knocked up, and it made me feel good.

I used to pull armed robberies. The Family paid me to do certain jobs—not paid like a salary, but when I wanted money I could walk into a Family-owned restaurant and bar and say that I was going on a date. They would throw me fifty.

My first armed robbery was a movie house. I was nervous; I always got nervous. If you don't get nervous then there's something wrong with you. Being nervous puts you on guard. Then I started using drugs.

I was about fifteen when I began smoking pot. I used heroin at almost the same time. Between fifteen and eighteen I wasn't into drugs very heavily. I had money always, so I didn't realize I was developing a habit. As long as you can buy drugs whenever you like, you don't get sick from withdrawal and you aren't aware that you're getting hooked.

When I was eighteen I stole a car and got busted. It was my first conviction and they put me on probation. Shortly thereafter I was arrested for armed robbery. It was my first felony, and on conviction I was sent to prison for five years.

I was frightened on the way to the prison, which was in Upstate New York. I had heard stories of prison, about the fights and the homosexuality. I was young and I figured I wouldn't know anyone so far from home. I soon met people from the City. After you know a few people and case the joint, you get more comfortable.

You can only survive in prison by breaking rules. Some of them are little rules, like not eating food from the mess hall in your cells. I would steal bread and eat it later during the long nights. If the inmates didn't take advantage of privileges, some of the rules in prisons wouldn't be necessary. It is almost an obligation in prisons for the inmates to get away with whatever they can in order to be considered a big man. Another sick rule they had was that you couldn't talk to anyone from 6 P.M. until 7 A.M.

We smuggled in money and bought alcohol from the guards. Prisoners sneaked drugs out of the infirmary and we'd take them, some of them sleeping pills, some of them amphetamines, some of them chemicals we didn't know. We got high off nutmeg stolen from the kitchen. Cigarettes are money in prisons; a pack of cigarettes is like having a dollar. We did all our buying with cigarettes.

I never got involved in the homosexual thing. After the first few weeks in prison I wasn't bothered, not after one day in the bathroom. I was approached by a guy who said that he ran the prison. Whatever he wanted he could get. He would protect me, he said. I had been warned and I knew what he wanted. I picked up a handy mop-wringer and cracked him over the head with it. There was no trouble after that.

Not that I wasn't in other fights. There's a lot of petty stealing in jail. If you know who did it, you have to fight him to save face. You fight to set an example. If someone does something, makes a crack or pats you on the rear end, then it's a license for the next guy to do the same thing unless you fight.

You have to give the message that if they meddle with you, they're going to have to fight. If you do, you're respected and not bothered. I was hurt a few times, but it's not winning or losing that matters. It's better if you win of course, but you're looked up to even if you lose. They test you in the beginning to see if they can trust you, to see if you're a rat, if you'll stand up. They thought I was all right: "Good people," they call it.

Two years after I arrived in the prison, I was due to appear in front of the parole board. They told me to come back in another two years. They said I was a wise guy and wasn't doing well. After that I got more drugs from the infirmary and got more involved in the prison network. One of the things we did was rent out pornographic books for a pack of cigarettes a night.

Since I had served seven months of my sentence in a county jail before my trial, my five years were almost completed by the time I could next apply for parole. I decided to pass on it. I would stay the final five months and then walk out without having to worry about reporting to a parole officer. So I served the full five years, going in at eighteen and coming out at twenty-three.

When I was sent to prison, my mother became ill. No one else in the family had ever gone to jail. She passed out when they told her about my arrest. She loved me very much. She'd do anything for me. She's very Italian, *my son, my son.*

When I left prison it was October 1959. I moved back into my old bedroom and celebrated New Year's by taking my first shot of heroin in five years.

From then on shooting drugs was a regular part of my day, except when I was going in and out of jails and hospitals. Heroin made me feel that I was making up for the time I lost while in prison. I was going to enjoy, enjoy, enjoy; nod and enjoy. There wasn't much else for me. The way I felt about myself, I didn't even have the confidence to apply for a job.

I started working with the Family again. I would go into stores and bars and tell them to take out their juke box and put ours in. If they said no, I would tell them that it would be a good idea for all concerned if they did. Windows would be broken, accidents would happen. I would help with the accidents every now and then.

I got my gun again and pulled some armed robberies. I had a partner and we did some big jobs. One time we robbed a payroll and got $32,000. I bought a car with part of my share.

I got smarter as a robber. I had learned much in prison, how to case a place, look it over, watch the people going in and out, do a thorough job. Prison is good for that. You can pick up a lot of things that make you a more successful criminal. I even developed an instinct for avoiding trouble. Once I refused to join a friend who was planning to rob a jewelry store. He went ahead without me. There was a struggle with the owner. My friend killed him. During the struggle, though, a match book had fallen out of his pocket. The police traced him to the bar where he hung out and arrested him. He was sentenced to the electric chair.

The Family found out that I was using heroin and asked me about it. I said, "No, I'm just smoking pot. You think I'm crazy? I wouldn't use heroin." That was fine. They didn't mind smoking pot and they didn't know that I was using about a hundred dollars of heroin a day. The Family wasn't dealing in dope any more.

I pulled a burglary one day and couldn't get back to my car. The police identified me because of it, and there was a warrant issued for my arrest. It was 1963, and I was twenty-seven years old. The Family I was with was having some trouble with another Family at that time, a big feud. People were being shot on both sides and a few shots were fired at me.

I thought about it: Well, I'm using a lot of drugs and I don't like that; and there's a warrant out for me, which isn't good; plus I'm getting shot at; and I am living with a girl who has grandparents in Macon, Georgia, so we might as well go there. I figured it was a good place to hide. Who the hell knows where Macon, Georgia, is? They'll never find it.

Macon was so small we left. We went to Augusta and lived there for about six months. I kicked heroin in Georgia. You couldn't get any there. There was nothing but cough medicine with codeine in it. You drink it and, if you're clean and it's a good brand, one bottle is enough.

When I went back to New York a cop who knew me all my life grabbed me on the burglary charge. I was surprised. The Family had lost power during the feud, and the cop was getting back at us for the years when he had to take orders. I did eight months at Riker's Island. It wasn't too bad. There were some people there I knew from prison and it was like Old Home Week.

In the two years that followed I was in and out of the hospital seven or eight times. Whenever my habit got too big, over a hundred dollars a day, I would decide that I needed a rest to put a little meat on myself. Periodically I would arrange to take the twenty-one-day detoxification at Metropolitan Hospital. When I got out, my habit was smaller for a while.

When I went to Met in 1965 it was my eighth time in the revolving door. I planned to get myself on the methadone maintainance program. After fifteen years of addiction I was resigned to the fact that I was never going to get off drugs, so I might as well be getting them free and legal.

While I was waiting for methadone, they chose me to test the cyclazocine. A few months later, in January 1966, Judi came.

When I split later rather than mess up the program Judi was running, I went back on heroin. Eventually, fifteen months after leaving Met, I was arrested for possession of drugs. When my urine was tested and found to be positive, the State certified me an addict. This meant that the courts could send me away for three years to the Rockefeller Program. I didn't want to go, so I kept turning up in court without a lawyer, so the judge would have to postpone sentencing. Finally he became fed up with my game and said he would send me away the next time—and if I didn't have a lawyer, he would assign one.

I had my mother call Judi. I was embarrassed and ashamed that I was re-addicted. I didn't want to talk to her. Judi told my mother, "He's a big boy. Let him speak for himself." I got on the phone and said, "How's everything?"

I reluctantly told her what had happened. Would she accept me into Odyssey so the court wouldn't put me in the Rockefeller Program? She said, "All right, come in tomorrow at three o'clock. If you're one minute early or one minute late, we won't take you."

That was Monday, November 20, 1967. I came in promptly at 3:00 o'clock and they inducted me. The "Great Split" had just occurred. There were only about five or six residents in the house; it holds seventy. Mel Williams was there; he came in the day after the split. Tommy Turner, one of the original seventeen, returned the same day I did. Then Louie Cascio turned up, and after him came Jimmy Murphy.

When I came in I was kicking my habit and felt sick. I told the others that I was too weak to work. I needed a few days to recuperate. Judi held a group of the whole house, which including staff amounted to about ten people. She asked, "Who agrees that Louie has a legitimate beef and should have a rest?" Ellen, who is now married to Tommy Turner, raised her hand.

Judi said, "Fine. He's too weak to work, he's a baby. Babies can't work. Babies stay in their cribs." She put me to bed in the living room in my pajamas and gave me a rattle to shake whenever I wanted to be taken to the bathroom. She assigned Ellen and another resident to stay by my bed day and night; babies have to have constant care. I couldn't have solid food to eat because I should conserve my strength and, anyway, babies can't eat solid food. I would be fed only milk and baby food—no coffee, because babies don't drink coffee. Babies don't smoke cigarettes either.

The next day was Thanksgiving and the thought of that strained baby food instead of turkey and the trimmings didn't appeal to me. I grew up fast and went to work.

We worked all the time. The house was still a shambles with a lot of plastering to do and most of the rooms still to be painted. We had to scrape tiles from the floors. It was back-breaking because we had only a little one-inch scraper.

I stayed because I had made up my mind that Odyssey represented the only way I would ever stop using drugs. I was going to do it right this time. While I had been at Metropolitan Hospital, I considered treatment something of a joke. I was negative, I didn't talk much, I broke the rules, I smuggled in drugs, I shot dope whenever I could. I cared about Judi, but the rest of it didn't impress me. This time I was taking Odyssey seriously. It was my only hope.

It was easier because I felt close to many of the people in the program—Tommy, Louie Cascio, Jimmy and later Matty Ancona. And there was Judi. I love Judi. I love her.

In those days we looked after one another. Tommy often came down hard on me, gave me an awareness like scrubbing the kitchen (Odyssey doesn't use the word punish, or the concept of punishing but rather exercising one's awareness like a muscle), but I knew he cared. Yet I would curse and complain. *How could he do this!* But I really knew that he did it out of concern, and that's what kept me there. That and, most of all, Judi.

Addicts were crazy characters in those days. We often say that they aren't making addicts like they used to. One night when I was night man and the whole building was dark, a resident came down about three in the morning and said he wanted to leave. I said, "Okay, but wait until morning."

"No," he said. "I have to go out and conquer the dark."

I was nervous immediately. I said, "There's plenty of dark in here. Can't you just run around in the house and conquer the dark?"

He said he couldn't. He had to conquer the dark outside. I went upstairs and woke Tommy, who was House Supervisor then, and he said, "Handle it yourself." So I played pool with the guy the rest of the night to keep him from going out.

We had another guy who had an imaginary girl friend he called Dora. He would get on the floor and go through the motions of making love to her. He was very hostile most of the time. Judi gave him a feather and told him that whenever he felt hostile toward anyone he should tickle him. It seemed to work. Judi uses a lot of imagination.

Addicts who come to Odyssey have to be serious about getting well. For one thing, we usually don't give any medication for withdrawal. But if they are about to have a convulsion which can happen if they are barbiturate addicts, the doctors give them medication. Heroin addicts kick cold turkey unless they are pregnant, have a serious illness or are epileptic.

When I entered Odyssey, most of the addicts were around twenty-five years old, which is old for an addict today. They came mostly from the streets, self-referrals, but we were getting more and more probated to us from the courts.

A few weeks after I had entered Odyssey, it was time for my probe-in. A probe-in is a group that decides whether or not you can stay in the program. Formerly, when she had more time, Judi ran them all; she enjoys probes. She says it's the first time an addict gets any real attitudinal therapy because until then the group deals only with his behavior.

My behavior hadn't been good. I had tried to smuggle out a letter to the girl I had lived with for eight years. You're not allowed to communicate with anyone on the outside until you are a Level II in Odyssey. The reason is that communicating increases homesickness and could lead to the person splitting.

In sending the letter, I involved about five other residents. It was a long letter and I needed advice. The staff caught us and we were busted at a general meeting. It was the first time anyone had ever tried to smuggle a letter out of Odyssey. We received a smoking ban for the next month and bald heads. It didn't mean that our heads were shaved, just cropped close to the scalp. The program was so small that it wasn't embarrassing. So many of us had bald heads that people with hair looked as if they were the ones out of step.

During my probe Judi did most of the talking. She said I was to stop my nonsense, stop breaking rules and being negative. She remembers everything you tell her. She mentioned the deaths of my father and brother, exactly as I described them more than a year before at Met. She explained that I had been feeling guilty all these years about their deaths. I used drugs to punish myself.

Even if I was responsible, she said, which I wasn't, my brother and father would have forgiven me long ago. They wouldn't want to see me using drugs for another fifteen years. I should stop punishing myself and stop the nonsense and get well. Suddenly, much of my life, why I was hurting myself, was clear to me.

It took about two hours, and then I stepped out of the room and waited. When they called me back they said I had passed the probe.

Getting well is a slow process. I was learning that I could do without drugs and that there were people in the program who had confidence that I could make it. They really cared. There's no flash of lightning and there you are—cured of drug addiction. You just get a little better every day, and gradually the crap you're going through gets easier and then disappears.

I had less desire to act out in stupid ways or test people—games that addicts play. I found myself just living.

One of the things that affected me strongly happened during a marathon. Matty Ancona, whom I knew only slightly at the time, was asked who would he like for a big brother. He looked around and said, "Louie." I felt good about it, being picked, and a sense of responsibility for Matty. A few days later when I was in the auditorium reading The Prophet, I called Matty over and we read it together. I'd never done anything like that before and it was nice. Matty is now the closest friend I have.

Judi was tough with me all the way. If I sneezed, she'd chop my head off. Once when they took away my proposal for candidate-out, I was going to split. I stormed out of the meeting. I was standing on the stoop outside the building thinking I should leave at once.

She came out and said she knew they were hard on me. I said I was going. She said, "You want to know why I'm so hard on you?" I said, "Yeah." "Because," she said, "I love you." I said something like, "Then don't love me so much. Hate me a little." We laughed and I went back in. What could you do? She has a way about her.

Many times I'd get angry about something. She'd say, "I want you to make it, you know." And I did know it.

My proposal for candidate-out kept being rejected for one reason or another. In a candidate-out proposal you're supposed to list your plans in four areas: family, employment, education and future therapy. I wrote that I would be seeing my family often and that I

Louis Sarra.

would go to college. I didn't really think I would, but it looked good to say so. They caught me at the game.

I said I wanted to work for Odyssey in either treatment or administration. That's what caused the difficulty. Judi said I should make up my mind where I wished to work and she turned it back.

Within a week I requested a meeting with the staff and said, "Look, you've got to hear my proposal!" They did and accepted me. That's how I got to be a candidate-out at Odyssey. After fifteen years on drugs, I had been clean for a year and a half. I had stopped the nonsense.

LOUIE SARRA'S DEDICATION

Judi pulled me together after the death of my nephew, Carl Ljung, in Vietnam. Carl was only eighteen when he was killed. We had been very close. He was home on leave during the time I was going to court, trying to avoid the Rockefeller Program. He suggested on the telephone that he'd visit me in the courtroom. I didn't want him to see me there, so I said we would make it some other time. I never saw him again.

I felt the familiar feelings of personal guilt mixed with the grief when I heard he was dead. Judi consoled me, saying I could make some sense out of it if I devoted my life to helping other eighteen-year-olds, those who might die of drug abuse rather than war. It helped me to look at it that way. I am glad we have the Boys Adolescent Unit.

If I could separately dedicate my part of this book, I would like to dedicate it to my nephew, Carl.

There is the enemy—
It's in, within—
There is the cause
Of the dreadful sin.
There the disease
Which cripples man,
Stops his thinking of future plan.

Find the chemicals,
And cure the soul.
Let it free to enjoy growing old.
Freed on grace, knowledge and prayer,
To become fully aware.

—TOMMY MOTT

Induction

Induction into Odyssey House is run by the ex-addicts with token participation by the professionals. It isn't that the professionals can't work with the incoming raw addict, it's that the raw addict can't work with us. They can't hear us, they're threatened by us, we're foreign. We're the authority they're rebelling against. They have no way of identifying us as themselves, and if there is no mutuality of self, there can be no rapport.

We have an ex-addict conduct the induction because he can act as a role model. He represents *I was once where you are and now look where I am. If I could get well, you can get well.*

Addicts often feel that they can't get well. They are hopeless with despair. They rationalize that it is all over for them, they're resigned that addiction is all there is for them, that they have fallen so low there is no possibility of rising. The ex-addict sitting across from them, poised and confident, is a demonstration of hope; there is a way out.

This is not to say that ex-addicts are better than professionals in treating addiction. That's a myth perpetuated by ex-addict-run programs. They claim the professionals have no place because only ex-addicts can understand addicts and break their games. Some of the professionals I know are among the best game-busters around, and what is even more important, they can recognize what is not a game.

Not everything an addict does is a game. For instance, schizophrenics really do see and hear things that aren't there. It's not a game for them, it is a terrible reality. A non-professional is not likely to know the difference. A patient once was referred to us by the City Addiction Services Agency from one of the ex-addict-run programs. He was an epileptic and that program decided his seizures were a game. They refused him his medication, Dilantin, and he almost choked to death on his own dentures during a consequent seizure.

There is danger in allowing the ex-addict the tyranny—and it's a true tyranny—of insisting that all of life is a game. That attitude is the basis of Synanon's encounter-aggression therapy. There is a place for that type of treatment but not an exclusive one. It belongs within a whole series of treatment techniques. Because in most ex-addict-run programs there is no psychiatric evaluation or diagnosis, appropriate treatment is often not even known, much less given.

However, it is useful to play the aggression game at the time of induction. The game is hostility and challenge, and it's an important game. One of the reasons a majority of addicts like drugs is that they must cop them. Copping isn't easy, so they have a feeling of accomplishment when they obtain their drugs. Addicts denigrate and do not value what comes easily. Induction attempts to reproduce that dynamic in order to make the program enticing to an addict.

The jive do-gooders, people who give them things, are looked on by addicts as stupid and foolish, people to be taken advantage of. I am convinced that if you give something to an addict that he hasn't earned, you make him sicker.

What we say as a challenge in induction is that we don't have a nickel tied up in whether he, the addict, gets well or not. It's up to him. We couldn't care less. He's a despicable, loathsome, non-productive parasite on the community. If he would like to grow with us, using his head and his hands, we'll let him come in. If he can't, ph-f-f-f-t, *out*. We don't care. We present him with an existential choice: Does he want to live or die?

The responsibility is on him to get himself into Odyssey. Of course, once he is in, the community has concern. But only while the addict is in the community. If he splits, he is no longer part of us. In effect, he doesn't live. The only thing we will say to him if we meet him on the street is, "When are you coming back?"

There's a total tribal rejection until he does the right thing and returns to Odyssey. What parents do again and again and again is maintain the consistent attitude, either of acceptance or rejection, whether the behavior of their child is good or bad. Parents must learn to respond appropriately to their children. It's difficult for them, and also for people in the helping professions, to reject or make demands on patients. It's important to realize that it is just as harmful to the individual to be accepted when he is behaving badly as it is to be rejected when he has accomplished something good.

In the Induction Center at Odyssey, ex-addicts serve another function; they are bridges. There's a misconception that because we speak a common language everything we say can be understood by everyone. It's a great mistake to believe that.

Take some common words; for example, *money*. Money produces one set of reactions in the rich, who have never been hungry, never had to worry about the future, and another in the middle class which is constantly conserving, banking and saving for the years to come, and yet another for the poor, who know they will only have enough for three days of the week no matter what they do. They reason they might as well spend today because they cannot possibly save.

The poor are forced to live like rats, surviving on whatever is available. The middle class are squirrels always preparing for winter. The rich are domestic dogs and cats who are unable to exist on their own, if conditions change.

Time is another word with different meanings. Time is endless to the young, misery to the bored, precious to the busy, threatening to the trapped, meaningful to the confident, irrelevant to the oppressed.

We learned early in Odyssey's history that we weren't being understood. We had a mixture of middle-class professionals, hardened criminals, ghetto poor, spoiled brats, college dropouts and illiterates who spoke a common language but weren't communicating. It resulted in anger, hostility and paranoia. In order to trust one another, we had to find a way of being understood.

Our first efforts were absurd. We decided we professionals would work at menial tasks along with the patients. We would get closer to them by scrubbing floors beside them. It was like the campaign visits of politicians to ethnic neighborhoods, where they are photographed eating pizza or knishes or cuchifritos. They are no more accepted as Italians, Jews or Puerto Ricans because they eat the food than we professionals were accepted by the residents as being like them because we washed dishes.

We were noticing, however, that a few of the patients identified with the professionals better than the others and naturally had assumed the job of explaining us to the residents and the residents to us. The concept of people being bridges of communication was not so much invented at Odyssey as noted and used, like the apple hitting Isaac Newton, or the penicillin mold on Alexander Fleming's bread.

Clifford Robinson, who once was third in command at Odyssey, worked with me and with our Public Information Officer, Donald Dougherty, on a paper, "Bridges and Communication" which we delivered in May 1971 before the annual convention of the American

Psychiatric Association in Washington, D.C. In the paper Clifford used himself as an example of a functioning bridge:

"At the age of twenty-one, I help to bridge the gap that exists between the incoming raw addict and the professional, whom he finds very difficult to trust. The incoming addict identifies with me because I myself once used heroin and am now a graduate of the program. I am trusted by the professional and have earned his respect because during my treatment I was easily able to accept and understand his expertise. . . .

"I am a Black man who has succeeded in competing in a White man's world. I have not had to ask for special allowances or special favors. I am accepted by the White man because I can do anything he can, sometimes better. I am accepted by the Black man because I am Black."

Clifford Robinson and the Robinson family are bound up in the history of Odyssey. Clifford is one of four gifted brothers, members of a middle-class, intact family, and all four of the brothers became heroin users and all four came to Odyssey. There is also a sister, Rosemary, who is drug-free and played a very little part in the family dynamics.

Clifford gave an example of the usefulness of bridges during our presentation to the APA. He described the need to explain to professionals that newly inducted addicts shouldn't be wakened roughly in the mornings. In most cases, it results in the patient being hostile and threatening. Clifford commented, "Nothing in the professional's experience has trained him to continually ward off violent attack or defend his life and property. Most of our patients have lived in a world where the need to physically defend oneself is constant."

After a while in the program, when the patient is more relaxed, a rough waking is not so alarming.

Sometimes, I have great difficulty accepting what bridges such as Clifford and some of the others tell me. One time the staff, mostly ex-addicts and community workers, wanted to carry weapons whenever they visited our Bruckner Boulevard facility in the South Bronx. They explained that they needed the weapons not only to protect their lives, but that they wouldn't be respected in that area unless they showed themselves to be capable, aggressive men and women who understood the problems of survival. Otherwise they would be viewed by the ghetto dwellers as jiving do-gooders, out slumming. I gave permission, reluctantly.

I have an example of an effective bridge in my own family, my Mother. A generation ago, she was a corporation attorney, a woman who dared to keep her single name when she married. What she

CHINOOK WINDS
P.O. Box 794
Mill Valley, Calif. 94941

THE BRIDGE

passed on to me was the absolute assurance that a woman can be just as capable as a man. I've never doubted it in all my life, never imagined that anyone would question it. I know better now, but for a long time the hot protestations of the women's liberation advocates simply amazed me. Mother understood it well—their struggle is the one she fought thirty years ago. She bridged that battle to full person-hood for me.

One of the best examples in Odyssey of paramedical bridges at work is found every weekday in our induction center, where ex-addicts in the program talk one language to the raw addict who has just come in off the street and write another in the reports that will be read by professionals.

We induct children under the age of sixteen into Odyssey any time, day or night, but all others must attend induction at precisely one-thirty at our East 22nd Street facility, an old apartment house where Odyssey has been given a few apartments, rent-free.

On a Monday afternoon in July 1971, for instance, there were seven people waiting in induction for Steve Wasserbach to arrive. Steve is a gangling, laconic, drawling blond who had been in the program since early in 1970 and was currently assigned to induction, under the supervision of Ellis Williams. Steve was upset because his partner on the induction team, Peter Winston, had split Odyssey on the previous Friday night. Peter was reported to be applying for re-admission that day.

Readmitting splittees presents special problems. Usually we re-quire that they show motivation beyond merely appearing in induc-tion and asking to be admitted. They must indicate why they left the program and what they learned about themselves in the interim. They must use a process of self-examination. In the case of Peter Win-ston, however, we had other factors to take into consideration. Win-ston had been in Odyssey for more than a year and had done well. His leaving was an impulse and he was returning immediately. If he appeared honest, if he hadn't used drugs in the interval, if he took part in the induction, if he seemed to come across, we probably would accept him back without delay. If his attitude was one of indifference, we might require him to wait.

Induction was located temporarily in a first-floor apartment that was about to be renovated. There was no electricity and the light in the room was dull because there was heavy rain on the windows. A lamp had been placed on the floor with an extension cord connected to a socket in the corridor.

Steve took his place behind a long rough trestle table. He greeted two others on the induction team already there. They ignored their former associate, Peter Winston, who was sprawled on a folding chair facing them, grinning with discomfort.

All seven people waiting for induction to begin were Blacks. Besides Peter, there was Fred Beavis, another splittee from Odyssey, making his third attempt to get back in the program; a bleary-faced man almost asleep; a tense young girl; an elegant, sardonic youth with a Satanic beard, leaning against the wall propped by conspicuously new crutches; with two well-dressed women hovering over him.

Steve began by determining that the two women were relatives of the youth on crutches. He asked them to leave since induction is confined to those directly seeking admission. They hesitated, expressing concern. "You can come back at three o'clock," Steve told them, his eyes on papers he was sorting. He was giving a deliberate message to the watching addicts: matters were to be conducted on his terms, which were that the addicts had to get themselves into the program —no one else could help them.

When they left, Steve leaned back and looked at Peter Winston for the first time. "Why don't you run it?" he offered dryly. Peter looked amused.

He turned to the bleary man, asking routine questions about his name, age, address, and drug use as Steve wrote the replies on a form.

"Have you worked?" asked Peter.

The man beamed drowsily. "I was thirty-three months in the reformatory, and you work *there*," he drawled.

Peter told him brusquely that he would work hard at Odyssey. His own labor paid for the therapy he would receive.

Someone came in, a young White man in shirt sleeves with a polite, anxious expression on his face. Steve looked at him coolly.

"Do you want to come in?" he asked.

The man nodded brightly.

"You're too late. Come back tomorrow. At *one-thirty*, sharp."

Steve was impressing on the others that Odyssey has rules and makes demands. Because raw addicts tend to be cynical and are always testing, they require a repetition of concrete examples before they believe that we mean what we say.

The latecomer left, flustered.

Steve then asked the name of the man on crutches. He replied that he was Conrad Jones. When Steve told him to sit down, he did so, wincing. He was eighteen, he told Steve, and his heroin habit was up to thirty-five dollars a day. He indicated the girl beside him and said they wanted to come in together or not at all.

"You understand that you can't see one another in the program and can't communicate in any way," Steve warned. Even married couples are not permitted to live together at Odyssey until the staff decides that they have developed sufficiently as individuals to be able to have a positive mutual relationship.

Conrad and the girl weren't dismayed. They knew the rule already, they said. It was simply that they didn't want one of them to be in the program while the other was out on the street.

Steve turned to Fred Beavis, who had been staring stolidly into space. Fred explained that he left Odyssey "because I got fucked up in group. I wasn't verbalizing my feelings. I wasn't coming across."

This was received with some skepticism. How did he know that he wasn't going to fuck up in group again? And how about the people he had let down, the people who sat in group with him before he split and tried to persuade him to stay? Fred looked depressed.

Just then Ellis Williams, Administrator of Induction, came in and stood behind the table. Ellis can be a warm, supportive individual, but now his manner was cold and angry. He wanted to know why Fred had taken drugs after he split. Fred shrugged.

It happened only once, he said, the night after he split. He overdosed. "It was available," he told Ellis, his face gloomy, "so I said *fuck it* and got high."

"Who forced you to come here?" Ellis asked sharply.

Fred lifted his head and met Ellis' eyes squarely. "The streets," he said simply.

The induction crew turned to Peter, who appeared humorously resigned, a favorite defense with him. He had split, he explained, because he was uptight about a staff decision to discharge a resident as an example. After a fire in the 12th Street facility, attempts to discover the arsonist had failed so a resident was chosen by drawing straws to be the sacrificial stand-in. This resident, Richard Shanner, a Level III, was discharged to begin the program again. Peter, confused and upset, left.

He said he knew at once that he would be coming to induction immediately. He had taken no drugs. Peter has three small children and his wife, Joan, is a schizophrenic in treatment at Odyssey.

"What if Joan had split behind you?" Ellis demanded. "Did you think of that?"

Peter stopped smiling. "Then she'd be right here today with me," he said with conviction.

Splittees are aware that their return will be accompanied by hardship. They lose their Level, whatever it was, and drop down to what is called a *boarder,* who has no privileges whatsoever. They must work hard for their keep, spending weeks in the lowest jobs and staying up two hours after the rest of the house retires at night to complete whatever chores are asked of them. Men have their hair cropped close to their heads; women wear no make-up.

It's done to indicate to other residents that the splittee has such commitment to the program that he is willing to earn his acceptance back. It's proof of intent and serves an important attitudinal function.

When the inductee is a stranger to Odyssey, the induction crew outlines the four Cardinal Rules of Odyssey; no knowledge of or participation in the following: actual or threatened physical violence, contraband, sex or stealing.

No physical violence means exactly that, Steve explained to Conrad and the girl. The bleary man seemed disinterested. "It also includes threats. We don't think threats are a constructive way to relate to other people." No one is kangarooed at Odyssey.

No contraband means drugs, money, any personal possessions that you are not given permission to have. "Everything you need, clothes, food, etcetera, will be given to you. Your own clothes and everything else you have when you come into the program will be taken away. You enter the program as you enter the world. All of us are equal. Personal belongings are returned when you reach Level III. That takes from seven to nine months, depending on the individual. You can't leave the house without authorization, you can't receive visitors, write or receive letters until Level II. You concentrate on getting yourself together without worrying about what's happening outside."

No sex includes either homosexual or heterosexual conduct.

No stealing means what it says. "If you want something in the community, ask for it. If you aren't given it, it's because you haven't earned it yet or shouldn't have it. And, of course, before you all test and game, let me tell you that a conspiracy of silence—namely, *knowledge of*—is no better than doing it yourself."

Addicts protest that this goes against the street code; it means ratting on a friend. Steve tells them, "That's negative thinking. The program is not like the streets where you shelter people who are breaking laws and rules. Here you're part of a community. In our home, the individuals help one another to get well by making sure those in charge know about it before anyone messes up."

Steve advises inductees that their working hours might be as long as twenty-four in a day. "Your regular hours will be from seven in the morning until seven at night. If you think that's too much for you, it shows how little you know about yourself and what your body is capable of.

"Actually, what you've been doing is short-changing yourself. That's what you've been doing all your life. If you realized the capacities you have, you wouldn't have wasted your time in high-jiving and bullshitting out in the street."

Conrad Jones slouched deeper in his chair, his long narrow hand gripping his side.

"Take your hand down," Steve ordered.

"I can't," Conrad told him. "I'm holding my stitches." It developed that Conrad had fifty-six stitches in his side from a knife wound. His leg was broken in the same fight and his right eyeball was a livid scarlet because someone had tried to gouge it out.

Ellis and the others at the table concluded that Conrad had short-changed someone in a dope deal and had been beaten up as a result. Conrad managed a weak smile, his eyes sliding away, and said it hadn't been that way. It was a case of mistaken identity. The induction team laughed appreciatively.

In the end, Steve accepted four of the five inductees. He explained to each why he made his decision. The dazed man received the news that he had been rejected with equanimity; he had not participated. "Conrad, you were bullshitting about the fight, but we'll give you a chance."

He took the girl, though he didn't say so, because "you can't tell what is happening with a couple until you separate them. They back up one another's stories when they are together."

He took Fred Beavis because Fred had tried three times to get back into Odyssey, showing sincerity. "But he knows that if he splits again, it will be a long time before he is readmitted."

And Peter Winston was accepted because he met the requirement for honesty. "Besides," Steve said. "There's his wife, Joan. It would be too hard on her if we kept him out."

INDUCTION REPORTS

Sharon Ruder, accepted August 16, 1971. Age: 19. Birthplace: NYC. Date of birth: 10/13/51. Marital status: married. Hospital admissions: '67, gave birth, St. Vincent's, one week, '68, gave birth St. Vincent's, one week, '69 gave birth, St. Vincent's, one week, pregnant seven months at time of admission; '71 detoxified for heroin, St. Vincent. Education: Tenth grade. Addicted to: heroin. Number of years using: one. Cost per day: $45. Skills:

none. Referred to Odyssey by parole officer. Comment: Hot pants. She is seven months pregnant. She didn't want to come into the program. She left induction and came back in ten minutes and said she wanted to come in. Accepted. [NB: pregnant women are always accepted immediately at Odyssey.]

Susan Moses, aged 28, attempted suicide, separated, two children, illegal abortion, possible drug-induced schizophrenia. Must have a shadow, has fairly high potential for another attempt based on depressive reactions. Accepted: refer for emergency psychiatric evaluation.

Cynthia Serrarto, aged 30, three children, using drugs for 15 years, cost $60 a day. Husband left her, lost her apartment, cried in induction and expressed feelings so we accepted her, but she didn't stay.

Henry Fuller, aged 20; split four times; broken leg '65; detoxified '69; assault and robbery '67; grand larceny '69, served three months. Education: high school graduate. Drugs: heroin, pot, cocaine, cold medicine and glue. Started when he was ten. Cost per day: $35. Accepted: given an awareness, four months as a boarder, because he came straight from jail.

"The walking dead,"
    As the old-timer said.
The feeling of guilt, as I lie in bed.
    The addict walks, but never talks,
The addict steals, and constantly deals,
    The addict craves, and digs his graves,
The addict rants, and the addict raves,
    The addict sins, and never wins.

—TOMMY MOTT

John Cox 1

One night when I was out trying to cop some dope, I saw my brother copping too. That's how I found out that he was shooting heroin. I couldn't say much to him because I was doing the same. I was nineteen and he was fourteen.

It was jammed up because I would give him money to buy his dope. He'd phone me at work on paydays and say, "John, I'm sick. Will you come and help me out?" I thought that I should, as a responsible older brother, so I'd take a cab home and give him the money.

We used to shoot up together. After he overdosed the second time, I stopped getting off with him. The first time he overdosed we were in a hallway and I let him get off first. He passed out. Whuff. I smacked him on the face but he still didn't come to. Man, I did everything. But he still didn't come to. Even artificial respiration didn't work.

I hadn't gotten off yet so I was still sick. I went downstairs to our apartment and called the ambulance. Just before it came some older drug addicts helped me bring him around. They did something to him and he came out of it. I was scared, I was really scared.

By the time it was all over and I went back to my cooker, it was all dried up. I added water, relit it and shot the dope. It didn't hurt me. I wasn't afraid of it because I knew I had a higher tolerance than my brother.

The second time my brother ODed was in my cousin's apartment. We had a cousin living in our building. This time I was able to smack him out of it. His lips would move so it was easier to bring him to.

But I never got high with him after that. Never. I knew the one thing I couldn't face would be him dying in front of me. It's hard for me now to realize that I went through such experiences.

I overdosed myself plenty of times. I can't count them all. I would black out and friends would help me to recover. Once a guy, a very big guy, smacked me on the face so hard it was swollen afterwards. I'll never forget that, but he got me out of it. Once I overdosed all alone, but I'm still here.

We were living in a project, which is what we call the high-rise slums in New York. They're run by the city for people of low income. There were two children in the family, me and my brother. My father worked in a hospital kitchen. After I was twelve or thirteen, my mother started to work for the City as a clerk. Both of them were high school graduates.

They used to save their money. They wanted me to go to college and be a mathematician. When I was still a boy, I noticed that in our entire building, in which there were only Black or Puerto Rican families, there were no doctors, no lawyers, no teachers. There was no one of professional caliber, only laborers. I thought, "How far can a Black man go?" I didn't want the life of a laborer: I disliked the type of work my father did. Nobody else but me seemed to mind.

As a child I had severe asthma. I was always in the hospital. If I wasn't in the hospital, I was seeking some other type of attention. I seemed to have more needs than the average child, and my mother was somewhat over-protective of me.

I was jealous when my younger brother was born. I was five years old. By the time I was fifteen and he was ten, it was different. He had a great deal of respect for me and followed whatever I did. He followed me into addiction and he followed me into crime. I was successful in finding jobs while addicted, in manipulating my way out of jails, and in finding Odyssey House, but he wasn't. He was constantly in and out of jail. He's in now.

I've tried many times to get him into treatment at Odyssey, but he resists. It totally upsets me. I don't feel like beating him up or anything like that because I feel responsible in some measure for his addiction. He comes to see me whenever he's out of jail. Once, when he lived with me for a while, I talked to him about coming into the program. He didn't disrespect me; he just left. He said he wasn't ready to change, especially in a program that I had completed and in which I was an Assistant Director.

It might be a reaction to my mother. She always is comparing and playing one of us against the other—which he can't stand. He tries to prove himself to her by being self-destructive.

My mother makes many of the decisions in our house, which is a bad situation. It makes me sad that my father isn't more active in the family. When I was young I thought he was weak. Now I see that he does make decisions, but is reserved in his actions.

I'm the opposite of my father. Remembering how I felt as a child when my father didn't show much emotion toward me, I do the reverse with my daughter, Titi. We play like kids together. I sit her on my lap, take her for walks, talk to her a lot.

It's curious that my wife, Yvonne, is, at times, reserved. Judi sees us in private therapy and says that we can have a good relationship if we accept each other's emotional style. Unfortunately, I have great difficulty with rejection on any level.

One of the earliest rejections I can remember was in the sixth grade. I was constantly joking in school, attention-getting I guess. My sixth grade teacher gave me a hard time. As I think about it now, she was sick, with some kind of a psychological hang-up. Sometimes she threw my books on the floor, but most of the time she pretended I wasn't there. If I was the only one in the class with my hand up, she would totally disregard me. I was on the school swimming team, and she would wish every one luck before a swimming competition— except me.

It made me feel isolated. The school insisted that I needed psychiatric help and a psychologist gave me a test. Nobody ever followed it up.

In those days in my neighborhood, when I was about eleven, you had to be in a gang to survive. They had names such as Dutchmen or Assassins or Sportsmen. I was in the Sportsmen. It gave you a group identity. You would fight other groups, mostly with fists. Sometimes we used chains and knives.

I started to drink when I was thirteen. The drug most addicts start with is alcohol. I began with wine and progressed to whiskey, a brand called Kentucky Gentleman. We would get one of the winos who infested the avenue to buy it for us. He would do it for ten or fifteen cents. We drank mostly at parties on the weekends. I wasn't getting drunk, just high enough to be comfortable.

My asthma started giving me problems again in the sixth grade. It probably had to do with the static with my teacher. It seemed to me I spent hours in the house gasping for air and looking out the window at the other boys playing stickball on the street. That was isolating again and gave me the feeling that I was different. Besides that, my mother was strict and made me come home earlier at night than my friends did, which added to the isolation.

I started to run wild. I was rebelling, staying out as late as possible and drinking more. I began stealing to get money for whiskey. I smoked my first joint of marijuana at a summer camp that I was sent to to get me away from the bad influence of the city. It was the first time I was ever away from home.

By the tenth grade, I was drinking heavily and smoking marijuana on a regular basis. It was my main thing, smoking and drinking. I made money gambling and always won because I had it arranged with some other kids to peek at the cards against me.

I admired the guys who were driving around in Cadillacs and had fancy women dangling around their shoulders. I said to myself, "I'm not going to get involved in what my father is doing, I'm going to get involved in what these guys are doing." Money was a major value with me then, to get it and enjoy all the benefits of life as fast and as much as I could.

There was a White kid in my economics class at DeWitt Clinton High School who traveled all the way from Long Island every morning. He always had plenty of marijuana and we would smoke together. One day he asked if I could get him some heroin and I said, "Sure." I knew someone who was messing around with heroin. We went together to Harlem and bought some. He wanted us to shoot it together, but I said I wouldn't. The needle was completely outrageous to me then.

So we snorted it. I knew how because I had been practicing with Comet cleanser at home. It was crazy I know, but it was important to me that when the time came for the real thing I would look experienced.

I didn't throw up, as many people do with heroin the first time, and I really liked it. That night I went home, got some money and bought some more. I snorted it and again I wasn't sick. It gave me a mellow-type high, it wasn't sloppy. It gave me the feeling I was cool. I felt I was in some type of Utopia, that there was nothing but sheer existence. I can't explain it, but it made me feel I could do anything I wanted to do, that I didn't have to worry about things, that I could sit down for the rest of my life and relax. My isolation seemed very distant. I was on top of it. I was slowed down completely.

And I dug it. I dug it much more than I dug marijuana. Alcohol is a hassle, you can't work the next day. Marijuana gave me too many side effects, making me laugh and giggle a lot, which is uncool. After I started using heroin I disliked marijuana because then it made me feel paranoid.

When I was young I had millions of small-time jobs because I needed money for drugs. It wasn't my thing at that point to mug people. I was working in a cleaners after school and I made enough to support my Mickey Mouse habit. Four of us could get down on one five-dollar bag. When there was a panic in 1964 and heroin was scarce and expensive, I switched to pills, the depressants like Seconal and Tuinal.

Later I worked as a cashier in a department store. I was stealing money and clothing. They caught me with a sweater; I put all the blame on another guy and he was fired. But so was I. I was embarrassed to come back for my check, but I said, "John, you've got to get high for the rest of the week. You'd better just go and pick up your check and forget how you think people are looking at you."

Then I went to Mount Sinai Hospital. During the job interview they told me that they would put me in the inventory department and pay me about eighty dollars a week. When I reported to that department, where mostly Whites were working, they sent me to the kitchen where it was all Black guys. Blacks and Spanish guys. It meant carrying trays and putting my hands in filthy water. I quit.

Blacks and Puerto Ricans were performing all the menial labor jobs at that time, with no place to go. Because of drugs and not finishing school, I was in the kitchen, something I despised. It was a bottom of the barrel job, and I didn't want to be on the bottom of the barrel. There was too much to life, judging from what I saw on television—I had never experienced it directly—and I wanted it. I wanted it all.

My mother's ambitions for me seemed unrealistic. I decided I couldn't achieve them so why try. Instead, I would become one of the best hustlers in town and make money and more money. I saw two alternatives: a socially positive job with my hands in dirty dishwater, making no money, or negative hustling and driving a Cadillac.

Many young Blacks still feel the same way about the possible alternatives. Some go to drugs and some give in to the system. Today there is another alternative; some become militant. Hostility and the ventilation of the rage are something new; the low self-esteem and the frustration have always been there. However, just to demand without learning how is also destructive. Now it's all goal and no process. Through our history the goals have been obvious but the process was denied. There must be meaningful teaching and re-evaluating if we are to learn the process to control our own destiny.

We need two things now: Blacks staying in our communities working with our people, and Blacks confronting society at large by becoming successful within the mainstream but not in an Uncle Tom way. In past generations only a few Blacks reached satisfying goals. Yet their success was meaningless to our people because they abandoned us and we could not follow.

By the time I quit the hospital job, I was hooked. I was on the needle. The first time I used it was to impress someone. My White friend went first, and I watched how he did it and then put the needle in my arm. I didn't have any feelings about it. I wanted to get high and I wanted to impress him with the fact that I knew the ropes and all the tricks. To maintain my image, I did what he did.

The rush of heroin grabs you from the toes up. Going up and going up and going up—it envelops you, then it levels off. At a certain stage it's very peaceful. Nothing is bothering you, nothing exists but you. You think about nothing. It was for me then one of the most beautiful highs in the world. It probably still is.

It doesn't bother me now to think about it but, truthfully, it used to. Now it is an empty nothing. But that's the way it was. You stop functioning, stop existing. At the time I couldn't see anything better for me. Now that I think back about it, I know it was truly terrible.

I was the middleman between a dealer in Harlem and the kids I hung out with at school. I made money and enough drugs for myself that way. As long as they kept asking me for drugs I knew I wouldn't be sick, and they always kept asking. Sometimes, however, when the supply was short it got too long between shots and I would get sick. I would yawn and have a watery type of running nose and my back used to ache horribly. When I threw up it was a funny kind of greenish stuff. It was like having a severe case of the flu. I don't ever want to experience it again.

When my habit grew and I needed more money, I started getting more people involved in drugs. One time I put a little bit of heroin on a toothpick and said to my best friend, "Go ahead, try it. Just take a snort." He did. He's in jail now. He goes in, he goes out; he's in right now.

That's normal practice for addicts. Turning friends on is a source of revenue and makes for companionship. I saw nothing wrong with it then.

I've talked with my friend about coming into the program at Odyssey, but he won't. He's decided not to change. I've tried with other friends in my neighborhood with more success. Three have stopped using drugs, two haven't. Close friends.

It bothers me like my brother's addiction bothers me. Once, when Fred Cohen was in a candidate-out group with me, he said it was obvious I was in extreme pain because of my feeling of responsibility for my brother and my frustration at not being able to help him and, in part, relieve my guilt. My brother followed me as a negative role model into addiction, but he won't follow me as a positive role model out of addiction. It's painful to think that part of the reason he won't come to Odyssey is because it is mine, but I know of no other program that can help him.

I went quickly from being contact man to dealing. Sometimes I came back short without all the money. The people I was dealing for got tired of my appropriating an added commission and scratched me. They wouldn't give me any more drugs. I found someone else, a crazy guy, and started hanging out with him.

My arms were bad, tracks down both of them. I had a thing about people seeing the needle marks so I used to switch around. I would hit one place one day and another place the next day. I got off so much that the tracks ran down to my wrists. My arms were swollen because of abscesses.

One day a friend, Dutch, suggested that we rob a store. He was wild then. We had two girls with us. I was real real scared. We went to a clothing store and pretended that we had a gun. We told the lady to get 'em up and she laughed. Dutch smacked her in the face. We threw her in the back. We locked her in the bathroom. We cleaned out all the good suits and about one hundred and fifty dollars. We went back and got high.

After that we did many little jobs—drug stores, butcher shops, small stores of all kinds. Someone loaned us a gun and we robbed stores in our own neighborhood. Whenever we had the gun I was petrified because it meant that if someone made a wrong move we'd have to kill him.

I was living at home. My mother never knew what I was doing because she didn't want to know. She would find dope in the house, fifty or a hundred bags, and I would explain that I was dealing, trying to make a little money, but I wasn't an addict. I told her that if I were an addict, I would have had only one or two bags. She'd believe it because I was her son.

I was wild on the streets but I didn't want any part of being violent, because I often thought that the people we robbed could be my mother or my father. I didn't want anyone robbing my parents, hitting them or hurting them.

We were robbing stores all over town. When we went to dances at night we were well dressed, very well dressed. Nobody could ever say, "Those kids are drug addicts," because we never looked that way. It was just not us.

We had progressed to bigger stores. Now, we had handcuffs and rope and tape. We were beyond drug stores. We'd take off a shoe store or a school office where we would need to tie people up and put tape on their mouths.

When I was eighteen, I was called for the service. I told them about my asthma and got a note from my doctor. They gave me a 4F deferment because of being an asthmatic. They never looked to see if I was an addict.

The day the statement from the draft board came a group of us were planning a robbery; it turned into a real jammed up day for me because of Howard. Howard was highly intelligent and was planning to go to college. He hung out with us, but even though he was an addict, he belonged to fraternities in Harlem, groups of positive, respectable people. He was the basketball star of one fraternity.

He had borrowed five dollars from me the night before to get high. I was uptight for money, so when we met that evening I asked for it back. I don't know why I said it because I owed him three dollars from a month before, but I said, "I want my five dollars." Since he was a nice guy he gave it to me and never mentioned that I owed him three dollars. He was that type of person.

We left to do the job. It was decided that it would be a liquor store. I never decided what we would hit. I just hit with them. They picked a liquor store on a main avenue and I didn't like it. It was too open, we couldn't get away without being seen, and we didn't have a car. I said, "I'll walk to the corner and check it out."

Howard and Dutch went in. As I was standing on the corner, I saw the cops driving down the street. Just then I heard something go *pap, pap, pap, pap, pap*—five shots. I said, "Oh shit!" We didn't have the gun that day. Therefore, it had to be that Howard and Dutch were getting shot up.

Instead of running to the store, I ran to the cops. I didn't know what I was doing. I was crying. I told the cops that someone was killing my friends. They jumped out of the car and ran to the store.

It was a terrible scene. Howie had been shot in the chest and he was dying. Dutch was shot through the leg and was holding Howie's hand. Howie was still breathing. I got out.

I cried all day. The crazy idea kept going through my head that I should put the three dollars on Howie's grave. It was real jammed up. I thought the cops would be coming for me, but they never did. No one squealed. We were that tight a group. All but I went to jail.

I started hanging out with a group, all of us in our teens, all high school dropouts, all from the same economic level, all Black. If someone wanted to join the group who didn't take heroin, we would get him on it. We were all feeling the frustrations of life. There wasn't anything meaningful as far as work for us. All of us could hold jobs even though we were addicted, but there were only menial-type, low kinds of jobs available.

After Howie's death my life got harder. I don't want to mention some of the things I did. I sank into the gutter and had no self-respect. I stopped robbing stores. I was robbing people on the streets. That's a drop. Even though all robbing is negative, you have different levels just as for prostitution or anything else. I was mugging the guy on the street, which is the most degrading and the lowest.

Fortunately, I never had to hurt anyone. The people I ran with weren't overly violent—at least I didn't see them that way. Other people definitely would look on them as overly violent, but we never put anyone in the hospital.

You have to carry a knife or a gun or a pipe or a blackjack or something with you, and you have to look as though you really will hurt the people you are taking off. You push them and you tell them to give it up. Most people will hand it over. You read in the papers about people who try to fight. They only do that if you're nervous. If you appear solid to them and they feel there is no way they can deal with you, they give in.

I could appear tough. I changed myself because I knew what I must do. I had to appear strong, forceful, dangerous and very aggressive. I would hold the pipe up to their head and say, "Give it up!" And they gave it up. Sometimes it was as little as ten dollars and a watch. Sometimes it was a hundred or two.

At the same time, I was working for McCall's Corporation. There was only one other Black. We were doing scut work. The heroin wasn't working the same way any more. It wasn't peaceful, it was a stimulant. I was not the suave cool John Cox. I was a different person, a person who didn't care, who didn't put controls on himself, who despised and hated himself. I kept on working and mugging and using because my habit was up to forty dollars a day. There was no stopping.

Incredibly, I was going to night school at the same time. When you've been an armed robber for two years and guys see you carrying books, they don't laugh. I was holding down a full-time job, attending night school, and robbing people. I had switched back to mostly snorting because on my way to work or school I was too rushed to stop and main. So, I began sniffing heroin in subway stations instead.

Everything fell apart at once. One of my friends went away to college, two others went to jail, one of my drug contacts was out of drugs, another left town. I caught hepatitis from a dirty needle. I learned that my brother was addicted.

There was one good thing. A guy at McCall's became concerned about me. He was very frail and intelligent, a thinker. It was one of the first times in my life that I liked a White man. He talked to me about what I was doing to myself. It was a father and son kind of relationship. He didn't know about the drugs. He said that I had potential to be someone, and it would be a shame if I wound up at the bottom of the totem pole like he was.

Being addicted and having a shaky attitude, I didn't pay too much attention to what he said. It was all meaningless. I didn't dig until after I came to Odyssey how he was reaching out to me. He's still there and now I go around to see him once in a while.

My mother found out about my being a heroin addict when I passed out in the bathroom at home with the works in my arm. When I woke up there were two policemen there and my mother was crying. Really, really, really crying. My father looked as though he couldn't understand what was happening. They took me to the hospital and from there to jail. When I appeared before the judge, he asked my parents if they wanted me paroled in their custody. My father said, "We don't want him."

I yelled, "What do you mean, you don't want me?" The guard pulled me away. I couldn't believe it. It was the first time I felt any feeling from my father toward me, and it was negative. Or at least I interpreted it as being negative.

I felt tremendous rejection. I thought my father could have shown he cared by helping me, but instead he had been cold. He seemed satisfied to see me going to jail. All my life his indifference to me had been a non-verbal rejection which I had grown used to, but this was the first time we had a strong verbal communication and what he said was, "We don't want him."

I wanted to cry, but I said to myself, "I can't cry, I can't cry. This is jail and you can't cry in jail."

They sent me to the Brooklyn House of Detention. For the first five days there I went through withdrawal. I wrote my mother that I would lose my job if she didn't bail me out. She got my father to put up the money. The court gave me a suspended sentence on the charge of heroin possession.

After that time, there wasn't much affection between my mother and me. She would say things and I would tell her to get off my back. I started borrowing money from her to buy drugs. She would say "No, no, no, no, NO!" I would persist, and I'd always win. I tried to pay her back, but I wound up owing her about a thousand dollars at the end.

My parents were getting sick and tired of me. I was becoming increasingly bitter. Out of spite and not concern, I told them my brother was an addict too.

At home my mother's not too controlled with her feelings, especially if she's disturbed. However, I'm sure the neighbors never knew the pain she was going through because she can conceal it quite well in front of others. When she's in front of my father or myself, she can't. He is optimistic at times and my mother is not. I guess in this situation she was more reality-oriented.

I went to the hospital because of the hepatitis. I diagnosed it myself from a book. The symptoms were plain: the jaundiced look, the pain in the region of my liver that didn't go away even after I got off, changes in my stools, urine and eyes. I told the doctor that I had hepatitis and he agreed. He admitted me to Bellevue Hospital.

Recognizing that I was an addict, the hospital staff tried to persuade my parents to send me to the Rockefeller Program. It was something new. It involved civil commitment for three years to the State's drug program. I convinced my parents that I didn't need psychiatric assistance. While I was in the hospital, as a favor, my brother brought me drugs. He turned up every night with five bags. He was strung out then. He would take two and sit with a comic book nodding. I took two and left one for the guy in the next bed. The hospital ignored it. Two weeks later I was discharged.

Next, I went to another hospital where there was a twenty-one-day detoxification program. I stayed only four days. There was nothing there for me. They had as much drugs as on the street. People brought in heroin. I was taking five or six sleeping pills, people were robbing the dispensary, girls were being raped. It was a madhouse. I decided I might as well keep using heroin as everybody was full of shit.

I returned to taking from my parents; taking, taking, taking. They finally swore out a petition sending me to the Rockefeller Program.

On the day they buried Martin Luther King, my mother came into my bedroom and woke me up. She said there were two police officers to see me. While I was getting dressed, I sneaked into the kitchen and drank some vinegar. I had been told that vinegar cut the quinine in the urine. Therefore, the test results would not be positive and prove my addiction. It tastes horrible and isn't worth it—it doesn't work.

They took me away in handcuffs with all the neighbors watching out the windows. I felt ashamed.

I met a fellow addict in the detention room of Edgecombe Reception Center shortly after I arrived. He had been there ten months and was on his way out. He advised me to refuse to give

11

up urine or blood or anything that might incriminate me. He told me to keep insisting that I wasn't a heroin addict if I wanted to avoid being sent away for three years.

I took his advice. I refused to give up urine or blood. I insisted on my constitutional rights. There was nothing they could do about it. They asked if I wanted methadone for withdrawal, and I said no. I told them that since I didn't take heroin I wouldn't have a withdrawal. So I kicked cold. I mean, I *kicked*.

Judi says it takes three days, but it was a week before I got myself together. I told them after I kicked that I was ready to give up blood and urine. By that time, obviously, they were clean. Any addict who was sent on a voluntary petition could have beaten the system the same way.

My mother came to the court's rescue. After talking to my father, she testified to a whole list of things I had done, proving that I was a heroin addict. They decided to put me away for three years.

Odyssey House interviews anyone who wants to enter the program. They had talked to another inmate at Edgecombe the day before. I knew the game was up and I had better try to go to Odyssey. My Legal Aide lawyer, Mr. Fuchs, told me not to bother because, he said, there were no more beds at Odyssey. As I learned later, this is never true. There is always room for one more. I'll never forget that guy. I went ahead anyway and told the judge that I wanted to go to Odyssey. He suggested that I get it straight with Odyssey first, and then he would see what he could do for me.

Obviously, he was a judge who had some knowledge and understanding. Possibly there was some addiction in his family. I don't know.

Odyssey accepted me. They asked in my interview if I had any motivation to get well. I lied and said I did. I didn't really want to do anything for myself. I had heard that Odyssey's doors are never locked. Anyone can leave when they want to. I figured it was a good way to get back out on the street.

I never did. I changed.

I didn't want to go back to my parents. I was feeling bitter and guilty. They didn't like me being at Odyssey anyway; they wanted me in jail. In addition, my brother had just been arrested for armed robbery. It was a bad time for them.

My first impression of Odyssey was that the people in it were a bunch of lames. They used to call me "Radio" because I isolated myself by listening to music so much. I must have projected what I was feeling. People who came into the program after me were getting their probes-in and starting to move up, while I was still a candidate-in at the bottom. I got tired of it. Since I wasn't going to split I decided, "I'm going to get something out of this."

I started progressing, but it was hard to do. You can't play games and manipulate people when all of them are ex-addicts or professionals who know what they're doing.

Finally, I had my probe. I learned a great deal about myself that day. They explored my feelings of dislike for myself. I had doubts about being able to satisfy women sexually, which may have been related to my inability to meet my mother's career expectations for me. They told me in the probe that these doubts were unfounded, which made me feel better. They also talked about the hostility I was projecting all over the place. They helped me to gain sufficient insight to realize that my anger came from feeling trapped and being unable to influence my own destiny.

I'd never known anything like it. It was the first time in my life that I'd ever discussed myself that way. I went away thinking that I wasn't completely off the wall. I wasn't so isolated or different after all.

I said, "Damn, this is great."

POSTSCRIPT FROM JUDI
ABOUT JOHN COX

I don't remember any first impression of John Cox. While he was going through the program, Coxy was overshadowed always by Clifford Robinson. Until CR left Odyssey there wasn't a real relationship between John and myself. I did have some interaction with John, however, during the Starvathon.

The Starvathon was a marvelous experience. Jimmy Murphy and I invented it because the house was filled with depression. The residents were cynical and apathetic. The only emotion that can be stirred in a depressed and apathetic person is anger. We decided we should do something to make the residents angry. The best way, we figured, would be to take away one of the basic human necessities. We stopped feeding them.

All a resident had to do in order to be fed was to encounter us and ask why there was no food for him. The reason we would give was that Jimmy was too thin and I was too fat. Then he would counter with: "That's the most absurd thing I have ever heard. I want to be fed."

That's all they had to do, but you can't imagine what went on. Here's the scene: We went through the house eating all the time.

John Cox.

When we talked on the intercom we were chewing. We had popcorn and ice cream vendors going through the building. When they arrived for work, the staff conspicuously ate enormous breakfasts. There was never a moment when the pressure wasn't on; but it took some residents three days to ask for food. Toward the end almost everyone was eating, but a few still wouldn't ask.

On the third day one resident complained that he wasn't being allowed to listen to jazz on the radio. We replied while eating steaks, "Aren't you hungry?" False pride got in his way and he answered, "No. It's just that I want to listen to jazz." We agreed and gave the order that jazz should be played. He left, thanking us.

It was ridiculous. The residents knew it was a game. They knew we weren't just being cruel. But some of them couldn't figure it out for the longest time. All we wanted them to do was demand their rights and stop accepting our outrageous behavior. Some were so apathetic. We lost about five people who split because asking was too painful. For the rest it worked beautifully. For weeks after the Starvathon, the house was filled with laughter and fun.

My first memory of Coxy comes from that time. He was one of those who demanded and got his food early in the Starvathon and he therefore was running induction. One of the residents, a Jewish boy, had sneaked in the kitchen and eaten the dog's food. We discharged him for stealing. I instructed Coxy not to permit him back in the program until the Starvathon was over.

John came in my office and immediately sat in the probe chair. He released the worst anger I have ever experienced: pure, vituperative rage. It was transferential anger, and the pain of a Black who identified with a White boy who was at the mercy, as he perceived it, of power. It was racial, full of everything that has to do with master and slave, oppressor and oppressed. He called me *a farmer* and every other insult he could think of.

I ordered him to be quiet. It was the only way to stop him. And he stopped immediately. So I knew that fundamentally he still trusted me.

I call him Nelson Rockefeller Cox now to get even with him. Coxy is Odyssey House's *farmer.** He is in charge of our real estate holdings, and the tools of the establishment hang from his back pocket—the keys to two and a half million dollars worth of real estate.

He strives to be part of the establishment without compromising his Black identity or leaving his people. He is driven to see that his children go one rung higher on the ladder. I identify in Cox and his family—his wife, Yvonne, and daughter, Titi—the ambition of the Black to become part of the mainstream of American life, if we let him in. Not against us, but as part of us. If we allow him the opportunity which is his right, his rage will go.

But my first memory of John is him yelling and screaming epithets at me. John I remember as angry and energetic, Jimmy as silent and passive, Louie as directionless and seductive, Fred as hungry and appearing in need of a cup of chicken soup, and Charlie as security and reassurance.

* By *farmer,* Coxy means the keeper, or money behind the Establishment "pigs."

From the depths of the ocean floor
Comes my feeling of love and war
To the feeling I can relate
This my sorrow I do debate
The answer seems to be in all
Be my brother and I'll not fall

—TOMMY MOTT

Time	Monday	Tuesday	Wednesday
7:00 A.M.	Wake Up	Wake Up	Wake Up
7:15 A.M.	PT Begins	PT Begins	PT Begins
7:30 A.M.	PT Over/Breakfast	PT Over/Breakfast	PT Over/Breakfas
8:00 A.M.			
8:15 A.M.	Breakfast Over	Breakfast Over	Breakfast Over
8:30 A.M.	Morning Meeting	Morning Meeting	Morning Meeting
9:15 A.M.	Morning Meeting Over	Morning Meeting Over	Morning Meeting Over
9:30 A.M.	To Job Function	To Job Function	To Job Function
10:15 A.M.	Coffee Break	Coffee Break	Coffee Break & Level III Group
10:30 A.M.	Coffee Break Over	Coffee Break Over	Coffee Break Over
10:45 A.M.	To Job Function	To Job Function	To Job Function
12:00 P.M.	Lunch	Lunch	III Group Over & Lunch
1:00 P.M.	Lunch Over	Lunch Over	Lunch Over
1:30 P.M.	To Job Function	To Job Function	I & II Group
2:00 P.M.			
3:00 P.M.	Coffee Break	Coffee Break	I & II Group Over
3:15 P.M.	Coffee Break Over	Coffee Break Over	Coffee Break Over
3:30 P.M.	To Job Function	To Job Function	Concept
4:00 P.M.	Spanish Group		
5:00 P.M.	Dinner	Dinner	
6:00 P.M.	Spanish Group Over		Dinner
8:30 P.M.		Wisdom Group (Over 30)	
9:00 P.M.	Coffee Break	Coffee Break	Coffee Break
11:15 P.M.	Prepare for Bed	Prepare for Bed	Prepare for Bed
12:00 A.M.	Lights Out	Lights Out	Lights Out

Thursday	Friday	Saturday	Sunday
Wake Up	Wake Up		
PT Begins	PT Begins		
PT Over/Breakfast	PT Over/Breakfast		
		Wake Up	
Breakfast Over	Breakfast Over	PT Begins	
Morning Meeting	Morning Meeting	PT Over/Breakfast	
Morning Meeting Over	Morning Meeting Over	Breakfast Over	
To Job Function	To Job Function	Morning Meeting	Wake Up & Breakfast
Coffee Break	Coffee Break	Morning Meeting Over	Breakfast Over
Coffee Break Over	Coffee Break Over	GI Begins	Light House-cleaning
Lunch	Lunch		Free Activities
Lunch Over	Lunch Over / To Job Function	Lunch Begins	Light Lunch
Candidate-In/Boarder Group		Lunch Over	Lunch Over
Coffee Break	Case Conference & Coffee Break		Visits Begin
Candidate-In/Boarder Group Over/Spanish Group Begins		Coffee Break	
Dinner	Dinner	Dinner	Visits Over / Dinner
Spanish Group Over			
Coffee Break	Coffee Break		Cross Con-frontation
Prepare for Bed			Prepare for Bed
Lights Out			Lights Out

Key: PT—Physical Training
GI—Intensive Cleaning of the Facility

The Group Method

One of the reasons we developed the group method at Odyssey House is my belief that reality is best understood when seen through many eyes. I have a great need for consentual validation. As an only child of two strong-willed parents, both lawyers trained in the adversary system, I never felt that I was right. In the frequent struggle to make my own decisions concerning my life, they usually won by convincing me that I was wrong.

My odyssey has led to a feeling of confidence in my own decision-making, but to this day I use the opinions of others as prime factors in reaching my conclusion. The group method is the ideal setting for listening efficiently and comprehensibly to various points of view.

Odyssey is based on the trained ear hearing many different viewpoints and then synthesizing them through education and experience. Group is my reality. I'm not threatened by differing opinions as many people are. My ego doesn't insist that other people see things the way I do, probably because my early years presented me with so many different life styles in the people I loved. The great benefit of the group method is that it presents so many alternatives to the individual. He experiences that there are many acceptable ways of being a person, many kinds of equally acceptable ways of functioning.

Group is the antidote to the nuclear family, which appears to be an unhealthy way to raise children. The nuclear family—one father, one mother and the children—is one of the etiological factors contributing to the drug-addiction epidemic in this country. The nuclear family is ripe soil for addiction because the male child has for a role model only a single adult male and the female child has but a single female adult. All kinds of issues of control are created. The child feels he is personally failing or hurting the parent if he doesn't behave and think identically to the parent.

In the old days, we raised children in a cluster of relatives, an extended family setting but with breeding couples. Extended family units and promiscuity are no more synonymous than the nuclear family with fidelity or morality.

In the extended family living situation there wasn't a single role model—there was Uncle Charlie who liked to whittle and Aunt Sally who didn't marry and so on, all of them different and all of them functioning, all of them available to the child to be picked as a role model. They were a naturally occurring group. Because there were so many of them the burden on each child to conform to a single life style or be robotized was much less.

That isn't to say that a child could do as he pleased. Each group or extended family has its own rules and puts limits on its members. But the child had more choices within that framework.

A group-living situation, a group-sharing of responsibilities, a group method of problem-solving, all provide the maturing person with a choice of styles and, therefore, afford the most enriching developmental environment possible. Individuals require an opportunity to choose from a variety of constructive, feasible alternatives within a setting of love and concern.

From the parents' point of view, the nuclear family is also destructive. Parents are chained to their children in the tight isolation of the modern family. Their conflict comes in vying for the child, each parent, consciously or unconsciously, seeking the child's loyalty, seducing and demanding that the child join his or her team against the other parent. Parents need a range of peers with whom to share their burdens. This would help to displace their dependency on their children to the more appropriate dependence on peers. In this complex urban techological society, we all have dependency needs. Mankind is a herd animal. But we must not depend on our children to provide the necessary comfort and support.

We need one another in order to cope; therefore, trust must play a strong part in the group process. This is particularly true at Odyssey. Addicts are not only lonely, empty, depersonalized and fragmented, but they have almost no ability to trust. An atmosphere of trust must be developed. It begins with trusting the group because it is less threatening to trust a group than it is an individual. Once the addict is able to trust that the group cares about him, he can accept being hurt by the group, and this is crucial to his growth. He tolerates the pain of criticism knowing that it is done for his own good. Addicts, like most people, consistently turn away from censure. In order to change, they must endure it. A tolerance for criticism is part of mature functioning. The addict realizes that he will have to be hurt if he is to get well, and he trusts that the group hurts only with this view in mind. The group will not hurt intentionally for its own needs, it will not act out against the individual.

We gathered ideas for running groups from everywhere, from all the therapeutic communities, psychiatric disciplines, and sensitivity groups that we knew of. Some of the most dramatic techniques were learned by Jimmy Murphy and me in a prison hospital for the criminally insane at Penetanguishene, Ontario, Canada. There, Dr. E. T. Barker created a therapeutic community from one tier of males, most of whom were murderers. He and the prisoner-patients experimented with long-term marathons under conditions of sensory deprivation. Dr. Barker felt deprivation would quickly break down defenses. There is much experimental work to indicate that distractions help patients to maintain their defenses. The men entered a locked and windowless room for five days, where they remained naked and almost sleepless. There they sorted out reality from rationalization; there they learned about themselves.

When Jimmy and I returned from Canada, where he had presented a paper on the therapeutic community modality treatment of addiction at the Fifth International Meeting of Forensic Sciences, we were anxious to see what the effect of a long-term marathon with minimal sensory input would have on some of us. I wanted to experiment with it because, in a sense, people in the slums live in non-stimulating environments. I wanted to peek into the private core of my staff and myself as we regressed. We would know one another as closely as non-schizophrenics can.

My staff of approximately one hundred had the opportunity to take part in the experiment. Five accepted the conditions we had agreed upon.

The marathon would have a definite time limit of thirty-six hours. We had to make some modifications on the Penetang method in order to suit a heterosexual, non-criminally insane group—namely, my staff and myself. We would wear loose robes to cover our nakedness. They became a powerful dynamic in the marathon because they resembled shrouds. We would have only liquid Metrecal as food. We would wear no watches. We would not read. We would not play with anything in the environment. We would have only mattresses to lie on. We would not even look at one another. There would be no attempts to problem-solve. We would only free-associate, speaking without blocking. Pacifiers would be available. Halfway through, an opportunity would be provided for each of us to leave the room singly for an hour of sleep and a half-hour visit to a whirlpool bath (symbolizing a rebirth experience), after which the robe would be changed and the person would begin the marathon again.

One July day six of us went into the room: myself; Angela Green, a nurse; Jimmy Murphy; Clifford Robinson, an Odyssey graduate; David Anderson, a psychologist; and Herb Goldberg, a school teacher. We agreed to co-operate with the mandate: We would allow our anxieties to run wild, we would not block or filter or defend, we would let it all hang out.

After the first ten minutes of nervous settling were over, we began talking about death. I've been in groups for five years, and I have never known a group to begin with existential questions about death or God. But individually and spontaneously we began to speak of: *Who am I? Where am I going?* and *What is life about?* Within the half hour on that hot July day, we were all on the pacifiers.

For the first three hours the conversation vacillated between religion, sex, poetry, singing and death. After that Clifford hypnotized himself for the first time in his life. He remained in a trance for the rest of the marathon. We threw water on him, we stuck pins in him, we covered him in ice, we threw him in the bathtub. We did everything we could, but he had blanked out. Although he responded to questions we put to him with unguarded candor, revealing himself totally to us, he could remember nothing of it afterward.

Jimmy waited for it to end. Always co-operative when called upon, he hibernated and allowed time to pass through him. David Anderson began with aggression. He wanted to fight Clifford in particular. As a White man, he resented Clifford as a symbolic Black stud. The rest of us remained friends throughout the experience, but David unleashed hate. After a while he began to hallucinate actively. As usual, Angie did not play by the rules. She became totally self-centered and depressed. Herb, a scout master type, organized us into drills, into work crews to clean the room; he kept giving brisk orders.

I felt desperately trapped. I was caught between playing the game by the rules, which I did conscientiously, and a restless need for action. I had to do something. I needed motion, so I beat my hand on the wall rhythmically and one time nearly put it through the window. Jimmy came over to me and gently took my arm and told me to stop before I hurt myself.

The marathon became so threatening and painful to us all that we had to revise the rules. It began with Jimmy leading a raid on the refrigerator in search of solid food while I was responding to an emergency telephone call from Louie in another room. Next we decided that we needed a sleep break. Unlike any other marathon, the others chose to huddle together in the middle of the room, all in a row like biscuits in a baking pan. I stayed awake in a corner, fighting the urge to flee the unbelievably confining room. I felt I was in a coffin. Because I was the leader, I kept telling myself, I have no right to break the rules. Yet I had to escape the room to preserve my sense of self. I needed distance desperately.

When I did leave, rationalizing that I was justified on the grounds that I could not provide leadership if I were destroyed, I fled in such panic that on the way out, I stepped on Herb. He didn't stir. I slept in a side room, awakening a short time later. I returned to the room. No one had missed me, but I told them of my needs for privacy and seclusion.

The experience was the most amazing I have had at Odyssey. I look forward to a second one. It was a chance to penetrate inner space, a journey young people say they are taking through drugs. I had decided to search as deeply into myself as possible. I had been reluctant to try it alone because I didn't know where it would lead. I wanted to be among friends.

I turned inward as far as I could, and the farther I went the less I found. Inside, sadly, there is nothing. It made me feel that we can know ourselves but only through others. We know our own being, our own identity through relationships to other human beings, to nature, to books and to objects.

If you go into yourself too much, there is nothing you can relate to. After a while you no longer know where you are, what you are, who you are. That's what is happening to those on drugs. They lose their contact with reality. They digest themselves so much that there is no self left.

We know ourselves through the experiences we have. If we do not have any meaningful relationships, we are a *tabula rasa*.

Part of the Odyssey Concept says, "I see myself best through the eyes of my brother." We know ourselves best by listening to how we appear to others. In looking at ourselves we lie to ourselves, we deny, we create false images. We don't see ourselves as we really are, yet we feel something is wrong.

We called the experimental marathon Odyssey Trip Through Inner Space, or OTTIS. Afterwards each of us was entitled to be called an "Ottis." I was chilled when I was told months later that Ottis is the ancient Greek word for nomad, the wandering man without roots, a nothingness of being. There must be a primitive unconscious for us to have chosen that name. I had a sudden reverence for Jung.

In spite of the terror and desperation of that OTTIS, we still had some fun. One of the ways we attempted to revive Clifford, for instance, was to drop him head and shoulders into a platterful of some forbidden scrambled eggs that was set on the floor.

Many people who run groups make the mistake of emphasizing the pathology but never the health. All marathons and groups must run the full emotional gamut. There must be sadness, there must be laughter, there must be anger, there must be hostility, there must be joy. You cannot have only one emotion because it doesn't represent life. The group is life in a microcosm and must contain all its textures.

What delights me is that Jimmy, Louie, and the others tell me that my groups are the most fun. Therapy should be fun even though it hurts. If we tear down, we always build up. We never leave the person down. Many times in attack-and-encounter therapy, particularly that run by ex-addicts without professional guidance, there is only attack. They expect the subject of the attack to be able to go forward without any reaching out or giving from the group's members or leaders. Honesty is helpful to growth, but it is not enough. You must give the individual acceptance and hope. You can't leave him stripped and shivering.

Many therapists decide before they start a group where they'll be at the end. It really doesn't matter to me. Before there can be an obtainable goal there should be a process, and the goal may be modified by the process. I don't care where I am at the end of a group. What difference does it make? It's all part of experience, and we'll get wherever we're going at the very end. Each group, like Odyssey itself, is direction, at the end of which is the goal of a full-functioning human being.

THERAPEUTIC COMMUNITY

It's the unreal reality of an experience as seen through self
    and Brothers, related to reality.
It's the acceptance of love and trust to equal the losses.
    It's the reaching out of the isolated thin man who cries out,

but now identifies with his Brothers.

It's the injection of being, but now belonging.

It's the equation of end to beginning.

It's the end of the wish, and the unfolding of the answer.
It's the revolving world, but now you reach the brass ring.

It's the drawing up of love, trust, confidence, understanding,
with the unending booting.
It's the feeling of feelings, but knowing who and why.

It's the skelton of man offered a banquet.
It's the crossroads of lie and hate to love and trust.

It's the lit candle in the dark soul.
It's the delay of the ferris wheel, so you can get on.

It's the collar of love with the seepage of trust.

It's the combination to the deep secrets of soul.
It's the reaching for stars, but now knowing they're beneath you.

It's the crawling of a child in a play pen, to grow and walk the
streets as a man.

It's the journey to inner space.

—TOMMY MOTT
September 16, 1966
(written 4 years before the OTTIS was held)

J.E.S. GROUP

We began the Junior Executive Staff (known as J.E.S.) of
Odyssey in June 1970. It was started partly because the regular
program makes demands on the residents to conform. When working
with gifted patients, conformity frequently represents underachievement or an intolerable rigidity. A different program had to be
designed to meet the needs of residents such as Fred Cohen who
have unusual talents. The J.E.S. also functions side by side with
Odyssey's Senior Executive Staff. They are the pool from which we
draw future ex-addict staff members. And finally, as one of the
J.E.S. put it, the group was established "because Judi wanted to
have some fun." I no longer had time to conduct all the therapy at
Odyssey, and I missed it. The J.E.S. gives me an opportunity to
work with groups again.

The J.E.S. is constructed like a fraternity, with rushees and a
crazy initiation party and mock titles, but it has a serious goal. It is
designed to prepare gifted people to make the contribution to
society that they are capable of making. It's wrong to be gifted

and throw it away. It is a betrayal. I am convinced that human beings are interconnected; all life is one life.

People are not equal—some are more gifted than others. These few have a moral responsibility to shape the world and care for others. We have allowed the mediocre to lead. We can't permit it any longer. The gifted must lead, and they must be taught a moral commitment based on responsibility. That's part of what the J.E.S. is all about.

They meet in my home, a beautiful five-story nineteenth-century town house crowned by a greenhouse and an opulent marble bath I had built for me to luxuriate in. I like to be linked to the past. I see both life and time as a continuum. John Barrymore once lived in the house, and his daughter Diana wrote of it with fond nostalgia in her autobiography.

The J.E.S. gathers in a brick-walled room on the ground floor, reached by a dizzy descent of sheer plexiglass stairs. The room is a small softly lit square with a good fireplace and an alcove retreat containing a heated water bed. My private patients make themselves comfortable there.

I sit on the floor, sharing a copious vinyl beanbag with Fred Cohen. The J.E.S. crowds in, some fifteen to twenty of them. The early-comers grab the other two beanbags and the rest sit on folding chairs or stretch out on the floor.

In April 1971 we were to hear Richard Klein's candidate-out proposal. Richie, a gaunt young man with tousled hair, was sitting in his wheel chair in the middle of the room. He has been paralyzed ever since he jumped off a bridge while on an LSD trip. I lounged in the corner, wearing one of the loose floor-length robes I wear to allow me maximum freedom of movement. Fred Cohen, a graduate of the J.E.S. and now cotherapist, had folded his long length beside me.

I asked Carlton Martin to describe the J.E.S. for a visitor. He grinned, "I don't really know what we are . . ." The group laughed appreciatively. "I just know that we're here, that we're a very close-knit group, that we don't care what Level we are—we're all Level II or up—because we don't function on our Levels in the J.E.S."

His expression was droll. "Everyone here has no problem functioning . . ." A whoop of laughter. "We all function very well, more or less at the Junior Executive Level. And we work with Judi as our therapist and Fred the cotherapist and Richie the co-cotherapist, and we just have a lot of fun and we're great."

"Does the co-cotherapist want to add anything?" I asked Richie.

He answered in a crisp, businesslike tone. "We're too sick in the J.E.S. to get well in the regular program, or even in an abnormal-type program, so what we did was create an abnormal-abnormal-type program."

"Which makes it normal," I suggested.

"No," he responded gravely. "No, it doesn't make it normal and it doesn't make it abnormal. What it does is create hysteria." There was another burst of laughter.

We began with Solly Goldstein's composition: three pages of his considered thoughts on why he should not go to the Fillmore East Theater again. Odyssey House discourages residents in treatment from attending these rock concerts because of the availability of drugs. Richie Klein had ordered Goldstein to write it as an awareness. An awareness is an exercise which is frequently repeated just like a muscle exercise, to help develop one's perceptive faculties. In other words, "you exercise your awareness." It is always given by a higher level to someone lower in the community. Goldstein's awareness, as read by Carlton in the tone of a schoolboy's recitation, was hilariously pompous. The group howled throughout while Goldstein sat stoically staring at the gargoyle figures on the mural facing him.

"Solly," said Fred, "before you start to look like you're in a number, which is another of your sympathy-maneuvers that you pull all the time, or assume the patronizing, whining attitude that you do at the end of these confrontations, which is 'I can see what you mean, everything is clear, a total revelation, the sky has opened' —forget all that shit too."

Fred continued, "First of all, I don't believe a fucking thing you wrote in there. The attitude, the prevailing attitude in it, shows through quite clearly. I don't think you believe anything that you wrote. I think you did it as an exercise, a ten-finger exercise."

"It's so ridiculous and so off the wall that it's thumbing your nose at Richie," I said, "or anyone else, for saying that you can't go to the Fillmore. There's a kind of childish sarcasm in it which no one can miss."

Ralph Drew said softly, "What I picked up about Solly is that he's very frustrated because he knows what's happening and it's really hard for him to get out of this . . ."

Carlton turned to Ralph, a lanky tow-headed teen-ager flat on his back on the rug with his feet neatly crossed. "Can you tell Solly what's happening? Do you *know* what's happening?"

"I don't think it is really intentional," said Ralph less surely.

"I don't think his selfishness is as intentional as the group makes out. Besides . . ."

"Ralph," I interrupted, "even if it's not intentional, how do people react to it?"

Ralph pondered. "Yeah, I can see what you're saying."

I explained, "People react to his behavior with hostile feelings. Solly's going to be handicapped all his life by people moving away from him, which will drive him back to drugs. The problem is that he doesn't know how to make friends. He's going to remain isolated unless he changes his behavior patterns."

"Why don't we concentrate on the part that *is* intentional," Klein said urgently, "and that is sitting down at the typewriter and typing something like that. Solly, I felt it was a suicide note."

Steve Wasserbach, also flat on the floor, lifted his head and looked at Solly. "This morning you said to me that everybody's not understanding you," he drawled. "You claim you're so critically *sick!* You're just basically a lazy, inner-directed bastard. Honestly, your facial expression kills me. It looks like you want people to start feeling sorry for you. They'll *do* it. They don't see where you're coming from and they'll do it. And you and they will get fucked up."

"I don't mean to come across like that," protested Solly. "I just get very defensive." He looked aggrieved, sitting in a Popeye jersey in a pool of light from a nearby table lamp, his long sideburns flaring from his pale face.

Leonard Shapiro, a chunky, balding man with nervous hand gestures, spoke up. Shapiro is a rare type of addict. He first used drugs at the age of thirty-five after many years of homosexuality. A lover insisted he join him in drug taking, and Lenny, desperate for love, could not say no. Six months later he came to Odyssey asking for help. He was the head of the J.E.S. house, describing to the group Solly's indolence about making his bed and keeping his room tidy.

"That's one of the ways that he shows hostility to the group, by becoming messy," I commented. "So-o-o, what are you doing Goldstein?"

Solly spoke in a low voice. "I don't think I was aware of what I was doing at the time."

The group exploded. "There he goes!" "Don't look at his eyes!" "Don't look at him!"

"It's like infinity," I said soothingly. "He's caught in the endless loops of never getting out of this maze of experience . . ."

"This cosmic essence," agreed Fred.

29

Angela Green, enthroned on a beanbag in the corner, shook her head. "*Cosmic essence* and *endless loops* I can't put together," she complained.

Carlos Rivera spoke crisply. "I'll be much more concrete, Solly. First of all, you're in the exterior maintenance group and you're talking about getting close to people. But countless times when you're in a working relationship where you have to get close to someone, you louse it up. When you get yourself all fucked up you go into your bag and you do your whole number. You have groups, you threaten to split and you talk with everybody. You're constantly draining people, needing all their attention. We can explain this to you in a million different ways, we can really go through a lot of different analogies to try and help you see things. But you don't change."

"Wait, I don't quite agree with you, Carlos," I said. "I think you're better, Solly.

"I think he *hasn't* changed," Fred declared.

"No," I said. "I think he is better. He's not quite as obnoxious. He's not *totally* obnoxious."

Solly was intensely studying the gargoyles on the wall again.

"What are you going to do about the basic fact that you and people don't get along?" I asked.

A long silence. Fred said dryly, "Solly, we wait." More silence, broken by derisive comments from the group.

"What is it that you do that moves people away from you?" I demanded.

"I guess it's my attitude towards people," Solly responded finally.

"All people?"

"The majority of people."

I thought about it. "Is it basically that you don't like people, or is it a defense against the fact that people bristle with you, react in some way?"

"It's partly that," Solly replied, considering what he said carefully. "It's also my negative outlook on life . . ."

Bob Smith spoke up. "Solly, everybody who comes to Odyssey has a negative outlook on life. But it doesn't mean that we hate people."

Solly mumbled that he couldn't agree with some of the things he was supposed to do in order to be considered improving. It was a fact, he said, that he didn't like many people.

"It doesn't endear you to people when you say things like that," I chuckled. "Most of the people in here are people, and they resent it."

"You can't get away from it," Richie Klein observed. "Without people you get lonesome."

Solly said stubbornly, "I don't get lonesome." He looked about to cry and murmered something about being defeatist.

"You're not a defeatist," I said vehemently. "You're not a cynical or skeptical person. It doesn't seem to me that you're the kind of person who walks around questioning the meaning of life."

Richie quoted, "Life is nothing more than an unpleasant interruption in an otherwise idyllic state of existence," and the tension in the room dissolved.

"Is that one of the things you get out of bubblegum?" Fred inquired.

"Out of that existential bubblegum produced by Jean Paul Sartre?" I asked.

Carlton took over. "Solly, I know you like people. You like me, you like Smitty. I notice you have a lot of good laughs together. You like Johnny Cox. I notice you like Rivera. You like Judi. In general, you like people." Solly nodded, relieved.

"Solly," I said, "we've ruled out that people don't like you because you're defeatist, or cynical, or questioning the meaning of life. Got any other ideas on why people may not like you?"

Solly looked at me and spoke clearly. "Because I'm a self-centered bastard."

The group sighed with relief.

"You're always offensive and defensive," I said gently. "You are afraid that there'll never be enough to go around for you, enough affection, enough caring, enough concern, enough freedom. Why are you always looking out for Solly? Is it because you're afraid nobody else will?"

Solly's voice was broken. "I think that's so," he said. "I am always looking out for myself . . ."

"You're just not perceptive," I told him. "You keep dancing like a Mack truck when you're on the point, you flatten everybody under. You don't take cues from your environment, you don't take warnings from other people's reaction tones. You don't sense the normal distance testing: *May I, May I Not?* You never ask, *May I?* You must have been terrible at Giant Steps."

"It's that he's self-centered, totally disregarding everybody," suggested Steve Wasserbach.

"That's not true," I objected. "He really doesn't have an understanding that other people have different tastes, different things they like. Solly can't imagine that if he likes sugar on the beef, the world doesn't like sugar on beef. It's one of his basic fundamental problems. Remember his favorite dish of herring and peaches? We always had to watch him when he was cook."

Solly's body drooped and he made comments.

"Solly," I asked, "why are you so threatened?"

He denied that he was.

"You are. You're in terror. I perceive it. Not because you're arrogant, as some have said, but because you don't seem to know the answers and you're very afraid that because you don't know the answers, the ax is going to fall. . . . Relax."

Solly straightened and asked curiously, "Why do I always feel the ax is going to fall?"

I smiled. "I don't know, and to tell you the truth I don't care. Eventually the ax will fall unless you stop fearing it so much. It's like wish fulfillment." I paused and studied him. "In the next few weeks, Solly, do you think you could make a maximum effort to try to understand other people, and forget about their understanding you?"

He nodded.

"Then do you think in these coming days," Fred asked, "we will see a noticeable difference in the way people relate to you and, in turn, the way that you react to people? Do you know the distinction?" Solly looked confused.

"In other words," I explained. "Let Fred relate to you and you react to Fred, rather than the other way around. All the people in the room will relate to you and you will react to them, rather than you relating to them and they getting annoyed at you."

"In other words," said Solly, perking up, "I react first and then relate later?"

"No, no, no, no, *no*," I told him. "You don't understand. *They* relate and *you* react. They go first. You will be very quiet and you'll try to understand what Carlton is like, not that Carlton should understand what you are like. You will try very hard to stay on the right side of Carlton, on the right side of everyone in the room. You'll learn what they like, where they're at, and then you'll try to adapt your style, just for a brief period of time, so that for once in your life they don't have to accept your style.

"Try to be a totally well-functioning nonentity," I concluded.

Fred said admiringly, "That was beautiful!"

I watched Goldstein, whose face was clearing. I said, "Another thing that turns people off is bragging about what you do. Let the machine run magnificently well without anyone knowing that Goldstein did it. And you know something, Goldstein? People *will* know that Goldstein did it. You don't have to go around selling yourself."

"I see," said Solly with composure. "All I should worry about at this point is just to do what I'm told and function . . ."

"NO!" I interrupted, feeling depressed. I turned to Fred. "He thinks all he has to do is subjugate his entire being and do what he's told to do, and he says it with resentment. It's still an authority hang-up, a feeling that he's going to lose himself." I turned back to Goldstein.

"With you, Solly, everything is an issue of who's in control. Why are you fighting for control so much?"

Solly was flatly honest for the first time. "It's like everything I do. I'm in a debate. It's very important for me to win the debate, otherwise I'll crumble. Or perish."

"Why don't you practice losing the debate," I suggested, "and see that you won't fragment? Seriously. I believe you. I don't think what you're saying is a fake. I believe that you truly feel that if you're not in control, you won't *be*. And that's not true."

I had an aside for Fred. "His pathology is the exact opposite of yours. Do you see that? You felt if you exerted yourself, you'd be destroyed, and he feels that if he doesn't exert himself, he'll be destroyed." Fred nodded in recognition.

I studied Solly's troubled face. "It's very interesting," I told him gently, "because Fred's way of dealing with life before he came to Odyssey was to back off from it. Frederick felt if he made any demands, he would be destroyed. And you feel that unless you make constant demands, constantly assert yourself, constantly win, you'll be destroyed. Neither one is real. It's important not to fear every moment that you're going to disintegrate or dissolve or fragment if you decide to be yourself, whatever that may be. You don't have to fight other people, Solly. They can't destroy you."

There was a long peaceful silence.

"A penny?" I asked.

"I was thinking of myself," Solly replied slowly. "The areas I get into. I see myself in extreme areas, doing extremes, and finding myself at the other end of a sort of spectrum . . ."

Carlos Rivera rolled over. "I think he's just testing now, to see if we like him."

We had started at nine o'clock that night, four hours ago. "We'll leave Solly," I decided. "He's had oodles of time in this huge room." The group, packed tightly in the small space, was amused.

We talked next with Leonard Shapiro, warning him to be on

guard against laxity developing in the J.E.S. house. Then we discussed who among the Odyssey residents should be inducted into J.E.S. next, and we finally moved to eighteen-year-old Ralph Drew. He had been selected for the core group that would open the New Hampshire house. Ralph's past experiences made it difficult for him to accept a concept of love that doesn't involve a sexual assault on him. The group and I, in easy good humor, worked for an hour to bring Ralph to the point of being able to say that he was aware I loved him as a son and would miss him when he left New York.

However, he was at first too blocked to see it, and Fred began to work with him. Fred knows very well that saying the word *love* is exceedingly difficult for some. "What's happening on a feelings level, Ralph?" Fred said coldly, adding, "If you're not full of shit."

"I feel that Judi will be apprehensive about me going so far away," Ralph said hesitantly, still uncertain of what was required.

"Why?" asked Fred, rolling a thin cigar in his fingers.

"Because she likes me."

"She *likes* you?"

"Come on!" protested Ralph, flushing with embarrassment.

"Be more specific Ralph," Fred demanded.

"It's a four-lettered word," someone prompted.

"Loves? Cares?" tried Ralph.

"You said it the first time, Ralph," Fred told him sternly. "Don't cement it over with a less important, easier-to-handle feeling. What is the real feeling Ralph?"

"Love," he replied reluctantly. The group was delighted, congratulating him boisterously. When they settled down I asked, "Why did I decide to talk to you about this tonight?"

Ralph thought. "To reassure me, I think."

"How do you feel about that?"

"I feel better, a lot better. It's not the type of feeling when you go off to college and your mother is checking up on you. This is not a badgering or anything. It means a good feeling dwells at home in case I'm lonely."

"At least write," Solly told him.

Said Fred, with a Yiddish accent, "Make a phone call, it wouldn't killya for godsake."

I said fondly, "This is the sickest group of people I've ever met."

The group ended around four in the morning, everyone tired, low-keyed and feeling good.

Carlos Rivera had been in the Odyssey program for three and a half years, an interminable time. I call him Non-Commonsensical Rivera, because no matter what happens he always homes for the self-destructive course. When there is a fork in the road and he wants to go to the right, indubitably you know that the left-hand road is the correct one. I have never seen Rivera make a correct choice.

He's a sociopath, someone who can't think in terms of consequences. I fear that he might not make it because, unfortunately, he's so much smarter than the staff, and they have to be perceptive enough to set limits for him. He is always gaming, which is typical of this disease. Rivera completely hoodwinked Charlie Rohrs, who

J.E.S. meeting.

once allowed him to be proposed for candidate-out, which is one step from graduation. I'm livid at Charlie for having been taken in—because Rivera functions well, the professional staff gets confused and believes that he is improving. I moved Rivera to John Cox for private therapy. Cox can see through the games.

When I turned down his proposal Rivera must have been deeply disappointed, but on meeting me the next morning he said, "It's good to see you." Mad as he may be at me, I have no doubts that he knows instinctively that I'm looking after his best interests, that I'm not acting out of some personal reason. I'm probably the only one he trusts. A sociopath knows there's something wrong with himself. He knows he needs someone to protect him from himself, and to protect others from him because he treats everyone as objects. Sociopaths cannot make good decisions, but they do get well at Odyssey.

About Solly Goldstein

I have stayed away from finding out much of Solly Goldstein's background because he was always demanding analysis. He wanted to use the past to justify the present. I gather he comes from a typical Jewish home with one of those overpowering mothers. Solly ran away when he was thirteen or fourteen, just after eighth grade. This is unusual.

He's uneducated, but he's a mechanical genius. He can do everything: fix plumbing, wiring, cabinets, design and make stained-glass windows. All sorts of things. He was married once. It was a very negative relationship with a lot of group sex, and finally he became involved with drugs. He had court cases pending in Florida, as well as in New York, and his New York lawyer sent him to Odyssey. He represents the addict who functions well, has a steady income, but always feels terrible about himself.

About Ralph Drew

Ralph Drew has so much pain in some ways he reminds me of myself. He comes from what would be classed as an ideal WASP home environment in the Midwest, but his was one where the parents were viciously cruel in the raising of their seven children. His father is a pathologist who earns six figures a year. He used to withdraw to the bathroom and read his medical journals for hours while the mother tried to attack Ralph sexually.

Once in New Hampshire, we had a wonderful group with

Ralph—Fred and I working together as one therapist. There was no division, we worked as one person. Fred led for the first several hours while mostly I listened to Ralph talk about his childhood. The fact that his parents were totally concerned with their own needs and demanded that at all costs the child behave aroused such feelings of identity in me that eventually I had to go out of the room. As in the OTTIS, when I become depressed I must withdraw.

I soothed myself by eating a whole roast chicken. It was driven behavior—it's fortunate that I understand myself and can interpret my actions and what I'm feeling. I fled the room because it would have been very destructive to Ralph if I had stayed and shared with him my distress. I was finding it difficult even to breathe.

One of the J.E.S., a teen-ager who came to Odyssey in a terrible state of depression and who is a sensitive, lovely person, knew that I was upset. He followed me and asked if he could help. We didn't talk but sat together for a few minutes. I sent him back to Fred with a message that I would return to the room in half an hour. I needed the solitude, which I filled by eating.

Whenever I feel isolated and reminded of the loneliness of my childhood, I feed myself. I eat voraciously. This is one of the reasons why my life has been a constant battle against overweight. If in a sense I'm not being fed, not being nourished, I feed myself.

Ralph talked about his mother seducing him, being soft, making him feel that he could open up, letting him cling to her. And then, when he did, she would say, "Can I put my tits in your mouth?" She would grab his testicles and beg him to suck her nipples, while all the time, her pathologist husband was in the bathroom defecating past his hemorrhoids.

Fred and I had decided before the group that we would need a commitment sign from Ralph. We often use commitment signs: with Clifford Robinson it's shining shoes, with Silas Whitfield it's standing on his head, with Fred it's verbal—he must say *I love you*, which the first time was so difficult for him to say that it took three hours to get it out.

In Ralph's case I knew we had to tilt him, set off the bells and lights like some pinball machine. I didn't know how I could do it, and I asked Fred for suggestions. We discussed some symbolic use of baby food, but rejected that. The problem was to reproduce, at a strategic moment, the deception of Ralph's mother, offering love and tenderness and then abruptly making a sexual demand that the child could not meet without destroying himself.

I had a vague perception that Ralph's commitment sign would only come out of a situation that would go against my natural inclinations. But it would be something that I would have to do for Ralph's sake.

We were about six hours into the group. Fred had done most of the questioning, with the group quietly watching. Since Ralph's arrival in New Hampshire he had been depressed and unable to cope with the separation from me. For him, the Odyssey program was me. He desperately needed a good mother.

I changed places with Fred, who had been sitting on the edge of the couch where Ralph was lying face down, weeping. He was responding to Fred, saying a lot of analytic garbage about his parents, and I rubbed his back and made cooing, consoling sounds. Ralph turned toward me and I took hold of his chin. It was very quiet.

I hit him across the face as hard as I could.

He screamed and began deep crying which lasted about an hour. The crying became deeper and deeper as the layers peeled away. This kind of crying is called the primal scream. There is a theory in one school of psychiatry that if you can get a patient to reach that level of pain, he will begin to heal. With certain patients it is necessary to go that deep. Once you hear that kind of crying, you can never forget it. I never in my life heard anything like that boy's scream. I think everyone in the room wanted to get out, but we were all paralyzed. The human pain was so intense we couldn't look at one another.

What I had done was repeat his mother's action, being very close and very soft and very warm, pretending to be really listening, and then from nowhere I gave him unexpected, inexplicable pain.

After he had cried profoundly for an hour, I told him to turn over. He had curled into the fetal position with his face buried in the back of the couch. People can get deeper into the cry when they can't see anyone. He turned around and said, "Judi, I'm sorry I made you mad," and began a long apology for forcing me to hit him.

For a second, I was stunned by his response. Of course the hit had come out of nowhere. It wasn't that he had made me mad, *he had done nothing.* Yet his reaction was understandable, for this child had tried for eighteen years to blame himself for the fact that his mother tried to stick her breasts in his mouth. He couldn't tolerate the idea that it was her sickness. It was easier to blame himself. I realized that my tactic had worked even better than I had known when he first screamed. He had transferred his feelings about being hit to his unconscious memories of his mother's assaults, which enabled him to release the pain. Then when he came back to the reality of the room, he brought with him his deep-seated feelings of guilt and apologized to me, symbolically apologizing to his mother.

13

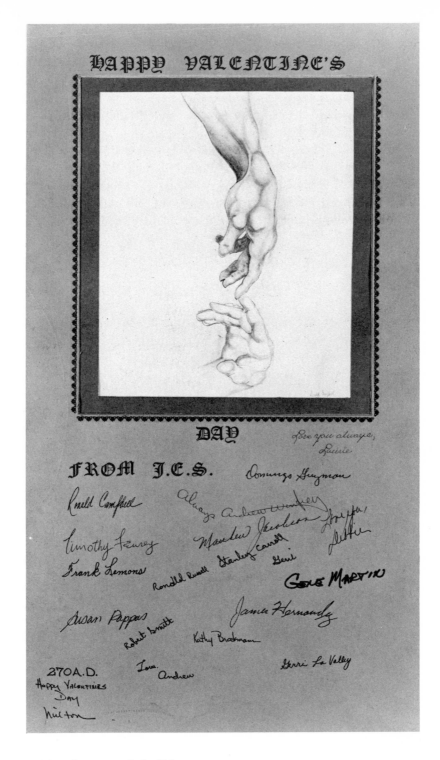

39   J.E.S. valentine to Judi, February 1972.

It was so off the wall that it provided Fred and me with a welcome, necessary release. Spontaneously we began to laugh and cry at the same time.

Fred explained to Ralph that it was irrational, that it wasn't because of anything he had done, that he bore no responsibility for the slap any more than he did for his mother's behavior. Ralph heard Fred and his face lightened.

I suppose my commitment sign with Ralph will have to be hitting him, but in the future I'll remind him of the hit rather than do it again. I don't like striking patients. I've done it three times, always deliberately, never not thought out. It's not a normal therapeutic technique, but it can be very meaningful.

About Richard Klein

Richie Klein, or Circle-Legs, is another illustration of Odyssey's unique approach to mental illness, which is sometimes at extreme variance with the rest of the world. Richie was sent to us by Dr. A. Ronald Sorvino, whom I worked with at Metropolitan Hospital in 1967. Richie's transfer note explained that his doctor did not expect him to last more than two weeks because he was acutely suicidal.

Richie had been in care at the South Orange Hospital in New Jersey for several months because he was suicidal and addicted. They had given up on him. Seven years before he severed his spine when he jumped off a bridge under the influence of LSD. He claims it wasn't because of a fantasy that he could fly, a delusion frequently experienced by hallucinogenic users, but rather he jumped in order to kill himself.

As a paraplegic, he continued taking heroin and dealing. He found it very easy to deal from a wheel chair. There are many places to hide the dope, and the police won't bother a cripple. He pretended to sell pencils while the glassine envelopes went back and forth and nobody knew.

When Richie arrived for induction at Odyssey, he was dirty, unshaven, completely depressed and whining. He had a huge pressure ulcer on his buttocks which he couldn't feel. Just as he can't move below the waist, he can't feel there either.

I responded to his suicidal wailing and demand for pity by saying, "Look here, Richard Klein, you have a perfect right to kill yourself. You succeeded in doing it halfway. If you're going to go the full route, *do it!* Let's not talk about it any longer. I don't want to hear about it. The day you want to commit suicide, go quietly and com-

Richie Klein (Circle-Legs).

mit suicide. It's perfectly understandable to me that you would want to kill yourself. Perhaps, if I were in your position, I might want to commit suicide too.

"But if you're not going to do it, don't waste time talking about it. If you want to do it, go ahead. Don't hang around. But while you're here, even though your legs are dead, you've still got your head and your hands. Use them."

He says I'm the only one who never argued with him, who didn't try to persuade him that being paralyzed wasn't so bad. "You understand that I might want to kill myself and you don't make me feel guilty about it," he told me. "You say if I want to work at living, you'll help me, but if I want to die, it's my right to do so.

You truly understand my existential reality. You don't take away from me the right of free choice."

One day after he had graduated Odyssey, he returned to me briefly for some problem-solving. He was depressed and suicidal again because he was having a relationship with a girl and felt guilty that he couldn't meet her needs. He felt that to ask anyone to be married to him was a terrible imposition, though he longed for a permanent relationship.

I said to him, "I can't give you back your legs and I can't give you back your pelvis. I want you to make one commitment: If you decide to kill yourself, will you please first write a copy of that poem you dedicated to me? It is the most moving poem I have ever seen. I must have that poem."

He stared at me for a moment and then laughed. He said, "I've busted your game. What you're telling me is that if I can write poetry like that, I can be romantic and, therefore, I shouldn't kill myself. You are IMPOSSIBLE!"

We had two sessions together and he is no longer suicidal.

ABOUT FRED COHEN

My brother-in-law was working for Odyssey when Fred Cohen was inducted. He told me that an addict finally had been admitted with whom he could identify. This addict was capable, bright and in great difficulty in the regular program. He felt that Fred Cohen had more potential than 99 per cent of all human beings but was totally self-destructive.

Some time later I was faced with the problem of finding a Level I who was sophisticated enough to participate in the probe of a transexual. Odyssey was going to force the transexual, Randi Stewart, to choose which sex he wanted to be. We didn't care which he selected, but he couldn't remain in the twilight zone of existence with both breasts and a penis because that way no one in the community could comfortably relate to him.

The fact that Odyssey would permit someone to choose whichever sex he/she wished to be was going to be a difficult concept to get across to a resident just beginning treatment. This idea had been almost impossible even for our Medical Director, Charles Rohrs, to accept. I was concerned if a Level I, because he was on that part of his journey which needed rigid structure, would be able to understand anyone with breasts and a penis. I didn't want a Level I in the probe but if I had to, and according to Odyssey rules I did,

Fred Cohen.

I remembered what my brother-in-law had said about Fred Cohen. I picked him on the basis of his reported intelligence.

I had never seen him, and when he walked into the auditorium my first impression was that he was unbelievably tall and unbelievably thin. He looked as Lincoln must have looked as a young man. I thought, *we've got the gentleman-addict from Springfield*.

He had a crew cut and was twenty pounds thinner than he is now, which is still appallingly thin. He is six feet two and weighs 135 pounds. He was bent over so you couldn't see his face. He resembled somewhat an overgrown turkey. In later days, I was to propose him for membership in the British Society for the Preservation of the Giant Bustard. He was extremely polite, but distant. I wasn't particularly impressed with him. He said very little during the probe. I didn't see him again for a month or so.

My brother-in-law kept bugging me about Fred Cohen so I decided to give him another chance. I was going to Tannersville, in Upstate New York, and needed a spare driver. He was a Level II at the time and I reasoned that it would give me an opportunity to evaluate him. During the entire drive, however, he never spoke. Not once.

Fred Cohen 1

I walked into Odyssey House at one-thirty in the afternoon. I was inducted on the spot because I came from out-of-town, from Boston. It had been my intention to look the program over and then go away, smoke some pot and think about it.

The induction staff, however, considered the visit an enlistment and told me I would be called a splittee if I left. My main motivation not to leave was that they said if I ever wanted to come back, I would have to have my head shaved.

So I stayed. The alternative facing me was a prison sentence of from eighteen to thirty years. I didn't believe for a moment it would happen. I was charged with six felonies, three for drug sales and three for possession. This would allow a judge to impose such a sentence, but my infantile omnipotence was in full flower and I took it as a joke, as something too unlikely even to be considered.

The part of the Odyssey program that was going to have a life-changing impact on me was its Executive Director, Dr. Judianne Densen-Gerber. I had no intimation of this on the day I arrived and saw her for the first time. Her office door was open and Seymour Domaclang, who was House Co-ordinator then, pointed her out. He told me her name. I thought, as usual, *So what?*

The next time I saw her was in a general meeting. She struck me as very intelligent, highly controlling and far removed from my lowly status. I wanted some attention from her. I was thinking, "Take a look at me, you've got something special here. A college student, *a guy who never used heroin.*" I thought that was a big deal because I was one of the few people in the program then who had never used a needle or tried hard drugs. I wanted to think of something pro-found to say to impress her, but I couldn't.

The third time I saw Judi was during the Randi Stewart probe. I had wanted to participate, but I hadn't spoken up. That's my passive-aggressive thing.

I was working in the kitchen when I was called to the auditorium. I figured they wanted me to clear away the dishes. I walked over to the stage to gather up the trays. Judi stopped me and said I had been selected to take part in the probe. It turned out to be an exhausting, enlightening experience.

As I learned later, Judi had worried that the participants in the probe wouldn't be flexible enough to allow Randi to make a decision about what sex he would be. He had both breasts and a penis. She thought the males would demand that Randi remain male, and the females would be threatened if he didn't continue the sexual transformation he had started to become a female. It took the probe group four hours to work through their varied anxieties and become sufficiently objective to send for Randi.

I stayed awake throughout the probe, which lasted a total of twenty-four hours, dozing only during the last hour or so. Randi wanted to live in the female dormitory but keep his male genitalia. He refused to make a decision so he had to be discharged. We never saw him again.

Later, as a Level II, I was told that Judi needed a driver to go to Tannersville. Since I had a driver's license, it would be me. It turned out that she drove all the way. I sat beside her, silent, uptight and confused, for three and a half hours. My only thought was, *What am I doing here with the Executive Director of Odyssey House?*

Tannersville is in Upstate New York. Odyssey was using a massive old house there as a staff retreat. Judi and the rest of the executives were working out new lines of authority. "Off the top," she explained casually, "you need a vacation and that's why you're coming with me. You've been working very hard."

It gave me something to fret about compulsively. *What does she mean? What does she mean?* This occupied me for the next five days.

Perhaps I should describe what I was like then. I didn't believe anything I was told. I related very easily to a function, but not at all to people. I didn't believe in anyone. I knew in my soul that everyone had a hidden demand to make on me, some ulterior motive no matter how simple it seemed. In order to preserve myself, I had to figure out what was wanted. In the interim, my technique was to withdraw into work and watchfully wait.

I did most of the cooking. I was compulsively fastidious with

146

those dinners. *Perfection.* Except that when I would have the meal ready, Judi and the others would still be conferring; by the time they came to the table the food was cold. I believed that it was part of their plan to get me uptight. They were disregarding me deliberately, I thought.

The night before we were due to leave we were sitting at the table having dinner. I made a motion to get up and clear it. Judi said, "Sit down. Somebody else will do it." I decided they were still trying to box me into a situation: *now I was going to get it.*

Judi told Louie Sarra to put wine in my glass. She proposed a toast to me: "To the new Level III."

I almost shit in my pants. Judi didn't clarify why I had been made a Level III. Of course I wouldn't ask. She told me my job function would be Ramrod of the Mother House, which is second in command at Odyssey's headquarters on East Sixth Street and one of the highest positions you can hold in the program as a resident in treatment. From kitchen to Ramrod! My God, where could I hide? Even worse was how could I relate and make demands on other people?

"You understand," Judi told me, "that there will be resentment among the II's because you have been promoted so quickly. And the Level III's are going to feel very threatened." I shuddered. The Level III's were all strong aggressive people. I would be destroyed.

Fortunately, it turned out that because of my driver's license, I spent very little time in the Mother House. I was always out picking up donations and delivering supplies. I would come in about two or three in the morning and get up at seven. The lack of sleep was worth it as long as I didn't have to interact with people.

I was a Level III for about two weeks when I was called into Judi's office. I knocked, I entered and I stood there. They pointed to the probe chair and I sat down. I was the last piece of business in the regular Tuesday Executive Staff meeting and they were all there—Judi, Louie Sarra, Clifford Robinson, Jimmy Murphy, and the others.

Judi asked me how I thought I did on the IQ test that Jerry Katz had given me. I said sincerely that I didn't think I did very well. Everyone laughed. I didn't know what to make of it. I explained that I was nervous, that I didn't remember some of the backwards numbers, that I couldn't concentrate. I began making explanations all over the place. The more I said, the more they laughed. Judi was pounding her desk excitedly and making faces like *I can't stand it! I can't stand it!*

I had changed somewhat since Tannersville. I no longer felt

that Judi was going to hurt me in any way. Whatever she was about to do, it would almost certainly be something I wouldn't like, but it also would be something I needed. I liked her, a new feeling.

When they had finished howling, she informed me that I had tested 177. Jerry Katz had never heard of such a score. He was so upset he locked the test in the safe and phoned Judi at home that night to tell her about it. She said to me, "What do you intend to do about this potential?"

I was thinking that it was a mistake. I was hoping that it was a mistake. I've always known that I'm intelligent, but this was absurd. *Who needs it?*

They went through a big group thing and I was fairly non-verbal. As it progressed I could see that Judi wanted something from me. I didn't know what it was. "What do you think it is?" she asked. I didn't have a clue.

She then asked if I ever felt warmth toward anyone in my life. My mother, my father, my sister, anyone. I responded with a half-hearted yes. She wanted to know how I felt about her and everyone else in the group. I went around from person to person, describing everyone negatively, picking out their faults. I left her for the last. Finally, I described Judi in terms of Odyssey House. She had built it out of nothing, she was an amazing person, she deserved a lot of credit, and things like that.

There was about two hours of such nonsense before I finally realized what she wanted me to say to her. I had to say, "I love you." The conflict that was going on in my head was that if I said I loved her, I would have to mean it. There would be no sense otherwise, it would be just a farce.

Judi explained that once I said the words, I would mean it. Apparently it's an existential reality. Eventually, mostly to discover what would happen, I choked out the words, "I love you." I felt self-conscious; I felt relieved; I felt happy. There was a sensation of warmth and affection toward Judi.

She gave me an ultimatum. She said there wasn't really very much that the regular Odyssey program could do with someone with an IQ of 177. What did I want to do? She gave me three choices: one, to become a Level IV (which I didn't want to do—I was totally insecure as a Level III and dammit why should I become a Level IV?); two, she could discharge me with medical advice from the program, since there was nothing she could do for me at Level III; or three; she could discharge me from the program and then see me as a private patient.

It was a setup. Knowing that having to make decisions im-

mobilized me, she was pushing me to the wire. I was being compelled to make a choice. Of the three alternatives, two were obviously impractical. I could choose neither one involving discharge
from the program. The program represented a secure environment for
me. Therefore, I told her I would become a Level IV.

There was a lot of prestige in being a Level IV. At that time
there weren't more than nine or ten of them at Odyssey House.
Suddenly I was an Assistant Administrator sitting in at staff meetings,
in a peer group with John Cox and David Winters and other big
people in the progran. No one liked me. They were all threatened by
me.

It was all part of Judi's design for Frederick Cohen. My intelligence had been isolating. She was making that isolation concrete to me by moving me through the program so quickly that I
could not avoid being aware that I was different. All my life I had
preferred to be second best. She was making me live with excellence.

She understood how isolating a high IQ can be. She uses her
high IQ in a healthy manner, while I had totally fucked up on mine,
ignored it, never used it. Her goal was to develop my self-esteem.
It was a very hard, slow process. But all I needed was to be told.
Because I trusted Judi, I never resisted.

My whole life had been spent going from one dependent relationship to another. I never learned to use the tools of existence. I
knew what I needed, but I wouldn't ask for it. I manipulated others,
instead, to give me spontaneously what I wanted.

I was born in Boston in 1945. My father was a sign painter and
there were two children, myself and a sister six years older. My
maternal grandfather was a fanatically Orthodox Jew. Actually, he
is somewhere between fanaticism and insanity, a man the family
says is brilliant. He never went to medical school but he wrote homeo-
pathic medical tracts. I look exactly like him.

My mother was always sick. First there were spinal problems
which required her to wear a heavy leather brace. Her terminal
illness began with breast cancer when I was three. Eventually, both
breasts were removed. The cancer kept spreading to new places
relentlessly. There were operations and radiation treatments and
stretches of months at a time when she was hospitalized.

She had a favorite, beloved doctor who, to my horror, used
to display her to his students as "the woman who won't die!" He would
remove the sheet covering her and show the amphitheater her
mutilated body, with all the raw tissue and scars. I felt then that it
would be better if she didn't live, rather than be made a spectacle

for the curious. I developed a lifelong distaste for the medical profession.

I tolerated the constant presence of death in our home only by setting up a distance in my relationship with my mother. She underwent a living death—a woman who loved people and loved the arts enduring intense pain and disability year after year. Day by day, over a very long period of time, that loving woman was totally destroyed.

Except for when I was very small, I never thought of us as a family. We were an existence of four people. I had a difficult time when I first started psychoanalysis remembering anything but the negative parts of my childhood. Gradually I started to examine it in a more realistic light. My father was one of the most devoted husbands imaginable. He stayed by her side throughout those years of sickness.

I was a precocious child and did strange things. I set fires in my own home. Once I ate a box of match heads and had to have my stomach pumped. Another time I blinded myself temporarily with chemicals.

My mother kept a kosher home, but I never believed what happened in the synagogue. I loved the ceremony, but I thought the dogma was unreasonable. I looked at it very concretely. My sense of the futility of religion was influenced by my mother's sickness. I used to ask myself, "Why is it *my* family? Why can't I have a healthy mother like everyone else?"

Everyone who knew me thought I was going to grow up to be a physicist or chemist or mathematician, some area of science. I had unbelievable curiosity about science, but I was lazy as hell. I was only an average student. The constant comment on my report card was, "Fred has a lot of potential and should be doing better."

My parents were very upset by my marks and I would catch hell at home. I was looked at by our whole family as the one most likely to succeed, so my poor report cards caused a big scene. My mother would cry and withdraw and my father would yell and scream. I would be silent and go up to my bedroom and cry. Emotionally I am very much like my mother. I became accustomed to bearing pain alone.

My greatest sense of guilt comes from the fact that I didn't know I loved my mother at the time she died. I had been preparing for years for her death and I was determined not to let it bother me. I braced myself as she went through one relapse after another. I was rigid about her. I couldn't make a distinction between loving her as a person and loving a sick person. Since I totally hated her sickness, I believed I hated her as well. I always see things in absolutes.

My father could only deal with my sister and me in terms of our mother. It all came out of his pain. He never asked how we felt or tried to help us accept it. Only a short time ago he told me that it was "necessary neglect."

One of my realities is that I grew up insensitive. I was a nasty little person, I can't deny it. I didn't like my attitude. It was abhorrent to me. But it was stronger than anything I could do against it. I alienated myself completely from any kind of mothering and it had a chilling effect.

For some strange reason, I wasn't suicidal. Even when most depressed it never occurred to me to kill myself. I chose the living death of withdrawal instead.

My mother died a month after I left home for the first time to attend Southampton College on Long Island. I returned home immediately. She had died alone, which still hurts me. Death itself is a totally singular experience. I regret that I had not reached the end of my adolescent selfishness and insensitivity so that I could extend my hand to her.

I reflect now that she lived so tenaciously long because she loved her family. She endured terrible pain to be with us. I can demonstrate love for her by doing my best without wasting time on guilt.

It was an accepted fact that I would go on to college after high school. I attended the two-year Basic Studies program at Boston University, transferred and was accepted as a second semester sophomore at Southampton College. I did well during my first semester there but after that everything went downhill. I liked the idea of education, I liked to learn, but I was stretching out socially for the first time. College otherwise seemed meaningless.

After my mother died I went drinking every night. My grades got worse and worse. During my second year at Southampton I was told I had flunked out. My father and his bride came down to see me in great concern but I was able to get back in school on a part-time basis. I moved in with some friends and started gambling heavily, supporting myself by playing bridge and hearts for high stakes.

I was having an affair with a woman who was a year or two older than I. She had no qualms about taking the initiative with me. I perceived our sexual relationship as an unfair demand she was making on me. Though I complied, I resented it.

I wouldn't go out when my friends went out, I wouldn't eat when they ate. I ate alone and went out by myself. The withdrawal had begun again. My grades were so bad that the school told me I would have to take a year off. I spent the beginning in Southampton working at being a butler during the summer.

There are a number of big parties given by wealthy summer residents in Southampton and they always need servants. I started to work through a local domestic employment agency. My first job at a formal dinner party turned into a catastrophe, since I had no experience whatsoever. But for twenty-five dollars I thought I might as well try it. After a while I caught on and became quite good at it.

For a while I worked full time for Magda Gabor, the oldest of the Gabor sisters. She had a house that looked like something out of Disneyland, with turrets, fountains, indoor pools and statues. I worked for a number of the Southampton society—an architect, a Broadway actor, a publisher who never urinated indoors. He used the bushes in the garden. They all seemed to be as screwed up as I was. It was all meaningless.

Deep inside I wanted to respond to people, but I didn't know how. I was afraid that if I responded, I would be rejected. To avoid that, I never responded. I couldn't even say thank you. I manipulated situations to my advantage without committing myself in any way.

I moved into a two-room apartment in a motel with a girl and three guys. The three of them slept in the one bedroom and I slept on the couch in the living room. It was supposed to be a temporary arrangement because I didn't have any money. I didn't even have any possessions. Everything I owned but the clothes on my back had been stolen in a burglary. My friends said I could bunk in with them until I got myself together.

I stayed there and just about died there. For four months I negated my existence. I never left the room. I didn't even bathe during that time. I never ate with my friends. I would wait until they went to bed and then I would carefully raid the refrigerator so they wouldn't notice food was missing. I was taking satisfaction in living on as little as possible, in existing at the lowest level. That's how I survived, by almost not existing.

Judi observes that withdrawal is still my defense mechanism. It happens less and less often and each time now I am able to allow her or Jimmy or Charlie Rohrs to reach me. But it still happens and it probably always will happen.

I stayed in that room until they moved out, which made my massive withdrawal no longer possible. I decided to go back to school.

I arranged to share a house with some friends, and I was anxious to come up with my share of the rent. I finally wanted to meet my responsibilities and not be so dependent on others. But I was broke.

So one night I set about finding a place to rob. Stealing was quicker than working. I had been stealing since I was ten years old. My parents never gave me a realistic allowance so I stole from them. They were aware that money was missing from time to time but said nothing to me about it.

In Southampton there was a hamburger joint I frequented. I knew where they kept their money. So, one morning about three o'clock I collected the necessary tools and some gloves. I was very cautious. I made certain I had no identification on me and I wore clothes without buttons. In mystery novels and movies, buttons fall off people's jackets and are traced. I also wore hard-soled shoes that wouldn't leave a distinctive pattern.

I sneaked over to the field behind the restaurant and squatted there checking it out for about half an hour, hiding behind an oil drum. I was wary about what I was going to do but excited at the prospect. There wasn't a doubt in my mind that I was going to rob the place and commit the perfect crime.

It was well lit, like the Fourth of July. I waited until there were no cars on the highway and then crept over and, one by one, unscrewed all the outside lights. I can't believe even now how stupid that was. If a police car had come along and found the place totally dark, they would have known something was wrong.

I put my fist through the window in the door—I was wearing heavy gloves—and unlocked it from the inside. I used a crowbar on a locked cabinet in the kitchen and got the money, about two hundred and fifty dollars. It was a rewarding experience and I felt good about it. The next day I paid my share of the rent.

I robbed the place twice more. I enjoyed the irony of paying for my hamburgers with the money I stole from them. The third time I robbed it there was no money. I thought of breaking open the juke box but I was eating there almost every night and I liked the music, so I left it alone. I took a can of money that the owner had labeled MARCH OF DIMES. Everyone in the place knew damn well that the intended charity was the owner himself. There was about fifty dollars in it.

I had started using drugs in the motel room. My friends had some marijuana and asked me if I wanted to try it. Without much hesitation I said yes. I knew absolutely nothing about drugs. I thought marijuana could hurt you, but I smoked anyway. They had some hashish too, and I smoked that as well. I felt a little tipsy and I had the impression that this might be the right thing for me because for a change I was enjoying myself.

It wasn't long after the robbery that I started experimenting with downs like Seconal and ups like Dexedrine. I tried what was sold to me as mescaline, but which actually was acid cut with speed. I loved it and the real mescaline. I was totally dedicated to both. I hallucinated only once but it was mild, a kind of glowy and shiny and awkward look to things.

I had no money. I wanted into drugs so much that I got involved with some other people who were doing drugs on campus—one person especially—and we would fantasize how we were going to start our own business. That was 1969, the year of the shortage of marijuana because of the Federal Government's Operation Intercept at the Mexican border. We figured we would get rich from marijuana if we could raise two thousand dollars and buy it in bulk. We had a capital of only about one hundred and twenty-five dollars and, as it turned out, we were both small-time, unimaginative businessmen. Our plans went nowhere.

I began delivering flowers because I couldn't find any butlering work the next summer. I was sleeping on a mattress on the floor of a head shop. My bedroom was a little alcove full of luminous black light posters. Another fucked-up situation. I was dealing drugs from the flower truck, nothing very big. Enough, I hoped, to pay my college fees that September. Mostly I did it as favors for friends. All I ever cleared, total, was about fifty dollars. I liked the status of having drugs to sell—that was the principle attraction for me; people coming to me needing something I could provide.

At the end of the summer I went to Woodstock for the music festival. I brought some mescaline. I spent three days just stoned out of my skull listening to all that heavy rock. On the third day, when it started to rain, I wrapped a piece of plastic around me and jammed myself up against a fence with just one little eyehole.

It was pouring all around, but I was dry inside this little shroud, listening to what I think was the Grateful Dead and the other groups who played during the rain. It was a very strange experience. I was neither dead nor alive.

I got busted two days after I returned to Southampton. Suffolk County had a drug squad who set me up. I knew a girl whom everyone said was an informer. I refused to believe it. I continued to sell to her and told her exaggerated stories about my drug deals. One day when I dropped in to see her, she was smoking pot with three strangers. I met them and left. The next day her three friends came

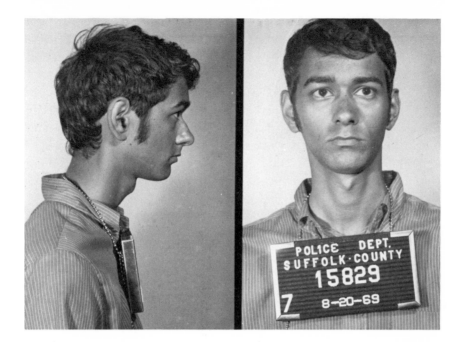

around and scored. They turned out to be undercover men and she an informer.

I went to jail along with some twenty other people from all over Southampton. I had three charges of sales and three of possession against me, six felonies in all, for acid and speed. While I was being interrogated the detective pulled out a folder full of pictures of me—me at the head shop, me with the truck, me all over the place. I had been under surveillance for a long time.

I co-operated in answering all their questions except whether or not I was a student. I expected that after the game with the police was over I would be going back, and I didn't want to involve the college. I was threatened with big unco-operative, but I kept saying there was something bigger at stake: a big ethical issue.

I couldn't make bail because I didn't want to tell my father about the arrest. I was put in the old Riverhead jail for two weeks and then transferred to the new jail. The conditions in the new jail were so much worse than the old that the whole tier got together and decided I should write a letter to Governor Rockefeller complaining about it. It was a gorgeous letter describing the conditions, and how jail was a dehumanizing experience, that it was one thing for men to be criminals but another for them to be regarded as animals. We got signatures from everyone.

The next problem was getting it mailed. My father had learned about the arrest and posted bail so I was getting out. It was decided I would take the letter with me and mail it. I threw it away instead. I don't know why; I guess I didn't want to get involved in anything.

I went home to Boston. My sister talked to a friend who had heard of Odyssey House, where people received some kind of therapy. I knew I needed therapy. I figured it was a place where I could obtain treatment while I worked at a job and made some money. I figured that Odyssey would square my court cases and everything would be cool. I took a bus to New York City to look it over and suddenly I was inducted.

After that I went back to Suffolk County court four times. An Odyssey staff member came with me and explained each time to the judge that I was making good progress in the program and that it would be detrimental to take me out. Each time we negotiated about reducing the charges and eventually the prosecution was convinced that it was better to do so and let me complete treatment. They dropped the six felonies to two misdemeanors, to which I pleaded guilty.

Judge Gordon Lipetz of Suffolk County Appellate Court sentenced me to three years probation at Odyssey. He said that if he ever saw my face again in his courtroom he would put me in jail and I would never be seen again by the outside world. I said thank you. He had given me the chance I needed.

Almost two years later I was sitting next to a Utah judge at a dinner where I was to speak. He had read the background notes about me mentioning the six felonies, and he asked about my case. He was obviously shocked and disturbed when I told him the details. After long agonizing, he had just sentenced a young college student to life imprisonment for the same charges. He murmured unhappily, "Have I made a mistake?"

On May 25, 1971, a year and a half after I was sentenced, Judge Lipetz wrote me that he had terminated my probation. Judi had notified him that I had completed the Odyssey program. Previously, my probation officer had hinted that he wanted a job with Odyssey. Unfortunately, I had nothing to offer him.

My original intention at Odyssey was simply to stay to exist, again. If Odyssey would let me live there, I was not going to jeopardize the situation. I had nowhere else to go. I therefore never put myself in a position where I would be discharged, never once verbalized the feeling that I wanted to follow any negative course. I remained withdrawn. Everyone said I was a model. I was like a model prisoner who tries to get himself some good time, only I didn't want out.

When I was at Level I, my therapist observed that I never asked for anything. He astutely decided to put me in the position of participating actively in my life. My therapy actually began with that. He decided not to promote me to Level II until I confronted the entire staff and demanded it.

They left me at Level I. I knew that I deserved to be promoted and finally I wrote a request for a meeting with the therapist. I lost my nerve and carried it around with me for about two weeks before I could even hand it in. I was summoned to the staff meeting, where I declared that I had done as much at Level I as it was possible to do. They made me a Level II, but when they noticed that the date on my request was two weeks old they put me in the kitchen.

Whenever I started to withdraw I was put there. I hated it, but I was good at it, fastidious. I was in the kitchen three times; I think I spent four out of my first five months at Odyssey cooking.

I had a horrible time at Level II because I didn't want to be an authority figure. I would have to call Caesar Lumpkin, another resident, down to the kitchen at one or two in the morning because he hadn't cleaned the stove properly. It seemed to me, being six foot two and weighing 135, that Caesar weighed about three hundred. He had a terrible temper. I therefore would tap him softly on the shoulder and say, "Caesar, Caesar, there is something wrong in the kitchen. Would you mind coming down for a minute and look at it?" Once I got him down to the kitchen I was all right. I'd stand back and roar, *"Clean the fucking stove!"*

I'm able now to make demands on people and ask for things. Having to confront the staff for the promotion to Level II represented a major break-through for me. And so was the time I choked out the word *love* to Judi and began to mean it.

A flower grows;
Eventually dies when it snows,

As, in time, man knows
Steps to his death, as sure as wind blows!

For man is the measure, but not of all things,
For it is God who determines what men shall be kings!

Whether Heaven or Hell, soul or not,
We all end in the man-measure plot!

So let it be known to one and all,
That man can determine his rise or fall! —TOMMY MOTT

Fred Cohen and Jimmy Murphy.

Judi and Fred running a group. Fred is on far right.

Jimmy Murphy II

I'm looking forward to the day when I can be replaced by Fred Cohen and move on from Odyssey to something else. I understand now how Judi felt when Charlie Rohrs joined the staff and gave her the secure knowledge that there was medical backup for her.

Given Fred's gifts, his rapid rise in the agency was inevitable. He couldn't have been cured going through the program as the average resident. That's just not Fred. I never have the feeling, though, that Fred will pull me down. My feeling is that he will push me up.

At Odyssey, we're free of ambition at one another's expense, despite the fact that the Senior Executive Staff has some of the most ambitious people on it that you could find anywhere. Even in the outside world where people haven't the common bonds of loving one another or loyalty or a shared past, still they should realize that it is much more advantageous to push the people above them up, rather than pull them down. There is more than enough of the pie to go around.

It was my idea that Charlie Rohrs be made a Director of Odyssey on the same line of authority as myself. Coming out of my own bag, I reasoned that it would be better for the world to relate to a physician as Executive Director, should Judi ever leave, than to an ex-addict. Judi said that this idea was outrageous: it would destroy the concept of the program.

I am influenced against ever wanting to be Executive Director because I observed that society tends to stereotype ex-addict administrators of drug programs. I am tired of being regarded only as an ex-addict, with no other dimension. More than tired of it, I'm enraged when it happens.

I sometimes remind Judi jovially that my name, James, means "The Supplanter." That's only in recent years, of course, because after the "Great Split" she was sensitive about teasing like that. In truth she isn't threatened at all by me, and I'm not threatened by Fred or Charlie. That's one of Odyssey's major strengths.

I came back to Odyssey on December 13, 1967 after the split, and faced Judi's only demand on me. She asked me to say I was sorry, which she knew was the most difficult request she could make.

I interpreted that she wanted me to apologize for leaving. I wasn't sorry that I had left, thinking my action was good because I was helping the group, a step forward for me after being isolated all my life.

I became aware that Judi wanted me to apologize for something different, for following people rather than an idea. She felt it demonstrated that my judgment around people was still messed up. That made it even harder for me. I had been mute in the group but respected—I knew that as a leader I should have developed sufficiently to understand where my commitment belonged.

Judi didn't express this but the message was beginning to come across. I was discovering, finally, that the dispute had been more than a clash of personalities and a fight between ex-addicts and professionals. The leaders I had followed had not been concerned about the group, as I thought, but about themselves. Suddenly I appreciated how much pain Judi had endured and apologized. She said simply, "We'll begin again."

Later I learned that Judi's real disappointment in me was my failure to come to her and ask for her side of the story. I owed her that, certainly.

There were only a dozen people in the program when we began again. They felt I should start the program all over again. Judi held a group and said I would return at the level I left, Level IV, because I misunderstood the situation. The others accepted her decision, but they treated me like an enemy agent—someone who had betrayed a trust. They were right. It wore off after a while, but with Judi it took almost four years.

Judi was more mature after the split. She more readily showed that she was strong. She was realistically less trusting, though not in a bad way. The first thing everyone in the program had responded to with Judi was her unbelievable ability to trust, even when it was clear to her that there was a possiblity that she might be hurt. To the majority of drug addicts, that's not sensible. It's idealistic to trust, but to trust knowing there is an excellent opportunity you're going to be hurt and still go on trusting—well, it used to make me wonder. Judi went on trusting after the split, but she was more wary.

People learn to trust in one of two ways, either totally on a feeling level through the gut or totally on a thinking level through the head. Judi is one of the few people I know who balances both perfectly.

As a result of the split, I became more rigid. No deviation in Odyssey's rules would be tolerated, no matter what it involved, even throwing out a friend. I once voted to discharge Louie Sarra.

Eventually, the idea or concept behind the program became most important to me, more important than Odyssey's structure or its people. I learned that finishing the program wasn't the real goal: It was the process that mattered, and the process never stops.

In reality, graduating the program only means starting the program in a new way. All through life you start new programs. It is continuous. There may be stopping-off points or resting points, but you should never go backwards. If that happens, you should review why.

The majority of people tend to strive for something in life that they conceive of as a goal. The only goal I can see definitely is death. And I am involved in living, in the *process* of living.

I'm often described as "Jimmy Murphy, the ex-addict." The split was based in part on that nonsense, ex-addict expertise versus professionals. If people say, "What do you do?" are you supposed to answer, "I'm an ex-addict?" Many wouldn't even answer the question "Who *are* you?" with "I'm an ex-addict." People stop using drugs; some of them are sane, some are insane, some are mature, some aren't. It's much more important for the answer to be given in terms of what the person has become or accomplished since he stopped using drugs.

People on the street always want to hear all about your sordid past if they know you are an ex-addict. Many of them are sincerely interested, but a few get a vicarious thrill out of it. I usually say, "It wasn't a very good life"—and leave it at that.

There are heroin addicts who love to live in the past, remembering the good times, the euphoria; but not the 90 per cent of the dying that goes with the euphoria. There weren't too many romantic happenings once I was truly addicted. There's nothing romantic about waking up in the morning sick and knowing that you won't be able to sleep that night unless you cop: and between is the circus of how to get money and stay out of jail.

We have addiction, in part, because this society thinks there is a magic cure for everything, some kind of pill you can take to make everything all right. We've reached the point of total ridiculousness when we think there is a magic pill you can take to cure the magic pill of addiction. There isn't. The cure for addiction is a process that is painful sometimes but very good sometimes. It's called living.

To handle the problem of drug addiction in our country we must set up programs, using the expertise everywhere in all communities. Since addicts infect other people, there's nothing wrong in locking up an addict who refuses help. But an addict should be given the choice between jail or a program that will rehabilitate him, particularly since the latter is much cheaper and more economical for the rest of society.

Programs that are run by ex-addicts with no professional input are not too meaningful. At Odyssey, the confrontation with many alternative healthy life styles among the staff members is very significant. There shouldn't be only one type of person, ex-addict or professional, for the residents to look up to as a role model.

The group method is mandatory in drug-treatment programs. Most addicts haven't developed sufficient trust in anyone else or in themselves to participate in one-to-one therapy. The presence of professionals in the group is essential because they act as bridges between the society and the ex-addicts, helping them with their re-entry problems.

The encounter-group process is intended to remove defenses. It functions best with the sociopath, who knows who he is but has no thought for the feeling of anyone else. However, the encounter-group method can be wrong for others. If you rip away the defenses of a schizophrenic, for instance, you destroy the fragile ego he has and he'll begin to hallucinate. Neurotics must hammer away at their defenses themselves for insight to be integrated and used to make effective change. It's therefore vital to have someone in control of the group who can make the diagnosis between a sociopath, a neurotic and a schizophrenic.

However, an all-professional staff would also have failings. There would be no bridges. Ex-addicts aren't the only possible bridges to the residents. Non-addicts who have been working in the drug field for a long time can be good at it.

A professional, however, will not understand why when there are five addicts on a rooftop and one collapses after shooting up, the others will take the dying addict's heroin and use it themselves before getting him help. The professional's reaction—the non-addict's reaction—would be to help the person and throw the lethal dope away. The addict thinks this is extra good stuff; he can't wait to take it. Someone has to bridge that vast gap in attitude and behavior.

When the agency was asked to evaluate a drug-addiction treatment program in Flint, Michigan, called Rubicon House, Charlie Rohrs and I represented Odyssey. We observed that this program suffered from an absence of bridges. The staff was excellent and the residents were motivated to get well, but there were no translators. We left with a feeling of great sorrow. The behavior of the residents was terrible, but the professionals were ignoring it and working only on attitudes.

We advised them they could either find responsible graduates of other programs to act as bridges, or struggle futilely for another year until they developed three or four from their own residents. Recently, Rubicon House merged with Odyssey to become Rubicon-Odyssey House.

Most sociopathic patients in treatment will readily develop great insight and superficial attitudes, but they still don't control their impulses. It's a shame because behavior is easy to pull into line, if you use good leaders and peer-group pressure. It must be done. We've all seen programs to which the addict comes every day for therapy for five years. He runs his Oedipal conflict and passive-agressive attitudes backward and forward, but he continues to use heroin every day.

Good drug programs can come in a variety of shapes and sizes, but unfortunately they are all too uncommon in the drug field. Odyssey often is asked to evaluate other programs, and we usually find that they are well-intentioned but ineffective. Some of the essential elements a good program should have include: ex-addict *and* professional involvement, psychiatric diagnosis, regular urine tests examined by an independent laboratory, fiscal accountability, and good group techniques. There is a proper size factor as well —thirty residents is the minimum number in order to avoid an incestuous, masturbatory intimacy that rapidly will lead to stagnation. Seventy residents in a single unit is perhaps the maximum size, just this side of becoming impersonalized.

By the time I was ready to graduate the program at Odyssey, we had about fifty residents. I was one of the first graduates and it was lonely out there. I had one day off a week. I spent it walking around wishing I was back in the house. One day I sat on a car fender outside Odyssey for several sunny hours. Tommy Turner said, "Why don't you come in?" and I said, "No, no. I just want to sit here in the sun for a while." I needed the reassurance of the street's familiarities, and yet going in the house would have symbolized failure to me.

Graduates face many problems, one of which is serious doubts about sexuality. Many people turn to drugs in the first place because of sexual problems. Since Odyssey demands celibacy during treatment, sexual difficulties can't be resolved until the resident begins resocialization. I had been abstinent for a year and a half. This raised various doubts in me. They ranged from whether I would be able to function adequately to whether I would be able to successfully integrate my newly developed awareness that a satisfactory mutual sexual relationship involves more than a physical act.

Most addicts are afraid to be close, on an emotional level, to someone of the opposite sex. It is preferable to maintain a purely sexual exchange, a sort of mutual masturbation, if indeed it is mutual.

Heroin affects sexuality greatly. When you're young and high on heroin you can sustain an erection for several hours but you can't climax. It is frustrating and unpleasant. Climax is impossible until the drug wears off. After you've used heroin for a while you become depressed and disinterested in sex. Any sexual urge is almost non-existent.

Prior to graduating from Odyssey, I began dating the girl I later married. She had used heroin for five years and was a graduate of another program. She had been divorced twice and both of us were having trouble adjusting to the outside world after being in treatment so long. She was as rigid as I was. We built a relationship based on our mutual weaknesses rather than our strengths. It's a very easy thing to do.

We were married in the auditorium of the Mother House in December 1968. The marriage lasted seven months. Our first fight occurred while we were cutting the wedding cake. Eventually our differences became too much to handle. We couldn't agree about children, about religion or about our ambitions. We're divorced now.

Judi had accepted my candidate-out proposal with the stipulation that I would go into group therapy with people who never had used drugs—squares. She said it was important for me to realize that I had an identity other than being an ex-addict. My reaction to the group I joined was negative. I thought they were crazy. They were acting out all the time and in many ways seemed to be sicker than I was. I observed, though, that people could work through serious emotional problems without resorting to drugs.

After graduation, I became Associate Director, second in charge of the agency. We had expanded to a second house, this one on 122nd Street, which Louie Sarra ran. There was also a storefront in Harlem where raw addicts came in order to enter the program.

Our budget was about $300,000 for the Mother House, which was government-funded. Our other two facilities cost $100,000 and were unfunded. We raised the required money from the private sector, by means of donations. The East Flatbush Civic Association gave us funds to open a storefront in Brooklyn. Then Father Gigante broke down the door of the nuns' residence in the South Bronx, and we started admitting children under the age of sixteen.

By that time I was certainly a less rigid person. I loosened up when I separated from my wife and went to live for a while with Louie Sarra and Matty Ancona. They had an apartment in New Jersey. Matty had recently been divorced and Louie separated from the girl he had lived with for about eight years. Living with them was a circus: It wasn't the Odd Couple, it was the Ridiculous Trio. There would be notes on the bedroom door: "Don't proceed any further, bedroom in use." We went out every night drinking someplace where there were girls—two Alka-Seltzers for breakfast and off to work. My rigidity went out the window.

One morning in the summer of 1970 I got a telephone call asking me to be a member of a task force for the White House Conference on Youth. It sounded very impressive, a White House appointment. In fact, I was to be co-chairman of the Drug Task Force along with Dr. Richard Blum, a Stanford University psychologist. He's a very bright man and working with him was one of the few good things that happened in that whole fiasco.

There were supposed to be seven other Task Force Youth members, demographically distributed as to ethnic background and regional representation, with some variety in age within the prescribed range of fourteen to twenty-five. My first jolt came when it was suggested that I should include a using addict on the committee. I was shocked. I asked in amazement, "What could he contribute, his nodding?"

I selected seven young people from a list of résumés I was given. They were good: one of them, José Colon, later came to work at Odyssey. All the adult representatives were chosen by the White House staff without consultation with Dr. Blum.

The White House Conference on Youth was made up of ten task forces, all of them with the ratio of three young people to each adult. One committee was assigned to report on race relations, one on the draft, one on poverty, and so on. Mine, of course, was drugs.

I was discovering, to my consternation, that I wasn't selected as chairman by the White House Committee because of my Odyssey expertise. They could have chosen me to contribute as a person who had served on several boards of directors, or because I was a consultant and adviser to senators and congressmen. They might have chosen me because I was director of an agency treating more than three hundred people, or because I was a guest lecturer at several universities and presenter of papers at scientific gatherings. But, none of those qualifications figured in the choice of James Murphy. The interest in me was purely because I was an ex-addict: They wanted me as a public relations gimmick.

This was later made obvious. The résumé of my career which was distributed to the press and public stopped with my arrival at Odyssey House. The rest of my life didn't matter. The résumé used by Odyssey is as follows:

JAMES P. MURPHY   1435 York Avenue, New York, NY

Telephone: (212) 288-1801

PROFESSIONAL: August 1968–	National Director of Organization and Co-Founder of Odyssey House, Inc., a therapeutic community for drug addiction treatment and rehabilitation. Responsible for the treatment of 350 residential patients, 10,000 monthly community contacts, thirty-three centers, all budgetary and fiscal matters, new projects and expansion (in the states of Connecticut, Michigan, Nevada, New Hampshire, New Jersey, New York and Utah), directly reportable to the Executive Director.
February 1968– August 1968	Graduated from Odyssey House Program and became Induction Supervisor. Acted as liaison with all agencies referring people for treatment. Developed admitting procedure for all new patients. Was promoted to Assistant Director of Induction and Community Education, which also included establishing a Speaker's Bureau that reached more than three thousand people each month.
September 1966– February 1968	Resident in Odyssey House Program. Held positions with varying responsibilities as a core-group member. As Office Manager, wrote first fiscal budget upon which Odyssey was funded ($243,000—June, 1967). Assisted in instituting methods of behavioral change in patient population as House Manager.
June 1963– September 1966	Immediately after high school graduation worked in various banks. The positions varied from Junior Officer in the Bank of Montreal (responsibility for

167

thirty million dollars in negotiable securities) to Documents Examiner for the Bank of North America.

PAPERS PRESENTED: 1969—Palo Alto, California, "The Therapeutic Community Psychiatric Treatment of Addiction Through Professional and Ex-Addict Teamwork," (with Judianne Densen-Gerber, J.D., M.D.) at the Committee on Drug Dependency, Division of Medical Sciences, National Research Council.

1969—Toronto, Canada, "The Psychiatric Therapeutic Community Approach Reviewed," (with Judianne Densen-Gerber, J.D., M.D.) at the International Academy of Forensic Sciences.

1970—Chicago, Illinois—"Different Experiences vs. Double Messages," (with Judianne Densen-Gerber, J.D., M.D.) at the American Academy of Forensic Sciences.

1970—Lausanne, Switzerland, "The Changing Face of Addiction: An Adolescent Confrontation," (with Judianne Densen-Gerber, J.D., M.D. and William J. Record) at the International Council on Alcohol and Addiction.

1971—Ann Arbor, Michigan, "The Therapeutic Community: The Odyssey House Concept," (with Charles Rohrs, M.D. and Judianne Densen-Gerber, J.D., M.D.) at the Drug Abuse Proceedings of the International Conference.

1971—Phoenix, Arizona, "The Changing Face of Addiction: An Adolescent Confrontation Reviewed," (with Judianne Densen-Gerber, J.D., M.D.) at the American Academy of Forensic Sciences.

1972—Atlanta, Georgia, "The Phenomenon of Adolescent Addiction," (with Charles Rohrs, M.D. and Judianne Densen-Gerber, J.D., M.D.) at the American Academy of Forensic Sciences.

ADDITIONAL: 1972—Worked in co-operation with Judianne Densen-Gerber, J.D., M.D., in composing a book about the story of Odyssey House, to be published in 1973 by Doubleday.

OTHER PROFESSIONAL: 1969—Member of the Board of Directors, Simpson Street Development Association.

1970—Appointed Co-Chairman, Drug Task Force, White House Conference on Youth.

1971—Granted the "World Prize Dr. Circuns," on Alcoholism and Toxicomania. Barcelona, Spain.

Served as Secretary, Treasurer, Second Vice Chairman, and Member of the Board of Directors of AVANT, (Association of Voluntary Agencies for Narcotics Treatment).

Have acted as Special Narcotics Consultant to Senators Charles Goodell, Jacob Javits and James Buckley of New York, Harrison Williams of New Jersey and Thomas McIntyre of New Hampshire.

MEMBER OF:
1. American Academy of Forensic Sciences
2. American Public Health Association
3. International Academy of Law and Sciences

GUEST LECTURER AT:
City College of New York
Northeastern University
Michigan State University
New York University
Ohio Wesleyan University
Harvard Law School

EDUCATION:
Theodore Roosevelt High School—Bronx, New York
Graduated in 1963
Pace College—New York, New York

PERSONAL:
Born—March 3, 1946
Marital Status—Divorced

Nevertheless, in spite of my feelings of being exploited by the White House, I needed to believe that something useful would be accomplished. I stayed with it and tried very hard. It really mattered to me.

The expectation of most of the young people on the committees, some of whom had competed for the right to represent their state, was that we would hammer out sensible recommendations to meet youth problems. These recommendations then would be forwarded to the White House, where they would influence future attitudes and legislation. We also anticipated that we would be meeting the country's most distinguished politicians and academicians, working with them in a mutual-learning experience to solve the problems confronting the country. The reality was nothing like that.

I got another chilling warning of the disaster ahead when I went to the White House to consult with Presidential Adviser Bud Krogh, seeking guidelines for my task force committee. The meeting lasted ten or fifteen minutes. He suggested I study the drug bill sponsored by Senator Hughes, since it had the endorsement of the Administration. It was hinted that it would be helpful if the Task Force recommendations coincided with it. It was politically realistic advice, but it had a poor effect on my morale.

The ten task force committees met for the first time at the University of California campus at Irvine. Our group wanted to put together a good preliminary report in the short time available, but we spent the first day in a disorderly ramble about drugs. The next morning Dick Blum pulled us together by suggesting that we list everything we wanted included in our deliberations. It resulted in a list of about sixty-five items. We eliminated one after another until we settled on a workable ten.

There were two concurrent developments. The first was the formation of a minority caucus group, most of whom were Black. I anticipated there would be some unexpected political pressures. There was a task force on race relations, but the Drug Task Force was being confronted in a very lively way with the problem as well.

José Colon went to the conference with the firm intention of upholding the principle of racially integrated problem-solving. Many of us agreed with him; we would not permit intimidation of that goal. The intimidation, José noted, started at our first meeting at Irvine. The first demand was for an equal number of Black and White representatives. This would have totally broken down the demographic balance which was to mirror that of the United States' population at large. José and I fought against this unrealistic demand, and words like "prejudice" were thrown around freely.

During the next few months, as the recommendations were changed and polished, the atmosphere of tension, chaos and fear heightened. Two members of the task force resigned, both Blacks.

The second disaster at Irvine involved President Nixon. Just before our meetings began, a distinguished Mexican-American journalist, Ruben Salazar, was killed by a police miscalculation during a protest demonstration by *Chicanos* over the disproportionate number of Mexican-American casualties in Vietnam. President Nixon was scheduled to greet the task force members, so the demonstrators went there to call his attention to the situation. They crowded around our conference building and the participants voted to meet with them.

José Colon had personally known the journalist and identified with the demonstrators. Twenty-four years old at that time, he is the son of a former Foreign Service officer who was an adviser in high government circles. José, though American-born of a Panamanian-born father, has worked for the American Civil Liberties Union as an investigator in the Mexican-American community and speaks fluent Spanish.

He was deeply affected by what happened next at Irvine. He told me, "The *Chicanos* and some American Indians were waiting peacefully for the promised visit of the President. A helicopter arrived and whisked away five or six hand-picked delegates, all of whom were non-threatening to Establishment kind of people. I saw it as a defeat, another defeat." President Nixon never did set foot on the Irvine campus; he never saw us and we never saw him, except for the selected few.

The site and time of the White House Conference on Youth were chosen by the White House. It was decided that it should be held in Estes Park, Colorado, in April. It was an interesting choice. In that part of the country, the heaviest snows and avalanches occur during April. Estes Park is a YMCA camp. Though it was built to house three thousand, most of the facilities hadn't been used in years. The accommodations for the two thousand delegates were totally inadequate.

In addition, there had been a vigorous attempt by Washington to diminish the impact of the Conference by having the ten task forces meet consecutively, rather than all together.

The Conference on Youth was planned in 1970 to be companionate to the White House Conference on Children, which was to meet earlier in 1971. The Conference on Children has been a mandatory conference, once every ten years, ever since the time of Teddy Roosevelt. It has a good reputation.

The Nixon Administration felt that the President could improve his rapport with youth by innovating a White House Conference on Youth. However, after the decision was made, the killings at Kent State and Jackson State occurred. This exacerbated the unrest among young people. There were riots throughout the country and a nationwide student strike. From that time on, it appeared to those of us involved in the youth task forces that the administration dreaded any additional embarrassment and wanted to bury us. The stabbing and violence that attended the Children's Conference held in Washington before ours didn't help much either.

We arrived at Estes Park to find two feet of snow on level ground and four or five feet in the drifts. Few of us were prepared for the weather since the Administration had sent a brochure suggesting spring clothing. Indeed, the frostbite that occurred necessitated the Administration to respond in an emergency fashion. Army planes flew in jackets and boots for the participants. Judi was one of the few adequately prepared as she was arriving from Fairbanks, Alaska.

The press complained that the Conference site was so remote and the number of telephones so few that they would have great difficulty getting their stories out. It fit with everything else that had happened to us.

As I have mentioned, our preliminary sessions had been rocky because of racial pressures. By the time the Conference began, the Drug Task Force had little minority-group representation left; our final recommendations attempted to rectify this by including those resolutions we thought absent members would want. One had to do with addiction in Vietnam and another concerned drug research.

I had two favorites among the recommendations. One was the establishment of National Awareness Advisory Councils, a concept that Odyssey had worked out months earlier while sitting around one afternoon at Judi's house. The other had to do with setting up multi-modality treatment centers throughout the country, focusing more on what would work for adolescents and young adults than on being mere replicas of any single program.

The Drug Task Force had one hundred and fifty delegates in attendance. We opened with an introductory meeting on Sunday night, during which I, as chairman, explained that we had only three days to work. Therefore, the task force recommendations should be used as a frame of reference to expedite matters. The delegates were not there to give automatic approval, of course, but the initial report would serve as a helpful guide.

That night it snowed. I woke up feverish and sick. I was staying at a motel several miles from the Conference site. Judi had insisted on it because we had been advised that the camp was dangerous if it snowed and the avalanches began. Also, the site had been chosen because it had only one bridge of access, and if rioting started it could be blocked off and the riot contained. Judi was attending only at my insistence and she kept repeating in a joking but serious manner that she had three small children and was too old for campus disturbances or worse. She was recovering from having lived for a year with the fear of facing a separation from her children—six months in jail.

I was late getting to the meeting because of the drifts. I found when I finally arrived about an hour late that the minority group was in one room and the majority, mostly White, was in another. I had missed the fight. The minority group had wanted general plenary sessions, but the majority wanted to stick to our original concept of a workshop working on each of the recommendations. The Black strategy, I believe, was based on the fact that they would be able to manipulate a large meeting more effectively. All hundred and fifty of us were to sit in the room for three days, they insisted, problem-solve and eventually write resolutions. It obviously was insane.

I was told a lot of shouting and screaming and hissing had gone on. A vote was taken eventually, and the proposal for a general meeting was rejected. The minority group, numbering about thirty, walked out deciding to boycott the sessions and meet separately. They would work on a list of proposals by themselves, they said.

The next two days were full of tension. I was getting sicker. I was sleepless and my cold was becoming the flu. The list of ten recommendations prepared by us during months of the work of distillation were being expanded by the delegates to almost a hundred. Some of the ideas now contradicted others. To me it was a nightmare. We had no idea how many more would come from the minority group.

The minority group was supposed to present its resolutions at six o'clock of the third day, by which time we expected to have finished the work of the majority group. They arrived at eight, two hours late, along with television camera crews. While waiting for them, we had gone on to other business and were in the midst of voting. I ruled that we would finish our motions before taking up theirs. This seemed to me a democratic decision, since we represented the majority and we had already begun. They were, after all, two hours late.

People began screaming about when the minority report should be presented. The term *participatory democracy* was kicked around like toilet paper. The television cameras left, followed by the minority group. We completed our business and sent someone to advise them. They sent a message that they wouldn't return since we had not stopped for them. They would file a separate report. Judi was calling it "the tyranny of the minority."

A White woman delegate went to them on her knees, to apologize for three hundred years of oppression, and to beg them to join us. They refused. My feeling was that their behavior had nothing to do either with drugs or race relations. It was a power play to get control. Interestingly, the minority caucus leadership was totally adult, not youth.

The majority group was discussing sending someone to negotiate again, for the fourth time. José objected and someone called him a "racist." Jeff Donfeld, a White House aide, yelled at Judi, "You're a hysterical woman, and I'll see that you're put away." I tried to get order and failed. I then resigned.

"I can't continue to act as chairman with this type of attitude," I said. "I find it much more discriminating, much more biased, much

Jack Anderson

Jeff Donfeld, a former escort of Tricia Nixon and now a White House aide, infuriated liberal Republicans when he called Rep. Bob Steele (R-Conn.) a "liar" and compared him to a "moron" for using narcotics figures with which Donfeld disagreed.

Now the 28-year-old hotshot has upset conservative Republicans by suggesting that a prominent conservative New York psychiatrist, Dr. Judianne Densen-Gerber, should be committed.

Dr. Densen-Gerber and Donfeld clashed at a White House youth conference in Estes Park, Colo., earlier this year over who started a row with black delegates. As tempers rose, Donfeld told Dr. Densen-Gerber to "shut up and sit down!"

The psychiatrist, face flushed, retorted: "Why don't you admit . . ." but she was cut off in mid-sentence by Donfeld who again snapped: "Shut up!"

"Be quiet and dig yourself!" spat back the infuriated lady.

Donfeld exploded. "Maybe," he said, "you should dig yourself! You're a hysterical woman and I'll see that you're put away."

Dr. Densen-Gerber stalked out fuming.

Donfeld tells us he remembers the argument, but not the exact exchange. For the attack on Rep. Steele, he ate crow and apologized. He has not apologized to Dr. Densen-Gerber.

more racist, than I can handle. All dignity is lost. To ask them to return once is okay, twice is okay, three times is depressing and the fourth time is ridiculous."

My departure was almost unnoticed in the rabble. José and Judi left with me as did Eileen Angileri, the Executive Aide representing Governor Ogilvie of Illinois. Dr. Blum had resigned his chairmanship in disgust prior to the Estes Park meeting.

Thinking about it now, maybe it wasn't control they were after but just chaos. If you can't win, the next best thing is to disrupt and prevent anyone else from winning.

I left feeling depressed, defeated and hopeless about the future of this country. The youth of America hadn't been given an opportunity to learn how to work within the system. The reality was that we were given the brutal experience of a jungle, created by the Administration, and no positive tools with which to survive. At all times, violence appeared only moments away. The next day, though the Conference wasn't over, the buses to the airport were full of disillusioned delegates of all ages.

The White House didn't care about the Conference on Youth, didn't want it and didn't want its recommendations. There has been no sign of implementation.

I suppose they know that I resigned, but I remain on the mailing list. Perhaps the machinery isn't set up to acknowledge resignations. My strongest feeling now is extreme cynicism. I know who I am, thanks to Judi and Odyssey, but I don't know where I'm going, thanks to Washington. Wherever it is, though, I know I'll handle it, though at times I may have to walk away and withdraw.

I worked on the task force business while maintaining my active role at Odyssey. The agency was going through a hectic period of development and change. We negotiated to open two new residences, one in New Hampshire and one in Utah. We were learning how to treat adolescent addicts. We were experimenting with a separate residence for girls, the first in the country and a totally new treatment concept, a program for pregnant females and then for the new mothers and their babies. They were turning up on our doorstep and Judi felt committed to help them. She was talking about a Mothering Program where the girls would live together with their babies and learn how to mother. In turn, Odyssey would attempt to discover if the art of mothering can be taught to women who themselves weren't mothered properly.

Clearly we were branching into new fields. We were more than a service agency dealing in treatment. We were becoming a conceptual agency where community needs were being recognized and concepts for change developed. It meant that Judi was going back and forth from New York to Washington as regularly as the hourly air shuttle.

She too was becoming increasingly disillusioned. She no longer believed that the mess the nation was in was a matter of ignorance and that if you showed politicians what is wrong, they would fix it. Yet, she kept trying anyway. She hoped it would be effective to bring Washington dignitaries to New York City and show them the kids, show them the slums, show them the garbage.

On a hot morning in July 1971 she took Washington on a bus tour of Fun City.*

* "Fun City" is the term John V. Lindsay chose to describe and publicize New York, while at the same time crime and addiction soared, education and public sanitation deteriorated, and responsible government disappeared.

ADDICTION SERVICES AGENCY
HUMAN RESOURCES ADMINISTRATION
71 WORTH STREET, NEW YORK, N. Y. 10013
Telephone: 433-2020

LARRY ALAN BEAR, *Commissioner*

C E R T I F I C A T I O N   B O A R D

This Is To Attest That

JAMES   MURPHY

On The Sixth Day Of March, 1970, Has Been Duly Certified As A

Rehabilitated Ex-Addict Under The Provisions And Regulations Of

The Certification Board Of The Addiction Services Agency Of The

City Of New York.

_____
James C. Higgins, Ph.D.
Chairman, Certification Board

_____
Larry Alan Bear, Commissioner
Addiction Services Agency

Effective Date: May 1, 1970
Expiration Date: April 30, 1971

James P. MURPHY

DIRECTOR ODYSSEY HOUSE   NEW YORK — NEW JERSEY

To explore and discuss the growing problem of psychological and substance dependencies (drug addiction) in our society, the problem in Utah, and some possible approaches to prevention and cure.

Monday
April 26
12 noon
Lobby U.B.

The Bus Tour

United States Congressman Benjamin Rosenthal of Queens once went on Odyssey House's special *Fun City for Whom?* tour, which we run periodically to acquaint influential people with the facts of life in New York City and to demonstrate that heroin addiction can be cured. He had been very impressed. He returned to Washington promising us that he would persuade others to make the same tour.

On July 23, 1971, we found ourselves hosting a bus tour that would include seven Congressmen, three Assistant Secretaries of State, the Special Assistant to the Secretary of State for Narcotics Matters, representatives from the Justice Department and assorted others. The first tour that had included Congressman Rosenthal had been planned by Odyssey and two other New York Congressmen, Seymour Halpern and Edward Koch. This tour was designed much like the other, permitting a leisurely visit to the Odyssey facilities and ample time for information gathering and discussion.

The day before the scheduled tour I was in Odyssey House in Newark, New Jersey, trying to pump some enthusiasm for Odyssey into a languid meeting of community leaders. We had been dismayed a few weeks previous when only two people arrived for a meeting of our New Jersey Advisory Board. New blood was needed, as well as a broad base of community involvement.

We made a mistake in how we opened the New Jersey Odyssey House. We had been invited there by the New Jersey College of Medicine and Dentistry to run the psychiatric therapy community component of its comprehensive drug program for the National Institute of Mental Health. The grant carried with it funding for 75 per cent of our staff, with the remaining operational costs to be paid by private donations. When we started we believed we would be able to obtain sufficient grass roots support, but we made the unhappy discovery that private donations rarely follow Federal funding. It's an error we will never make again. We know now that the first step in setting up a viable Odyssey House must always involve the community.

Some thirty influential citizens of the State had been invited to an informal meeting and buffet dinner in our New Jersey House. We hoped to intrigue them enough that they would commit themselves to inviting two others, each, to a second meeting. These would in turn invite two others to a third meeting and so on, until we achieved a healthy Advisory Board.

All of us were sitting in the upstairs living room. It is a high-ceilinged, handsome room in a mansion sold to us at one third its purchase price by its doctor-owner because the neighborhood had become raw and dangerous.

I was interrupted by a telephone call about the bus trip. The caller said Mayor John V. Lindsay had heard of the tour and insisted that some of the stops at Odyssey facilities be replaced by other drug centers. He used his influence and changed the itinerary, eliminating Spanish-speaking Odyssey in the South Bronx entirely. He had arranged for the tour to culminate with a luncheon and press conference at City Hall, hosted by him, to which I was explicitly not invited. I was instructed to leave the bus on the last stop before it proceeded to City Hall.

I could do nothing about the altered itinerary. Actually, I approved of the idea of Federal officials seeing a variety of programs. But I was not going to tolerate being excluded from the luncheon.

John V. Lindsay and I once were friends. Yet, for a year and a half Mayor Lindsay had been refusing to see me, ever since the Odyssey Choir sang in front of Gracie Mansion in an attempt to persuade him to fund a program for child addiction. He protested to me then that I embarrassed him politically. I retorted that he couldn't get to the White House by only looking ahead. Instead, he must look around in awareness at what was happening to New York City's children. Some of us would vote on what he had accomplished —on his record—not on how he appeared on television.

The way I handled the exclusion from the City Hall luncheon was to notify Rosenthal's office that if I were put off the bus I would call a press conference to ask why I couldn't break bread with the Mayor. Rosenthal's office said it would see what could be done.

I composed myself and returned to the meeting in the living room. I made some opening remarks about Odyssey House.

"Odyssey House," I explained, "is a treatment center for acting-out disorders. All kinds of acting-out are treated, but particularly drug use. Ninety per cent of our residents have used heroin. We've had prostitutes, we've had pipe-bombers, we've had . . ."

Louie Sarra prompted helpfully, "We've had a theatrical producer as a volunteer."

"A theatrical producer?" an urbane guest chuckled. "Is this a form of acting-out behavior?" The room responded appreciatively.

"Tragically, this one was," I said. "He committed suicide, clutching a copy of the Odyssey House *Concept*. We have taken pipe-bombers from the courts. We take anyone who primarily acts out his problems through some type of anti-social behavior. In 1966 we started with heroin addicts. We faced a medical establishment and community which believed that drug addicts were not treatable. Once an addict, always an addict."

Some late-comers joined us, waving and smiling to people they recognized.

"Based on government figures in 1966, doctors were saying that only five to thirteen per cent of addicts remained drug-free after treatment, the rest returning to drugs. By a strange coincidence, Odyssey has almost exactly reversed the figures for failure and success. I'm proud to tell you that about eighty per cent of the people who have entered the Odyssey treatment program are now drug-free and well. Ninety-eight per cent of those who have finished the program are cured. With good court co-operation and meaningful treatment, there *is* cure for adult addicts."

Fred Cohen tapped me on the shoulder. There was a phone call from Rosenthal's staff, and I excused myself to take it. Mayor Lindsay graciously was extending me an invitation to join him and the Washington guests for lunch at City Hall. I accepted dryly. I said I hoped I could bring some of my staff along. It didn't appear that this would be possible.

Returning to the room I began again. "The next problem which Odyssey began to attack was that of the juvenile addict. It was quickly realized that the therapeutic community would have to be modified to meet the special needs of these young people. Unfortunately, we still do not have the same success rate with children as we have with adults. Odyssey methods are still being modified.

"One of our major group-therapy methods is much like Synanon, Daytop or Phoenix confrontation therapy, with the important difference, however, that a trained professional is part of our groups. We run psychiatric groups. It's not all gut; it's also head. In addition, great attention is paid to case histories, to statistical data-gathering. We have the richest data banks on addiction available."

Fred interrupted me again. Congressman Edward Koch was calling from Washington. He was upset because he hadn't been invited on the tour and was afraid that for political reasons he wouldn't be allowed on the bus. I was beginning to feel paranoid about that bus myself. Since Mayor Lindsay would know full well that my remarks about his Administration would not be kind, it seemed entirely possible that I would be excluded. I perceived that the goals of the tour were political rather than information-gathering, and I was furious. After all, the tour of *Fun City for Whom?* had been designed and developed by Odyssey. I felt exploited.

I told my good friend Congressman Koch that under the circumstances I planned to leave my house early. I would board the bus before the shuttle plane from Washington landed. Since I would be on the bus when they arrived they could only get me off by removing me forcibly. Congressman Koch asked if he could join me. He felt it was the only way he could be certain of getting aboard as well. I was feeling excited at the prospect of my first sit-in.

This time when I returned to the New Jersey meeting I was asked if Odyssey House statistics were available. "Unfortunately, we've never had the time or the money to put this valuable data in the computers as we should. We're negotiating with the State and Federal government for grants to analyze the information. We're so busy fund-raising for service and treatment needs we haven't had time to do it ourselves. But we continue to be squirrels in the number of profiles and family histories we keep on our patients. If we don't do it now, these facts will be lost."

I described the testing daily of urine samples by outside laboratories. "We don't ask people to believe our patients are free of drugs because we say they are clean—they're clean because their urines say they are."

Odyssey, I added, is a type of half-way hospital in which the patients do much of the work. "But they don't try to be physicians, they don't try to be accountants, they don't try to be lawyers. The problem in many self-help programs is that the ex-addicts extend themselves beyond their expertise.

"The majority of programs are run by do-gooders at best and con artists at worst. 'The road to hell is paved with good intentions.' There's no research being done, there's no data collected, there's no evaluation, there's no staff conference. Most often it is no more than a group of people rapping together. Unfortunately, they're wreaking havoc."

To me it's like choosing to go to Blaiberg for a heart transplant rather than to Dr. Christiaan Barnard. "Blaiberg could certainly reassure the next heart transplant patient that surviving the operation is possible, but who would let him do the surgery? I wish the same were true in the field of addiction."

There was another phone call. This one came from Congressman Seymour Halpern, who is the man in political life to whom I feel closest. He was indignant that he, a member of Rosenthal's committee, had not been informed of the bus tour. He wanted to know what was happening. I clued him in on the Densen-Gerber-Koch plan, and he asked if he could be a co-conspirator. I was delighted that he would be joining us and invited him to begin earlier with breakfast at my house before we set out.

Again I went back in the living room. I resumed the description of Odyssey, apologizing for the interruptions. They asked me if there was an advantage to having patients seek treatment voluntarily rather than having it forced on them. I could see that my answer jolted some of the guests. "The longer the commitment from the court, the better our success rate," I declared. "Patients ordered to Odyssey House facing the alternative of going to jail do slightly better than those who come to us voluntarily."

Fred had been working on the problem of expanding my luncheon invitation to include a few of the Odyssey staff. He returned from the telephone and whispered that he had been refused firmly. Dr. Densen-Gerber alone could attend. No one else from the agency would be admitted. It appeared to me that the luncheon would be in extremely hostile territory and I didn't care to be there alone. Fred said he would keep trying.

I resumed by stating Odyssey has found that Blacks from New Jersey are much more estranged from Whites than those we see from New York. I stressed the point to our New Jersey guests, many of whom were Black, that Odyssey is a fully integrated agency, unlike the majority of drug-treatment programs.

"We do not believe that only Blacks can treat Blacks. Only through Black and White sitting down together is there any problem-solving or meaningful exchange. It is the only way we can build a healthy country. We are not for apartheid in any way. We are militantly integrationist.

"Much of addiction, particularly in the Black middle-class individual, is his own rage—his own justifiable rage turned inward. He is not able to engage the White community at his rightful level of functioning. We must let the Blacks and all second-class citizens enter the American mainstream."

There was some uneasy stirring. This is a livid issue in New Jersey. It was necessary to confront the community with it, but I was hoping that it would not estrange support. Odyssey New York had lent $70,000 seed money to the New Jersey House, and we wanted it repaid in two years in order to seed another facility, this one in Utah. Odyssey has a policy of revolving seed money from one new state to another. We urgently needed people to believe in and fund raise for us but not if we had to compromise by having an all-Black —or all-White—program. Both suggestions were intolerable to the Odyssey life style and commitment to serve all peoples. Years before some people from Massachusetts had offered us money for a Massachusetts house if we agreed not to take Boston Blacks, and now Newark appeared to want only Blacks.

Fred came back from the telephone. City Hall positively would not permit me to bring anyone else to the luncheon. Desperately, I decided that we would all go in together, holding hands. I learned later that Fred then privately called Halpern once more. He was worried for me. If Judi had to attend the luncheon alone, would Halpern, kind as ever, watch over her? Halpern promised he would.

The shuttle plane carrying the Washington contingent was scheduled to arrive at LaGuardia at nine o'clock on that hot, hazy July day. Three carloads of Odyssey people and the uninvited Congressmen were waiting for them at the shuttle arrivals building. Charlie Rohrs and Bob Smith leaned casually against a post in the parking lot, surveying a row of empty buses. Smith, with considerable experience at sit-ins as Stokely Carmichael's bodyguard, suggested that it was possible that the Odyssey House people would all board one bus and the officials would have it driven in some other direction away from the rest of the tour.

"And they'll seal the doors and drive it off the dock," Charlie commented.

These helpful remarks did nothing for my nervousness. I went inside where it was cooler. Congressman Rosenthal greeted me warmly. He advised me that the bus tour was intended purely for observation purposes. It would give the visitors a feel of the drug problem and nothing more. "We don't want to get into any criticism," he said in a warning tone.

I was noncommittal in my reply, but I seethed. I had been told to behave. The plane landed.

An officious girl from Rosenthal's office guided us all to the bus, together with reporters and sweating men with television cameras on their shoulders. I had instructed the Odyssey staff and residents not to sit together—they were to leave vacant seats beside them each time they boarded the buses. The Washington delegation would have to fill the empty seats. Odyssey would then have the opportunity to chat with them about addiction and governmental neglect.

The bus was noisy and hot. The air conditioning struggled impotently against the July heat. As the bus lurched through the morning traffic, Congressman Rosenthal held on to a strap and made some opening comments into the hand-held microphone and television cameras. I caught fragments of what he was saying—"President Nixon . . . narcotics traffic . . . world-wide problem . . . grave situation . . ."—but the rest was lost in the din of horns and grinding gears. He introduced me. I was amazed and gratified. I stood up and took a firm grip on the overhead strap.

I have a carrying voice. I acted as a sightseeing tour guide. "Look at the garbage on your right," I commenced, "and the children playing in it. There is no recreation area for the children in this neighborhood because the vest-pocket parks here are full of garbage. There is no garbage pickup. This is where the children spend their time, day in and day out—in the street."

The first stop was at SERA, a Hispanic center for addicts in the Bronx that is fully funded by the State for over a million dollars a year. It's an astonishing building to find in a slum heartland, full of newly tiled floors, fresh plaster, space, chrome, expensive desks and filing cabinets. The Washington group shook hands with the SERA staff and was invited to talk to the residents who shyly lined up for inspection.

Odyssey people remained in the background at SERA. We wished them well. On the whole the visit was an affirmative one.

We returned to the bus and Congressman Morgan Murphy, a lawyer from Illinois, sat down heavily. Murphy became a politician, in part, because he was distressed to find heroin addiction among the children of his friends. He and Halpern spent the Congressional recess that spring conducting separate study missions in order to learn about the drug problem at its source. They each wrote reports on their findings and submitted these documents to the House Foreign Affairs Committee, on which they both serve. Murphy observed that he believes these reports had some influence on the President's decision to take a greater interest in addiction, particularly in the military.

Murphy was exhausted and sad. He said he had no answers, but what he saw horrified him. He looked out the bus window at the slum around him. "It starts with a field of poppies in Turkey that looks like it must have in the time of Jesus. People still ride donkeys."

184

A Black man slumped against a building lifted his head and glared balefully at the bus. "And look where it ends," Murphy sighed wearily.

I resumed my travelogue as the bus made its way to the Odyssey storefront in Harlem. I said, "I think it is very important that a whole generation between the ages of eighteen and twenty-five is not feeling a meaningful involvement in America. This country has the twenty-third lowest infant mortality rate in the world, instead of the lowest. Young adults are rightfully demanding explanations for this kind of statistic.

"Heroin flows like water in New York City. There are *thirty-six thousand* addicts here on methadone.

"Take a look on your left. There's someone nodding, and over there on the corner someone is buying drugs." They craned and looked at the sights of Harlem. Sophy Burnham wrote in the New York *Times*, "Harlem is an area where heroin is legal tender. It pays the painter, plumber and the police lawyer defending a man on charges of drug possession."

I continued briskly, "The homicidal way that young people outwardly express their rage and anger is pipe-bombing. Drug addiction is the same rage and anger turned inward—it is the suicidal equivalent of trapped frustration."

I described the ripple effect of addiction and its contagious nature. An addicted Vietnam veteran returning to his home community in California addicted fifty high school students within the first six months after his discharge. "Several of the Congressmen present have told us that seventy-five thousand Vietnam veterans are addicted to opiates. Extrapolating from what one California veteran accomplished, we can anticipate that within two years after the seventy-five thousand partially treated heroin-addict ex-servicemen return to their home towns we will have one or two million children addicted." The bus was glum.

"I suggest that you go home tonight and think about what we are going to do if we are presented with a problem of that magnitude," I declared feelingly. "It might mean the end of American concepts of freedom, and/or the American way of life, for we will have too few young people left to carry on."

We had almost reached the Odyssey storefront. I explained that it is an outreach center we established in Harlem in 1967. "It costs us approximately twenty thousand dollars a year to run, and we have never been funded. Every year for five years we have sent a funding request to the appropriate city agency. The City does not even reply. There are political reasons for that."

I paused. I didn't look in Congressman Rosenthal's direction. My comments, I felt, had been models of restraint. I had not mentioned any of the material found in the New York *Times* on May 12, 1970, where it was reported that Mayor Lindsay's Addiction Services Agency had thirty-four million dollars to spend in 1971. ASA had six hundred and five people on staff and treated only about one thousand of New York's estimated one hundred to two hundred thousand addicts. By its own reports, the official city program, Phoenix House, had rehabilitated only about one hundred and thirty addicts. That works out to about a quarter of a million per addict.

The *Times* added, "Pathetically small as this figure is, it is suspect because the ASA has no follow-up program to determine whether those supposedly rehabilitated actually remain off drugs. In fact, it does not even require those actively undergoing treatment to submit to routine urine tests, the only sure way to determine that they are drug-free, according to many medical authorities. The whole ASA program is a slipshod operation devoid of essential checks. It has never had independent outside evaluation."

The *Times* asked pointedly, "Where does all the ASA money go?" More than a year later the question remained unanswered. The only change was that the newly appointed Commissioner, Graham Finney, is a man of the highest sincerity and integrity.

"Our Harlem storefront sees four hundred and fifty raw addicts a month," I informed the men from Washington. "These addicts are responsible for an estimated $393,000,000 worth of crime in a year." There were some raised eyebrows, but the figure is real. I based it on the amount of property Odyssey's original seventeen addicts used to steal in a year. They estimated that they needed $1.2 million worth of crime every year to support their $400,000 golden arms. There are other estimates around. Dr. David E. Smith of San Francisco's Haight-Asbury Clinic studied thirty-five heroin addicts who stole ten thousand dollars a day to support their habits. The Johns Hopkins Hospital Drug Abuse Center reported that the average addict seen there steals about fifty thousand dollars in property annually. The Harlem storefront saw 450 new addicts each month. They could easily account for that much crime.

I rarely miss an opportunity to put methadone maintainence in its proper perspective. It is my view that it is useful in only a small percentage of cases and is far from the panacea that many believe it to be. "In 1804," I related, "morphine was heralded as a cure for opium smoking. In 1904 heroin was heralded as a cure for morphine addiction. And now, only fifty years later, we have methadone, another narcotic, which is heralded as a cure for heroin addiction.

We are behaving like addicts, who never learn from experience. Already there are drug dealers who sell illegal methadone and people addicted to and overclosing from it. Lately, there have been an increasing number of deaths due to methadone abuse throughout the country. One wonders what is next. Another narcotic to cure methadone addiction? There are more than three thousand drugs of abuse. Do we intend to find a substitute for each? And then substitutes for substitutes?"

The bus stopped by the littered curb in Harlem. We climbed out. Ted Tann, who runs the Harlem storefront, was waiting. He is a lean, light-skinned Black with an intelligent face and a talent for irony. He left a job in the food-processing industry and joined Odyssey's staff at a salary cut of six thousand dollars a year. He wanted to do something meaningful. In addition to the storefront responsibility, he conducts sensitivity sessions with our schizophrenic residents.

Speaking as loudly as he could in the confusion of Congressmen and reporters, Ted outlined the function of the storefront. It tries not only to persuade addicts to come into the Odyssey program, he said, but also, it works with parents of addicts on a counseling basis and directs an extensive drug-education program in schools and the community. Much work is done with children before they use drugs, such as rap sessions, but even more important—help with homework is given youngsters who have no one interested at home. The storefront, he added, is not funded and must rely completely on private donations to survive.

I had planned to walk the Washington group around the block, pointing out the picturesque features of Harlem. Rosenthal looked at his watch and remarked that he didn't think there would be sufficient time. I placed myself beside an Assistant Secretary of State and set off.

A straggly parade followed us, passing utter misery every step of the way. They stared at the garbage tottering out of bashed cans, the young men and women with dulled eyes slouched on the steps of tenements, tiny babies crying bitterly, ragged listless children, flies, dog excrement, beer cans, empty wine bottles, the pervading stench, everywhere garbage and the sense of heavy hopelessness as the well-dressed, well-housed, well-fed White and Black sightseers moved by.

A drunken man clutched a reporter by the arm. "*Hey*, what's the difference between Manson, Calley and Nixon, eh? Tell me that, what's the difference?" The reporter pointed out a Congressman. "Ask him," he suggested. In minutes everyone had heard of the drunk's question.

The bus was waiting for us at a corner and the group climbed aboard gratefully. An unsteady young girl, obviously stoned on drugs, looked contemptuously at the perspiring dignitaries. "What good do you think these politicians are going to do for people on drugs?" she asked angrily. "No good at all," someone from Odyssey told her. She stepped back with a look of satisfaction. "That's just what I was thinking too," she said.

A tidy precise man, whom I later learned was from the Bureau of Narcotics and Dangerous Drugs, said wanly as he found a seat, "I've got more information about drugs here this morning than I have in the past six months in Washington."

During the next leg of the tour, I introduced Fred Cohen, who told the passengers that when he came to Odyssey he was facing from eighteen to thirty years in prison. I added, "The greatest motivating factor for an addict to get well is a good civil commitment law that is enforced. Also it protects the public by removing the addict from the community so that he cannot spread his disease. Gentlemen, addiction is not only *epidemic* but it is a *contagious* disease. We need training programs to prepare all kinds of people to run treatment agencies, to work in the community, to do ghetto medicine. The country is facing a national crisis. Like Hamlin, if we economize, we will have no children to follow us."

The next stop was at Odyssey's East 52nd Street facility, where we housed the Mothering Program. The choir was waiting, dressed in crested blazers. The dignitaries arranged themselves on sofas and chairs where they could watch. The space was cramped and stifling. Cameramen were becoming testy. I explained that the house was used for the Odyssey nursery and the new Mothering Program we were undertaking. The choir was visiting.

In a voice that cut through the babble around me, I informed the Washington people that this too is an unfunded house. "The choir helps to support this house by singing in churches or wherever it is asked," I told them. "That these sick children have to sing for their supper says something about our country."

We had arrived at mealtime so I picked up Serena Hyatt's one-month old baby and gave her her bottle. It was a needed respite. I was tired. I turned to Fred and asked him to take over.

The choir lined up in three rows and sang two of its best numbers, "Stony End" and "Hey Jude." Their voices are beautiful. The choir brings me endless joy. Part of the impact it has on people lies in the fact that almost all the child singers once were drug addicts. They live in the Odyssey adolescent units.

Rosenthal expressed appreciation on behalf of the others and said it was time to leave. It was ten minutes after we arrived. "We'll have to hurry," he said, looking at me. I retorted firmly, "First, we will introduce the choir. It is very important that our guests meet the children."

I instructed the choir to step forward one at a time and give their name, age, and home state and indicate when they began using drugs. Television cameras moved in and reporters were scribbling in notebooks as the children introduced themselves.

Julie Ojeda from New York was holding her ten-month-old daughter, born in Odyssey. She said in a steady voice that she couldn't count how many acid trips she had taken, although she had never used heroin. Doris Silverman of New Jersey said she was sixteen and had begun using heroin at the age of eleven. Laurie Palmer of Connecticut, a stunningly beautiful teen-ager, said she came to Odyssey at fourteen after an unsuccessful suicide attempt. She had used barbiturates regularly. She had never used heroin. Monique LaVoie of New Hampshire said she was an alcoholic and drug user at fourteen. Cassandra Jones from Harlem said she started heroin at thirteen and bought her drugs from her teacher.

The Washington people were aghast. "Will you tell us the name of that teacher?" Congressman Koch asked. Cassandra did. The police authorities present were given the name of the teacher alleged to have furnished the drugs.

John Roberts stepped forward and said he started heroin at the age of twelve. Juan Figuera also started at twelve, he said. Rosenthal asked, "How do you feel now?"

Juan considered for a moment. There were important Whites from Washington in front of him, television and newspaper cameramen around him and fourteen years of living in a New York slum behind him.

"Right now I'm scared," he answered simply.

William Record, Jr., two years at Odyssey, reported that he had finished the program and would be attending prep school in the fall. He was followed by a fourteen-year-old deaf child probated from the courts in Oregon. A twelve-year-old introduced himself and said he used heroin for six months.

The Washington group was shocked and stunned. I heard one say, "Nixon doesn't realize how bad this is," and another nodded.

I dropped demurely into the background for the rest of the tour. The next stop was Horizon House, another of New York City's official drug programs. The residents there formed a reception line to greet the guests and then sat in a circle of chairs and couches answering questions. They were asked, "Where did you get your drugs?" "How much do they cost?" "When did you start taking drugs?" "Why did you take them?" These are the usual questions for which addicts and ex-addicts have rote answers for strangers.

We next drove to City Hall, where Rosenthal's officious aide had posted herself at a swinging gate, deftly and definitely separating the invited guest, me, from the uninvited, all the others from Odyssey. I went in alone because we had decided not to create a scene. The children had made our point.

We were dining in the Blue Room under a portrait of Martin Van Buren on a feast of cold cuts and pickles served on paper plates with soft drinks in plastic cups. I chuckled inwardly. Fred Cohen had predicted exactly that. The night before he had said, "After all this fuss you've made to attend that luncheon, you know what you're going to wind up eating? Kosher cold cuts and pickles."

Halpern sat next to me as he had promised Fred he would. It was reassuring. Mayor Lindsay had greeted everyone except me. Later, when we were finished and the press was admitted, he introduced everyone at the table with the single exception of me. I expected nothing else.

The Assistant Secretary of State (East Asia and Pacific), Marshall Green, informed the press on behalf of the group that he had been assured that the government of Laos was passing its first laws against narcotics and Turkey had promised to cut back on poppy growing. It was a prepared statement.

Mayor Lindsay had some comments. It had been a very important tour, he announced. Congressman Charles Rangel, who represents Harlem, expressed his gratitude that the tour had taken place.

"Millions of poor people are struggling to become part of the North American dream," he said earnestly. "Heroin takes away that dream."

It ended abruptly with no opportunity for questions from the press or comments from the rest of us. Lindsay eased himself through the cluster at the door and disappeared. The Washington delegation returned to the bus, which drove them to their shuttle plane. The tour of Fun City was over.

We returned to Odyssey Mother House with an overwhelming need to ventilate. We wanted to be with real people again and say real things.

During the regular Friday Case Conference which followed, Louie Sarra asked me what happened on the tour.

"I can tell you," I reported to the crowd of about seventy staff and residents in the auditorium, "that we had a delightful day. We have now informed our members of Congress and the State Department of all the horrors of addiction and all the solutions of addiction, and they have learned everything there is to learn between the hours of nine and two.

"Knowing everything—which finally was summarized by our Mayor in a seven-minute 'thank you' in which he forgot to mention my name—we meaningfully solved every problem. And they have gone back to Washington understanding that the problem is the poppy fields of Turkey."

This got a big laugh.

"And now that we have decided that Turkey will no longer grow any poppies, we have nothing more to worry about, and so all of us should begin to think seriously about finding work in another place. For in a few weeks, obviously, there will be no more addiction problem."

Everybody howled.

"What we will do with countries such as Laos, Cambodia and Burma, with whom we have no diplomatic relations or to whom we give very little aid, we're not quite sure. We may tell them we won't talk to them any more.

"I don't know what else to tell you except that it was a pleasant day with very nice people. I think it was best summarized by one of the Washington dignitaries, who shall remain nameless. This dignitary has three sons. One is a lawyer, one is a psychiatrist and one is nuts."

The auditorium exploded with laughter.

"The one who is nuts," I continued, "is nuts because his older brother is a psychiatrist. Unfortunately, the brother who is a psychiatrist used to demand of the younger brother insight into his problems. And the reason, according to the father, that the younger brother can't cope and can't get ahead is that he has too much insight."

There was a roar of disbelief.

"This is honest," I said, holding up my right hand. "The solution therefore, ladies and gentlemen, is *no more insight*. And since that happens to be the solution, I can assure you after spending some time with many of our leaders that there is nothing to worry about. They have no insight."

City Drug Scene Rated a Shocker by U.S. Aides

By JAMES RYAN

The three top State Department officials who deal with the drug-producing areas of the world got their first look at American junkies here yesterday and admitted that they were "shocked."

The three assistant secretaries of state, and members of the House subcommittee on Europe and the New York City congressional delegation toured the South Bronx, Harlem and the lower East Side. They saw addicts "nodding," and buys apparently being made. They also visited treatment centers and talked to youths attempting to escape the drug nightmare.

Was Shocked

Martin Hillenbrand, assistant secretary for Europe, said the tour "certainly shocked me. I've been in the most disadvantaged parts of Europe and Africa but never before have I seen the kind of community breakdown that I saw today."

The other assistant secretaries were Marshall Green for East Asia and the Pacific, and Roger P. Davies for the Near East and South Asia.

The tour, arranged by Rep. Benjamin Rosenthal (D-Queens), subcommittee chairman, grew out of a recent appearance by the State Department officials at hearings in Washington.

At that time, according to reports, the State Department people admitted that although they were responsible for top decisions affecting our relations with drug-producing countries, they had never seen firsthand the impact of drugs on United States communities.

The group arrived here from Washington at 9 a.m. yesterday. Their visit was capped by a lunch-eon meeting with Mayor Lindsay and Police Commissioner Patrick V. Murphy in City Hall.

While the group was on its morning bus trip, Lindsay appeared before another House subcommittee and called for the creation of a single federal agency to combat narcotics with a budget of $1 billion a year within three years.

Testifying before the subcommittee on Public Health and the Environment, Lindsay lauded President Nixon's bill to coordinate all federal agencies involved in drug abuse.

'Welcome Step'

He called the bill "a welcome step to achieve this same objective."

During his testimony, Lindsay said that from all sources, the city now is spending $80 million to combat narcotics abuse.

Observers recalled that during the Albany-New York budget battle last April 23, Lindsay said that proposed state cutbacks would slash the city's anti-drug expenditures to $20 million.

Questioned on this point later, mayoral aide Jay Kriegel said that almost all the cuts were restored in the final days of the legislative session following a "massive lobbying effort" by the city.

Also testifying before the subcommittee, headed by Rep. Paul Rogers (D-Fla.), was Howard A. Jones, chairman of Gov. Rocke-feller's Narcotic Addiction Control Commission.

Jones placed 17 recommendations before the subcommittee, including adoption of the President's proposal. He added, however, that he considered the proposed $155 million increase in federal anti-drug spending "to be insufficient."

In other testimony, Whitney North Seymour Jr., U.S. attorney for the Southern District of New York, said that "the single most important step to stop the spread of narcotics addition is prevention education."

"It is absolutely essential," he said, "to persuade the huge body of potential addicts that addiction is dangerous and undesirable."

Julie Ojeda, 18, with baby, Racquel, tells how she gave up drugs at Odyssey House.

NEWS photo by Jim Garrett

THE GAME ENDS

It's the unquestionable question, but you attempt an answer.
    It's the acceptance of the naked crutch.
It's the real picture, but you measure the frame.
    It's the torn foundation with the new brick!

It's the planting of seeds now breaking the earth.
    It's the giving for the sake of sake.
It's the step to the rhythm of making.
    It's the caution to the sign, "Dead-End Ahead!"

It's the circumference of the lie with the truth as the surface.
    It's the loaded 38 with the final bullet trapped in the chamber.
It's the broken glass-pane with the new picture.
    It's the extinguisher for the burning torcher!

It's the lying down on a clean bed, and growing with the dirty linen.
    It's the empty glass with the overflowing invisible substance.
It's the key to the locked files with you the Investigator.
    It's the cripple making a move!

—TOMMY MOTT

THE WHITE HOUSE

WASHINGTON

December 22, 1971

Dear Congressman:

This is with reference to your letter to Mr. Chapin suggesting
that the President consider inviting to The White House the
Children's Choir of Odyssey House of New York.

Regrettably, a time is not foreseen when these young people
could be asked to come in to sing for the President in view
of his pressing schedule and the continuing heavy official
demands upon him. We want you to know, though, that we
greatly appreciate your interest in contacting us about this
choir.

With our best wishes,

Sincerely,

David N. Parker
Staff Assistant
to the President

Honorable Seymour Halpern
House of Representatives
Washington, D.C. 20515

If You Clean Up the Garbage, You Save the World

I have an absolute thing about garbage. I see all of the world in relationship to its garbage, and I believe that if we solved the garbage-disposal problem everything else concerning the urban blight would begin to be solved.

In Freudian terms, the human being goes through three phases: oral, anal and genital—the oral being totally self-engrossed and manipulative, the anal compulsive and rigid, the genital mutual giving and growing. Because the problems the nation faces are overwhelming, at Odyssey we've developed the following interpretation in a light vein.

We've solved the oral stage in America. There's no question about that. We have plenty to intake. We have more consumption, more goods, more ways of feeding and stroking ourselves than any human group has ever had before.

We're fixated now in the anal phase of development in this country, which is a tragedy not only for us but for the rest of the world. Anal people are competitive, aggressive, status-oriented horrible people.

The hope of mankind is that we can become genital people, concerned with others, partners with all living things, aware that what happens to individuals and babies in our society reflects on ourselves as adult human beings.

Our problem is that we are the only species on the planet that fouls its own nest. We are confused as to whether we are tree or cave animals, and in addition there is the indifference of the anal arrogance. We put out a great deal of waste, and we don't know how to get rid of what we produce.

Human beings began as tree animals, who defecate wherever they are and move on to another tree. Except that now we're over-populated on this planet and we can't move on any more. The trees are full, and anyway because we were naked and cold we moved into caves.

We're surrounded therefore by our garbage, we're inundated by our garbage, our garbage is up to our noses. Everytime we open our mouth it gets filled with shit, in more ways than one.

If we could discipline ourselves to get rid of our waste out of consideration for ourselves and our neighbors and for future generations, we would move on to the next state of human development, which would be genital and caring. Cave animals conserve and protect their environment; it seems we can't learn to do the same, ecology notwithstanding. I think we're going to drown in our own garbage.

When you wake up in the South Bronx and see fourteen feet of garbage, the rats and the roaches and all the carrion that lives in the garbage, you can't help but think that you might as well give up. You destroy all beauty in that mess.

In New York City we could solve the garbage problem, but we don't. Odyssey once asked the Department of Sanitation for trucks for our ghetto medicine program. We would drive them, we would load them, we would dump the garbage. We weren't allowed to do it because it was against the City union contract. Garbage can only be picked up at certain hours once or twice a week. But we make garbage at all hours.

When we were given the building on Bruckner Boulevard, we removed twelve six-ton truckloads of garbage from the back yard. While the Odyssey patients and staff were shoveling out the garbage and my elder son, Judson, was killing rats with a baseball bat, people cooking their dinners on the top floor were throwing garbage on our heads.

They thought it was funny. Not only would they not clean up their own garbage, but they laughed at us for being so foolish as to be cleaning up their garbage. So they threw more garbage at us.

No society can live like that.

It is a scorching summer day in New York City. The sun comes through the pollution haze and cooks your brains. The Odyssey House headquarters stands out on its block, the one with the fresh paint, the one where the garbage cans have lids. All the windows are open and listless passers-by can hear the crackle of the p.a. announcements. A voice is saying sternly: *"Can I have your attention please. Will all male residents who have to give up urine go to the co-ordinator's office. Will all male residents who have to give up urine go to the co-ordinator's office. Thank you."*

Heaven has created,
So heaven can demand
For the payment, the soul of man!

But when man dies,
It's for the second time.
For myself, buried once,

This my hell,
This my love,
This my laughter,
This my chapter,

This my tear,
This my fear,
This my thought, the end is near!

—TOMMY MOTT

The Schizophrenics

Ted Tann meets with a small group of schizophrenics every Wednesday afternoon in the front office of the Odyssey House on East 12th Street.

Twenty per cent of the patients at Odyssey are schizophrenics. We are able to identify them because we have professional diagnosis, both medical and psychiatric, within twenty-four hours of induction. Schizophrenia is a disease that can't be cured at our present state of knowledge, no matter what treatment is given. However, chemotherapy and a long-term supportive enviromnent lessen the stresses that accelerate the schizophrenic process.

The therapeutic-community method of treatment was first started by the famous British psychiatrist Maxwell Jones to treat schizophrenics. To some degree, they are able to help each other when they are protected against competition and manipulation by people who don't understand their pain. The aggression-encounter therapy used in addict-run therapeutic communities is wrong for schizophrenics. They collapse under it.

Ted Tann meets with several of our schizophrenic patients once a week for a special group, which affords them additional support. Often their conversation is unintelligible to a normal person, but Ted is sensitive to the way they think. We selected him as the professional to lead the schizophrenic group for this reason. All the schizophrenics treated at Odyssey were once addicts, but drugs are not their fundamental problem. Ted Tann is quiet, gentle, patient and non-threatening. When the group goes nowhere, he doesn't become frustrated.

On a sultry afternoon in July 1971 he had stretched his lanky length in a tipped-back chair and was watching the group alertly.

There were six patients in the room. Joan Winston was sitting on a small sofa, a chunky, pretty girl in a flowered mini. While the others talked, she kept her head down and plucked at loose threads on the sofa arm.

Ted was concerned. Joan's husband, Peter, had split from Odyssey the week before. Peter had left because he hadn't understood why a resident had to be symbolically discharged after the fire on 12th Street. Ted wondered what effect Peter's departure had on Joan.

A pale, rigid teen-aged girl with a trancelike expression and braces on her teeth was the first to speak. The others were maintaining that the girl's actions during the past week had been unreasonable. She was denying it.

"Let's take it one step further, Cynthia," Ted commented. Cynthia Schwartz turned her wide-eyed stare to him. "With your history of being in and out of mental institutions and your own acceptance of your insanity, isn't the basic problem that many things that you have incorporated into just being you are quite different in your mind from what everyone around you sees you doing?"

There was a long silence and Cynthia said weakly, "I know. I know I'm acting out more and more lately. . . ."

Ted said patiently, "But that's not the question. Again you're *avoiding*. The question was, Isn't one of your basic problems that you see things one way and everybody else around you sees things another way?" Cynthia sat, frozen as a Barbie doll, and considered it.

"Last week in group," Ted persisted, "the question was put: Does each member of the group accept his or her own insanity? Everyone else in the group became quite defensive, but your concept was that being crazy meant you were more normal than the average person."

"No," Cynthia protested. "I didn't say I was normal. I didn't say that being insane means being more sane. But insanity gives a larger scope."

"You're saying that people who are insane have more going for them!" said Ted incredulously.

"I'm not saying it that way," said Cynthia in a drifting voice. "I mean that we see things much clearer. If you mean, do I enjoy being crazy? the answer is no. I don't."

As the discussion developed, Cynthia spoke of feeling alienated when she used her "own language" and found that others couldn't understand it. Ted seized upon this as an example.

"You have a way of talking that is not the way normal people talk," he said. "And you have a way of problem-solving that is not the way we problem-solve. Just like with Betty Agabedian . . ."

199

Betty, sitting across the desk from Ted, nodded. ". . . you have to learn to give up this way of behaving in order to move on."

Joan Winston was paying no attention, lost in her own thoughts.

Cynthia complained that Betty was projecting pity on her and she didn't like it.

"I think you're full of shit," Ted observed in a friendly tone.

Alice Stevens, sitting next to Cynthia, groaned. "What did I tell you?" she said to Betty, giving Cynthia a disgusted glance.

"You're not going to tell us Betty is projecting on you, so we will stop and find out why Betty's projecting," Ted told Cynthia. "We're not going for that! There are people in this room who have gone through things similar to this and you cannot play your game with us. They're not going to let you."

At Ted's urging, Cynthia recalled an early psychotic experience. She had been a groupie following a rock band, living in a hotel and being sexually used in common by all the musicians. "One time I was on speed," she related in a faint voice. "I was acting out. I took all my clothes off and I was dancing around. I thought I was a witch." The group was sad for her. "The next morning when I woke up they were all gone. There was a sheet over me and the manager said to get out."

"Since you were ten years old you have evidenced weird, bizarre behavior," Ted said consolingly, "which has gotten you into terrible situations like that hotel room. Now that you're among friends, you must promise us that you will never do this again."

Cynthia said without emphasis, "I promise. I don't like it when I do extreme things. I want to finish the program, get married, live a normal life. I want to be able to do things like other people, to carry responsibility . . ."

"That's beautiful!" Ted cried. "Is it true?"

"That's what I want."

"Then you will give up your fantasy life?"

"Yes," Cynthia told him, "I will still fantasize, of course. But in the proper way."

Ted sighed. "You step on clouds, with *no firm foundation*. You can't go through life that way. You know how to run the data, you know how to tell us what we want to hear. But it's not what is happening with you. The only requirement of this group is for you to be honest. That's the only requirement."

"I *am* being honest," Cynthia insisted.

"We don't believe you because we don't think you have made the commitment to get well."

Cynthia shook her head. "That's why I left the other program to come to Odyssey—to get well! Because Odyssey has, in the Concept, what I want. That's my goal."

"If you want to stay at Odyssey, you're going to have to prove it to us," Ted told her coolly. "If these are your goals, let's start building a firm foundation together. The only way we can start is for you to be honest with us."

She promised, but the group was still annoyed. Alice Stevens told Cynthia angrily "you have been grooving on things that you talk about." Pat James, a heavy youth in a wet-look jacket, commented in a tone of wonderment, "I've been thinking, Ted, that what she's doing is what I used to do."

Betty said indignantly, "You know what you do? To avoid what's really happening, you stick to your own self and you're trying to make everyone believe it."

This made sense to Pat. He said delightedly, "I used to do this. I used to come to group, right? and I'd think about what I was talking about, and I used to change it around, dress it up a little bit, right? and slide right through it."

Cynthia absorbed this, moving only her eyes in her fixed head to watch the speakers.

"That way," Ted explained, picking up the point without difficulty, "Pat got a Brownie point for talking about himself, but he didn't do anything for himself."

"Right," Pat nodded vigorously. "That's what I used to do. Instead of helping myself I was saying, Forget about Pat James."

"Who was a non-existent person," Ted said understandingly.

"Right," said Pat.

Cynthia acknowledged in her limp voice that she had been unreal. Ted abruptly turned to Betty and asked how the book was coming. He had ordered her to read *I Never Promised You a Rose Garden* by Hannah Green, an autobiography of a schizophrenic. Betty said she was having trouble. She hated the book.

"Why?"

"What she does is exaggerated compared to what I do," she complained.

"Betty," asked Ted, "why does that book present such a big threat to you?"

Betty pondered. "Because of the hospital. It's just the fact that she's in a hospital that bothers me. And she's more extreme than I am. I might be in another world at times, Ted, but I'm not like she is."

Alice Stevens asked, "What is it about the hospital that you are scared of?"

Betty's voice was choked. "I relate to the hospital and how my mother is, and I'm scared of being like her." Ted looked skeptical. "I'm trying to come across! I'm trying, *I'm trying!*"

Ted said, "Do you want your five minutes now?" He had decreed some weeks before that Betty could cry for five minutes during every group, but no more. Betty grinned at him and declared that she didn't need the five minutes.

"But I feel sorry for myself," she confessed. "I feel scared."

"But when the situation is uncomfortable, you shouldn't retreat to your fantasy," Ted told her. "It's no solution. It's only temporary relief, and you jam yourself on it."

"I've been trying," Betty said, tearful again. "I just don't want to face a lot of things."

"That you're scared of."

"Yes."

"Finish the book," Ted advised her in a tone of kindness, "because if that book scares you, it's good. Yet in the end, it offers hope."

"I know," Betty responded, sniffling and then giggling. "I'm laughing at my behavior," she explained, "because I think that I'm ridiculous."

"I'm glad you realize that," Ted told her, smiling. "And now you are being very serious with us. You've been talking about the real problems that you have. But you're now, what—sixteen?"

"Seventeen."

"And it's time to grow up and accept the world for what it is. That's more real than using drugs."

He turned and looked at Joan Winston, who was, as usual, remote, withdrawn and silent. "Mrs. Winston," he asked softly. "Could we get some feedback from you about the past week?"

"It's not been very good," said Joan in a low voice.

"You'll have to speak up."

She cleared her throat. "It's not been very good." Unconsciously, she began swinging her leg vigorously. She kept her head down.

Ted rose and turned off the noisy air conditioner. He opened the tall window on the street and the radio in a passing taxi blared that one of the Mets just had a two-base hit.

Alice said with concern, "Why don't you tell them what happened, Joanie? How you're really feeling?"

"What day was it?" Joan asked distractedly.

"Monday," Alice prompted. "You got a reprimand that day for not doing your job."

"A lot of things were breaking up," Joan began. "There were just a whole lot of things I didn't like, like people would ask me, 'Why, Joan, are you looking around? Why are you walking around?' Like that, you know? It would be hard for me to come right out and tell them why. I just know they wouldn't believe me, you know? You know, I hallucinated. And when it started, it was *for real*."

"When did it start?" asked Ted.

"It started on Monday, before I got my reprimand."

"What did you hallucinate?"

Joan's head sunk. "People were calling me."

"What did they say?"

"I don't remember. It was like they were there when they were calling me, but I guess they weren't there."

Cynthia was looking panicked, her head held stiffly. She watched Joan out of the corners of her eyes. Betty looked concerned, Alice was leaning forward sympathetically. Pat turned his chair around to face the hunched-over figure of Joan. Rafael Gonzales, a handsome Puerto Rican sitting on the couch beside Joan, was scowling.

"Joan," said Ted very quietly, "I have to confront you. Hearing voices means that you're in trouble and everybody in this group knows that means you're in trouble. You tell us someone was calling you, but if I hadn't asked about it you never would have copped!

"As I've told you before, the agency's policy when you're in trouble is not to send you off to a mental institution, unless you attempt suicide. There's nothing and no one here for you to be afraid of." He got up and sat on the arm of the couch, touching her hand. "We'll give you medication to relieve the tension which you've built up over the weekend because Peter split."

He stayed beside her for a moment and then returned to the desk and picked up the telephone. He spoke in a low voice, part of which —"auditory hallucination"—could be heard. He put down the receiver.

"My call was not to Bellevue to see if you're going cuckoo," he assured her. "I was checking with the Odyssey psychiatrist, Antonio Domantay, to see if you need the additional help of medication."

Joan's voice was stronger. "I still have those feelings," she said sadly. "What came down came down real slow, and I felt I was going down really."

"Is it a shape?" asked Ted.

"No, it's nothing big. It's little. And as soon as it came down, well, I shook my arm and I was still there. I shook my leg and . . . you know? I knew I was hallucinating. I just didn't react to anything. You know, calm. I didn't tell Mary Lou, I didn't tell anyone it was happening. It was just, well, so slow."

Ted mentioned the medication again and perceived that Joan dreaded it. "I accept it," she said reluctantly. "But I don't like drugs. They mean I'm sick . . . different from other people."

"There's a difference when a doctor gives you drugs and when you medicate yourself," Ted told her. "Some people who suffer your kind of problem medicate themselves with heroin to relieve the pain. But now you're safe in a therapeutic community; here there are qualified people to help you. Don't turn away from us."

Joan was aroused. "No, no, no! It's not so much the taking medication. I always felt the reason I started taking heroin was because, well, it was because I started using barbiturates. That was the reason. I feel that if I start taking medication, I would become addicted again, you know?"

Alice Stevens identified with Joan's distress and said comfortingly that she was taking the medication and it was good. "It slows everything down," she explained.

Joan listened, twirling a pen in her fingers and watching it intently. It would help Joan function better, Alice continued.

"How can you function better if it slows down the action?" asked Joan.

"You function better because you take your time and you know what you're doing. You don't try to do too many things at once, like I used to try to do. Too many things *fast*. It just slows you down, and as far as going to bed it knocks you out. You won't dream too much. There's nothing to be scared of, Joanie, it doesn't harm you."

Joan didn't look up but she nodded acceptance. The room was heavily quiet. In a weary voice Ted chided Joan for waiting for three days "in a living hell" before telling about the hallucinations.

"Do you wait until somebody asks, 'Are you hallucinating?' Or do you tell the doctors or myself, or anybody, that you're in trouble?"

Joan answered weakly, "I feel bad."

"We all feel bad about being here, Joan. If anyone in this room had a choice of being anywhere else, he would be there. But we are here to get ourselves together so we can meet the hell out there in society without running away from it," Pat said.

He paused. "And the one way we can do that, Joan, is by helping one another. And the only way we can help one another is just by what we told Cynthia earlier—we have to be honest, we cannot play the sociopathic game. We cannot act like dope fiends. The fact that our sickness is not the same as everyone else's in the program is very evident to us all. And you waited *three days!*"

"If it happens again," said Joan, "and Mary Lou ain't there, who

Ted Tann.

could I tell?" Mary Lou Evans is easy for Joan to seek out because she is also a schizophrenic, also Black, and also female.

"Tell the staff," Ted advised.

"Tell the Level IVs," suggested Alice. "They'll tell the staff."

"Staff can help you, there's plenty of staff in the house," Betty said, leaning forward urgently. "I'm sure Yvonne Cox would help. You're going half nuts, you know, with thinking that you're going half crazy. You don't know what the fuck's going on, and you're not telling anyone about it. Something might happen to you, Joan. You might jump out of a window, you know."

"This is serious," Alice added. "It's *very serious*."

"But nobody in the house is like that but me!" Joan protested.

"I question how many people are having similar problems and have not said anything about it," Ted observed. "And there are several others you could go to, Clayton Taylor for one. Clayton is now a Level IV, and he's worked through where you're at now. He's found a way to establish a basic firm foundation for himself so he doesn't have to live in a living hell; namely, the confusion of his own mind. Joanie, you are taking the initial steps. You should be proud that you have begun working on your problems."

They talked briefly about her husband, Peter, who had split on Friday and returned Monday afternoon. She was distressed that he would have to start the program over again.

"Instead of saying 'Why me?'" Ted suggested kindly, "you should be thinking that you're in a place that can help you. You're not out on the street shooting dope."

Joan nodded thoughtfully.

"Can we have a small smile from you?" asked Ted.

She lifted her head and managed one. The group applauded her.

BRONX FEMALE ADOLESCENT TREATMENT UNIT SCHEDULE TUESDAY

TIME SCHEDULED	EVENTS SCHEDULED
6:45 A.M.	House wakes up
7:00–7:15	Physical Therapy
7:30–8:15	Breakfast
8:30–9:30	Morning Meeting
9:30	Coffee break and go-to-work assignments
10:00	Medication administered
10:00	Level II group starts Inez Tann (therapist) Janis Williams (unit leader)

	Level I group starts
	Barbara Brenner (therapist)
	Laurie Palmer (unit leader)
	Rest of the house
	work activities
12:00 P.M.	Groups over
12:00–1:00	Lunch served
1:30–3:30	Cross Confrontation
	Work activities
3:30	School—tutoring for Marguerite Sono,
	Julie Ojeda with Herb Goldberg
	Level III groups
5:00–6:30	Dinner served
6:30	Medication administered
	School—tutoring for Serena Hyatt, Monique La-
	Voie, Pat Jones
	Teacher—Mary Jane Mott
7:30	May Stevens—school downtown
	Candidate In-group
8:00	Nightladies go to bed
9:00	Coffee break called
10:00	House prepares for bed
10:00	Medication administered
11:00	Nightladies get up
11:00	House goes to bed

° Candidate—In-group is held at night with the staff on duty and May Stevens as unit leader.

QUARTERLY REPORT
18TH STREET MALE ADOLESCENT
TREATMENT UNIT
JUNE 15, 1971

Name: B.N.   Level I
Age: 14
Race: Puerto Rican
Date Admitted: 12/2/70
Years Using: 6 months
What Used: Heroin, Acid, Barbiturates
Physical Disabilities:

Mental Status: 1. Possible anxiety neurosis
2. Character disorder, characterized by poor self-image, tension release
3. I.Q. 92

Personal Evaluation:

B.N. has been in the program about six months and just made Level I about a week ago. In all the time he has been in the program, he has had a very hard time accepting from people and getting to trust them. In the work area, B.N. does very good. He puts a lot of pride in the house and things for the house. He confronts his peers a lot on the things that they do wrong; he also confronts the upper house. In group, B.N. helps out his peers a lot but he still hasn't brought out his problems to the group, which probably comes from the lack of trust that he had.

Submitted by: Roger Sayers
                 House Supervisor

B.N.'s anxiety has decreased somewhat. He has a good deal of anger towards his parents because of rejection feelings that he has picked up. He appears to be doing well in the program. He required a great deal of attention and has been placed in a group of fourteen-year-olds who relate to Roger in addition to the regular groups.

                                          Carl F. Lazzaro
                                          House Psychologist

QUARTERLY REPORT
GREENWICH ODYSSEY
DECEMBER 15, 1971

Pat James   Level III
Job Function: Head of Kitchen
Age: 20
Race: Black
Admission Date: 5/26/70, 4/1/71
Drugs Used: Marijuana, Cocaine, Heroin
Years Using: Three years
Mental Status: Schizoid Personality; Rule out chronic undifferentiated schizophrenia
Evaluation:

Pat has been having some difficulty since he came to 12th Street from the Spanish House. He is not handling his responsibilities, and he is complaining that he feels very insecure as a person. He has come to group with some problems that really don't make sense. I don't know how to judge him in relation to the peer group. His Special

Group feedback is about the same. I am not certain if we can expect him to function on the same level as his peers. This presents a problem as to what we should look for in order for us to propose him for the next level. My feelings are that we should place him in some type of vocational rehabilitation position, so that he can get some meaningful direction for re-entry.

Yvonne Cox
House Administrator

QUARTERLY REPORT
MOTHER HOUSE
MARCH 15, 1972

C.A.   Level III
Research Assistant
Age: 22
Race: White
Date Admitted: October 29, 1970
Years Using Drugs: 2
Drugs Used: Marijuana, Amphetamine, Cocaine, LSD
Mental Status: Impression: Paranoid Schizophrenia
Personal Evaluation:

There seemed to be a change in C. around the second week in February. He became less defensive in groups and in confrontation, though not, of course, consistently accepting. He reported "feeling better" about himself. Perhaps he has come to trust some of us; in any case, he seems less threatened now by people. He has since expressed interest in forming friendships with his new peers (he was *ecstatic* about being made a Level III) and has really tried to interact with them on a human level, minimizing his intellectualizing. And they seem to accept him.

C. must receive solid support as a III and not be permitted to regress. I feel he will be doing better, and soon.

Submitted by Wesley Avera
House Counselor

Name: W.B.   Level II
Age: 17
Race: White (Irish)
Date Admitted: 4/30/70
Years Using: Two and a half (2½)
What Used: Heroin, Pot, Cocaine, Speed, Acid
Physical Disabilities: Arthritic condition of the hands
Diagnostic Impression of Mental Status:
        1. Anxiety Neurosis—300.0
        2. Drug Dependence—304.0
        3. Passive/Aggressive Personality—301.81
Personal Evaluation:

    W.B. has done a great deal of growing, going through Level I again. His awareness of wearing a laughing bag around his neck and having everyone pushing the button when he looks depressed has made him come out of his depression somewhat. In group, he is more verbal and reaches out to his peers, but he should talk more in terms of what is going on with him. He has been confronting his peers and staff on his feelings and seems to be getting them. Resolved in terms of the program. I think W.B. feels much better about himself at this point in his treatment. Could see Level III in the near future doing a lot for him.

Submitted by: Harold Robinson
House Counselor

I agree.

Carl F. Lazzaro
House Psychologist

MENTAL STATUS REPORT

Name: M.D.   July 3, 1970

APPEARANCE:

    Patient seen at the request of the Gramercy Park Staff, because of suicidal ideation, inappropriate behavior and parental thought disorder.

    Patient is a 21-year-old, white female of Italian extraction with a 3-year history of drug use, primarily amphetamines and hallucinogens.

210

She has occasionally snorted heroin and taken barbiturates. Ingestion was by mouth and there are no signs of needle marks or skin popping.

She is an attractive young woman, pleasant and co-operative to the examiner. There is marked dilation of the pupils and questionable exophthalmus. She has an inappropriate voice which is flattened, and an idiosyncratic giggle and nervous laugh, particularly at times when she talks about death. There are wide swings in her mood patterns.

THOUGHT CONTENT:

Delusional thoughts and auditory hallucinations, particularly, hearing the voice of God telling her to talk to us are present. There is a marked negative relationship with another female patient, Jean Young; with lesbian overtones and submission to the control of the latter patient, even to the extent of asking her for permission to go to the bathroom in front of the other residents. However, she was able to transfer these feelings very quickly, in group, to myself. Thoughts of death were dealt with by having her make a commitment to each figure in the room, that she would not, under any circumstance, kill herself. She actively asks for help and seems in great pain. There is marked loosening of association and very poor concentration.

GENERAL INFORMATION OF INTELLIGENCE:

Within normal limits, and additional tests for abstraction are not done at this time.

RECOMMENDATIONS:

1. Patient to be transferred to the mother house, in order to separate her from the negative relationship, and to reinforce transferance to psychiatrist.
2. Thorazine, 50 mg TID and 100 mg H/S. Reports to be given by the medical staff weekly as to the effect of this medication and as to the need in increase or decrease.
3. Deepening of transferance relationship and dependency on house to be encouraged.
4. Refer to Medical Department for work-up for possible thyroid disfunction, and for follow-up blood test monthly for blood dyscrasia post-Thorazine use.

DIAGNOSIS:

1. Schizo-affective Schizophrenia active with suididal ideation and paranoid features.
2. Drug Abuse—Amphetamines and hallucinogens.
3. Rule out thyrotoxic psychosis.

Respectfully submitted,
Judianne Densen-Gerber J.D., M.D.
Psychiatric Director

Charlie Rohrs I

It took me about five months to reach the decision to become full-time Medical Director at Odyssey House. This represented a complete change of direction from the one for which I'd been planning and training throughout the twenty-two years of my formal education.

I'm trained as an endocrinologist, a specialist in glandular disease. At the time I took a part-time job at Odyssey in 1969, I was working on a research project at New York University Medical School on energy production and utilization at the sub-cellular level. The project wasn't anything earth-shattering, but it was a good piece of fairly sophisticated biochemical research, because it was being done under the supervision of a fine scientist, Dr. Edwin E. Gordon, a Professor of Medicine.

Choosing Odyssey meant giving up my future in traditional academic medicine and a good deal of anticipated independence. Most doctors function as individuals, even when they work in large hospitals; at Odyssey, we work as a team.

It also required an attitudinal change. In medicine we are taught to consider one thing, and one thing only: what is in the best interests of the individual patient. In Odyssey, we make occasional decisions that aren't for the individual's good. But the decision is made because it is best for the other members of the program as a whole, such as when Richie Shanner was discharged from the program after the fire on 12th Street. To hurt an individual patient because of the needs of a group of patients isn't easy for a doctor to do. It is similar to medicine on the battlefield or in a catastrophe, where we are instructed to treat the least injured first.

The dispassionate, scientific role I had always imagined for myself in medicine is not possible at Odyssey. Doctors don't ordinarily involve themselves with human beings as people, with the exception of the field of psychiatry. They involve themselves in an organ system or a disease process, which permits them to remain aloof from the patient. I wasn't certain that I wanted to be involved intimately in the lives of patients.

But as soon as Judi asked me to join the staff, I knew that I was going to do it. My wife, Barbara, and I spent the months between October of 1969 and February 1970 discussing all the things that would be different. I wondered if she was urging me to take it because she thought it was what I wanted or because she really thought it was a good move. In the more than ten years of our marriage we have had the habit of making decisions together. This was not one I would make alone.

Usually, the doctors who come to Odyssey on a part-time basis plan to stay for a few years and then go on to something else. At the time of the decision, I was twenty-nine and sick and tired of training and preparing. It was time to determine what I would do for the rest of my professional life and stick with it. No more shopping around—Odyssey represented permanence.

However, I don't regret those years spent in the laboratory. They taught me to think critically, analytically. I have an internal discipline I didn't have before. You learn to use the scientific method in sizing up a situation, and to be ruthlessly honest with yourself about facts. There's an application for science in the clinical situation.

Anyway, I realized that I wasn't cut out to be a good scientist. The research project was good experience in methodology, but I hated the obsessively meticulous side of it. You have to write down the tiniest details, keep records, concern yourself with the temperature of the room or whether the sun's coming in or not. Everything has to be done today exactly as yesterday and the same as tomorrow in order that the results be useful. I couldn't force myself to adhere to the routine and rigidity. Besides, I was more and more turned on by the part-time job at Odyssey.

I had begun moonlighting because I needed to supplement my income in order to support my family better. Physicians in training are often paid very poorly.

My first moonlighting job was running a coronary unit in a small hospital, sleeping there two nights a week. There was little work to do and I was bored. I quit when I was hired for the part-time job at Odyssey. The work consisted of giving routine examinations to the inductees, handling sick call for the residents and being available for emergencies. It paid seven thousand a year, which was only one thousand less than I was making at my full-time position in the lab.

The way I got the job was by telephoning a *Dr. Judianne Densen-Gerber* and telling her I was interested. She said to come down and see her.

I arrived in the middle of a candidate-out group meeting; Louie Sarra was reading his candidate-out proposal, which eventually was turned down. It was the weirdest thing I had ever seen in my life, and Judi struck me as one of the most uninhibited people I'd ever met. I really didn't know what the hell was going on. She was sitting on a couch in a bag of a dress, laughing and smoking a thin cigar. There were about fifteen people in the room and there was some yelling about furniture, urine specimens and dinner. All the time, Louie was reading his proposal and people were coming in and out. It was like a Fellini movie. After about fifteen minutes of this, Judi turned to me and said, "Well, what do you think of us?"

"Well," I said, "that's kind of an unfair question. I just don't know."

At that point Judi introduced me and everyone introduced themselves and there was a nice relaxed feeling throughout the room. They returned to the candidate-out proposal, and I sat there watching them. At the end of it, Judi said, "Do you want the job?" I asked, "What job?" because I didn't know what was involved. She described my duties and told me many things about the agency.

I had called Barbara around five o'clock that day to say I'd be a little late for dinner because I was going to see about another job. She was expecting me about six-thirty, and I arrived home at one in the morning. That's Odyssey. It always bothers me when that happens and I know it bothers her, but there's not one damn thing we can do about it.

I agreed with Judi to come in on a regular basis, taking responsibility for medical problems and the physical examinations of inductees. The actual work took ten hours a week, but because I became so involved I stayed closer to forty—plus the thirty hours a week in the laboratory.

In school or during their training, doctors aren't taught about addiction except in the same negative way that a policeman sees it. You see the worst aspects and get a picture of addicts as operators, hostile people demanding treatment, criminals, smugglers of drugs onto the ward, people you couldn't possibly identify with and shouldn't waste hospital beds on. Actually, it is the mark of a good hospital resident physician if he can prevent the admission of sick addicts to his ward because they are such a nuisance to handle.

That's not the way they're seen at Odyssey. Here we see them as human beings who have a sickness that's different from other

214

people's. I learned to consider the drug addict as a person with a treatable disease rather than someone sub-human.

There's a different concept of the doctor-patient relationship at Odyssey. I'm not a person who is regarded as all-powerful because I am a doctor, a man on a mission of importance in a white coat. In fact, I don't wear a white coat, and all the patients except the children call me Charlie.

I'm one of several specialists here with a specific expertise, but John Cox can be considered a specialist in a certain situation, or Louie Sarra, or Fred Cohen, or Jimmy Murphy. Odyssey has freed me to learn from people I was closed to before coming here. John has enabled me to gain insight into the problems of the Blacks, Louie enabled me to see addicts as people of sensitivity and warmth, Fred has resourcefulness and preciseness, while Jimmy provides enlightening perception. From all of them, I've learned the importance of commitment, dedication and mutual problem-solving.

We have the team approach to treatment. The residents aren't patients lying in beds; they are people we have to interrelate with in order to find out their problems and help them. It is liberating to begin to learn from everyone around you, not just fellow doctors. The reason we doctors have been ignorant so long about addiction is that we've shut our minds to any meaningful exchange, particularly with the patients themselves. Except for using the escape mechanism of drugs, the problems and attitudes of medical students or visitors who come to Odyssey are often the same as those of the addicts. Only they express them in more sophisticated ways. For instance, many exhibit the same fear of closeness that is fundamental in the addict. People don't usually listen to each other's talk in order to perceive truth, they listen so they can retaliate. They play the same game that the addict does.

This is seen often in medicine. If one physician attempts to give advice to another, it is usually taken as criticism. Intellectual fencing frequently goes on in a hospital, people always needing to be right, or to get in the last word. It exists elsewhere, on Wall Street or attorneys' offices or in business—wherever people are in competition. This alienation in the "real world" is readily perceived by the addict who uses it as an excuse to justify his own anti-social, self-destructive behavior.

The concepts of a therapeutic community like Odyssey House are applicable to absolutely everybody. There's no one who couldn't benefit from it, and I'm including the professional class most definitely. The addicts aren't people who can't function, as is so often expressed. They function very well, manipulating and exploiting to change situations to suit themselves. The problem is their functioning isn't constructive functioning. Their tragedy is that they destroy other people—every single patient in this program has torn his family to pieces—and in the process of destroying others, they destroy themselves.

They problem-solve in an inadequate way rather than a healthy way. And so do many others in society who are considered well. In their case, however, society does not demand a change.

I had to unlearn a good deal of what medical school taught me when I came to Odyssey. Doctors are taught to accept, understand, hold back from making judgments or demands on patients. In a therapeutic community, we make judgments and we put stringent demands on our patients. We tell them, in effect, "We cannot consider you an acceptable human being if you continue to act this way. We in the community do not approve of what you're doing. You'll have to change if you want to travel with us."

Medicine, as I learned it, is all New Testament: love and forgive, no matter what. If you get slapped in the face, you take it and then you turn your cheek and you get slapped in the face again. Odyssey House represents in some degree the reality of the Old Testament. There is "an eye for an eye and a tooth for a tooth." A mature person learns to accept responsibility for the consequence of his actions.

The basic pathology in most addicts is that they treat other people as objects, not as persons. They are insensitive to other people's feelings, and therefore they can't monitor their own conduct by the pain they may cause other human beings. In short, they don't care. They are isolated because they can't appreciate feeling tones in other people. They're two-dimensional, ego and libido, missing the third dimension, which is superego; they are self and desire without concern and caring. We have to supply values to the residents in Odyssey House.

I admire the New Testament style because mercy and forgiveness are fine qualities. But too much of it kills people. Usually when the addict is at home with his family he is forgiven over and over again, which permits him to cling to his disease. The same thing happens on the street, in hospitals, in courts, and in too many drug addiction-treatment programs. Here, we tell him that he has to pay the consequences. He cannot continue to hurt others. Kindness is withheld when kindness is not deserved. He can't get well unless we make demands, and we can't treat him unless he faces reality.

This represents the most profound attitudinal change Odyssey has made in me. I had a very liberal Democratic orientation when I left college. I believed the 1930s concept of liberalism should be expanded, and I never analyzed the problems the New Deal had created.

In 1932 welfare was marvelous and it worked. There were people on welfare who knew how to problem-solve and make decisions, who could function independently. The Depression had thrown them on the rocks through no fault of their own and they needed help badly. They had self-dignity, most of them and a sense of direction. Welfare was regarded as a temporary expedient while they attempted to get themselves out of the situation as quickly as possible and back to functioning independently again.

We still retain that 1932 concept, but we're dealing now with people who don't have a previous experience of functioning and have no motivation in moving away from the lassitude of dependency. I couldn't have understood that when I arrived at Odyssey. I thought that anybody who criticized the present welfare system was a reactionary bigot. Now I think about what I believe and say, rather than just throwing out hunks of programmed dogma. I have become, in this sense, a socially responsible conservative.

My mother is a 1932 liberal. She believes that if you want to help a person, you not only find them a job but also a house and clothing. And you tell them that they should be able to function on their own because they are adults. But you don't demand that they function because that would be "unkind." Her innate kindness was good for me when I was a child but not, unfortunately, for the welfare clients she has worked with for the past few years. She is now beginning to realize that herself.

The therapeutic community demands that people function in a healthy way or suffer the consequences. I call that real kindness.

My whole upbringing was in the liberal Democratic tradition. I was born and raised in Oregon by people who were second- or third-generation American from German Lutheran stock. I was the oldest of three brothers and it was an uneventful, happy Hoosier type of childhood like those in James Whitcomb Riley books.

My mother has her Master's degree, and my father never finished fifth grade. They were married in their late twenties and it was a very happy marriage. She had been a school teacher. She's a brilliant woman. She was the youngest person ever to graduate from Oregon State College at the time she was there. My dad was a semi-skilled laborer. He had a number of jobs, iron worker, logger, truck driver, that sort of thing.

He was a very domineering person. There was never any question about which of them made the decisions. He was authoritarian and made us toe the mark, but he was also a warm, loving man. He would come home exhausted from the hard work he did but faithfully, every night, he took his sons out to a game, or to play catch, or to Scouts. He didn't just accompany us—he involved himself in what we were doing. I always sensed that his life was limited and demanding, but he kept his problems to himself and gave us nothing but the feeling of safety and happiness.

The tragedy of my whole life was the death of my father. He contracted cancer and died at the age of forty-nine while I was away at school. That's the only time in my life when I've been terribly unhappy.

My mother influenced all three of us to go to college. She worked as a librarian and in book stores, and we had a tremendous collection of books at home. My father too was concerned that we do well in school. He was very conscious of the fact that he lacked an education. I decided to be a doctor as soon as I got over wanting to play professional baseball, which was around the age of ten. To study medicine wasn't difficult financially because I'm what is known as "geographical distribution." Eastern colleges like to have someone from states like Oregon in the student body, and therefore I received a very expensive education that didn't cost me a penny until my final year of medical school, when I had to put up $428. My spending money came from summer jobs in logging camps, on railroads, at dude ranches. It was heavy work but it appealed to me, and I look back on it nostalgically as a lot of fun. I still thrive on the kind of hard physical work my father did. I enjoyed renovating our home myself recently.

When I was eighteen years old, I came East and started at Columbia. New York City was a hell of a cultural shock for someone who had never been east of Idaho. The size of the city and the pace of it frightened me. I was a long time figuring out the subways. Together with that, the academic demands were another shock. I'd never had to work very hard in school to get high grades. I quickly realized that I couldn't coast any more. I would have to work to succeed.

I received a B.A. in liberal arts, began additional work for an M.A. in history and then entered medical school. It was another jolt. The vocabulary is different, the environment is different, the people who teach you are different from the teachers you've ever had before. In the first four years you get exposed to each of the specialties and everyone is very enthusiastic. While we were learning about pediatrics, we all wanted to be pediatricians, during hematology

21

everyone wanted to be a hemotologist, then an obstetrician, then a child psychiatrist.

I spent about six months flirting with the idea of being a neurologist and then thought of becoming a chest surgeon. Following that I wavered between psychiatry and internal medicine and finally decided on the latter. There are sub-specialties within internal medicine, such as gastro-enterology or hematology, and I chose endocrinology.

By this time, my brothers had followed me to Columbia also benefiting from "geographical distribution." My middle brother, Gary, majored in political science and got a Master's in sociology before he went into the Peace Corps. He speaks fluent Russian and Spanish and now lives in a commune in Upstate New York. My youngest brother, Gale, got an MBA, a Master's in Business Administration, went into the Peace Corps and is presently working for Odyssey in our Great Neck storefront. We are even closer now than when we were children; we love each other.

Barbara and I were married at the beginning of my senior year in college. She had left college in Ohio moving to New York on exactly the same day I arrived here to begin at Columbia. Between my freshman and sophomore year, my roommate and I sublet our apartment for the summer to Barbara and four other girls. However, he had made all the arrangements. I would never have met Barbara except that I had to return three weeks before the fall semester began to take a re-examination, having flunked organic chemistry. I moved in with all the girls. Barbara and I went together for two years and then did a smart thing: We married.

Neither of us planned on an early marriage. We were seeing one another often, enjoying each other and discovering a number of mutual interests. After a while we realized that we loved each other. Mutuality is important to us both, but we were always aware that we were able to be independent of one another as well. I had always wondered how I would propose, but as it turned out, I never did. It seemed a natural process one day to call her parents to tell them that we were going to be married.

We had a delightful first year of marriage with plenty of time to spend together. It was fortunate that we did have that leisurely first year because once I started medical school—at Columbia University's College of Physicians and Surgeons—we didn't see much of one another for the next eight years.

You can't warn anyone about what it's like to be married to a medical student or intern. No matter how much I told Barbara about how often she would be alone, it still came as a brutal shock. Barbara and I survived it partly because we'd had that good first year and partly because Barbara enjoyed her work. She had been to design school and was a showroom model. She was successful and well paid. She became a buyer for a chain of department stores and traveled as a result. She did so well that once there was an article about her in *Women's Wear Daily*.

In 1968, while I was deciding whether to take a second-year residency, I got my draft call. It was time to pay back my student deferment. Many physicians take a different position, and I have no quarrel with them, but I didn't fight it because I reasoned that as long as I wasn't asked to kill anyone I couldn't ethically withhold my services. I was assigned to the Marine Corps and ordered to report to Camp Lejeune.

They discovered as soon as I arrived at the camp that I had tuberculosis, most likely contracted at Bellevue Hospital where I had done my training. I was deferred for treatment to be recalled when cured. I spent ten days in the hospital and six months recuperating. I am still taking medication.

Barbara had quit her job to go with me, and our ties with New York had been severed. When we returned we were lucky to get our former apartment back. I started back to work on my Fellowship. After eight years of marriage we decided it would be a good time to have a baby. Barbara opened a boutique about the same time she became pregnant. We were living in New York the way you should, mixing with a variety of people and dining often in restaurants. My friends were almost all in medicine, but Barbara knew creative people who were designers, painters, architects, dancers. Our life style didn't change even with the birth of our son, Alexander. We still frequently dine out. Occasionally, when I come home at midnight, we go out somewhere to have a drink together or just a piece of pizza. We enjoy one another's company and we can talk for hours.

Odyssey consumes time. There is the ordinary work load of a doctor who is Director of an agency with five full-time doctors, twenty doctors on a part-time basis and ten nurses in his charge. There are administrative responsibilities and meetings, such as the Tuesday Executive Staff meetings that can run until midnight. I also run a special group that meets twice a week, at night. Barbara gets annoyed every now and then when I'm not at home when she expected me. I think that happens in most households. The time we do have together is all the more valued and appreciated because it's hard to come by. Sometimes I get away from the pressure, and everyone understands, and have lunch with her or spend part of an afternoon playing with the baby.

I didn't want to be a businessman, or a lawyer, or a real estate broker, or write for a newspaper, or be an accountant, but at Odyssey I'm learning to do a bit of all those things. I forced myself one time to stay up for eighteen hours learning how to read account ledgers. If you have to know law, I've discovered that what you do is teach yourself some law. If you have to be a policeman, you'll learn to function like a policeman. You find you do a great many more things than you thought you could, and feel much better about yourself in the process.

I'm asked sometimes how I feel about working co-operatively with ex-addict staff. The question surprises me. I problem-solve, Jimmy Murphy problem-solves, we problem-solve together. I don't think of him as an ex-addict anyway. To me, he's a very accomplished, gifted person who overcame some psychopathology, just as I overcame tuberculosis. There is not much difference.

POSTSCRIPT FROM JUDI
ABOUT CHARLIE ROHRS

My first real memory of Charlie is simply of his being there and my being grateful that I now had a medical person I could depend upon. There isn't any particular incident I recall during those months that he worked part time at Odyssey, beyond the fact that I was aware he was well qualified, had a good sense of responsibility and was trustworthy.

When I think of my early impressions of Charlie, there are two that come to mind. The first was during the probe of Randi Stewart when we asked Randi to choose whether he would be a female or a male. It was impossible for Randi to continue in the Odyssey community without a sexual identity. He had both breasts and a penis.

Randi had been born male, but he took the first steps to becoming female by having hormone shots which caused breast development and testicular atrophy. However, he did not complete the process.

He was an endless source of difficulty to the community since we were obliged to make decisions about with whom he showered and where he slept. He wanted to sleep and dress with the women and urinate with the men. He had to choose which sex to be because none of us could relate to him otherwise.

It was my opinion as a psychiatrist that he had the right to choose either sex regardless of his genotype. Charlie was adamant that what you're born you stay. On no level could he understand a man wanting to have his penis and testes removed. I informed Charlie that if Randi so chose, it would be Charlie's responsibility to arrange for the operation and to maintain Randi on female hormones so long as he remained at Odyssey. Charlie told me that he would wait to see the outcome of the probe, but if Randi chose to be female, he might have to resign on an issue of integrity. He summed up his feelings with the statement, "No man in his right mind would want to be a woman."

Charlie isn't hostile to women. His remark was a natural spontaneous thing. My Husband, Michael, joined the Odyssey doctors in a group discussion. He informed us that he had autopsied a number of sex-changed individuals who had committed suicide. To his surprise the pathologist may discover in the middle of the autopsy that the person he thought was a female had begun life as a male. In fact, many of these unfortunate people work as prostitutes, and the men dating them don't know it either. Apparently their problems are not solved by the symptom-relief of hormone taking. As with addicts, it appears that one must treat the underlying problems.

Fortunately for Odyssey, the difference of opinion between Charlie and me never came to issue. Randi preferred to remain in the "nether-nether" land of sexual confusion. He decided to remain female-appearing—a drag queen—while strapping down his penis. Randi was discharged, but he has returned many times with a group of five friends in a similar predicament. He has asked us to open a special therapeutic community for transvestites and transsexuals. Someday we will tackle this problem.

I liked Charlie for his integrity in that situation. One of the basic tenets of Odyssey is that even if you disagree with the top, you follow the order, unless it is an issue of integrity. In that case, you first inform the authority, who may reverse the decision. If the authority does not, you resign rather than destroy what another has built. Charlie disagreed with me, but he was willing to be part of the probe and learn. He felt he might receive new data to enable him to make his decision.

It is the only time in our many years of close professional association that Charlie and I have ever had a clash of integrity. We have been able to agree on everything else, which perhaps is one of the basic strengths of Odyssey.

The other incident involving Charlie that I remember is when I sent an Italian-American patient to him for examination. The patient

Group session. Charlie Rohrs is second from right.

had said in group that his penis was less than an inch long, even when erect. I assumed that this was a delusion, part of his schizophrenia, because he had fathered four children, but stranger things have happened. I thought it would be better if Charlie examined him rather than I. I sent Charlie a note reporting that the patient had complained that his wee-wee was very wee. Would Charlie please advise?

Charlie came to me afterwards, sheepish but very concerned. "I think I've done something very wrong," he said. "I've gone beyond my expertise. Could you interpret whether what I did was right?"

He said he had taken a look at the patient's penis and that it was a normal size. However the patient was so pathetic and so insistent that it was small that Charlie wanted to reassure him. He dropped his pants to show him that he was no different. "Look," he said to the patient. "We're just the same!"

I agreed with his after-thought that his spontaneous impulse was wrong psychiatrically for a number of reasons. The patient, for instance, might have construed it as a sexual attack. But from the human point of view, from the soul point of view, I said to myself that

Barbara, Alexander and Charlie Rohrs.

this was one of the nicest men I'd met in a long time. It was such an uninhibited, generous act.

Charlie and I are amazed that we have come to think alike on so many issues, he from a long-time Democratic workingman's home and I from several generations of wealthy Republicans, he from Oregon and I from New York. He observes that he's a liberal Democrat and I'm a conservative Republican, and yet we come to the same conclusions on almost everything. We have been called Jeffersonian Libertarians. On humanitarian issues there is no difference. We're physicians who listen to the patients' need without allowing political ideology to get in the way.

Attendance:

Louis Sarra	Eugene Pryor	Josette Fils-Aime
Neil Kitagawa	Willie Ross	Joe Forcinito
Charlie Canizio	Arto Woods	Mary Jo Ford
Margaret Ward	Yvonne Cox	Patrick Royster
Kathie Price	Jerry Meyer	Henry Berry
Erica Novsam	Ralph DeLucia	Peter Terry
José Colon	Marty Blaustein	Bob Fernandez

6TH STREET LEVEL III'S

Nothing extraordinary with the IIIs; very little to report.

Yvonne feels that W.T. should not go out on pass alone unless she is going home; she will receive a job change.

L.C. is functioning very well.

12TH STREET LEVEL III'S

Charlie said that V.A. has feelings for J.S. that appear to be an infatuation.

S.H. is questioning why she has been a III so long (10½ months). She is wondering what is holding her back. The group consensus expressed their feeling about her attitude as the main fetter to her moving.

G.R. having just become a Level III, is having his problems. Having been a Level II in Exterior Maintenance and now moving to III in Exterior Maintenance has not been much of a difference to him. He still is identifying with his old peer group and finds it hard to delegate. He is in need of teaching and some direction. G. also needs to have demands placed on him.

It was brought up by Josette that B.B., C.A., J.W., R.R. and B.L. are still playing "tit-for-tat"—acting out on each other in a "playful" manner. However, it has gotten to the point where C.A. is getting fed up with this game and is very uptight especially about B.B. and R.R. touching him. It should be noted that B.B. is a homosexual and J.W. a latent homosexual with one experience. Giving rise to the suspicion that this might be a sexual acting out. This problem will be taken up in group.

Other Changes—R.E. is moved to procurement.

R.R. is moved to housekeeping.

A.B. will get a sponsored probe.

D.Z. will get a confrontation probe.

12TH STREET I'S

Nothing spectacular to report except that M.J. was moved to Level II.

12TH STREET II'S

L.C. needs a lot of work with relating to people. He has been moved to Assistant Head of Maintenance.

R.G. wants to know if he could visit his sister in jail or at least write her. Arto will present this in Assistant Administrators meeting tomorrow. Louis later said no on this question since his sister is negative. R. is also unhappy with his job function. He says he is constantly out of the house.

6TH STREET LEVEL II'S

R.B.—Joe feels that R. is very slow and should be tested. Ralph has noticed his extreme defensiveness and sarcasm when confronted.

W.L.—Joe feels he is doing better in Exterior Maintenance, but W. is still not felt in the house.

No 6th Street Level II is at present ready to move.

Bob Fernandez had to leave the meeting early and asked the group how they felt about his request for J.S. to move to New Jersey. No objections were raised and he is moved.

Arto proposed F.L. for III. Objections were raised from Josette, Erica, Joe, Ralph, Willie, Henry and Yvonne. From the subsequent discussion, it was decided that we would wait till next Monday when he will be re-evaluated. In the meantime, F. will be moved to Assistant Head of Kitchen, where he will be given more pressure.

All Level IIs will get their responsibilities back.

6TH STREET I'S

J.G. finally is proposed for Level II and is unanimously approved by the group.

No other moves were made.

J.S. was discussed. He has a big attitude problem and continues to be very negative. He had been given an additional awareness for not completing the original one he had. It was decided that we would lift his awareness and try another dynamic.

The Executive Staff Meets and Meets, and Meets and Meets

Of the Odyssey staff of 140, the top executives from the three Eastern Seaboard states meet on Tuesdays. During the spring and summer of 1971 the meetings were attended by: Judianne Densen-Gerber, J.D., M.D., Executive Director; James P. Murphy, Director; Charles C. Rohrs, M.D., Director; Frederick Cohen, Associate Director, Executive Division; Louis Sarra, Associate Director, Treatment Division; Rowen Hochstedler, M.D., Associate Director, Medical Services; René Casaclang, Associate Director, Community Education and Information; Matthew Ancona, Associate Director, Re-entry; John Cox, Assistant Director, Development Services; Robert Smith, Assistant Director, Special Programs; Richard Klein, LL.B., Assistant Director, Legal Services; Donald Dougherty, Assistant Director, Public Information; Lew Garely, Assistant Director for New Jersey; Thomas Scott, M.D., Administrator, Medical Services; David Winters, Assistant Director, Community Services; David Sandberg, Administrator, New Hampshire; Carol Sarra, Secretary.

APRIL 27, 1971

John Cox and Rowen Hochstedler had been in Mobile, Alabama, to investigate that community's request for the establishment of a branch of Odyssey House there. Coxy prepared the budget, $200,000 a year for a forty-resident house, but his presence in Mobile also served a less direct purpose. Coxy is a Black; I wanted Mobile to be aware that Odyssey is militantly integrationist, not only in its residents but throughout its staffing, including the top executives. Rowen went to Mobile to be a bridge to professionals in the city.

At roughly 10 A.M. the Executive Staff meeting had its usual lazy start with some people pouring themselves coffee from a battered outsized percolator, others using several of the five telephones scattered around the office, Dave Winters making cheery comments about Louie Sarra's new checked shirt.

Coxy was sitting on a lounge chair, his feet up, telling Jimmy Murphy that the Mobile committee had difficulty comprehending a fully integrated program with Blacks in authority. Kayser mills are integrated, he explained, but Blacks hold only the lower jobs. "It was the first time some of those middle-class Whites had ever talked to a Black on an equal basis," he said.

Lew Garely, a big, jovial man who runs Odyssey in New Jersey, came in and called to Cox, "How was Alabama? You look a little pale."

"I *felt* a little pale down there," drawled Cox.

While there would be no government money available in Mobile for Odyssey, Rowen didn't think funding would be a problem. Somberly dressed and mild spoken, the Mennonite doctor looked worried. "The attitude of the community bothers me," he said. "It wouldn't surprise me too much if Odyssey went down there with an integrated program and got bombed out. The more isolated the project, the more danger."

Cox confirmed this. "It's a real shaky community," he agreed. "When integration came they set up these private clubs—they've got *millions* of private clubs."

"And there's a real problem among the physicians," added Rowen. "They just don't accept the idea that the community at large must take care of citizens who cannot take care of themselves."

Louie mentioned the Mother House marathon that would be starting at midnight. Bob Smith, sprawled loose-jointedly on a straight chair, worried that there were not enough bridges. "You need more Level IIs and IIIs in there," he told Louie. "The lower Levels are so full of fear, they don't know where you're coming from."

Charlie Rohrs stood up and stretched. "My feeling is that the Mother House is just one angry act after another."

Louie was disturbed. "I don't want a fear marathon," he said. "You don't change attitudes with fear."

A small quantity of what we thought was heroin had been found in the 18th Street facility. It had been turned in by a fourteen-year-old resident, who said it was in his drawer and he didn't know how it got there. Louie was excited, his arms flailing out, words jammed together. It was unthinkable to him that a former drug user would stash heroin and not use it.

"If I'd been in this program a short time and I had a stash, I'd be going out of my mind," he said. "I don't see how those kids can have it stashed there for a month, or whatever. It can't be done, psychologically."

"I can't understand them not using it either," I remarked. "But I have known kids to give heroin to someone else. There was Carlton who shot up his rabbit to see what would happen when the animal got high. No adult addict would waste heroin on a rabbit, would he?"

There was amused agreement that it was unlikely. Louie was not so sure. "Well, I don't know," he grinned. "If you've got enough . . ."

"I just can't picture someone with a stash not using," I continued. "People who use drugs, *use drugs!*"

But the urines tested in 18th Street were clean.

"Louie," I teased, "is it possible to beat the urine test?"

We exchanged smiles, remembering. "Sure," he responded. "You get someone to piss for you."

I brooded over the possibility that someone had found a way to beat the test, tight as it is at Odyssey House. Ever since Louie got someone to urinate for him, we have insisted on a direct witness whenever urine is collected. "There was one addict on a methadone maintenance program who used to void and then inject someone else's urine through his abdomen into the bladder, so he could urinate clean," I informed the meeting. "There *are* ways of beating it."

Charlie Rohrs thought the hiding and finding of the heroin might be part of the adolescent rebellion. "I can see a fourteen- or fifteen-year-old angry at the staff and doing something like that. It's like pulling a fire alarm."

Dave Winters nodded vigorously. "Or like writing on the wall *Fuck the Marathon.*"

"That's a good possibility," I agreed. "Some of these kids have backgrounds that would make you shudder. There are many totally deprived children. They need emotional love and closeness, and we have to give it to them. And they have to test us."

Fred Cohen was standing with a coffee cup in his hand. "I don't think it matters to an adolescent what the quality of the closeness is. Any sign of closeness is enough. The security and safety of the Odyssey facility is sufficient for them. They don't need it to be a warm type of relating facility."

"Most of them are there because they have to be," Louie reminded Fred. "They're there under some sort of court hold or parental threat."

"Normal adolescence is yearning for a healthy sense of belonging," I commented, sorting memos, splindling some and putting too few in the wastebasket. "They're in identity crisis and they're in great pain. Adolescence is that time in human development of greatest pain, even in those who are fortunate.

"The first group of adolescents in Odyssey had severe difficulties," I recalled. "But they were able to make positive commitments. There was yearning there."

I considered the possibility that the problem at 18th Street might stem from the presence of a small negative group with a hold over the other kids. "Maybe we just haven't found the negative leader," I suggested.

I looked at Louie. "The same thing happened when we were all at Met," I reminded him. "Rosado and the others never used drugs from the day they were admitted. They waited around for a positive ex-addict leader to develop whom they could follow. They themselves were too weak to be leaders. But they never were involved in all the negative nonsense you were doing. They wanted to get well. They believed I might become strong enough to begin a meaningful program if I could find the right ex-addict. And they waited, some of them for a whole year. There was no indication that anything good would come of it, or that a leader would emerge, or that I could do it."

"Sheer desperation," Fred commented.

We would have to find the negative leader among the adolescents in 18th Street, shape him up or ship him out. I was reading and signing letters. "Actually what I did at Met was to bring in the world's biggest bully, Enriquez. Tony came in to bully in a positive direction. Then Murphy developed. Now he knows how to bully." Jimmy grinned at me.

We discussed a number of suggestions for improving the adolescent program. Matty Ancona had an idea about house parents, two people from each Level who would do their normal jobs elsewhere in Odyssey during the day but who would return to 18th Street at night and sleep there, as working parents do. I suggested we should move all the adolescents together, pulling in those who were now scattered in other facilities. Carlton Martin, a Level IV who had graduated the adolescent unit and relates well to his peers, would return to work with them.

Rowen cleared his throat and said in his mild voice, "It's throwing bad money after bad money."

"Carlton's not bad money," I objected.

"No, no," Rowen explained. "I mean you're pouring in so much and nothing happens, or it gets worse, so you pour in more. We need new ideas."

I disagreed. "Maybe we poured in a single individual and were demanding too much of that individual, and therefore he failed. There's a depressive reaction to failure. If it's a shared failure, like a shared success, it's not so bad.

"Maybe we should pull the adolescents out of the Third Avenue storefront, out of Great Neck, out of every other place. Take them to live in the Adolescent Treatment Unit and see what they do. See who is picked as a role model. Let the adolescents experience the texture of each other."

I opened a letter from a woman who had volunteered to work with the Girls' House in the Bronx on a poetry therapy experiment. She was subsequently hired. It started me thinking in another direction.

DREAMWALKING

to something new/we touch
25 foot HIGH
Ice Bag in American museum/bumping
into Hide & Seek/up Pavel
Tschelitchew's TREE OF LIFE
& HEY
Pavel/did you ever imagine 20 of us
stretching across your canvas
into allegory/into universe/into us
on the last day of June
                    DREAMWALKING
into your TREE OF LIFE
smack into sanctuary/smack into
Armstrong's last trumpet solo
on Avenues of Straight Ahead
I appear as guide
with children for awhile/LOOSE

at my side/LOOSE outside
the big public eye/LOOSE
like jazz notes in blood & chemistry
of Puerto Rico/Congo/Indian
tribe/Native Land/USA like
jazz notes parachuting
rainbows/crying out
no tears
           DREAMWALKING
to something new/I am disturbed
with their memory of cocaine
with their misspelling of love
with their wondering who they are
with their look at Hell
in nightmares of syringe & needle
in nightmares of pimps & politicians
starting on Jump Street
like deer crossing/DAZED
in games of "dope is big business"
in games that chloroform their minds
in opium mist & breakneck speed
jiving/jigging/flagging
assaulted
in swivel chairs/in reports & reports
in a world of witnesses
in the karate chop of who cares
about children/HURT
in shooting galleries of lobotomy
where the pure forms of childhood
collapse
DREAMWALKING
           through lunch hour of executives
           through lunch hour of secretaries
           through lunch hour of messengers
up against glass city/blocking sky
           & What's your birth sign?
past Madison/Park/New York City
never noticing us/released
from heroin/EXHAUSTED
with the weight of unspeakable
infection/we pass
no time of day/never noticing

the weather on the last
day of June
                    DREAMWALKING
to something new
at 2 in the afternoon/we touch
25 foot HIGH
Ice Bag/USA/in brushstrokes brighter
than red/Marilyn Monroe parts
her lips/suicide/near families
coming out of stone/surprised
with Marisol/larger than life
marble woman/down
at the wading pool/her hand
half in/half out of it
on the edge in a courtyard
off 5th Avenue
                    DREAMWALKING
with 20 children
inside of me/retching Hollywood
Love Story/MYTH
where I appear as guide/STUMBLING
with teenage baby faces/SMACK
into your TREE OF LIFE/Pavel
healing us/for a moment/all magic
leaves/tumbling/popping newborn
SHOCK before our eyes
                    DREAMWALKING
to something new
at 3 in the afternoon/bumping
into angels & apostles/we hold
to each other like new thought
carved in silence
at the corner Cathedral of St. Thomas
for a moment/in the crush
of our loneliness/& TRUTH is
a family/holding on/for a moment
to love/love/love.

                              for Judi—
                              RUTH LISA SCHECHTER
                              June 1971
                              Odyssey House, New York City

"Are we giving the residents beauty?" I asked. "How much are we working on developing what is healthy in the children and how much are we concentrating on what is their pathology?"

Louie was intrigued. "What was important, Louie, in the initial program," I observed, "was the constant emphasis on health, on building. Now what building blocks are we giving these kids for a good life? What are we showing them that is beautiful?"

I polled the room, asking what each of us did in adolescence that was gratifying. For me it was reading poetry, Kahlil Gilbran in particular; Charlie Rohrs enjoyed scouting and remembered the television program "Omnibus"; René Casaclang, who came to Odyssey from the Philippines under a U. S. State Department grant, liked sports. John Cox grinned when it was his turn. "At sixteen," he told us, "I was strung out." We laughed.

I thought about it. "Do we need therapy at all?"

"Just what I was thinking," Rowen commented.

"Beauty therapy could enrich the whole agency," Louie said. "Kids get on the point in a group, and they don't know what their problem is. You ask them about their problems and they just . . ." He gave an exaggerated shrug.

"Their problem is that they don't know how to be adults," I declared. "That's a normal problem for the adolescent."

Louie beamed. "Quite a few adults have the same problem."

We'd been working for three hours. Lunch was brought in on trays: a tomato and macaroni dish, salad, buttered bread and cake. We served ourselves. The discussion turned into a major overhaul of the adolescent treatment program.

"Let's change all the therapy to exploring what is and what is not meaningful," I said, pushing aside my plate. "For example, what did we experience today? How does it enable us to grow? Therapy should be limited to that. There shouldn't be extensive aggression such as there is in the usual encounter groups nor deep exploration such as there is in traditional therapy. Even though it meets the therapist's needs, the kids can't tolerate deep therapy. It makes them sicker."

Rowen agreed and added, "There should be less pouring out of their guts."

"Why shouldn't kids do that?" I cried, slapping my desk. "Kids are *all guts!*"

"Yeah," said Louie. "They sit in group and they get badgered. *You're not telling us about your problems, you're not giving!* They get confused because everyone is coming at them from different directions, and they don't know what the hell's going on."

The solution was coming through. I said, "They're too young for analysis, even in group."

Louie approved of that, his blue eyes thoughtful under his long forward-combed gray hair. "When a kid relates to you that his father chained him to the radiator, how can you analyze that away?"

I related a time when my Husband had spent an hour or two trying to explain to a resident that he, Michael, had no need to hit me in the teeth when we have a dispute. A healthy individual does not have the need to subjugate the female that way. The resident was truly amazed. He'd never seen a relationship between a man and woman in which physical force was not the determining factor.

"They need more explanations like that, adults showing them a good relationship and how it works," Louie agreed. "And more hobbies . . ."

"But only if the hobbies and recreation are used therapeutically, and not for busy work, not to keep them occupied," I warned. "Which is what it can easily become." I remembered the time at Met Hospital when we sent the patients to occupational therapy to make collages. They got high on the glue.

I turned to Rowen. "Your staff is going to have to share in the process. They'll have to share themselves in order to provide real examples to follow." Rowen nodded.

We ended up accepting all the suggestions. It was much easier than having to decide between them. "We'll do it all at once," I said, "rather than do a consecutive research project to find out which method works.

"We will bring the adolescents together, attempt to find the negative group leader, provide the house parents Matty had recommended, dump the traditional therapy, inject some beauty, and ask the staff to interact closely with the kids to provide them with a picture of healthy adult behavior."

"How long will we do this?" asked Fred.

"Until we see what happens," I decided. "We can evaluate it in a few weeks."

And what about the heroin? Rowen asked if the 18th Street house should be searched to see if more drugs had been concealed.

"No," I said. "Let them work it out."

We don't search for drugs as a rule so long as the urines test clean. Our concern is whether or not the residents use drugs, which shows up on urine screening.

We learned several days later that Charlie Rohrs had been right. It *was* an adolescent prank. The "heroin" turned out to be talcum powder.

Some members of the Italian-American community had approached Odyssey to start a storefront in the Coney Island area. I was pleased. There's nothing in the Odyssey program that is in conflict with the strong Italian family style. We teach residents to respect their parents, to make peace with them, but to live their own lives. When I worked with addicts at Metropolitan Hospital, a few of the Italian-American patients were members of Mafia Families.

Louie Sarra, who spent half his life working with the Mafia, was explaining that drugs horrified the Families when some of their own children became addicted. "Drugs are the worst disgrace," he said. "When their kids started using drugs, it was the worst thing."

I told the story of Sammy No Legs who walked on bilateral prostheses—two artificial legs—after his own were severed while he was sitting on the edge of a subway platform too stoned on barbiturates to care that the train was coming. After the accident Sammy was a drug dealer, stashing his drugs in his wooden legs, in places he had specially hollowed out. He frequently was admitted into Met that way, loaded with drugs, to sell to the patients.

I made him angry one day when I refused to give him a prescription for drugs. A little later, I was writing at my desk and I heard breathing behind me. It was Sammy No Legs, stoned out of his mind. He put his hands around my throat and started to choke me. Fortunately, one of the patients heard the scuffle and came to my rescue.

That patient was one of the most handsome Italian men I have ever seen. He had a girl friend who supported him and who liked to scratch him during sexual play. One time we had to admit him to the hospital for loss of blood from the scratches.

"A gorgeous girl!" I recalled. "She just had this need to scratch! Those were the days of the great patients, remember Louie?" Louie, hand clutching his forehead, shook his head.

No Legs left the hospital but said he'd be waiting for me in the parking lot. I called a Mafia member who had sent me one of his sons to treat. He also sent me fresh cannolis each week. I told him what had happened. He offered protection. They came immediately and found No Legs in the parking lot. They told him he was never again to make me afraid. I never saw No Legs after that. He's probably living in fear that if I ever get hurt, he's dead.

Louie said, "It's good to have connections. But it's not like the old days. Breaking heads don't do it no more. Everything's changing."

Executive Staff meeting.

Coffee and doughnuts were waiting for the first arrivals: Matty Ancona, looking pale and worried in a striped sports jacket; Lew Garely from New Jersey, big, rumpled and talking in a rush of deeply felt unfinished sentences about Vietnam addiction; and Donald Dougherty, describing in an educated Eastern accent the most recent Odyssey art gallery opening.

Jimmy Murphy arrived, wearing a custom-tailored blue blazer over a white turtleneck sweater and gray flannels. He removed the jacket and folded it carefully, with the paisley silk lining on the outside. Dave Winters came in, noted that the room was too warm, and aggressively punched on the air conditioner.

The wide black couch was filled, Louie almost flat on his back with a pillow folded under his head, Matty sitting erect and tidy beside him, John Cox in crisply clean blue shirt and pants lounging beside him. Lew Garely squeezed himself between Matty and John.

Louie was complaining about the Girls' House in South Bronx. "I don't really know what's going on there," he said, his voice rising. "It seems to me they just run rampant. Everybody's running around like maniacs. It's like one of those old-type films where they speed it up and everybody's running. That's what it looks like."

"Tell me," asked Jimmy, "what does the staff do when they go up there at night on duty?"

Louie looked baffled. "I don't know what the staff does. I listen to them in staff meeting; they claim they're always doing something —they got girls' group and this group and that group, but I don't know what's going on."

"So what are you going to do? Are you afraid of them or what?" said Jimmy.

"I'm not afraid of them," Louie answered indignantly, sitting up.

"I think you are," Jimmy told him. "I think you really are."

"It's easy, sitting here," Louie protested, "but you go up there with twenty broads running around, maniacs!"

"What will happen when you have a daughter?" Lew Garely asked with a wide smile.

Louie looked at him through his hair. "I'm going to have one daughter. I'm not going to have twenty."

I asked, "How are things going with New Hampshire?" Finally we were opening in Hampton, after one of the most remarkable funding campaigns in Odyssey's history. Forty per cent of the population of the state contributed. The average income in New Hampshire is $3,100 a year, so there was considerable sacrifice involved. The citizens did it by putting up highway billboards asking for Odyssey House support, sponsoring Boy Scouts walkathons, holding public meetings. On the eve of a long-delayed opening of the Odyssey facility, Hampton had planned a Town Meeting.

Simultaneously, while they filled me in on New Hampshire, I was checking the chart of the new lines of authority and the new proposal for the Department of Defense on Vietnam addiction— Seymour Domaclang had been up all night preparing them. David Sandberg, blond and tanned, was describing the arrangements for New Hampshire.

I listened. "We should bring residents and staff up there ahead of the Town Meeting," I decided, when he had finished. "Bob Smith can drive them up. He can play the token Black." Bob grinned at me, standing by the coffee table about to pour himself a soft drink.

Sandberg said what little opposition to Odyssey that still remained in the town, represented chiefly by a member of the school board who lived across the street from the Odyssey residence, would be evidenced at the meeting. It was being offset by the enthusiasm of the Hampton Selectmen, who had visited Odyssey in New York and returned home greatly impressed. "A whole week in June has been declared Odyssey Week in New Hampshire by the Governor," he told us.

I instructed Dave, "Get as much press coverage for our four staff members as possible. Bob Smith, you give them your life history, how thrilled you are to be coming to New Hampshire. You're a corn-fed North Carolina boy, right? You're so glad to be in the fresh air after New York City."

Smith's wide grin split his face. "It's going to be easy to do," he said in his summertime-and-the-living-is-easy drawl.

Smith attended college in North Carolina where he participated in pipe-bombings. Lithe and startlingly handsome, he was once a bodyguard to Stokley Carmichael. His father is a New Jersey police-man who held a gun to Bob's head, giving him the choice of death or going to Odyssey for treatment. Bob believed that he might pull the trigger. He came to us. That's true existential choice.

"I have an idea for that Town Meeting," I announced, folding up the military addiction proposal with a margin note for a change or two. "Let's publicize that everyone who comes to the meeting should bring one can of food as an admission fee. Peas, soup, any-thing. When you go on the radio, Bob, tell them that."

Louie found the idea hilarious and was collapsed, murmuring, "Eats, chickens, livestock—Judi, you're too much."

"Suppose people come without a can," I wondered, starting to eat. "How can we manage that?"

I thought about it. "Hmm. Bob, when you're up there go to the local supermarket and ask them to provide you with a box or two on loan. You'll pay for it later. Get mushroom soup, that's twenty-nine cents a can, or something like that. If anyone comes without a can they must buy one can to get in. That's easy. There's no one who can't pay twenty-nine cents admission."

"How about Mother's Chicken Matzo Ball Soup?" suggested Fred.

"Chicken with stars," offered Coxy.

"Minestrone," shouted Louie.

"Tomato is nice," Lew Garely said.

"It should be chowder," Murphy added.

We were having a good time. "Any can of soup," I told Bob, "even vichyssoise. It fits with our nitty-gritty poverty."

It was late afternoon when the dispute concerning the Odyssey nursery was raised. I had been fuming for days. The nursery is used by the pre-school children of the staff. The fee is adjusted according to income. Doctors Rohrs and Hochstedler have their sons there and pay the most, while other Odyssey employees pay less. Three female graduates of the program, Susan Dabney, LaVerne Whitfield and

Odyssey nursery. Alexander Rohrs is in foreground.

Yvonne Pierce, who was soon to marry John Cox, had had their children in the nursery since Level IV, but after they became salaried they did not increase their payments for nursery care. Angela Green, the nurse in charge of the nursery, claimed that they knew they should be paying more. The women said they had never been told about the increase. When I found this out, I was extremely angry.

I made it quite clear at the staff meeting why I was furious. "I like people who pay their bills," I said, cold and angry. "I don't like the feeling that people are with me because of my money. I feel personally that if I have to put any money into Odyssey—and this is an obsession with me—it would mean that my work wasn't valuable enough to stand on its own. I am here because I'm a psychiatrist, not because I have money to sustain the program.

"Candidates-out should be here as equals, paying their way, not taking advantage of the agency. This is a very sensitive area for me, feeling that I'm being taken advantage of financially," I said to the group.

I am equally incensed by capable, able-bodied people accepting welfare. The government should provide jobs for them, not subsidies.

There was a long, miserable silence. No one wanted to speak.

"I mean it's bad," I added, nervously twisting paper clips in a chain. "I'm smoking with anger."

Someone observed that Angela is very devoted to the agency and should be forgiven a mistake.

"She's not a patient," Bob Smith glowered. There was another dismal silence.

Dave Winters said, loudly and suddenly, "We've got to get a little rational, man, and tighten our belts. We can't let personal feelings get into play. I'm all for law and order, baby." He made me laugh, which relieved the tension. "The staff lives within the laws, they live within the fucking standards, *fine*. They got a job here. If they don't, get rid of them—across the board."

Rowen observed, with some rancor, "You've got one set of standards for the professionals and another for the ex-addicts."

John Cox was looking shocked and despairing, worried about Yvonne. No one knew for certain who would have to be fired.

"The thing is," Bob Smith said, slouched low, "Angela isn't a resident in treatment. She is supposed to be a responsible adult. If she doesn't function, she should be told about it."

"She's been here two years," I reminded them. I was in great pain, loving Angela as a sister. We've been through a lot together. I had met Angela when I was in the hospital with a septic thrombophlebitis of the right leg after walking barefoot while renovating my house.

I had stepped on a dirty nail. One night in the hospital, I didn't want to go to bed at lights out. I wanted to read. I told her to leave the sleeping medication ordered by the doctor on the night table. She refused to be intimidated by me and told me squarely to ring her when I was ready for sleep and she would return with the pills. I hired her for Odyssey shortly thereafter. She knew how to say "no" on important issues. At the same time, she had let Michael sneak the children in for a visit even against the rules because I missed them so much.

Angela is a big person, as I am, and we think of ourselves as the Scotties on the whiskey label, one black and one white. Jimmy Murphy was staring sadly into space. He has the same warm feelings about Angela. Two years is a very long time to be together at Odyssey.

Dinner arrived: pork chops, salad, rolls, pastries. Some decided they preferred to send out for pizzas or Chinese food.

There was talk of firing Angela.

"Everytime a professional fucks up," I commented, "Louis has profound anti-professional feelings of 'There they go again!' Right, Louie? Cop!"

Louie denied it. "No, I'm worried about her."

"I'm not talking about Angela," I interrupted irrationally. "Is it not true that when some yo-yo out there, one of our professional staff, fucks up, you get slightly anti-professional?"

"No," Louie insisted. "I get mad if *anyone* fucks up, but I'm a very tolerant person. Very tolerant." We all exchanged fond, skeptical smiles.

"Well," I said, stripping the case from a thin cigar and lighting it, "my feelings towards the ex-addicts at this moment are not good. I separate some of you in this room, but at the moment I am profoundly anti the ex-addict female, particularly one who is also a mother. If one shows up today needing my help she wouldn't stand a chance in holy hell." I was ready to transfer my hostility universally.

Dave Winters grinned. "There are ten in induction."

"What can I tell you?" I said, giving him a bleak smile. "My feelings are global. At one time or another, we all transfer feelings."

John Cox spoke in a taut voice, clearly having considered for a long time what he would say. "Judi, you have expressed attitudes here today that I don't understand. I would not react in that manner. I just wouldn't. It's just not me. I personally think that Angela is at great fault, and I want to out her on the spot."

"I agree," I said morosely, "I think Angela must speak for herself. My feelings are so bad . . ." I stubbed my cigar out, emptied the ashtray in my wastebasket. "I think that the decision should be made by all of you here. I don't think Jimmy or I can take part in any of it."

It is Odyssey policy that whenever someone in authority is emotionally involved, the decision-making must be turned over to somebody else.

Rowen looked up from his dinner. "We should send for Angela," he said.

Jimmy explained to John Cox that the failure of the ex-addicts to pay their bills indicated that "a great amount of dependency still hasn't been resolved." That was my concern exactly.

Angela arrived twenty minutes later as we were discussing a visit of Duke Ellington to the Odyssey facility in New Hampshire. He is a long-time member of our Board of Directors. She waited, a Black, huge, silent presence, breathing heavily, stunning in a dark red pant-suit and chunky gold jewelry.

We next heard Don Dougherty's report on his public relations activities. I listened to him while sorting through some memos and correspondence, giving some to Carol Rapetti, my secretary, a calm girl who retains her poise no matter how the work piles up. She was to be married within the month to Louie Sarra, and I love her. Angela sat motionless watching us.

It was around eight-thirty in the evening and dark outside when I announced, "This is the part of the meeting that Fred and Rowen will run. Jimmy and I will not run it." Angela shifted and Rowen began to explain what we had been saying about the nursery mess. I kept my attention on an order of blintzes and sour cream that had been delivered to my desk. I was feeding my pain.

Angela insisted that she had advised the three mothers to increase their payments.

I was unable to stay out of it. "Angela, what's happening? We repeat a story and you say it's something else. Are you trying to create bad feelings?"

Louie was full of rage, with characteristic suddenness. He shouted at her, "I'm not saying that you plan these things at night, you don't lie in bed figuring out how to set people up or how to hurt people. But I think you fuck up and then you manipulate to get out of it."

Dave said somberly, "And it's females with kids too. Everybody involved is a mother."

Louie, standing up and brandishing his arms, warned Angela not to start crying. She, sullen and affronted, said, "I'm not crying, and I won't cry."

I told Cox, "Call the girls up. Let's have everyone involved present." He picked up the telephone nearest him and made the calls. He reported a few minutes later that LaVerne's husband, Silas, had insisted on coming with her. They were on their way and so was Susan Dabney. Yvonne couldn't be located, but a message was being left.

Silas arrived with LaVerne and Susan around a quarter to ten. The room was so crowded there wasn't a chair left, but they squeezed themselves onto the sofa and lounge chair. Fred crisply told them what the crisis was about, making it clear that if they had deliberately cheated the agency, they probably would be fired.

As soon as Susan opened her mouth to say she didn't know about the increased fee, I knew where the truth lay. That was it. I *know* Susan Dabney. I was quiet while the argument went on among Susan, an intense, slim girl with a haughty face and close-cropped Afro hair, LaVerne, paler, small and wide-eyed with horn-rimmed glasses, and Angela, whose tone was strong and emphatic. After a while Yvonne came in and John Cox made a space for her beside him. Yvonne has a beautiful, elegant face and superb chic. In moments, she too was yelling.

I said deliberately, "I have never known Susan to be untruthful. Never. I have never known Susan to ask me for anything, or mooch, or try to get anything out of the agency. I've never seen Susan be dependent or make unfair demands."

By eleven-fifteen, we started to sort it out. Angela stopped defending herself and admitted it was possible that the three weren't aware of the fee increase. "I could not expect people to respect me, Angela," I told her coolly, "if in the light of all this I continued to protect you."

I sat with wet eyes as Fred lashed into her. "It raises many questions about our two years of experience and close association and trust," he said, among other things.

We all stared at objects—ashtrays, our shoes, dirty plates. She began haltingly, "I apologize . . . for my behavior. It was not done consciously, it was not done to hurt anybody . . . I only ask that forgiveness . . ." She broke down. "I can only ask each of you . . . if there is any way at this time . . . I can do anything to make amends."

LaVerne listened with tears running down her cheeks. We had turned off the air conditioner in order to hear one another better, and the room, consequently, was full of smoke and hot people wiping their foreheads with handkerchiefs.

Bob Smith exploded, glaring at Angela. "I can't see how she can stay when the others were about to be forced out. I can't see that.

That seems fucking unfair to me. I happen to be a fucking ex-addict. That's just where the fuck Black people are really at now." He was erect and quivering, his drawl gone. "When you look and see who's over there"—indicating LaVerne, Susan and Yvonne—"there's three Black females. You know that statement about every Brother is not a brother? You're fucking right! *Every Brother isn't a brother!*"

There was a long silence in which only Angela's sniffling could be heard. Matty Ancona, sitting on the windowsill to be closer to the cooler air, suggested mildly that she might remain at Odyssey but be demoted. This had happened twice to him. I asked Rowen what he wanted to do. Charlie Rohrs was away on a vacation in Yugoslavia and it was therefore Rowen's responsibility because she was a nurse and part of the medical staff.

Rowen thought for a long time, head down and face strained. He looked directly at her for a moment and said, "I don't see how you can stay, Angela. I don't see how you can stay."

Jimmy looked as though he was about to break down. I felt as he did. Two years of closeness was being destroyed.

"There is nothing we can do," I said quietly to him. "If we delegate, we have to accept the subsequent decisions. That's Odyssey at its hardest."

Angela said brokenly, "Will you please explain to me on what basis I can't stay?"

"If Rowen as your superior feels he cannot trust you, I cannot ask him to do it," I explained, keeping my voice under control. "Rowen has to feel secure." I was looking for some way to manipulate the group and turn the decision around.

"Rowen," Angela said, turning to him, "your decision is made on the basis of what . . . has happened . . . but I ask of you . . . in relation to the things I report to you as a nurse . . ."

Rowen said firmly, kindly, "There has never been a problem. There has never been a problem. You're an excellent nurse."

"So why can't I be a staff nurse in a facility?" she pleaded. Rowen explained, his face desolate, "One, you got yourself in a position where you played the top against the people under you, and, two, you were willing to let three people be fired." She cried bitterly. No one moved, except those fanning themselves with paper napkins.

It settled into a sad exchange, Angela huddled over her handkerchief stressing that her ability as a nurse still was useful to Odyssey, the others dispiritedly saying that the situation appeared hopeless. I had never wanted more to find a way out.

I said at last, "She has asked to be busted and start again, just as a resident would. I am at the mercy of this room."

"Busted?" said Dave Winters. "What does that mean?"

"The lowest rank she could be busted to is a nurse in a facility," I told him. "It's the lowest one."

Dave observed, looking at the others for support. "You know, she's actually sitting here pleading and . . ."

John Cox couldn't contain himself. "And so did I sit here today pleading! And I was all off the fucking wall! And how *she's* pleading. *I* was pleading, man!"

"What I'm trying to tell you," Dave said soothingly, 'is that she's pleading for another chance. She's willing to get busted, she's willing to start over. I think it would be very cruel, inhuman, not to give her a chance."

"I guess I was very angry," John conceded, accepting this.

"We were all very angry," I admitted. The room was reflective. Louie wondered what would have happened if there had been a stalemate, if Angela hadn't copped to her guilt and admitted that she had never informed them to pay more. At the time she had simply forgotten and later was embarrassed to admit it.

I said I never doubted where the truth was, once Susan began to speak. "I totally believed her. It's not factual, it's not based on admissible courtroom evidence, it's based on cumulative experience, how I have perceived Susan and Angela over long periods of time. In addition, Angela was constantly re-evaluating, reinterpreting and redefining every word she said, which made me begin to doubt. Then Susan's free-flowing anger convinced me."

"What would have happened if she didn't cop?" Louie persisted, looking tense.

"Out!" I said. "She'd be out! Because her defensiveness would have taken three jobs with it. I'm suggesting, knowing Angela, that the psychodynamics at the time when she felt threatened were that she thought of nothing but how to get out of it. I don't think anything occurred to her except she didn't want to look bad."

"Yeah," Louie agreed, subsiding. "I don't think she did it maliciously. She just got caught up . . ." Carol, his fiancée, smiled adoringly at him.

"She did keep saying that it wasn't Susan's fault, or LaVerne's or Yvonne's," I reminded him.

Louie nodded. "She tried not to hurt them. I saw that. She didn't want to hurt them."

"I don't think the girls' jobs were on the line because of her," I continued. "They were on the line because of the kind of person I am. Much of the hostility you all feel toward Angela should be directed at me. There's an important message here, which Jimmy has learned very well, Louie has learned very well, Matty has learned very well . . .'"

Jimmy spelled out, "M-O-N-E-Y" and I gave him an affectionate glance. "The lesson is that every leader has idiosyncrasies and you shouldn't cross them," I finished.

"Know when to keep quiet," Louie grinned.

"Yes," I said, getting another cigar. "Know when to keep quiet. That's part of getting along in the world. And I do give ample warning. I say, *beware!*"

I summed up the situation, noting that Rowen would still have to make the decision, but the discussion had clarified some points. "Certainly Angela and I are exceptionally close," I continued with sadness. "I assume that regardless of what Rowen decides, we'll have to create some distance." She was weeping noisily. "Probably there will be more distance if she continues to work here, less if she doesn't. Friendship is a long, difficult process."

It was one-thirty in the morning. Someone suggested that trials should be conducted this way, with everyone concerned thrashing it out before interested observers. I asked Rowen what he wanted to do.

He stared into his thoughts briefly, then said, "I want her to start over, at the bottom."

"Which house, the ATU?" I asked without expression. Rowen nodded.

"You start at the bottom, Angela," he said, his voice tired and compassionate. "You start at the bottom at the trust level too, with no money in the bank."

Angela asked, "Rowen, do you think I lied?"

He studied her. "No," he said at length. "I don't think you lied. But I'm not sure."

She bent her head and wept.

"Truth is a strange subjective thing, Angela," I said, on the edge of exhaustion. "It's often very hard. What's true for you may not be true for another."

"Everything that was has to be rebuilt and you are asking for the right to begin again. It's never the same, but some feelings are strengthened by a crisis and others are weakened. Sometimes they can be regained and sometimes they're lost."

I looked at her bowed head. "Subject to your choice, we can do an odyssey again. Okay?"

She was still and we waited. She said, very low, "Yes."

The meeting was over a little before two in the morning. Dave

Winters reminded me that I had promised to do Robert Robinson's probe after the meeting. Everyone had gone to bed—did I still want to go ahead with it?

"Certainly," I said, "I promised Bobby he would have his probe tonight, and I never go back on a promise. Get them all up."

He turned on the air conditioner and called for a crew to clear away the dishes and pop bottles. In fifteen minutes, we started the probe.

JULY 27, 1971

My office had been freshly painted in the inescapable shade of orange I love. Lew Garely was among the first to arrive, wearing a becoming chin beard and longer sideburns grown on his Canadian vacation. Dave Winters and Louie Sarra discovered they both had chosen to wear brown checked shirts and ties. Louie wears his ties folded over rather than knotted. I arrived with Roger Lourie, who is a dedicated member of our Advisory Board and works for the Robert F. Kennedy Memorial Foundation in Washington.

Roger, a neat, well-tailored young man with a curve of mustache over his lip, was introduced around. I explained that he was interested in hearing about new programs that need funding. He couldn't have come at a more propitious moment—I was anxious to get the Mothering Program moving. I told him about it.

"It has a budget of about $400,000 a year, for forty mothers and forty babies," I began. He accepted this calmly.

"What we hope to do primarily is learn how to teach mothering. You know Prescott's experiments with maternally deprived monkeys show that if a young monkey isn't mothered before the age of one or two years, she in turn is unable to mother her own children. These children cannot develop normally unless they have a surrogate mother or tremendous peer-group interaction. We want to see if this is true of human beings. If it is, we want to know if you can teach people how to mother when they have had no mothering themselves. If you can't, we want to design programs so the infants are not damaged. It is our belief that many of the causes of addiction can be found in early nurturing."

Dr. Vincent Fontana, head of pediatrics at St. Vincent's Hospital, noted in an article that abused, battered and neglected children of today will become tomorrow's sociopaths and criminals. He also found that 50 per cent of battered children returned by hospitals to their homes are dead within the following year. Odyssey is hoping

248

to discover if the cycle can be broken by working with addict mothers in the program.

"But can you teach mothering to a young adult, or is it too late?" I wondered aloud. "Everyone assumes that you can, but all the animal experiments show that it can't be done. The real question is whether we are different from the great apes in this respect. I'm not so sure that we are."

Roger was intrigued and asked for an outline to take back to his Board at the Kennedy Foundation.

"Odyssey House is very existential," I told Roger. "We say it as it is, and if we find that mothering can't be taught, we are going to say so—even though it goes against the great Judeo-Christian mystique about mothering being a natural instinct. It will have profound social implications if mothering can't be learned by humans who previously were mother-deprived."

If that turned out to be true, another project I had been mulling over would be even more vital. It was called Child Advocacy. I asked Roger to consider it as well for funding and described it.

"First a pilot project is set up with the present good demographic distribution of Whites, Blacks and Puerto Ricans found on the Lower East Side. Someone who lives in the block trains as a Child Advocate. She is responsible for, say, fifty neighborhood children under the age of six. Ten such women could supervise five hundred children. These women work with, not against the parents. They watch that the children are not abused, are fed properly, and have no major medical problems that are being neglected. *These are the children no one sees!*

"A competent parent has two jobs. One is to provide love, which in the case of children is shown by constancy of care and affection tones. The other is to negotiate the system on behalf of the child. Many parents can provide one but not the other; some can provide neither.

"The Child Advocate will be trained to negotiate the system," I continued. "If the child or the child's parents are having difficulties, she'll be able to arrange a cerebral palsy work-up, or an examination for mental retardation, or whatever. If the child is wandering the streets at midnight, she'll do something about that too. If the child is being abused, she'll move to get protection. For the good parent the Advocate serves as a welcome aide; against the bad parent, as a needed protection for the child. I say 'she' for convenience, but the Advocate could as easily be a man."

There had been some preliminary talk in governmental circles about a health program for preschoolers in New York City. To my disgust, most of the direction seemed to be in the traditional one of building a huge, structured agency first to meet the conjectured needs and then gathering confirming data from the neighborhood. I thought it should be the other way around. One should start at the grass roots in order to find out what is needed, after which an agency can be designed to fit. The design should permit flexibility as needs change. Odyssey's role in the Child Advocacy proposal would be to train the paramedical grass roots Advocates. It seems that every group in our society has someone to fight for it, except children.

"Those are the two projects I'd like to see developed, Roger, the Mothering Program and Child Advocacy. If your Foundation isn't interested in these, we have nothing better to suggest."

"I think you very definitely should get action on one of these," Roger assured me. "Child Advocacy is right down our alley."

"Let me tell you," I grinned, "that Child Advocacy is no more than an idea in the heads of Dr. Louis Cooper at Bellevue Hospital and Dr. Judianne Densen-Gerber at Odyssey. We were sitting in the office of the Department of Health of the City of New York this week, listening to them talk about building an agency first and investigating the problem second, and we said, 'This is bullshit.'"

Roger realized that the Child Advocacy program had relevance to addiction, and Charlie Rohrs was quick to agree. "There are so many social conditions that guarantee that children will become addicts," he observed, leaning back in his chair with a big cigar in his mouth. "First is the fact that many parents are inadequate people."

"As with every other social problem, the situation is magnified in the presence of addiction," I added. "The addict mother is totally unable to nurture her child. Of the sixty-five battered children who died in New York in 1970, more than half came from addict homes."

The more I thought about the five hundred children in the Child Advocacy pilot project, the more delighted with it I became. "It will be fascinating to compare five hundred children who have nothing in common except that they live in the same neighborhood," I mused aloud. "It gets away from the selectivity that occurs when hospitals or clinics wait for the children to be brought to them. The ones who come, you must assume, have parents who are concerned and have some motivation. Therefore, you know nothing of what is needed back on the block."

I added that it might be interesting to compare the five hundred ghetto children with five hundred children of physicians, who know best how to negotiate the system.

"It's a logical extension of Odyssey," I told Roger. "We're treating the results of poor mothering, poor nurturing and bad conditions. We should get into the preventative aspects. It's time we stopped moaning about the rising rate of drug use and started planning and working toward children growing up strong enough to resist drugs."

We held a post mortem about the arsonist on 12th Street. A fire had been discovered late Thursday night in our Gramercy Park facility. It was three fires, two started in girls' beds and one in the girls' closet. After the fire department left, efforts to get the arsonist to confess failed. It was decided to use an established Odyssey technique: Someone would be "scapegoated," discharged from the program, as a symbol. He would have to begin his Odyssey again. Odyssey requires that someone be punished when a Cardinal Rule is broken regardless of whether we know who the guilty person is. The method, when applied against an innocent, also puts pressure on the guilty person to confess. Somebody must always pay, and often we must choose the person by lot.

Slips were drawn and the losing one belonged to Richie Shanner. He is a resident who has done well in the program, is much respected and liked; he was about to finish treatment with his promotion to Level IV in a few days. We were anguished to see Richie sacrificed, but the Case Conference the next day upheld the action. Richie himself said, "I think it's best for Odyssey if I go through with it." He loved Odyssey enough to be willing to start the program again, even though it would mean at least another year out of his life.

A matter of hours after the Case Conference, the arsonist, a fifteen-year-old boy, admitted his guilt. He had set fires in several other houses endangering countless lives, but he had never been caught. He said he confessed only because he couldn't watch Richie take the credit or the blame. He was removed to a more structured institution than Odyssey where he could be given greater supervision. Richie was reinstated.

We discussed the incident briefly and someone asked Dave Winters how the arsonist had behaved when confessing.

"He started by asking to talk, saying, *'Do you have a minute?'*" Dave related with relish. "He's a hyper-strung-out type, very, very competitive. His eyes are always open. He went to the staff, shaking, and he said, 'I think I lit the fires. I remember lighting a similar fire in the Bronx. When I was in military school there was some type of fire. I walk down the street sometimes with matches and I throw them in bushes. I throw them in garbage cans.' He thinks he remembers that he lit the fires. But his whole thing is 'I think, I think.' It's not 'I did it.' There isn't that. It's 'I think I did it—but I don't remember.'"

I was grateful, thinking of Richie, that the other boy had confessed. Some days something good happens.

AUGUST 17, 1971

Odyssey wanted to sue Metropolitan Hospital for six cents. Our medical staff was exasperated by what we considered the unethical research practices in the hospital. We reached the end of our patience when Serena Hyatt had her baby, Sonia, there. Serena is a seventeen-year-old ghetto Black who had been at Odyssey for six months before her baby was born. Despite the fact clearly evident on her chart that she had been drug-free all that time, Metropolitan Hospital doctors wanted to include her baby in a research project on infants born to using addicts. They obtained Serena's permission—her uninformed consent—to do an unnecessary potentially dangerous spinal puncture on her new-born daughter by leading her to believe that the infant wasn't normal, which was a lie. They said the baby needed to be "tested" for her own well-being.

I introduced the subject at our Executive Staff meeting because there were some details of the suit still to be clarified. The Odyssey lawyer thought there should be two suits, one for six cents for actual damages and another for a million dollars punitive damages for the mental distress suffered by the mother. The behavior of the doctors had been particularly destructive in this case because before coming to Odyssey, Serena had had a deep-seated hatred of all physicians, and she had been finally persuaded in the Women's Marathon to trust doctors. It was also very cruel because Serena had a morbid fear that her baby would be defective because she had used drugs during the first part of her pregnancy. It was this fear and the resultant guilt that had brought her early in her pregnancy to Odyssey to seek treatment.

I didn't agree with his suggestion. "It's bad for us to sue for money," I said. "It looks bad. This case probably will never reach the courts. It's going to be tried in the press. All I want is for Metropolitan Hospital to stop doing this kind of thing."

The discussion rambled. We formulated the idea of a fund resulting from the damage suit. This would avoid giving the appearance of Odyssey suing for reasons of financial gain.

"We might set a small amount, say a thousand dollars, aside for the baby and put the rest into the Serena and Sonia Community

Foundation for Infant Research," I offered, with growing enthusiasm. "And a clinic or committee might be started to protect other similar children. Or we might create an organization that would handle the claims against hospitals from other mothers and children who haven't got Odyssey to defend them."

Charlie Rohrs amended it, "Or even expand it to a patient advocate program. You don't have to limit it to mothers and children. This kind of shit goes on all over the place in all our hospitals."

"That's what the New York *Times* reporter who called me this morning wanted to know," Don Dougherty said. "He was asking for information about how other women who do not have support . . ."

"That's very good!" I interrupted. I was thoroughly pleased. "First of all, the jury will be more disposed to award once the jury knows we're suing for altruistic reasons. The proposed plan would be very good, *very* good. We'll form a committee with people, such as Judge Justine Wise Polier and other concerned citizens, who know how to negotiate the system to hear and follow through on claims for infant plaintiffs, who until now never had a chance. I *love* it. It's marvelous. It's about time."

Don Dougherty would tell the *Times* reporter that his question had helped us reach our decision. I said, "Tell him that whatever punitive award is received from Met Hospital will go into a program to which mothers and children and other patients can come and get advice concerning their rights. *Set it up!*" I was delighted.

Antonio Domantay, a psychiatrist who works for Odyssey on a part-time basis, soon to be full-time, had been assaulted by a resident. Tony, a handsome Filipino wearing glasses with heavy black frames, joined the meeting. He leaned against the wall as he described the situation.

"He's a homicidal maniac," he said. "I made the mistake while I was interviewing him of getting myself in a corner. He was . . ."

I interrupted hurriedly. Homicidal maniacs make me nervous. "Where is this patient now?"

"He was admitted to Bellevue," Tony answered, disgusted. "He was supposed to be transferred to Bronx State Psychiatric Hospital, so Bellevue gave this homicidal maniac the transportation money and . . ."

"He didn't show up at Bronx State, right?" I said, grimacing.

"Right," Tony nodded. "He came back to Odyssey and I told him we couldn't admit him, that he would have to go to Bronx State. When he heard that . . ."

"What's his name?" I asked.

Tony told me, spelling it out as I wrote it down. I handed the name to Carol, my secretary. "Tell Ellis not to readmit him," I instructed her. Carol picked up the telephone at once.

"Did he assault you or try to strangle you?" I asked Tony.

"He picked up a chair, Charlie's desk chair," Tony explained. "That was the second try. First he came at me with the secretary's hand mirror."

"He sounds very sick, very sick, particularly to be wandering the streets," I shook my head. "There's nothing we can do, since Bellevue released him. Let's not readmit him, Louie." Louie found a pen and made a note. "Smith!" Bob Smith looked up. "You will let Rivera know not to readmit him if he turns up at the Spanish House, all right?" Smith nodded, and wrote it down.

Anyone in Odyssey can be "encountered"—by which we mean challenged—by people on a different line of authority, and that includes me. Stewart Vexler, an Assistant Administrator, who supervised Odyssey storefronts, sent in a slip asking for an encounter with me. I sent for him.

Stewart is a Texan, a college graduate, intelligent, fluent in Spanish, with a good work record that includes some summers as a construction foreman. He applied for a job at Odyssey, and we needed someone with manual skills to be the counselor with the exterior maintainance crews. He turned out to be a fine addition to the staff, an honest, open person who always told me to my face when he disagreed with me, which isn't true of all of my staff. He had just notified us that he was returning to Texas to enroll in law school. Odyssey encourages staff to go on with education and to better themselves. I was pleased. It was late in the afternoon when he came in the crowded office, found a chair and faced me calmly. He's a wiry, capable-looking young man with a long, angular face and blond hair grazing his shirt collar. In a resonant, strong voice, he outlined his grievance: my behavior during the previous Case Conference.

He was referring to the reprimand I handed out that day, ordering the Assistant Administrators to clean the latrines for a week. I had been incensed to read the complaint in the minutes of their last meeting that when a Level IV resident had been asked to do menial work they felt it was beneath him. I don't believe that menial work is demeaning or that good attitudes will be developed by the patients if Assistant Administrators feel that way. I'm adamant in my belief that honest human labor is a basic ingredient of human dignity. Able-bodied young men and women, even if addicted, can work and not continue their dependency to others. I decided that as an awareness exercise all Assistant Administrators, who felt responsible, would set an example to the residents by cleaning latrines for a while, even though it would cost Odyssey several hundred dollars in staff time. It would be a meaningful, worthwhile lesson. Stewart had protested at the time but I overruled him.

"I felt that everything I said at that Case Conference was wasted words," he told me. "The rest of the people at the Conference all sat silent, rather than try to deal with your temper. I think when you lose your temper the whole structure of the agency is thrown out."

I shifted some papers on my desk, found my cigars and lit one. I am well aware of my inherited, notorious temper.

Stewart continued steadily, "I don't think any of your trusted advisers were any too rational, either. Rationality was out of the room . . ."

"I wasn't angry with you, Stewart," I told him. "I was angry about the Assistant Administrators' minutes, which I read over the weekend. My anger developed over a period of six or seven days; it wasn't impetuous anger. I was angry with what I consider a total distortion of the Odyssey philosophy.

"It's true that I knew before I went into the Case Conference that I was going to order latrine duty. If nobody showed up for it, I probably would suggest that Jimmy and Charlie and I become the latrine crew and prove a point in this agency that menial labor is not beneath even us."

"I understand that," Stewart said, "but that point isn't really my encounter. My encounter with you and the rest of the staff is that no one was listening, including yourself—who was really in a fine temper—no one was listening to what anyone was *saying*. In the past, like when you encountered me about that time I was misquoted in the New York *Post*, I explained what had happened and you went on to something else, and I felt better. But this time I was attempting to explain that what was in those minutes and what really happened were *two different things*, and I didn't get any-where!"

I explained again that there should be some concrete examples in Odyssey to the effect that no labor is beneath any of us, and whether the minutes were accurate or not didn't matter—such teaching was long overdue. "I don't punish," I told him. "Punishment to me is worthless. What I want to happen is a learning experience."

Stewart observed that the matter was clarified for him now.

I didn't want him to leave: He had raised a troubling point. If the staff was afraid of me, did I have a right to lose my temper?

"The very reason the encounter technique started back in 1967," I informed Stewart, "was not because the residents wanted a way of speaking to me but because I wanted to blow up at them. I couldn't stand this fucking bunch of addicts any longer. They were constantly pushing me into the corner as they do with everyone. It's part of the con game, their sickness. If I didn't yell at Louie or at Jimmy, I might have gone off my rocker. And there was no way within the limits set by my Freudian-psychiatric training that I was allowed ever to lose my temper. Little wonder most analysts don't want to work with addict/sociopaths. You can't last unless you ventilate. And so I created the Odyssey encounter system—which is a structured, controlled release of anger across different lines of authority."

I picked up paper clips and began making a chain. "You've raised an important issue, Stewart, and I'm grateful for it. The issue is can the top—on Friday afternoons, ever lose her temper when the top is as distant from the bottom as I have become? Can I ever be real now that Odyssey has become so large?"

"I think that's a valid question," Stewart responded, crossing his feet in soft cowboy boots.

I asked the group for their opinions and advice. We were all baffled and depressed.

"How do we solve the problem of making me real?" I wondered gloomily. The paper-clip chain was four-feet long and I had exhausted my supply. I dropped it back in the dish.

"I think what's wrong with the agency," Louie commented, "is that every time someone is overruled and they don't like it, they let the residents know. *They let the fucking residents know!* They say, 'I agree with you, but my hands are tied because of the fucking top.' That's not their job—their job is to reinforce us, not go against us."

"It's like what happens in a typical business," I commented, "with no one willing to take the weight and always shifting it upwards."

"Yeah," Stewart said, thoughtfully, "I agree with you."

"It's fucking ridiculous!" Louie cried, thoroughly heated. "We're breaking our fucking balls!"

"Wait a minute, Louie," Charlie admonished. "What you say is true, and Stewart acknowledges what you're saying. Most people on the staff feel that it's much better not to complain to the top, to keep their mouths shut. They're always afraid of their job security."

"They won't get promoted that way," I snapped. "Ted Tann and Stewart don't keep their mouths shut, and they're the ones who get promoted." I looked at Stewart, who was completely relaxed. "You're not afraid of me," I observed. "You never were."

"No," he admitted.

"Why are others afraid of me?"

Stewart considered. "The only thing I can think of offhand is that you are sensitive in very many areas, and people don't know what is going to offend you or bother you."

"Am I sensitive in many areas, or am I sensitive in a few?" I asked, intrigued.

Jimmy answered easily. "I don't think it's so much being sensitive. If there's something going on that you don't agree with, though, you don't lay back. The majority would, and it's that difference that frightens people. You are never afraid to say what you think."

I digested this. "Do I have more buttons than most people?"

"Yes," Jimmy nodded. "To me, you have more buttons."

"Louie?" I asked, "Do I have more buttons?"

Louie shrugged, "I don't know."

"I think your buttons are different," Charlie observed.

Louie beamed. "Yeah," he said, "that's it."

"That's it," Stewart concurred. "Its hard to anticipate your reactions."

"Do you think that's true, Fred? Do you think I'm unpredictable?" I was amazed.

"Right," he said emphatically.

"I thought I was predictable!" I protested.

"Only to people who think the way you do, who make the same associations," Fred explained. "Other than that . . ."

Stewart leaned forward. "You view the world on a completely different level than I view it, or most other people view it."

"How?" I asked.

"I don't know." He thought for a moment. "When we get into philosophical discussions in Case Conference, I find that you're more idealistic than most people are. I remember once you talking about your feeling that people would obey laws if they understood them, and that concern could be a reality."

There was a knock at the door and dinner was brought in, fruit and cold cuts. It was almost eight o'clock. Through the clatter of trays and plates I pursued the discussion. "What do you understand me to mean when I said that only by obeying laws can we get rid of drugs?"

Stewart answered, "You meant it was our task to bring our needs and concerns into legislation and that government cares about the governed, and I think that's idealistic."

Dr. Densen-Gerber and from left to right Fred Cohen, Jimmy Murphy, Louie Sarra, John Cox and Charlie Rohrs, in a relaxed moment.

"That *is* idealistic!" I told him urgently. "But I believe we can succeed!"

"I can't see it as reality," Stewart said flatly. "I can't. The Washington and Albany Legislature are self-serving jungles."

"We don't have a choice!" I insisted. "We *have* to reach our leaders and make them respond to us. Otherwise, we're going to be annihilated or annihilate ourselves."

Stewart said steadily, "I think through our apathy we are going to annihilate ourselves."

The whole session resulted in a marvelous idea: I made Stewart Vexler an Acting Director of Odyssey, with authority equal to that of Charlie Rohrs and Jimmy Murphy.

"You can run around, tighten everyone up," I told the astonished Vexler. "You might start by telling everyone honestly how you see them. The best thing you can do for the agency is give them all an honest feedback, get the honesty game started. What do you care what you say—you're leaving for Texas in two weeks, aren't you?"

He agreed, dazed.

I turned to Carol. "Send a memo," I instructed her. "To all staff: Stewart Vexler is Ramrod Acting Director of Odyssey, on an important assignment of special importance to me."

I faced Stewart. "Before you leave," I warned him, "I want you to write me all the things I should do. All right?"

Stewart let out a breath. "You always do that, Judi," he said in wonderment. "Every time I've encountered you, you've always said, 'Well, what would you do?' and you have left me holding the bag, as all good leaders do."

"Your encounters aren't against me or against Odyssey," I told him. "I perceive them as coming from a genuine wanting to resolve situations that could be made better. I don't find any hostility in you."

"No," Stewart agreed. "I don't have any hostility."

"And most of the time," I added warmly, "*you're right*. And we welcome any opportunity to do better. Now that you're Acting Director you must stay for the rest of the staff meeting. We usually go on to one, two or three in the morning."

As it turned out, I was wrong. We finished at midnight, only thirteen hours after we had begun.

Reprimands

W.B.:

reprimanded by:	M.M.	4/29	re:	Throwing a knife on the floor.
	M.M.	5/2	re:	For wasting paper and leaving the legal office messed up.
	J.R.	5/7	re:	For not wearing his awareness.
	J.R.	5/7	re:	For using Odyssey House envelopes for ash trays.
	C.N.	5/7	re:	For leaving his department without making J.R. aware.
	M.M.	5/8	re:	For wasting paper.

Child-rearing practices have undergone revolutionary changes during the past two generations. Until the 1930s, it was not difficult for all a child's needs to be provided by the parents. Population increases, urbanization, plus fragmentation and specialization of services have removed the parent as an intermediary in the child-system relationship. Essentially medical, educational, and social services are being provided on a catch-as-catch-can basis for those who neither understand their needs nor are capable of fulfilling them.

Odyssey House recognizes the growing need for child advocates—local community members who can objectively negotiate the system for the benefit of each neighborhood child. We would like to initiate the program in the East Village of New York City. This catchment area offers a population of varied racial and ethnic backgrounds. Attention will be focused on five hundred children to be divided into groups of fifty for whom a neighborhood child advocate is responsible. In this way we can ascertain the needs and problems of this population and the extent of service availability.

The Child Advocacy Program offers an opportunity to integrate the functions of theory and implementation within a mutually compatible and consistent framework. By studying the parameters, rather than focusing our attention on the individual, we can better develop a program that directly services children.

MOTHER'S PROGRAM ODYSSEY HOUSE

Odyssey House, Inc., has begun a new program for the treatment of young addict mothers and their children in the same facility. The experience of the Odyssey community in the treatment of young pregnant women clearly demonstrated the need for a venturous therapeutic modality that allowed the post-partum mother to receive adequate treatment for her anti-social behavior through the Odyssey House method, and at the same time take appropriate responsibility for the care of her child. The benefits of this program are great for both mother and child; the infant has the benefit of continued maternal care during the crucial early months of life, while the mother can obtain expert advice and tutoring in infant care. Consequently, her own dependency disease will not be reinforced through the institution of foster care. The mother and child are resocialized together at the end of treatment, rather than combining the transition from in-patient to out-patient care with the new parental responsibilities.

Initial experience with the program bodes well for its success. The young woman responds enthusiastically to the task of mothering within the therapeutic community, and motivation for her own treatment is enhanced by the physical presence of the child.

The problem of anti-social behavior among addicts—and whether, in fact, mothering can be taught—is now being confronted by Odyssey House in the Parent's Program. Essentially, the crucial problem of second-generation-dependency disease is being attacked at the source.

The nursery/day-care center is an integral part of the Odyssey House Services to Women program. It is staffed by professionals (experienced in child care and mother-child relationships and paraprofessionals whose important expertise is that they themselves are successful parents). They are, therefore, excellent role models and teachers.

When the newborn is brought from the hospital the mother and child live together in the facility with full supportive services. Odyssey pediatricians and nurses provide complete well-baby services. All essentials for adequate newborn care are assured. During the period of six weeks to three months, mother and child are constantly together, the mother performing as much of the feeding, caring, dressing and changing tasks as she is physically and emotionally able. Her relationship to the newborn is carefully evaluated and supervised as well as guided.

After an appropriate period the child goes to an on-the-premises day-care center. Here the child is with several other infants ranging from three months to two years of age. Residents in treatment are taught to be responsible for the care of children, and are closely observed and supervised. Each mother spends a considerable number of months assisting in the day-care center. When she is on duty, she is responsible for the care of all children in the nursery. However, except for the eight hours that her child is in day-care center, each natural mother is responsible for the needs of her own baby.

A unique feature of this program is the day-care facilities that are made available to staff and graduates who work at Odyssey and have small children. This small group of mothers arrange to leave their children and to spend time in the nursery when possible. This allows for further input where the residents are exposed to healthy mother-child interaction. This feature also affords the staff an opportunity to make evaluations of child development across cross cultural, racial, ethnic and social lines since doctors, nurses, staff and patient offspring are together.

Louie Sarra II

I never thought I would ever get married. I've been in love before, but for whatever reasons, I always pulled back. With my wife, Carol, it was different from the beginning. I didn't think anyone like Carol would marry someone with my past. She represents goodness to me, and most of my life I thought of myself as badness.

The quality she gives me, first of all, is security. I know she will never hurt me. I trust her. She tells me what I have for her is heart. That's nice. She's my dream girl; I don't mean I ever pictured a dream girl exactly, but if I had, she would be exactly like Carol.

The one thing that bothers me is that I'm fifteen years older than she. It's not difficult now, but in twenty years I'll be an old man and she'll be only forty. That's my biggest concern.

Carol began at Odyssey as Jimmy Murphy's secretary. Jimmy and I share an office, so I was with Carol frequently. After a while I wanted to ask her out to dinner. She's a good-looking girl and I liked her warm and kind qualities.

There's a policy at Odyssey that you have to get permission from Judi before you can date another staff member. I asked her and she said no. She said, "Carol's a baby. What are you doing, you dirty old man?"

Still Carol and I were attracted to each other and we wanted to date, but we accepted Judi's decision. I was living with David Winters at the time. We gave a party and invited Carol along with other members of the staff. She came with her sister. I spent all evening with Carol, danced with her, talked to her, hoping the others would tell Judi about it and I would have a chance to ask her again to let me take Carol out.

It didn't work, as it turned out; Judi didn't hear about it. But one day, she called me on the telephone. She said she'd heard that I was depressed and she wondered what was wrong. I told her that I still wanted to date Carol. "All right," she said, "but only if your intentions are honorable. If that girl is compromised, you'll have to deal with me."

At an Executive Staff meeting that week, before Carol and I had even gone out together, Judi asked, "When are you going to marry Carol?" She had a five-dollar bet with Clifford Robinson that Carol and I would marry. For some reason, I had the feeling I was being pressured.

We dated for about a month. It was the week before her birthday. I said, "What do you want for your birthday, an engagement ring?" She said, "Are you serious?" I said sure. She thought it over for about five seconds and said, "All right." I knew she would—there was a good feeling between us. It was the happiest day of my life.

The next problem was meeting Carol's parents. I don't like to meet a girl's parents; it gets me uptight. Carol warned me that her father is very conservative. Her father feels that no one on earth is good enough for his daughter. He calls Carol *pumin,* which is Italian for "little apple." She's the apple of his eye. At the very best he would not like my long hair, she told me. That didn't make me feel very good. There were a few other possible difficulties: my fifteen years of drug addiction, my eight years in prison, my association with the Mafia and our age difference. But I *am* Italian.

Carol kept reminding me that if I was to marry her, I would have to meet them, so finally I went over. I spent about five minutes talking to her mother, saying it was a nice day. I was sweating. Then her father came in and I said, "Do you think my hair's too long?"

I realized I would have to tell Carol's father about my drug addiction before we married, but it was several months before I got the courage. Judi was urging me to do so, saying that I owed him the respect of letting him know about it before the wedding. Carol was upset. She didn't think her father could accept it. She expected that he might disown her. Italians can be that severe. She agreed with Judi, though, that I must go ahead and tell him.

I decided to tell him one Saturday when he was helping me fix up our future apartment. We were alone. I said, "Why don't we stop and have a beer?" He said, "We have no time." I kept trying to get him to take a break and he kept refusing.

Finally an hour later, he stopped and sat down. I looked at him and said, "There's something I have to tell you. I used to use drugs." I was terrified. I feared I might lose everything.

Louis and Carol Sarra.

He sat silently for about two minutes. Then he looked up and
said, "No wonder your mother's so sick." He thought again and
asked, "Why?" I said, "I don't know. I was stupid." I added that I
hadn't used drugs for five years and he said, "Well, I guess you've
smartened up." That was the end of it.

Two months later, Carol and I were married. My mother came to the wedding in a walker. She was in her eighties and not very strong. She clung to Judi and thanked her for saving my life, giving her back her son. She told Judi, "Now that my baby is happily married, I can die in peace."

Our marriage has fulfilled me. It is the last piece I was missing in my life, and now I'm a whole person.

I sometimes think about the fifteen years I took drugs but never with the feeling that I would like to try them again. Now and then we go out as a foursome with Tommy and Ellen Turner. He was one of the original seventeen. He now works for the Manhattan Court Employment Project, which helps first offenders. Tommy and I occasionally reminisce about the times we were high or the times we were beat for some dope, the hard times we had. But I don't have the feeling that I want ever to get high again.

I have difficulty identifying with the new breed of addicts coming into Odyssey now. I can't understand them. I don't know what to do with kids who are only twelve, thirteen, fourteen years old.

In all the years I sold drugs to maybe two hundred different addicts, the youngest I dealt to was about nineteen. None of us would ever think of selling drugs to a child. In fact, we stayed away from places where children were because we didn't want them even to see us with drugs. When it came to children, we old-time addicts had some sense of standards. What is happening today both horrifies and puzzles me.

To tell the truth, I don't think these youngsters are addicts at all. I see them as confused babies. They take whatever drug is handy. They're just nowhere.

In part I am guided by the Case Conference and staff meetings where Judi explains about the dynamics of adolescence and why they have hang-ups. None of us adult ex-addicts have anything in common with these kids; none of us have any expertise where they are concerned, but no other program seems to be as far along in understanding them as Odyssey, and so we continue.

I'm learning, though, little by little. I feel good about the program expanding, about developments like the Mothering Program. I'm letting myself go. The agency's expanding and I'm expanding with it.

It bothers me that the kids in the program these days don't show concern for one another. They're so Mickey Mouse. If someone is two minutes late, they want to kill him with reprimands and punishments. There's no understanding. In our day, we looked out for each other. The time that Ellen Turner's urine report came back positive, we fought to keep her in the program. We insisted that it must be incorrect; therefore, she shouldn't be thrown out. Nevertheless, she was put out and we understood why. However, when the urine was retested it was discovered that there had been a mistake in laboratory procedures, so she was reinstated and we were

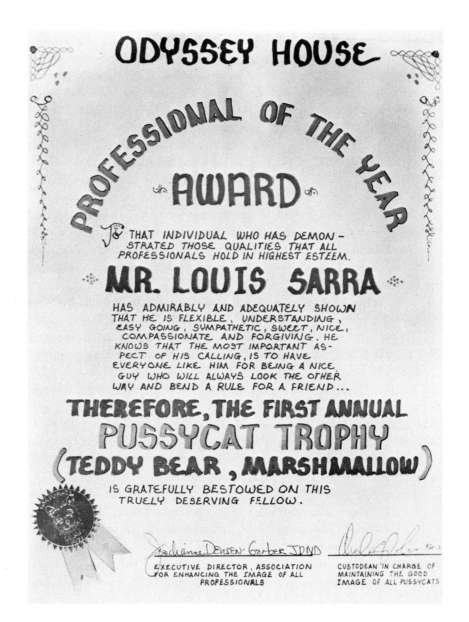

overjoyed. But in the meantime, we ex-addicts had fought to keep her in the program. Today if an ex-addict takes a candy, who wants to throw him out? The *ex-addicts!* The professionals today show more concern than the ex-addicts do.

Charlie Rohrs, one of the professionals at Odyssey who always shows concern, gave me the Pussy-Cat Award at Odyssey House's fifth anniverary party in October 1971. The Pussy-Cat Award goes to the ex-addict who has become soft and is, therefore, like a professional. I'm known now as Dr. Louis Sarra, P.C.

I watch Charlie and his wife, Barbara, with their son, and I wonder what it will be like when Carol and I have a baby. It means that some day I'll have to explain to our child that I used to be a drug addict. It wouldn't be good to try to hide it. I made a terrible mistake, and I pray our child will understand that.

I want to keep good communication between myself and any child we have. No parent can prevent his child from doing what he wants to do, and that includes taking drugs, but maybe it won't happen if there is good communication and concern.

Children have to feel that you love them, that you're concerned. I don't mean buying a bicycle or all the clothes they want; I mean concern from the heart, not the pocketbook.

That, and praying often that they won't take drugs.

If I found out my kid was taking drugs, I don't know what I'd do. I'd break his legs, I'd break his arms—I don't know. If I ever walked in and found my kid with a needle in his arm, at that moment I might break his arm. I don't know how I could bear such pain. But truthfully, I tell you, I don't know what I'd do.

A Night in New Hampshire

New Hampshire Odyssey is housed in what was once a New England inn, a three-story clapboard building with a wide screened porch across the front and long center halls lined with doors. It is built on the site of the first Whittier Inn where it is reported that Paul Revere began his famous ride. It was known as the Whittier until Odyssey bought it.

I was there late in June 1971, with Michael and our three children, partly to have a brief vacation but mainly to establish the newly opened residence. We were also going to celebrate the first anniversary of the founding of our Junior Executive Staff, the J.E.S.

The J.E.S., Fred Cohen and I gathered in the parlor after dinner, me in a loose flowered gown stretched out on a lounge chair, the others scattered on the splayed wicker furniture in the room or lying on the floor. Fred and I opened with an account of our recent visit to Washington with Secretary of Defense Melvin Laird. Congressman Seymour Halpern had arranged that we meet with Laird. Halpern was concerned at the lack of Federal involvement in the Vietnam addiction problem.

"I woke up that morning promptly at eight o'clock," Fred recounted, sipping a beer. He had special permission to drink beer in the facility because he was experimenting with a new method of gaining weight: a six-pack a day. He wasn't sure if it was working since he rarely could find time to drink his quota, and he still weighed 145 at 6′2″.

The Baden family on their way to church at New Hampshire Odyssey House.

"A member of Halpern's staff took me by car to meet with Melvin Laird," he continued. "We picked up Halpern, and he and Judi anxiously discussed the meeting ahead. Any of those here who are perceptive enough can tell by the tone of my voice that it was not a big-time thrill for me."

Fred went on, "Since December we have been keeping voluminous scrapbooks. Isn't that right, Wasserbach?" Steve Wasserbach agreed, his expression full of sincere scrapbook-keeping. "These scrapbooks contain articles on Vietnam addiction and anything to do with drugs in Vietnam or with legislation or government bullshit involving the situation in Vietnam, etcetera. In December we had submitted a budget to Laird and as yet had received no word from him. Now we cut to about six months later. The present situation is . . ."

"There's Fort Bragg," I corrected him.

Fred looked into his beer distastefully. "Yessss. The Fort Bragg caper. It is not exactly a government project, but it is funded by donations from the coffee hour run by the officers' wives."

I began to laugh helplessly. "They're good people and mean well," I said. "But the only program the Army has is *seven beds* that are funded by the coffee money from officers' wives. It's a good program. Right, Smith?"

Bob Smith, sitting on the floor with his back against the fireplace wall, grinned. "Right."

"They opened a head shop," I said. A head shop stocks supplies for drug users. The group was incredulous.

Smith told them, straight-faced, "That was their first project in rehabilitation."

"*A head shop!*" I cried. "*With water pipes!*"

No one believed us. "It's real," Bob insisted. "The addicts chumped off the jive do-gooders again. Squares can't cope with us."

"It's the first project of the Vocational Rehabilitation Fund," I said, trying to be heard above the laughter. "I'm *serious!*"

"Four different brands of Stella and other cigarette papers," Smith reported, "which we all know is used only to wrap Bugler tobacco in."

Fred explained that a group from Odyssey consisting of Judi, Jimmy, Charlie, Bob Smith, Senator Thomas McIntyre, Congressmen Halpern and Koch and Dan Buckley, executive aide to Senator Buckley, had inspected the government head shop and the entire government rehabilitation center at Fort Bragg the previous March. Congressman Halpern was so upset by the signs of widespread drug abuse in the military, as evidenced by what he observed at Fort Bragg, that he set out shortly thereafter on a world-wide study mission aimed at revealing the origins of the international heroin trade. "He found countless instances of corruption, including G.I.s who were openly dealing and a Laotian Air Force lieutenant who had been seized on an Air America flight—the CIA's air operation— with about 186 pounds of raw opium . . . in other words, almost 19 pounds of pure heroin."

One of the ex-addicts whistled in astonishment. "And because Laos had no laws against drugs at the time, there were no charges made against this lieutenant, except that he was carrying excess baggage. He was charged about thirty-five yen for being overweight." The room was howling.

"Then in June," Fred said, returning to his account of our Washington visit, "we received an urgent request to meet the Secretary of Defense in Washington, the seat of our nation's government. Actually it's the ass."

"Frederick, *please!*" I objected.

"Sorry," he said agreeably. "So, to continue, Judi goes out to buy two granny dresses for the occasion so she will look very very conservative."

Fred gave me a disapproving glance. "I have told you many many times," he declared, "that regardless of what you think you look like in those dowdies, once you open your mouth the impression is completely destroyed."

"I had on white oxfords," I remembered.

"And a nice little white handbag," Fred added.

"And I had a neat hairdo and the proper pearls . . ."

"Beautiful, beautiful," Fred reassured me.

"You couldn't tell me from Wisconsin cheddar cheese," I sighed.

Our appointment with Defense Secretary Laird was for nine-ten in the morning. It was stressed that we should be punctual. We were. We waited in his outer office until nearly ten, when we were ushered in to see him.

"For the next few minutes," Fred related, "a photographer took pictures—me and Laird and Judi smiling, Judi and Laird smiling, Judi and Halpern and Laird smiling, me and Halpern and Laird and Judi smiling. Then it appeared that the interview was over. They were edging us out."

I interrupted. "We were determined that we wouldn't leave until we had presented Odyssey's military addiction treatment program to the Department of Defense. Fred was holding two copies of it. I edged toward a chair. One of Laird's assistants, who must have been an ex-football player, blocked my way. I tried to get around him but he blocked me off again. So we stood still and decided to make the best of it. We went ahead, like Mack trucks. We stood there and Fred opened the proposal and showed it to Laird."

Fred picked up the story. "Laird takes the book," he related, "and he puts it on my arm. Since the book weighs a good four or five pounds, it can be very painful after a few minutes. He doesn't read anything but he thumbs through every single page. Slowly my arm goes numb. And then we make our final statements and he says it was nice to meet us and he says good-by and he'll see us again.

"We took the other copy of the proposal to Brigadier General George Hayes, whose function in the Pentagon appears to be innovative and to make decisions on new ideas. His decisions then are approved and implemented, if possible, by Roger T. Kelly, who has

To my friend
Dr. Densen Gerber
with best wishes Mel Laird

Mel misspells Judi's name.

matching authority and controls the purse strings. The Pentagon's arrangement seemed to us very efficient. Since it is rarely possible to see both men at once, no decision is made.

"The General's mood with us was cautious. It was eleven o'clock and he said he was waiting for the President's announcement about military drug addiction, which was scheduled for noon of that day."

"I assume you all know," I reported to the New Hampshire group, "that the Federal Government finally has decided to assume its responsibility. No young men will return to the United States untreated. They will all be treated with seven days of detoxification and three weeks of out-patient aftercare, after which they will be well. The President has so proclaimed." I was unable to be humorous about this. We were all depressed at its naïveté, inadequacy and threat to the youth of our nation.

"It's interesting to note," I added, "that General Hayes kept explaining that what was wrong with the Odyssey proposal was that it was designed to be a joint program for all forces. He explained that there is no way that can be implemented. We have to understand that the Army, the Marines, the Navy and the Air Force all work independently, and there is no way they can follow a joint directive. I interpret, therefore, that if one military service wanted to invade Okinawa and another preferred to invade Japan and another England, each would follow its own dictates."

I formed a different impression of General Hayes in the privacy of a walk through the Pentagon corridors while he showed me to the car and chauffeur he gallantly loaned me. "He said to me that his hands were tied, that what was happening was terrible, that he feared for the youth of our nation. He said the private sector has to yell, scream, carry on, because those within the system have to follow orders. He suggested that the Odyssey House choir should sit-in indefinitely at the doors of every Congressman and Senator until the situation was resolved. He said, 'Don't stop.'"

I had the feeling while he talked that I was in the presence of a deeply moral and religious man. I was sad that he was so powerless.

Following that meeting, we testified before members of the Republican Congressional Task Force on Alcoholism and Narcotics. "It was an unbelievably depressing meeting," I recalled. "Congress seems to be made up of a group of old men who are busy throwing the youth of the nation away while they play power-struggle games."

I find it difficult still to think about that meeting. It was a long time before I was able to go back to Washington again. First of all, they didn't seem to be able to hear me. I found myself becoming more and more emotional as I pleaded with them to give some thought to what they were doing to the children of this country with their inability to take action and their willingness to put dollars ahead of human lives.

I warned them, in fact I threatened them, that American women will demand a healthy soil on which to raise their children. And if the Congress does not secure it, their offices were no longer safe.

I was trying to break through their political games. "Why do you think someone yesterday tried to blow up Congress?" I asked them. "Are you going to answer that by more guards on the borders to keep drugs out and more guards in Washington instead of asking why?"

While I was talking they were taking turns posing beside me for local newspaper and TV coverage.

Finally, Halpern had the good sense to stop the meeting. He suggested we have lunch. As we were leaving I was asked by another

Congressman, jokingly, if I had observed whether or not one of the Congressmen from New York had his fly zipped while I was speaking to him. I said I presumed so.

"Well then," this man beamed at me, "that's the first time he's ever talked to a woman with his fly done up." It was obviously meant to be a compliment.

My immediate retort was that the Republican Party should have a primary fight for his seat. If all his blood is so frequently diverted to his phallus, what did he have left for his brain to make a reasonable decision on the SST?

The Congressman was surprised that I was angry. At that moment I was struck by a total overwhelming awareness that women, indeed, are second-class citizens. I had been talking to the Congressmen as a psychiatrist and lawyer, founder and Executive Director of one of the nation's largest social agencies, and a citizen. All the while some of them had been thinking of me only as a sex object.

I said to the group in New Hampshire in a broken voice, "You must all help me in the next few days with my decision. I must choose which is more important—fighting for my identity as a woman and the right to be a person, which is fighting for all women, or fighting for the future of the children of this country, which means that I must keep in the background and feed the data to Charlie and Jimmy. Men will listen to them—after all, they are men."

I turned to Bob Smith. "Smith, I have never felt closer to you— you, a Black man, and I, a woman, are truly second-class citizens."

"I was disgusted," he answered in his husky voice. "More than half of them weren't interested in what you had to say. There were a lot of excuses, a lot of P.R. handshaking and 'Oh that's good' and all that, but no one—or anyway very few—made any attempt to try to inform himself or even listen. I became very uptight.

"The hearing reminded me of my confrontations with The Establishment when I was a radical militant and pipe-bomber," he continued despondently. "It's what many young people today are sensing indirectly—they don't have the opportunity to confront it directly as I did. It's my conviction that if it continues the way it is going, the United States will be another Roman Empire that's going to fall."

He added, "The problem is compounded by the fact that the younger generation coming up, who might be in a position to correct this, is running around drugged and tripping out."

There was a long dreary silence. Fred said, "I don't know if any of us can accomplish anything, but at least we'll do it together."

It is one of my convictions that there is no hope for America unless gifted and concerned citizens become involved in running the country, putting an end to the rule of mediocrity we are seeing. I was preoccupied with this and so I decided to confront Russell Tompkins that night.

Tompkins is unbelievable for a number of reasons. First, he's a hemophiliac, so self-destructive that he used to play basketball, ride motorcycles, shave with a straight razor and shoot heroin—even though his blood doesn't clot. In his lifetime he's had more than five hundred occasions when he needed blood transfusions.

Secondly, he's totally bald, the result of radiation treatment for ringworm when he was a child. He's a Harlem middle-class very light-skinned Black. Because of the severe bleeding in his joints, one knee already has been fused. He walks with a limp.

Because he is enraged at being a hemophiliac, he tries to prove he doesn't have the disease by being self-destructive. Even after he came to Odyssey this persisted. For instance, when typing, he would bang the typewriter keys so violently that there would be bleeding into his fingertips. The group encountered him on this one day and told him that whenever he felt like hurting himself he should notify someone on the staff. We gave him our commitment that we would do a better job of it than he. As we anticipated, he never asked. It "concretized" his whole nonsense.

Odyssey received a spontaneous compliment concerning his progress from the staff of the Columbia University Physicians and Surgeons Hospital, where Russell has had one hundred and ten transfusions in the two-year period that he has been with us. After Russell had been in Odyssey for a year, the doctor who is head of the hemophiliac service called and said he'd never seen anything like the attitudinal change in Russell. He wasn't sarcastic any longer, he wasn't nasty to the nurses. He was co-operative. He seemed to have accepted his disease.

I was indignant at Russell that night. I had just been given the results of his I.Q. test. Russell had scored 138. That's extremely high. My I.Q. is 139 and Fred Cohen's, whose raw score is 177, is adjusted to a full scale of 140. Fred has promised me that next time he takes an I.Q. test he'll arrange things in order not to beat me.

Tompkins had shown no indication of his extraordinary intelligence while at Odyssey. I felt he was far from cured of self-destructive tendencies. He deliberately was suppressing his intelligence.

"How does an I.Q. of 138 affect the mess that is you?" I asked him severely.

Russell was lying full length on the floor beside Bob Smith and his thick glasses in gold wire frames caught the light as he looked up at me.

"It affects the rest of the mess by reaffirming that I haven't done very much to put it to use," he admitted. "Very little, if anything. Now I'm in a position where I have to use it."

"Now explain to me," I continued harshly, "how, with this excellent faculty of reason, did you do to yourself what you did."

"You mean on the street?"

"Sure."

"Acting out," he laughed unconvincingly. "Isn't that it?"

"I don't think you have been acting out."

"Sure!" he assured me. "Ever since I can remember I understood fully what I had to live with, and I didn't want to live with it. So I . . ."

"Let me hear you talk about that," I asked. "Frederick has asked me, 'Is Russell going to live long enough to exercise all his gifts?'"

Russell was startled. "Well," he began. He paused and thought. "I'd say last year at this time I would have said I wouldn't live long enough to be here now. I say now that I *will* live long enough. If something happens to me, it won't be because I was doing something I shouldn't."

"Has he been behaving well?" I inquired of the group.

Wasserbach answered, "He carries a knife."

I was amazed. "You carry a knife!"

"Certainly," Russell replied matter-of-factly, rolling on his side, propping his head on his hand. "Just last week they tried to rob me on Ninth Street. So now I carry a knife. I wish I had a license to carry a gun. That's real protection. If I was acting out, I wouldn't carry anything."

I was still dumbfounded. "You're going to get in a *knife fight?*"

Russell explained that he already had been in a knife fight during the attempted robbery, except that he didn't have a knife. His attackers cut him on the finger during the struggle, necessitating three stitches and three blood transfusions. "That's the reason I carry a knife now. If I'm going to get hurt, I'm going to take somebody with me."

We talked about his hemophilia. Russell has an outstanding bill for $36,000 at Columbia Presbyterian Hospital from the time when he had surgery, the fusion of his knee. His parents have paid other bills of $7,000 and $12,000. His father worked at two jobs simultaneously to help pay them.

I returned to the subject of Russell's intelligence. "What do you think of my confrontation?" I asked him.

"It's about using my intelligence."

"To control what?"

He was puzzled.

"To control your real sadness," I told him gently.

He closed his eyes and then looked at me again. "I promise you, it will be controlled," he said in a low voice.

"You've allowed your emotions to control your head," I commented. "Your head should have been able to overcome that, shouldn't it? It's such a very good head."

Russell said he couldn't follow me. Bob Smith was amused. "You didn't understand that?" he asked with friendly skepticism.

Carlton Martin, sitting on the floor some distance away with his arms around his knees, murmured, "Tonight everybody is a little full of shit. . . ."

"In reality," I said to Russell, "To a certain extent you *do* have a fucked-up destiny."

Russell agreed, expressionless. "Yes, it is."

"But it can be shared," Carlton told him, "to a certain degree. To lessen the pain."

"He doesn't believe that," I told Carlton.

Russell looked away. "No, I don't."

"Martin is reaching out," I said, chiding him softly. "None of this is bullshit. But it's your isolation and your bag."

Russell shifted uncomfortably. "With people who know me very well, I share some of it with them. But, ah, many times I find it very difficult to share what I'm feeling. There's no way of talking about it without going into the whole thing of apologizing why I can't do certain things. And it turns me off, it still turns me off."

"So why share your hemophilia?" I said.

"Well, I don't."

"You have to accept it. But you can share your fine mind, with me, with Fred, with others. You can create and accomplish. *That* others can plug into, *that* you can share."

Russell considered this. "I have been gradually overcoming the limitation that I've put on myself," he said thoughtfully.

"How do you feel," I continued, "about being such a phenomenally intelligent Black. That's Clifford Robinson's problem. How do you feel about being a member of the one tenth of one per cent of the entire human race? One of the few of us who are so gifted?"

"It's a fucked-up feeling," Russell admitted, "because I always wanted to consider myself Mr. Super-Average, more average than the average, than the average Black person. I'm as fucked-up about being so intelligent as about my hemophilia. I don't like to stand out."

Fred slammed down his beer. "You don't understand what a rare gift it is to have as fine a mind as you have," he told Russell curtly. "Remember what we talked about earlier tonight, about Washington? There are some fine minds in Washington that have been relegated to second best and have never exercised their potential.

"I've spent a lot of time on campus and seen students with unlimited potential waste it, asking questions that couldn't be answered and coming up with answers that were totally ridiculous; banging their heads against brick walls when they didn't have to.

"The fact that you're Black means shit. The fact that you're a hemophiliac means more. What I'm hearing tonight is that you're more self-destructive than anyone in this room. You still don't like yourself enough to commit yourself to using what you have to make your life meaningful. That's all it is. In the end, the disease becomes your reality. Eventually you will be another person lying in the morgue, but how meaningful your life has been up to that point is completely up to you."

There was a silence. Russell had pulled himself into a sitting position beside Bob Smith and looked reflective.

"I've indulged myself in my own nonsense many times," I observed quietly. "I've watched *him*," pointing at Fred, "indulge himself *ad nauseum*. But we have watched you indulge yourself in a life-threatening manner for almost two years. When are you going to stop?"

"Since it's out in the open," Russell sighed, "I can't fool myself and other people. In that order. I'll have to accept higher goals."

"There are a quarter of a million people of your intelligence in the whole of the United States," I informed him sternly. "And along with that, you're a Black hemophiliac. You're very unique. *You're it!*"

"And an ex-addict," Carlton reminded me.

"A highy intelligent, middle-class, Black, hemophiliac ex-addict," I marveled. Russell grinned embarrassedly. "Look at the life experiences you can share, the people you can identify with and bridge to if you decide to do so. You're a unique human being, right? And I am tired of waiting for you to come across, to be a colleague in the full sense of the word. You dilly dally . . ."

"You remember Dilly Dally," Fred murmured to Russell. Russell smiled weakly at the joke.

"There's nothing you can do about your Blackness," I went on, ignoring Fred's helpful aside. "There's nothing you can do about your hemophilia. But there is much you can do for your people. There's much you can do about race relations, since you are superior to most of the Whites in the world. Will you or will you not join us on our odyssey?

"You know and I know and Fred knows that you *can* make the choice. It's as much a choice as closing the door on drug abuse. I'm asking you to close the door on this kind of self-destructiveness, of constantly not living up to your potential."

I sat up, cross legged, tucking my skirts around me. "I'm not saying that you will not have recurrences, just as Fred has recurrences of withdrawing, but each time, as with Fred, they will be less pathological."

Russell sat with his head down, brooding.

"You have closed the door on physically injuring yourself by promising to let us jump on you if you have a need," I reminded him. "You have closed the door on drug use by staying in Odyssey. But you haven't closed the door on underachievement. You hold on to underachievement with tenacity. You are committed to being an average, indistinguishable Black."

I hitched myself toward him. "You can't be average," I said forcefully. "You're probably one of the most expensive Blacks alive in the country. How many thousands of dollars have gone into you? Keeping you alive has cost a lot, so when are you going to give back?"

"I don't even know how to begin," Russell said weakly.

"You don't have to begin," I told him. "Just close the door on underachievement. . . . So, Tompkins, what are we going to do with you? Do you want more time to be mediocre?"

"No," he answered slowly. "If I don't close that door now, it's probably going to be a long time before I do. Since it's out in the open, I don't have any choice."

Bob Smith spoke. "Plus the fact that at Odyssey House you have a golden opportunity to stretch out constructively, to get involved, to make something of yourself."

"Let me give you a commitment, Tompkins," I said, "that the road will be depressing, unrewarding, filled with failure, frustrating, bitter and difficult. You will have the most miserable days that you care to spend. I promise you that it will be filled with misery. You'll discover that Washington is made of shit. . . ."

"And there is always the guy with the busted zipper," Steve Wasserbach added.

Release and Consent Agreement

I, _____, recognizing that in the past I have had a problem with narcotic addiction, hereby request treatment by Odyssey House and recognize and/or consent to the following:

a) That Odyssey House uses its own form of treatment of addicts and accordingly, may vary from standard treatments of other facilities. In connection therewith, Odyssey House supplies staff, living facilities, equipment, and other provisions relating to the treatment and well-being of residents in accordance with its own abilities.

b) That Odyssey House is not a security institution and that residents are free to leave at any time. Odyssey House will undertake to notify the family or next of kin of the resident within 24 hours if a resident should leave provided that the resident has given the name and address of the next of kin and/or his family to Odyssey House.

c) That Odyssey House has my permission to act in all medical and psychiatric matters in my behalf, including but not by way of limitation, prescribing and conducting treatment and therapy.

d) That Odyssey House has my permission to use my name, image or voice in connection with any appearance in the news media, publications or before the public in connection with furthering the work of Odyssey House.

e) That Odyssey House will make every attempt to insure proper separation and conduct between the sexes but cannot be held responsible for any improper or consentious behavior and sequela that may occur.

f) That Odyssey House has made no representation to me with respect to treatment, therapy, facilities, or anything else other than disclosed herein. Odyssey House has made no promises or guarantees to me of any sort whatsoever.

g) That I freely and voluntarily wish to become a resident of Odyssey House and undergo the Odyssey House treatment. That I will abide by all the rules and regulations of Odyssey House.

I have read the above and understand what I am recognizing and consenting to by placing my signature below.

Signature:_____

Printed Name:_____

Address:_____

Telephone:_____

Release and Consent Agreement (Minors)

I, _____, the parent or legal guardian of _____ _____, recognizing that in the past he (she) has had a problem with narcotic addiction, hereby request treatment by Odyssey House and recognize and/or consent to the following:

a) That Odyssey House uses its own form of treatment of addicts and accordingly, may vary from standard treatments of other facilities. In connection therewith, Odyssey House supplies staff, living facilities, equipment, and other provisions relating to the treatment and well-being of residents in accordance with its own abilities.

b) That Odyssey House is not a security institution and that residents are free to leave at any time. Odyssey House will undertake to notify the family or next of kin of the resident within 24 hours if a resident should leave provided that the resident has given the name and address of the next of kin and/or his (her) family to Odyssey House.

c) That Odyssey House has my permission to act in all medical and psychiatric matters in behalf of my child or charge, including, but not by way of limitation, prescribing and conducting treatment and therapy.

d) That Odyssey House has my permission to the use of the name, image or voice of my child or charge in connection with any appearance in the news media, publications or before the public in connection with furthering the work of Odyssey House.

e) That Odyssey House will make every attempt to insure proper separation and conduct between the sexes but cannot be held responsible for any improper or consentious behavior and sequela that may occur.

f) That Odyssey House has made no representation to me with respect to treatment, therapy, facilities, or anything else other than disclosed herein. Odyssey House has made no promises or guarantees to me of any sort whatsoever.

g) That my child or charge freely and voluntarily wishes to become a resident of Odyssey House and undergo the Odyssey House treatment. That he (she) will abide by all the rules and regulations of Odyssey House.

I have read the above and understand what I am recognizing and consenting to by placing my signature below.

Signature:_____

Printed Name:_____

Relationship To Minor:_____

Address:_____

Telephone:_____

Fred Cohen II

One of my first responsibilities on completing treatment at Odyssey was to be in charge of the Drawing Board, a task with no reality. This assignment was designed to teach delayed gratification, perseverance, organizational skill and tolerance of frustration—a filing exercise. If anyone saw my files he would know exactly what I mean.

Judi chooses one person at a time to explore and develop new concepts to meet changing social needs. This is not an endurance game; it has a purpose. But given the reality of our bureaucratic processes, fruition is exceedingly slow. With great patience, we plan for twenty years ahead. We can wait forever. Judi insists that everything will come to pass eventually. Nothing is wasted in the universe.

The first of my Drawing Board assignments was called Treat the Streets. It's one long anguish. Everyone who runs Treat the Streets starts off thinking that he's going to tackle the world. He tackles nothing.

Treat the Streets was one of those ideas that emerged from several brain-storming sessions. Odyssey was totally frustrated about the ghettos and what was being done by ghetto programs—which is sometimes sinister and sometimes ludicrous and most times useless.

We developed a concept of rehabilitating people and property simultaneously using therapeutic community techniques. Everyone else deals with ghetto people or with ghetto buildings, and keeps the two separate. It's been a great boom to social workers and building contractors, but it does little for the problem. Judi calls Treat the Streets the common-sense approach. It recognizes, she says, "the interplay between man and his domain."

Odyssey's plan is for rent money from unprofitable slum buildings to be commonly pooled and to be used by the tenants to renovate their apartments and maintain the building. It is co-operative apartment living for the poor. Odyssey House would refer tenants with difficulties to such services as day-care, hospitals and counseling, guiding them to use community resources to meet their needs. Many slum people are block-bound, never leaving their street. The unknown outside world begins on the corner and is too threatening for them to cope with. I have a hard time deciding whether our current solutions to social problems are placebos or hosts of the problem. Certainly the current answers do not bring about healthy change.

Treat the Streets, however, is an idea that still had not gotten off the ground three years after it was formulated. Clifford Robinson did preliminary budgets, which were never approved by the City, or anyone else. The project was given next to John Cox, who handed it to me. I gave it to Bob Smith some months later, who eventually handed it to Ron Russell. It remained on drawing boards throughout the process.

At one point, we were close to achieving a Treat the Streets demonstration project in the Virgin Islands. Under the co-sponsorship of I.T.T., Odyssey and the Virgin Islands government, a small group of us studied the resources on the Islands for one week. This too came to nothing.

I was dismayed by the Treat the Streets project for an additional reason. While working on it in the South Bronx, I was persuaded by Clifford to carry a knife. I was depressed by the suggestion of this necessity: How could I help people if I had to carry a knife to protect myself against them?

Our concept of a National Awareness Advisory Council had a better fate. It reached the United States Senate drafting office in 1971 after beginning in the small basement room of Judi's house. Its conception followed a meeting between Judi and Senator James Buckley called at his request. She talked about the problems of the country, which she feels have to do in part with the great distance between government and the governed.

She uses as illustration an incident she has never forgotten: the afternoon when she was five years old and her Mother took her to meet the President, Franklin Delano Roosevelt. President Roosevelt opened his office to the public one afternoon every week and received citizens. As Judi puts it, "He took time to be a human being." Judi's Mother thought it was fitting that an American child should meet the country's leader, so she took her to the White House on visitors' day. Judi not only talked with President Roosevelt but she introduced him to her toy panda, Andrew, whose paw he gravely shook. In contrast, in 1971 when Judi wrote to President Nixon about the spreading epidemic of Vietnam addiction she didn't even receive the courtesy of a reply.

Senator Buckley asked her what kind of legislation she thought would help solve the problem of distance between voters and decision makers. Judi said she would report back to him. She then called a group of Odyssey staff together and we had a long, often funny, discussion, from which came a method to achieve attitudinal change. As we see it, people are frustrated because they feel powerless in the face of government. Whenever citizens have a problem or a reaction, it takes three years for the government to hear about it and two years for any action, by which time it is too late and the problem or reaction usually is different anyway. There is no quick communication between people and government.

We therefore designed a communication system of three levels along which information can flow. The President would be able to hear from the grass roots with as little as a week's delay, and the longest period of communication lag would be only three weeks. Reciprocally, citizens could be informed on what concerns the President as quickly and could receive explanations of his decision-making process. The design is a pyramid, with representation consistent throughout, from grass roots to White House and back. It is participatory democracy based on New Hampshire Town Meetings.

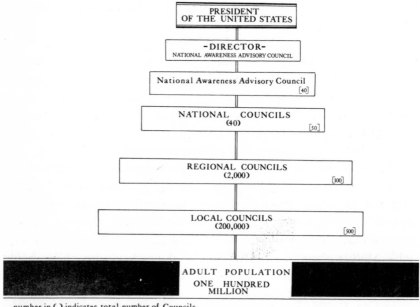

...number in ( ) indicates total number of Councils
...number in [ ] indicates total number of Members per Council

Senator James Buckley tentatively agreed to introduce the idea to Congress in the form of a bill, along with Congressman Seymour Halpern. Congressman Halpern is a real person; he was my first indication that there are hard-working, decent people trying to be effective in government. Designing the bill was one of our better moments at Odyssey. It is not often that a group of doctors and ex-addicts even dreams of designing a new Federal agency, let alone realizes that dream.

When I first started working on problems of that magnitude, I was concerned with my tangible work product and wondered if I could contribute something of value. Initially, I doubted my ability to offer anything significant. I also believed that I couldn't get gratification unless I did everything myself. I didn't like to share the credit. Gradually I came to appreciate that in the environment of Odyssey's team approach, self is not lost. In fact, it is enhanced.

Working on a team is more than an exchange of ideas. We truly like one another and enjoy being together. There is support and affection in the team, which often resolves my isolation and attempts to withdraw. Jimmy is generous to a fault; to an annoying degree, he's selfless when it comes to giving and uptight about taking. But I love him. Louie is more than a marshmallow—he's gentle and concerned and, in a sense, the conscience of the Executive Staff. Louie will shout and scream about patient care until he's hoarse. He keeps us in line; we need him. John is very distant and to me the epitome of the desire to succeed. I feel racially committed to him, deeply obligated to stand beside him and prove that the bullshit inside him isn't true. Charlie is the hardest of the group to describe. He reacts, but nothing affects him. He adapts with ease to every situation. Working with him gives me confidence. And there's always Judi.

I perceive that most of the qualities I observe in others are ones that I desire for myself and am slowly developing, with the help of my friends.

I came to understand gradually that you relate as you want to relate. My isolation was mostly my own invention. My participation in the Awareness Council design, in Odyssey's program for military addiction, in the new programs we are developing, has given me a tremendous boost. I feel self-confident even when meeting prominent figures throughout the country. But at first, it was difficult for me to believe I had anything worthwhile to say to them.

If you conquer the *a priori* fear of inadequacy, you can be adequate in all situations. You only have to have a desire to participate. Being right or wrong is not an issue. Doing the best you can is the point. The fault of parents is that they have to always be *right*. This is an outrageous expectation, one that the child knows the parent can never live up to. Our nation's leaders have the same fault. They fear admitting a mistake and so, to correct the situation, they must either hide their errors or justify them with more mistakes.

At Odyssey, on realizing our errors, we say, "Let me begin anew and do it better with this new knowledge." Inherent in this concept is the profound sense of freedom. If freedom be the goal of this nation, then we are faced with a great confrontation in humility.

SEYMOUR HALPERN
6TH DISTRICT, NEW YORK

WASHINGTON OFFICE:
2236 RAYBURN HOUSE OFFICE BUILDING
WASHINGTON, D.C. 20515
225-2536

DISTRICT OFFICE:
89-31 161st STREET
JAMAICA, NEW YORK 11432
658-0300

COMMITTEE ON
FOREIGN AFFAIRS

SUBCOMMITTEE ON
INTERNATIONAL ORGANIZATIONS
AND MOVEMENTS

SUBCOMMITTEE ON
ASIAN AND PACIFIC AFFAIRS

SUBCOMMITTEE ON
NEAR EAST

Congress of the United States
House of Representatives
Washington, D.C. 20515

April 12, 1972

Dear Colleague:

One of the most distressing problems confronting our nation today is the tragic gap between government and the mainstream of American society. It is evident on the streets of our cities, on college campuses, and in the homes of our senior citizens.

I cannot help but feel that there is a genuine need for a citizens' lobby which, through its own organization, would provide the Executive and Legislative branches with a direct avenue of communication with the people. It should be obvious to all of us that there is an estrangement in our midst which is evident in young and old, and is fed by the belief that the Federal government is a monolithic structure in Washington which is indifferent and unresponsive to the needs of too. .many segments of our society.

On April 25, I plan to introduce a bill which would create a National Awareness Advisory Council which would provide the people of our country with real problem-solving techniques based on a self-help program. The National Awareness Advisory Council would be a four level structure. The first level would be comprised of a neighborhood based organization which would meet once a month to discuss local problems. This local council would select one delegate to serve on a regional council which would define common neighborhood difficulties. In turn, the regional council selects one representative to serve on the national council. This level selects the National Awareness Advisory Council which reports directly to the President and the Congress.

In an age when alienation from the center of power is creating disillusionment among our citizens, especially the youth, we urgently need a new system of communication between the people and the power. Only if such realistic, two-way dialogue is restored can we maintain credibility in the institutions of government. I think that it is high time that this Congress makes an attempt to restore participatory democracy to its citizens.

The idea was conceived by Dr. Judy Densen-Gerber who is the Director of New York City's Odyssey House, a therapeutic community for drug addicts.

If you wish to cosponsor this bill, please contact my Administrative Assistant, Victor Kamber, (Ext. 52536).

With all my best wishes, I am

Sincerely,

Seymour Halpern
Member of Congress

SH:pev

Hayseed Cohen breaks soil on Odyssey Utah farm.

Fred Cohen in Washington when the Odyssey House Choir sang for the United States Congress.

John Cox II

For Blacks like myself, the militant racial integrationist attitude of Odyssey House presents problems. In my case, they have to do mainly with my relationships in my former neighborhood, which is all Black. People there wonder why I'm not working in an all-Black agency headed by a Black instead of an interracial agency with a White leader.

They see the Whites purely as oppressors, people who have put invisible barriers around Black communities that prevent the Blacks from developing. Frequently, I'm criticized for staying at Odyssey; most criticism is indirect.

One time, I was coming out of the building on 53rd Street, the Odyssey staff apartment building, where I was living at the time and met one of my friends who was walking down the street. We started talking. He told me that he was working in a bank while waiting for a job as a counselor in a Harlem youth group.

"I guess you're enjoying yourself," he said to me. "I see where you're living. I guess you're never coming back to Harlem."

He knew this charge of abandonment would hurt. Things of that nature really affect me. Many of my friends in my old neighborhood didn't get into drugs. They have become militants. When I visit them, usually remarks like that don't happen. That incident gave me pain.

My friend is looking for a total separation of the races. I'm not. I have a family now, my wife, Yvonne, and a little girl, Tenetrias, called Titi. I don't think we could survive in this country if there were separation. I'm certain there would be violence, and that's something I am totally against. I believe people must learn to live together in mutual respect.

The feeling of color difference doesn't happen much within the Odyssey program. Whites don't hang out with Whites or Blacks with Blacks. When a person first enters the program he might have that feeling, being fresh from the streets where Black addicts stick to Black addicts and White addicts to Whites, but after being here for a while he goes through different experiences which show him that he can identify with what other people are feeling regardless of their skin color.

After living in a house together for six months, you even build strong bonds. It was a big surprise to me, sharing with Whites, because all my life the only Whites I ever knew were persons in authority, the ones who made decisions. I wasn't used to relating to Whites as peers or of being in charge of them.

There's a good deal of separatist pressure from their friends and families on Blacks coming into the program. A great many Black families today are for total Blackness, and for a child of theirs to come into an interracial program can split the family. This creates conflict. Perhaps it is the cause of the greatest conflict a Black person has to bear during his odyssey. It surfaces again near graduation, when the Level IV must evaluate what he has gained and what he has lost. What he has gained is knowledge that all people can live and productively work together, trusting each other. What he has lost is a negative attitude that a Black man can't get ahead no matter what he does. For now he realizes that he is in charge of his own destiny.

I keep my Black identity by maintaining many of the traditional, familiar ways of Black culture. People in the community I come from are very free. I don't find that others open themselves up in the same way. Many Establishment Whites are closed and Blacks typically are not. The style of the Black is comfortable. There is free-flowing talking, a relaxed loudness, an easy breaking down of defenses, a special camaraderie.

Whites are more formal, but you discover in Odyssey that there are similarities on the feeling level. A man fears anything that he doesn't understand and with that fear goes hostility. Blacks in Odyssey House have overcome that.

Ellis Williams wrote something about this in the Odyssey newspaper that comes out bi-monthly. "Black people here at Odyssey are given a real chance to succeed," he wrote, "to get a good job, to go to school if they wish. The Black man just beginning the program sees that other Blacks in the program move up as quickly and as fairly as the Whites."

It is certainly true for me. I was asked one day to lunch privately with William Spencer, who is President of the First National City Bank, which represents more than 1 per cent of this country's Gross National Product. One night at Judi's I had called him a "Farmer," and he asked me to meet with him and explain the term. It was an opportunity to meet with an influential White on a friendly basis that isn't uncommon for Odyssey Blacks.

When I first came into the program I used to be deeply hurt by criticism. I found it humiliating to stand in front of twenty people and take it. At one point I almost burst I was so outraged. But I stayed with the program basically because people talked to me. Clifford Robinson in particular was very close. He was immediately ahead of me. He would calm me down and convince me that I should stay and keep on trying.

After the first year I stayed because I knew I was needed. It was apparent I could help other guys like myself and, besides, I had built up love for the program. Judi has greatly helped me. I

had an abundance of problems to deal with and I'm a funny type of person. She helps me understand the paranoia that I had as a frustrated Black and my conflicting need to please. Through her, I have insight into my great feelings of rejection, how they began with my father's seeming indifference and continue to the present. They still affect my relationships with others and sometimes give the impression that I'm a closed person. I respect and love her. If she's ever in difficulty, I will give her all the help I possibly can.

There's a big difference in me today from what I was when I came into the program. Before, I always used to manipulate everything around myself, told lies, whatever, to my best advantage. Now I am not so self-centered. I've learned through the agency that you may not always be able to get what you want, if at all, or you may have to work very hard to get it. You learn to live through the occasional disappointments.

While going through the program I was attracted to another resident, Yvonne Pierce. She had a daughter, Titi, who was being cared for by her mother while Yvonne was in treatment. Yvonne is a very beautiful girl with a cool, poised style. She's the type of woman who would enhance any man she was with. We weren't allowed to date until both of us reached Level IV, but when we did we found that we had fun together and shared similar goals for our lives. We decided to marry after we had known one another about two years. I gave her an engagement ring for Christmas.

We were married in July 1971. Titi was flower girl. Obviously, as with most newly wedded couples, we have our differences. Unlike many, we sit down to discuss them and work them through. Odyssey has been good for us both.

We've branched out in many areas since our marriage, doing a great many things we couldn't do before because we were addicted. We went to the Bahamas, for instance. I never went to the Bahamas when I was strung out. We're able to live like normal people now. We're close to Clifford and his wife, Diane, who also went through Odyssey. It's the same kind of friendship that I suppose former roommates in college have.

I think I'm a good father to Titi, who was four years old when we married. I talk to her, play with her. At the same time I'm rigid in my discipline about such things as telling lies, being disrespectful, showing off, not wanting to go to bed. I explain to her why she should not behave like that. Her mother felt that Titi was too young to understand, but I still took the time to do it. I figure that between the ages of one and five is when a person receives a foundation.

I don't know if I can protect her against drugs. Like Louie, I wonder what I would do if she ever used them. Since Yvonne was an addict too, we often discuss whether we should tell her that her parents took drugs. I suppose it might come up when she's a teenager and asks where we met.

Sometimes we think we will tell her and other times we think we won't. It depends on the relationship we have with Titi. If we have a wonderful relationship like we are having now, we'll tell her because we'd know that she'd understand. If our relationship is shaky, or if there is resentment and hostility, we wouldn't tell her. It's something Yvonne and I will have to work through over the years. It's a rough one.

We know we can't protect her against drugs. We can point out the evils of drugs and we can try to build a strong family foundation for her so she can live a constructive life. But it's impossible for anybody to protect their children against drugs. You can give children values, give children direction, give them insight, but they then move in the direction that is meaningful to themselves. That's what we're doing with Titi, giving her a foundation. It's the only protection I know.

Bobby Robinson's Probe

Bobby Robinson is the youngest of the four Robinson boys. All of them have used heroin, all of them have been treated at Odyssey with varying effectiveness. The Robinson family is the *Ladies Home Journal* family of togetherness, very gifted middle-class Blacks who did everything together, including fighting. The parents are religious and concerned about their sons. The mother, a teacher, remained at home to raise them while they were young.

What happened in that house was that all the sons and the father competed for the attention of the mother. The dynamic in the house wasn't love or understanding; it wasn't aggression either. It was competition. Each son competed against the other sons for everything. Bobby, as the baby, could not compete. He reacted with extreme depression.

We had an entire Case Conference devoted to the Robinson family. Stan, the third son, who came to Odyssey not for addiction but because he wanted treatment for homosexuality, presented to us the whole psychopathology, which he understands very well. All the Robinsons have incredible insight and almost no ability to put it to use.

The Case Conference was directed mostly at Bobby, who had been at Odyssey for more than a year by that time and was almost unchanged. We had not been able to break through his depression.

Stan told us, "We were all treated as one child. If something bad happened, all four of us were punished. If something good happened, all four were rewarded. We were never individuals, and there was little affection in the house. We seemed to be pitted against each other, fighting for my mother's attention, trying to stand out and be the strongest. We battled in every way, in vicious ways.

"Willie was the leader. He is almost eight years older than I and five years older than Clifford. Whatever Willie did, good or bad, we followed in his footsteps. He has a hand over us. We'll all follow him to the center of the grave. I used to feel that until Willie got well, none of us could get well. But when he bought Willie's birthright, at least Clifford got free."

The sale of the birthright took place in a group in my office. We were attempting to change Willie's profound hatred and resentment of Clifford. Willie had lived his early years alone with his mother while his father was away in the armed forces. When the return of the father and Clifford's birth happened within the same year, Willie turned his anger at the invasion of closeness with his mother against Clifford.

I asked Clifford to be the first to forgive past hostility since he owed his older brother that respect. Clifford very reluctantly, but courageously, did so. He used a symbolic gesture, offering to shine his brother's shoes. He said to Willie that he was sorry for the pain he had caused him.

Willie was asked next to forgive his brother for having been born. He refused. We said he couldn't remain at Odyssey unless he took that significant step, but he continued to refuse. We then gave him a choice: either ask forgiveness and get well with us, or give Clifford the right to be the oldest son in the family so that Clifford and the two younger brothers could get well.

We read the Bible to him, the scenes between Esau and Jacob and Cain and Abel, pleading with Willie not to sell his birthright, but to choose to forgive his brother instead. He said, "How much will you pay me?"

It was a payday and we had cash. Clifford said he would put up a hundred dollars and I matched it. Somehow, in our anxiety, one of us put in ten dollars extra. Willie took the $210 and sold his birthright. He went back on the streets and deliberately got himself arrested a few days later. Clifford now has his brother's soul. He paid for it.

The group between Clifford and Willie was the most dramatic and intense in terms of pain for two individuals that I have ever witnessed, but the group with the most passion was the one we remember as the *shoe-shine* group. We were having a walk-the-walk marathon, in which residents sit on the probe chair one at a time and come across, literally as well as figuratively. We group all the negative members of the community on one side of the room and the positive ones on the other. As each succeeds in demonstrating growth, he or she joins the positive side. Occasionally someone remains negative and he or she must leave the program.

The marathon had been going on for some time and most of the residents were sitting on our side. Bill Peters was on the probe chair, an older "yes, sir" and "no, sir" step-and-fetch-it type of Southern Black in whom no personal dignity had ever been able to develop. His behavior deeply affronted the younger Blacks in the program, particularly Clifford, who at the time was having personal difficulty with his Black identity.

Clifford wanted to get a rise out of Bill, something more than his usual servile docility. He tried insult. "When are you going to look us in the eye?" he demanded hotly. Bill didn't respond. Clifford, furious, took off his shoe and threw it at him. "Here, *nigger*," he cried, "shine my shoes!"

It touched rage in all the Blacks in the room. As Bill continued to slump, head down, ignoring the taunts and abuse that Clifford was unleashing, they took off their shoes and threw them at Bill. The whole room, all the Blacks, began to scream vituperative, racial hatred. It came from their guts and they unleashed it screaming.

The Whites withdrew. We were dumbfounded. Louie Sarra described it as walking into another world. We listened in agony as the Blacks did to one of themselves what Whites have been doing to them for centuries. Clifford had yelled, "If you want to act like a nigger, we'll treat you like a nigger." As the pack jeered around him, Bill Peters sat there, staring at the shoes lying at his feet. He didn't seem to know what to do.

Even in my bewilderment at what I was seeing, my instincts told me something was wrong. It wasn't the cruelty. I've seen lots of cruelty. There was something wrong about the therapeutic approach. I said to myself, *What would I do if I were sitting there instead of Bill?* I whispered to Clifford under the uproar and said, "You're giving him a conflict that he can't resolve. The Odyssey House structure says that he must follow your orders because you are the authority. If he disobeys you, he'll be discharged. However, your order is couched in such terms that his ego is on the line. You've given him the choice between his personal integrity and staying at Odyssey, which means his life. Who can choose between integrity and life? You've put him on a cross."

Clifford started to rage at me, saying that I didn't know what I was talking about. Any Godamned nigger with any spunk would say No and throw the shoes back. I should shut my mouth. No White knew what it is like. Silas Whitfield, an even darker Northern Black, sitting beside Clifford, listened to the exchange. He tugged at Clifford's sleeve. "Listen to her, Clifford," he said quietly. "She's right."

Clifford calmed down at once. Silas merits respect. I said to Clifford, "You must make amends now. You put Bill in an intolerable position. You must take his place." Clifford went over to Bill Peters and said, "Brother, I'm sorry. Let me have the chair."

He took Bill's place on the chair. I took off a shoe and threw it at him. I said, "Nigger, shine my shoes." Clifford picked it up and stared at it, just stared at it for a long time. Then he began to sob. There was total silence in the room, broken only by the sound of Clifford weeping and the scrape of the brush as he polished my shoe. He was painstaking with it and it seemed interminable.

When he finished I went over and said, "Let me shine the other shoe. This one is for me to do." I tried to take it from him but he held it tightly. "You mustn't do that!" he cried. "There must be no difference," I insisted. "We've got to do this together." He wouldn't give it up, so I ordered him to let me shine the shoe.

I sat there polishing as C.R. sobbed uncontrollably. Jimmy Murphy got up and tried to take it from me, but I refused. He said later that he appreciated that what I was doing had to be done for therapeutic reasons, but, on a feeling level, he felt only horror at the awareness it brought him of how trapped people can be.

Eventually I gave up the shoe to Jimmy and he finished the shine. By that time every Black in the room was crying in unison, in a primal scream of pain. The Whites were torn apart by it; none of us had imagined there was so much agony locked within the people we knew so well.

Suddenly, Whites and Blacks, began to sing. They started with "She's Got the Whole World in Her Hands," directed to me, and moved on to every song any of us could remember. There was the release of joy after the intensity of the pain. We started to dance. My partner was Richie Klein, sitting in his wheel chair. He danced by rocking it to the music so abandonedly that three times he fell out of it and had to be helped back.

We nicknamed him "Circle-Legs" that night. If a man with wheels for legs can dance, man can do anything.

Silas Whitfield had influence over Clifford at the height of his tormented shouting because of the kind of man Silas is. He's a Black with almost no racial identity problem whatsoever. He prefers not to interact with the world at all, which is why I think that heroin appealed to him. Life was just too much bother. He speaks so infrequently that we have dubbed him "Silas the Silent."

It came to a head, after Silas had been in Odyssey for a while, when I believed he should move beyond his need to weigh and evaluate everything before taking any action. He was becoming frozen, brooding about the ramifications of every deed. We were seeing a man who was totally indecisive. I said to him that I wanted him to stand on his head.

The reason, I explained, is that there wasn't any reason for him to stand on his head but, on the other hand, there wasn't any reason why he shouldn't. All he had to evaluate was whether or not it would harm him. If he decided it wouldn't harm him, he should trust me and do it.

"Trust your doctor," I told him. "I'm not asking you to do something like jumping off a bridge." If he didn't trust me enough to follow my ridiculous request, I added, there was no possibility of Odyssey being able to help him further. There would be many other things that we would be asking him to do that he wouldn't understand, so if he didn't accept the order to stand on his head we would have to discharge him.

He sat in silence for ninety-three minutes. The whole group sat in total silence while he thought about it. At the end of the ninety-three minutes, Silas silently got up, took the change out of his pockets, put it on a table, and stood on his head. His odyssey had begun.

It was the first time in his life he had given up his compulsive-obsessive rumination and turned over the decision-making to someone else. If I were to meet Silas in the middle of New Jersey tomorrow and asked him to stand on his head, he would do it.

At his wedding reception, when he was in a tuxedo, a group of us who knew what it meant took him to a private place and I said, "Silas, once more, stand on your head." Without hesitation he silently took the change out of his pockets, put it on a table, and stood on his head. I bent down and kissed him and said, "Congratulations. You've just graduated from Odyssey."

He has told me that it represents to him the single most meaningful experience in his cure.

I've spoken before of the importance of trust in the therapeutic process. It presents special problems for Blacks to trust a therapist who is White and for a Black man in particular to trust a White woman. Still it does happen.

Bob Smith is another example. He was hostile and negative when he first came to Odyssey, fresh from being a leader in bombings and other violent activist acts in the South. He was recognized by the staff to be J.E.S. material. When he was being inducted into the J.E.S., I asked him if he would ever be my bodyguard as he had Stokely Carmichael. He answered that he would like to reserve decision.

He began to spend a good deal of time in my home because I

wanted to understand him better. One day I was involved in a dispute with some men sent by a private contractor to work on my floors. I discovered that they were addicts. Using addicts, differing from addicts in treatment, are extremely dangerous. I asked them to leave and later refused to pay the maintenance company. I reported them to their supervisor.

They returned. When I opened the door they started yelling and screaming at me. Bob almost reflexively put himself between them and me and ordered them off. Because they were Blacks, I was struck by the decision he had made, without thinking. He said he realized then that he could have commitment and loyalty across color lines.

It was beautiful, mostly because it was so spontaneous. I find him one of the most perceptive and sensitive and kind individuals I have ever met. He wants to go to law school, and I hope he will go on to Congress. In 1972 he was nominated to be a Robert F. Kennedy Fellow. He has the capacity to be a great leader for his people.

The same instinctive protective act happened with Donald Mann, a patient from Virginia, who later had an Odyssey scholarship to one of our finest Michigan prep schools, Cranbrook. Don was in my home early in his treatment helping me and Michael paint. With us was a very disturbed patient, Jesse Hampton. The sickest patients used to visit in my home because I needed to observe them.

Jesse, a Black, had spent fifteen years in a southern prison for statutory rape of a sixteen-year-old Black girl, the daughter of a minister. His sentence began when he was eighteen. Thirteen years of it were spent in solitary confinement. In the South that meant in a hole in the ground with a grate on top of it. He was fed from a bucket that went up every morning with his waste and was dumped and then filled with his food. He spent thirteen years like that.

He was insane when they released him. He filed his teeth to points, like a wolf's, for effect. To control his murderous rage, he took heroin. He knew he was mentally ill. Because he wanted help, he voluntarily had himself certified as an addict by the New York State Narcotics Addiction Control Commission, which sent him to Manhattan State Psychiatric Hospital. He told us that he spent six months there with increasingly severe hallucinations and never saw a doctor or received any medication. So, he left and walked six miles to Bellevue Hospital and asked to be admitted. Bellevue explained that it didn't admit addicts. They suggested he try Odyssey a mile away. And so he walked to us.

Jesse, Don and I were painting my son Judson's room one night.

Jesse started playing with the idea that I was Dora, an imaginary Black/White female who had been in his cell with him for most of the thirteen years. He chatted lightly as he developed the thought that he could get rid of Dora by killing me. He left the room; Don and I heard him rummaging among the kitchen knives.

Don was only sixteen at the time, but he went downstairs and took the knife away from Jesse. He calmed him down and escorted him back to Odyssey House alone, a sixteen-year-old boy handling a homicidal maniac by himself.

Jesse later decided that our son Judson had everything he, Jesse, had wanted as a child. He was jealous. Therefore, he reasoned, he should kill Judson. He called a group together to tell me about it. Because part of Jesse cared about me, I extracted from him a commitment that if his rage became uncontrollable, he would leave the program rather than act out against Judson. I had no other choice, since no place else would accept him and putting him on the streets would only increase his anger and likewise the danger.

One day Jesse went to his house supervisor and said his rage was out of control, and he was leaving. He went to Bellevue and, as I expected, they discharged him in about a week. Then I got a very strange message. He wanted to inform me that he didn't want me to live in fear for my son. He was therefore going to kill himself. He disappeared. My Husband, Michael, went through the death records without finding Jesse, but no one has seen him since.

I have felt very close to many patients at Odyssey, Clifford Robinson for one. When he was third in command at Odyssey, he left the program because of his conviction that the expansion of the agency was destroying its warm, intimate family feeling. Since then he has had many good jobs, one of which was with the VERA Institute of Justice. All of us attended his wedding to Diane Silver, another Odyssey graduate.

Because of Clifford, I took a special interest in his youngest brother, Bobby. Clifford has asked me to help all his brothers but particularly the baby of the family. I hadn't conducted a probe-in for more than a year. But I agreed to do Bobby's for Clifford's sake as much as for his. There was the strange Robinson family bonding.

It started at two-thirty in the morning after the Executive Staff meeting ended.

I love probes. The probe is the first real therapy session the patient has. The addict enters Odyssey as a candidate-in. He stays at that Level while we get to know him and he learns about us. After he begins to do well we call a special group, a mixture of staff and other residents representing each of the Levels. Here we focus on his attitude.

Until now the patient has been confronted only on his behavior. Two questions are asked in the probe-in. *Does the patient want Odyssey?* and *Can we help him?* We concentrate on him as a human being and often the results are extraordinarily gratifying. During the process, the isolated addict is forced to allow himself to feel. Occasionally, the group decides that the patient with his present attitude can't be helped at Odyssey and discharges him. The patient almost always returns to begin again. I handled the most difficult cases when I was doing probes regularly. One time I discharged seven people out of eight consecutive probes.

Bobby Robinson's probe was in my office, with Bobby sitting on the high-backed gold-painted metal chair which is the probe chair. The only light in the room came from a white glass bubble about three feet in circumference. It throws a soft, relaxing glow. We call it the Nostradamus globe.

The residents came in sleepily, awakened after being in bed less than an hour. Fatigue is important in a probe, as in many therapy groups, because tired people let down their defenses more readily. Bob Smith and David Winters had stayed on with me from the lengthy staff meeting, both of them changing from business suits to jeans. I was wearing my usual floor-length dress, loose and comfortable, and I was stretched out on the couch with a cotton sheet over my legs. In the dim room, the others were sitting on the more comfortable chairs or lying on the floor.

We introduced ourselves around the room. Odyssey has grown so large that unfortunately this is necessary. Each participant was asked to express what he or she hoped to gain from the probe. We started with David Winters.

"A probe is one of the most intense learning experiences that anybody can go through," David told the group. "Besides being a gas and enjoyable and certainly profitable to the person on the point, everybody in the room can learn a lot and get closer to the program. They can learn how Judi and others of us at the top think. It's a good experience, so keep your eyes and ears open and try not to fall asleep. It's not one of these regular rinky-dink probes like I run."

"I'm asleep," I announced loudly.

"If we fall asleep," David said with dignity, "that's part of the problem-solving method."

When Ted Tann introduced himself he remarked that he had never been in a probe with me before, although he had run a number of probes himself.

I groaned, "God, I hope I do something."

"You can't go to sleep now," David grinned.

There was a knock at the door. The kitchen crew came in with trays of apples, cold meat, buttered bread and chocolate milk. We finished the introductions and Bobby was sent for. He came in, an apprehensive, handsome, small, dignified figure, eighteen years old; a lighter-skinned version of his brother Clifford. I asked him what he wanted to talk about and he looked confused.

"I don't know what you want," he answered tentatively. "Like, do you want me to run my background, or this or that? In all my other probes they told me to recall back as far as I could remember . . ."

"And now that you've got rid of *that*," I interrupted sweetly, "what would you like to speak about?"

The bullshit usually comes first. Bob explained that he was concerned about himself because he "didn't have a feeling for people." I dismissed that and asked him to describe the day I talked to him after he left Odyssey six months before. Reluctantly, he told the group that his plan when he left the program was to get a job, to find an apartment and, if that didn't work out, to kill himself.

We received a call at the time from his Job Corps office saying that he was there. Smith brought him home to Odyssey and Bob, in tears, agreed to make it through the program. In turn I promised to run his probe-in.

"I've been in the program sixteen months," Bob added, his face a careful mask, "and as long as I've been in the program my problem has been acceptance. I could never accept that I was really sick."

A diesel truck rolled past Odyssey, muffling Bob's almost inaudible voice. I peered at him sternly. "Let's look at this," I demanded. "An eighteen-year-old you go out and if you can't get a job and you can't get an apartment, you're going to commit suicide. Is that well or sick?"

Bob half smiled. "Yeah, I admit to that being sick."

I persisted. "What are we discussing? Are you sick or are you not sick?"

"I'm sick."

"Fine," I said, sinking back into the couch. "Now let's talk about how you're going to get well. . . ."

Hours passed. Some of the time I dozed, a part of my mind still conscious enough to monitor what transpired. David Winters was solidly asleep and snoring; others in the room dropped off gradually. Ted Tann, his voice light and at times mocking, wore Bobby down, prodding him through a series of retreats.

When I heard Bobby insist that he felt superior to his brothers, Willie because he had used heroin the longest, Clifford for a reason he didn't understand, and Stanley for being homosexual, I roused myself.

"You truly feel you are ahead of everyone else and that's why you feel depressed and suicidal?" I asked, incredulous.

"It has nothing to do with me feeling depressed and suicidal," he protested. "It's not totally a mental depression . . . it's, ah . . ."

"Physical!"

He nodded gratefully. "Partly physical."

"Oh, tell us why," I begged. "You're in menopausal depression? Your hormones are raging? You inherited it from your mother?"

He started to explain that his drug-taking may have "distorted my nervous system."

I rolled over in disgust and turned my back to him. "Wake me up when all this is over," I muttered.

Ted Tann continued with derisive questions, to which Bob responded stiffly, earnestly and with resistance. Toward four in the morning I sat up again.

I instructed him, "All we want you to tell us about, is the life essence of Bobby Robinson: his enthusiasm, his joy, his commitment, his affirmative dedication to help in getting well. And we'll pass you. Sell us Bobby Robinson."

He slumped. "As far as any positive turnaround or anything, that's still to come," he admitted.

A city cat appeared on the windowsill outlined against the streetlights, looked into the still room and went away.

"We aren't arguing with you," I said. "On the theory of existential crisis, every so often there come to people those moments in their lives when they must act, when they can't survive if they passively sit by and let life drift from one point to another. Right?"

"Right," Bob agreed, looking at me sadly.

"You're in existential crisis and you can't wait," I continued. "You must do something."

Bob sagged and after some more pokes at his unresponsiveness, I rolled over and went back to sleep.

Stoically Ted spent nearly an hour more drawing from Bob some stories about how he enjoyed making others feel uncomfortable and depressed, and the methods he used. Ted and the few others awake encouraged Bob by laughing delightedly at each example, congratulating him on his ingenuity. It was nearly five in the morning, with gray pre-dawn light outside, when I woke up and asked, "Have you had a break-through yet?"

"No," Ted assured me, "we had a laugh."

"Very good," I told him, closing my eyes.

Bob's voice was dragging, his face full of hurt, as Ted pointed out that he was failing the probe. "I wanted this probe," Bobby said wearily. "I wanted it a lot. But now that I've got it, right, it's . . . I just don't know what to put out."

I lay on my back, with my eyes closed. "Bobby," I asked abruptly, "do you think there might be something wrong in the orientation of someone whose enjoyment of others is based on how much he can goof on them? Rather than on how he and they can mutually benefit and move forward?"

"Yes," he said faintly, "yes, there is."

Around five-thirty Bob said, "I cop to having some type of sadistic need to make people feel uncomfortable."

"Fine," I murmured through a yawn. "Wake me up at the next break-through."

"That wasn't a break-through," Ted corrected me.

"A hobble-through?" I suggested.

"Yeah," he sighed, "a hobble-through."

The brick tenements across the street were becoming visible. The cat had returned to the windowsill when Bob brokenly assured Ted that he wanted to get well and that he didn't want to be discharged from Odyssey. Ted was unimpressed. He snapped that he would feel no guilt in turning Bob out of the program. "Maybe you'll find happiness on a cold marble slab," he told him ruthlessly, "seeing you want it so badly. You have already overdosed twice on barbiturates."

Bob, head down, replied slowly, "You've had it all. I simply can't think. I can't think anything. I can't feel anything, other than what I've already said."

"Don't do us no favors," Ted told him icily. "There's one hundred and fifty thousand drug addicts in New York City, right?"—Someone said sleepily, "More than that."—"So don't do us no big-time favor by staying here."

"I know I'm fucked up," Bob said patiently, his face miserable. "I know I'm a big jammed-up person. I do want to change that. I don't want to die."

"Then, there's only one alternative," Ted told him. "If dying isn't the choice, then help yourself."

"I'm tired," Bob answered. "I'm very very tired."

There was a bar of sunlight on the top of the buildings across the street. It predicted a beautiful summer day.

"What time is it?" I asked.

Ted lifted his head from the rolled-up pillow he had arranged. "It's six-thirty," he told me.

"Any more break-throughs?"

"I have had a revelation," Ted said with satisfaction. "Bob has set us up to kick him out, like his parents have kicked him out, like his brothers have kicked him out."

"That's right," I told him, pleased. "That's very good. Not nice, Robert." I pulled the sheet up to my shoulders and closed my eyes again.

Ted spent the next half hour leading Bobby to imagine himself going through the program, describing what it might be like. Bob had difficulty conceptualizing it.

"What would make you happy this minute?" Ted asked dryly.

There was a long dismal silence. Bob stared at the floor and said finally, "I don't know." Brokenly, his eyes wet, he said it would make him feel good to "look everyone in the face and smile—but I can't. I want to share but I don't know what to share. And I want help."

My breathing was noisy. Ted moved from lying on his back to lying on his stomach. The pauses grew longer. After a long stillness Bob asked softly, "Is anyone awake?" I sat up at once.

"What are we going to do with you?" I asked gently. "You must throw off the defense of intellectualization that maintains your depression. You don't need it any more."

Bob looked at me with a defeated expression.

"You're nowhere as vicious as your brothers," I went on. "You're not mean, as they are. You're just depressed. Of all your brothers, as the baby you come from the most difficult, most competitive, most destructive life situation. Give up your depression. Just give it up. You don't need it any more. You needed your depression in order to cope with your brothers, but you don't need it any more."

Bob began to sob, making deep tearing sounds. It wakened most of the group, who turned to watch him with compassionate faces. Someone pushed a box of tissues within his reach.

I stood up, moved around the people lying on the floor and from the wall I took down a picture of Clifford sitting in the probe chair. It shows him with his head back and his eyes closed. His face is full of intense pain.

"Take it," I told Bobby. "It's yours. It's your brother sitting where you're sitting now. He got well, and you can too."

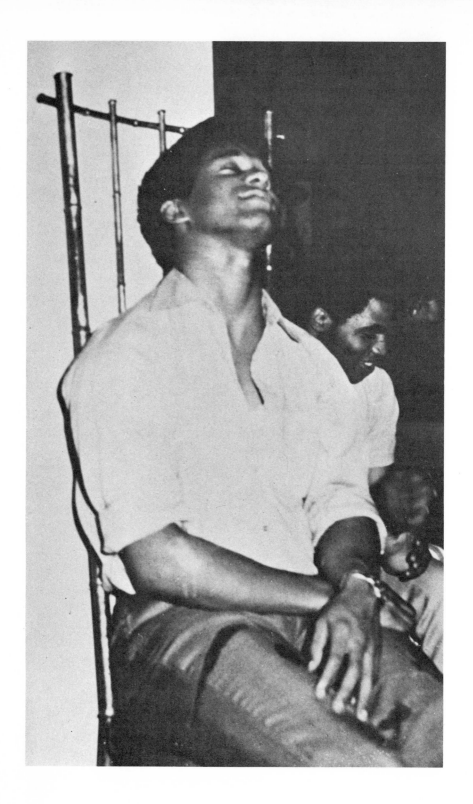

Bob's slight body was shaking. For a moment he didn't accept the picture. When he took it with one hand, the other curled into a tight fist.

"No wonder you were depressed," I said softly, sitting near him. "You were the runt of the litter and you needed your depression to survive. But you don't have to be depressed here at Odyssey. It gets between you and other people, between you and your feelings. You can't get well as long as you are depressed. It sounds easy to say, *just stop it,* but that's how it's done."

Bob cried hard, his body convulsed. I watched, not touching him. "Let it all hang out," I said soothingly. "Cry it all out. Willie is just a bastard, Clifford maintains his distance with charisma, Stanley maintains his through being effeminate and you maintain your distance with depression. But you all maintain distance in some way." I grieved with him for the four gifted Robinson boys.

Bob was beginning to recover. I said briskly, "We'll have no more feeling guilt, no more feeling bad, no more feeling uptight and paralyzed. It's time to start moving. Now let's have a nice, deeply resonant, gut-level commitment."

Bob gave me a wan smile. Sniffling, he said, "I guess the most important thing is that I stop feeling so bad about myself . . ."

"Let's put it in the present," I ordered. "Say, 'I have stopped feeling so bad, and I am not going to feel so bad again.' Right?"

"The most important thing," Bob began again, "is that I have stopped feeling so . . ."

I giggled. "Listen to him," I said fondly to Ted, who shook his head in disbelief.

Bob choked up. ". . . so bad about myself, so depressed all the time." He wept again.

"You can cry a little more?" I asked approvingly. "Good. You've got some crying left and that's good. Get it out. There's a lot of loneliness in there."

When he regained control I instructed him to sit up straight, his shoulders against the back of the chair, his eyes looking straight ahead. "Look us in the eye. See how much better that is? You look one hundred per cent more enthusiastic. I like the way you look. It makes me feel I have another positive Robinson in my midst."

Ted asked, "How does it feel to be human?"

His head back, his face exhausted, Bob answered slowly, "The main thing is that I have already broken through . . . well, the realities are . . . I guess there will be times when it will be hard. I never cried so much in my life before."

I was pleased. "Isn't it good! It's all done!"

Bob looked around the room. "I feel strange," he murmured.

"Can I do something unprofessional, Judi?" Ted asked me. "Something completely unprofessional?"

"Go ahead."

He turned to Bob. "You are going to help us with your treatment," he told him. "You are going to figure out what would be beneficial to you in the job function areas and what you would like to see done with you."

"I didn't know you were going to do that," I commented.

"Isn't it all right to ask a patient to tell me how to treat him?" he asked.

"I always do. It's the best way," I assured him. We exchanged smiles.

"You will now be meaningfully involved in your treatment," I informed Bob, who looked bewildered. "We'll see you Friday at Case Conference, and you'll have prepared the best treatment plan for you that you can. All right?"

Bob was beginning to like the idea. "How do I prepare it, in writing?"

"Yes," Ted said, "but not too complex. The staff has to follow it."

Bob was erect, relaxed, amused. He finished the ritual of the probe, asking each person in the group for a verdict. In Odyssey probes, the applicant must satisfy every member of the group. All of them, tired and serious and moved, voted to have him continue at Odyssey. We roused David Winters who had been asleep throughout.

"I vote yes," he said distinctly.

"We need to know why you feel that way," I reminded him.

David threw up an arm. "Because I *like* him," he roared.

It was shortly after nine-thirty in the morning when we finished. I gathered up my briefcase. I had to hurry home to shower, market and have breakfast with a Congressman who was interested in funding the New Jersey house. Then I was flying to Ohio to be on a television talk show. And it was looking like a scorcher of a day outside.

Roger Sayers and his bride, the former Dolores Ifill,
with Judi after their wedding at the Badens' house.
Each used heroin for eighteen years—
a combined drug history of thirty-six years.
Both are graduates of Odyssey.

Richie and Charlie Shanner before Odyssey.

Richie and Charlie Shanner after Odyssey.

Charlie Rohrs 11

Ted Tann has no academic background as a therapist—he learned his technique at Odyssey—but he has a commitment to our treatment method, and he has the ability to come across as a real, creditable human being who practices what he preaches. His importance at Odyssey demonstrates what must happen if medicine is to become more effective in the field of mental health, and certainly in the field of drug addiction. More physicians must learn to function as members of a team where decision-making is participated in by others.

Odyssey has a professional training program in which our somewhat unorthodox methods are taught. They are unorthodox so far as traditional medicine or social work is concerned. For one thing, we're demanding. We believe a person *can* control his own behavior, that he must earn the right to have therapy, that he must be held responsible for what he does rather than constantly be forgiven.

Medical schools should be training people to develop this attitude toward dependency diseases, among which drug addiction is now the most troublesome. They must also prepare professionals to listen to and share authority with para-professionals and others who have a different kind of expertise. This physicians haven't been too willing to do in the past. We must strive to achieve the goals of such men of science as Dr. Jack Geiger of Tufts University, who exhorts the profession to do more than just treat rat bites: It should be getting rid of the rats as well. There's a new breed of physicians who see their responsibility as exactly that, treating not only the symptoms of the diseases of social disruption but also the causes.

In addiction, and in many other fields of medicine, there may be seven or eight correct alternatives. What you want to find is the *most* correct for a particular patient. The group process of problem-solving makes it more likely that the leader will have sufficient input to arrive at the decision that is most correct.

People seeking employment at Odyssey sometimes apologize for wanting money to work in the drug field. They don't approach rehabilitation as a vocation, as something that will benefit and enrich themselves; instead they come here with the idea that they're going to do something to help somebody else. One of the things ahead of us is to make people realize that this is a vocation just as cardiology or law are careers and not simply pastimes to appease their social consciences. Odyssey's policy of paying well is based on the philosophy that helping people is as important as making automobiles, designing homes or writing television scripts. Also we want to attract the best talent available.

Someday, medicine will recognize that what we're doing at Odyssey is a new specialty. It might be called *Unnatural Diseases*. This country is rapidly approaching a situation where unnatural disease is as large a cause of death as natural disease: alcoholism, drug addiction, child abuse, suicide, murder, automobile accidents and that kind of thing. People are being forced to live in a society they can't understand. We all must work on new techniques for dealing with the ghettos we all inhabit. Everyone lives in a ghetto. The suburbs or expensive apartment buildings are as likely to be emotionally alienated jungles as any slum in which the individual must fight to survive.

Today many people dabble in the addiction field. The attitude is that they'll work in it for a year or two and then they'll get a *real* job. Until we professionals attach importance to this type of work, we aren't going to have many more Judianne Densen-Gerbers. Right now addiction is considered a second-rate specialty by the medical profession. It's one of Odyssey's responsibilities to make it first-rate.

We've learned to restrict the activities of volunteers. Our residents don't need the kind of help volunteers give in hospitals or nursing homes. They shouldn't be getting help to function. On the contrary, we're forcing them to function by themselves. Volunteers who want to *do for* the patients directly, rather than *do with* them, are definitely wrong for a therapeutic community. Treating addicts requires more than good intentions; training is essential.

I've been asked often about how I feel working for a woman. Is it a threat to my virile instincts or whatever? It never entered my mind when I came here that there would be any difficulty working for a woman, probably because I have a mother who is a capable person.

Judi is impressive. She's mastered three disciplines: law, medicine and psychiatry, which is an extraordinary achievement for anyone. But she's done more than just accumulate degrees. She has concepts and understanding of what each truly means, which I don't think many professionals do in even one area. She's able to put what she has learned into practice, as well as having a natural instinct for administration, for dealing with people, for politics and publicity.

She can deal with the most anti-social individual and the most Establishment person at the same time. She can be demure and feminine when the situation demands it, and she can also come across as hard-nosed and abrasive when necessary. She's the most fascinating individual I've ever dealt with just on the basis of total competence.

It's easier for a man to work for a male who has outstanding abilities and accomplishments rather than a female with them. This is where the man's problem of relating to women really lies: it's when women are deservedly in positions of authority. One of the things men have to learn is that we should be more concerned with the incompetent men who are in positions of power, rather than the competent women in ascendency.

At Odyssey, we are asked repeatedly to explain why people take drugs. We're aware that most of the time the person asking is thinking in terms of one answer, bad family environment, mental illness, permissiveness, lack of religious upbringing, something like that.

The fact is that there are hundreds of reasons why people are taking drugs. One of the true horrors we're facing is the number of young people from "ideal American families" who turn to drugs. They have had everything imaginable to equip them for a healthy productive life, but they still shoot heroin into their veins.

Studies of these adolescents show that acceptance outside of the family at that age plays a more important role than family ties. It's the time of life when nature intends young people to break away from their families. Instinctively they seek the security and conformity of a peer group in order to become strong enough to eventually emerge as full-functioning, independent, mature young adults. Therefore, if the peer group is taking drugs, the healthiest individual adolescent may adopt drugs as well. No child is immune.

Judi once observed in a speech to the American Academy of Neurology: "Sadly, in many areas across the nation, it has become a normal maturational development to use drugs. For instance, when you have a home-room class of thirty students and twenty-nine of them are mainlining heroin—as we had in a home-room class in New

York City—then I fear for the thirtieth child who must be schizophrenic or severely schizoid to be so different."

We have to solve the problem of how our society alienates people, isolates people, and increases their feelings of rage and frustration. Drug-taking, like many other problems in society, arises from our attitudes toward one another, from the way individuals relate to each other. In part, it has to do with the breakdown of healthy family life and the lack of responsive social institutions. Most of our efforts to improve the situation during the past thirty years have failed. We are now in the process of destroying a generation.

I wince when I see stereotype heroes on television who come across as stern, gruff and always in control of the situation. They are never inadequate, have no emotions and are without personal problems. That's not human, but that's what we give our kids as role models.

It is time to try some fundamentally new approaches. The techniques of a therapeutic community provide some of the tools to help the United States. We can't expect to clean up the mess with nickels and dimes. It's going to take a great deal of money, and it's going to require a great many trained people.

If I were to think of the United States as a person, I would describe her as someone with a very sheltered childhood, advantaged, privileged, spoiled. Americans grew up with the myth that no one can grow corn like the *people* in Iowa can grow corn. The reality is that Iowa has the best land in the world for growing corn—*anyone* could grow the world's best corn if he had been fortunate enough to live in Iowa. Fortuitous circumstances like that, however, gave Americans the idea that they are people who are more capable than any other.

Now the country is leaving the security of childhood omnipotence and is entering the identity crisis of adolescence. We are forced to deal with realities of poor housing, perpetual poverty, malnutrition, pollution, prejudice and consequent second-class citizenry, discontent, rioting, mediocre education, crime, violence, infant mortality, venereal disease, drug addiction, inadequate health care, abandonment of the aged, to name a few. Without change how can we any longer justify continuing to present ourselves as the moral leaders of the world who have a clean house at home, or to believe that we can be good role models to the other nations? We Americans are decent people who love our land, but only by facing our problems will we solve them—denial leads nowhere. I love America and I want to help create a better country for my son and his generation. We don't have immediate answers, and things aren't going the way we want. The situation can also be compared to a patient who has a potentially fatal disease and is still practicing denial, still taking drugstore remedies, still refusing to see the doctor. He suspects because he's coughing that he might have lung cancer, but he doesn't want to see the X-ray.

We must go beyond this ostrich attitude and sit down to listen to people who have some expertise about what's wrong. It is not going to be easy. No one has answers for these huge problems. We haven't even begun to ask the right questions yet.

At Odyssey we can only treat a limited number of people. We can't cure the whole world, but we're pulling enough out of the sick pool to clearly demonstrate that our methods work. We feel satisfaction with each of our successes, but we are aware that unaided we can do little toward prevention. Yet, our struggle to educate the people in power seems futile, and no meaningful attempts at change are in the offing. At Odyssey, Judi and I as well as others are bound together by sharing the mutual gratification of watching individual patients such as Jimmy, Fred, Louie, and John get well and the mutual depression of watching our politicians refuse to problem solve. We have storefronts and experimental programs, most of them unfunded, and we are begging the government to give us the necessary resources to explore and deal with the challenges that preventive medicine presents.

It isn't as simple as calling the problem lack of education or faulty law enforcement or generation gap. There's too much distance between groups of people, too little feeling of mutuality between people of differing ages, religions, ethnic backgrounds, education and/or authority. Until people can function again as a tribe or an extended family, all the problems we have today will get worse.

I'm fearful for my son. Louie Sarra says that he doesn't know what he would do if he found his child taking drugs. Barbara and I share his feeling. Right now we're doing the best job of prevention that we can. Alexander goes to the Odyssey nursery frequently where he has the opportunity to be with other children. He has parents who love and are honest and open with one another. He sees that we make mistakes, but we face them and deal with them. He also sees adults at Odyssey working together in a spirit of trust and co-operation. What I am doing at Odyssey not only has meaning for me but also for him. Because of it he'll see that adults don't necessarily hate one another or run from their problems. There is warmth and tenderness here, which we extend not only to our own children but to all children.

It's the best we can do for Alexander.

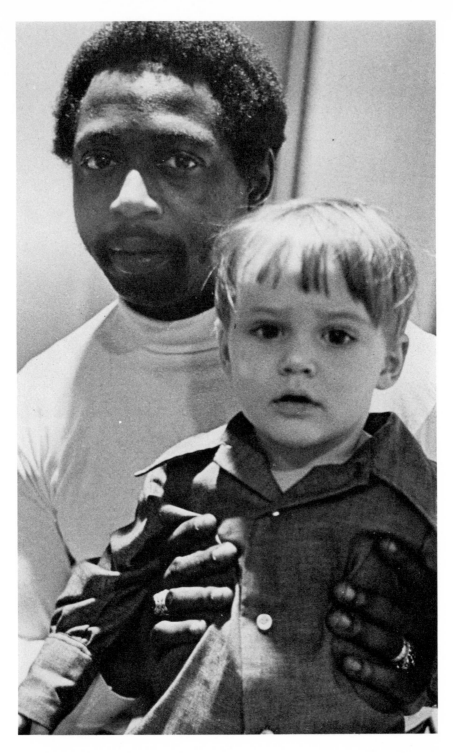

17   Ellis Williams and Alexander Rohrs.

Two Odyssey mothers and their children.

In June 1971 Odyssey House began a new development in the therapeutic community treatment of drug addiction.

Until the fall of 1970 Odyssey had treated adolescent addicts, both male and female, in the same therapeutic community setting. However, at that time, it was decided to separate the two sexes below the age of eighteen, in order that special attention could be paid to the problems of the female adolescent addict, notably very low self-esteem and inability to realize her female identity. Therefore, the young girls in the program were moved to an inadequate but livable facility in the South Bronx, the only building then available.

In addition, Odyssey physicians and others in the public health field had long been aware of the growing numbers of pregnant female addicts. Usually in her early teens and unmarried, such a girl knows nothing of pre-natal care and is likely to use drugs during her entire term. Her baby, if born at all, will be born addicted, with the con-

31

sequent medical problems that are still not fully understood by the medical profession.

When, in April 1971, an Odyssey House board member lent the agency a spacious townhouse on East 52nd Street that was ideal for use as a girls' residence, it was decided to combine the solution of the two problems in a comprehensive therapeutic community for young female addicts.

In the past, when an Odyssey House female resident gave birth the baby was put in foster care until the mother graduated from the program. She then had the option of making a new life with her child or placing it for adoption. Obviously, foster care at such a crucial time in the baby's life was not ideal, but Odyssey lacked facilities to care for both mother and child. There was no program in the United States designed to care for mother and child together. Odyssey House decided to meet the need.

With the acquisition of the new building, it is possible for young mothers to live in the community with their children. The inherent advantages are obvious: The infant has the benefit of its mother's continued care and attention, and under Odyssey's professional supervision the mother does not abdicate the responsibility for bringing up her child.

The program, of course, is entirely voluntary. No pregnant girl inducted into the program is required to give birth if she would rather have an abortion in accordance with New York State law. And no girl is required to keep her baby if she would prefer to place it in a foster home or for adoption. The choice remains totally with the mother. However, for the first time in the United States, she is afforded the option of long-term supportive help if she decides to keep her baby.

The program, of course, is expensive, although compared to the costs that would be incurred in a state or municipally run program, it is quite reasonable. Even though the girls do all their own housework, cooking and maintenance, the total cost for a mother and child for one year is $9,500.

The New York State Narcotics Addiction Control Commission has denied funding for the adolescent part of this project, even though there would be no need for new funds but merely a reapportionment of NACC funds earmarked for Odyssey's previously established adolescent program. NACC's grounds for refusing the reapportionment were that the girls were no longer living in the same building as the one for which the original grant had been made. This prompted Odyssey's Executive Director to remark that the state was obviously funding buildings rather than people.

Therefore, the survival of this vitally needed program is entirely dependent upon voluntary contributions. To provide the best medical care for these young mothers and their babies in a therapeutic setting in which the mothers can be cured of the disease of addiction and taught to lead productive, healthy lives and to be good mothers would cost approximately $190,000 for twenty such mothers and their infants. A small price to pay to help alleviate one of society's gravest social ills.

The Marathon

It's the soap-box of lie, and the concrete of truth.
    It's the game for concealing guilt.
It's the wish of another for fear of others.
    It's the twisted mind blaming Fate!

It's the reaching of bridges with magic pills as the toll.
    It's the fear of who and what.
It's the blockade to the revolution of soul.
    It's the steel covering, and the undentable shield!

It's the end of the twilight with the turning off of new current.
    It's the perverted moral, identifying.
It's the battle for the plus and negative on the ground of reality.
    It's the standing cripple!

—TOMMY MOTT

The Women's Marathon

The female addict is vastly different from the male. Generally she is much sicker and harder to treat. Rarely does she have a sense of identity as a female. Her relations with men have been terrible. She has been used, sold, beaten, violated, conquered, derided, exploited.

Despite this, women residents initially did very well at Odyssey House. We were surprised by this because no previous program had succeeded to any great extent with women addicts. We were not aware at the time that I was the decisive factor. I was providing a strong female role model. When pressure of Odyssey's expansion compelled me to move more into administration and I had less contact with the patients, women began to leave the program. The men in charge were permitting the normal dynamic of society to take over, and the women were relegated to inferior positions. Accordingly, the women became discouraged and felt they couldn't aspire to be important. When we recognized what had happened, we put women such as Yvonne Cox into authority, and women again began to succeed in the program.

It's important for adults to be in a coed treatment center in order to work through the relationships between mature men and women. There is no difficulty controlling sexual acting-out among adults. However, with adolescents there is the normal male need to prove masculinity by conquering females. It isn't easy for any adolescent girl to cope with constant sexual demands of her peer male, but most adolescents have strong enough self-concepts to be able to say *no*. Girls at Odyssey do not; they wouldn't be in need of treatment if they did.

We discovered in the coed adolescent treatment centers we

were unable to control the sexual puppy play. It was proving destructive to the girls, so we separated the sexes. The need for our experimental all-female house was confirmed by the good results. We now believe strongly that adolescent males and females should be treated in separate facilities.

Unfortunately, the New York State Narcotics Addiction Control Commission is not as flexible as we. It cannot learn from experience and appears to have a commitment to failure. For instance, when we realized we had made a mistake in putting adolescent males and females in the same facility, we moved the females to another house. There was no extra budget required—*not one additional cent.* We asked permission from NACC to divide the previously awarded staff and food budget between the two facilities. We assumed it would present no problem: We were treating exactly the same number of residents for exactly the same amount of money in more space.

Permission was refused on the ground that the building had been funded, not the program nor the people. The house where the males were being treated would continue to be funded but the female house would not. As a result, Odyssey's female house depends wholly on public donations. For a time, indeed, we were fearful because threats were made that the funds of Odyssey male adolescent house would be cut even though we were now treating sixty males instead of forty males and 20 females. This illustrates the need for agencies to be run by the private sector. The public sector, being unable to learn from experience, is an ass. It demands that programs know the answers before they begin and refuses to allow them to respond to new data or input. Experience is irrelevant, creativity stifled, helping oneself punished, and common sense nonexistent.

The Women's Marathon for the adolescents in the program was called mostly because I wanted to get closer to them. We would be female together. I didn't know where it would lead. I hoped that they would feel at the end that it's nice to be a woman.

It was planned as a traditional marathon, one with a time limit. It would start at midnight, run for twenty-four hours, stop six hours for sleep and then run twelve hours more. Most Odyssey marathons are open-ended. They last until everyone in the marathon has "come across," which is the Odyssey term for being honest about oneself and being committed to the community. Once on a summer night, we started a marathon that ended fifty-five days later on an autumn afternoon. Three hundred and fifty people came across.

The Women's Marathon was held early in June 1971 in the

auditorium of the Mother House. A floor of mattresses had been prepared within a hollow square of couches and armchairs. The girls waited for me nervously. Many of them had never had any previous contact with me. The necessary expansion of Odyssey is an endless sadness to those of us who must become even more distant from the residents.

The girls were dressed for comfort in jeans and loose tops. A kitchen crew, made up mostly of males, had arranged trays of coffee, raisin buns, oranges and apples on the edge of the chest-high stage. Cartons of cigarettes were stacked on a chipped, doubtful-looking piano.

I arrived shortly after midnight, bare-foot and wearing an ample floor-length gown. I always wear long gowns in group sessions in order to have freedom of movement. We closed the doors. The hallway outside was hung with OFF LIMITS signs so that we would not be interrupted except for the delivery of food.

I selected a soft sofa and put my feet up. Due to my seven pregnancies, I have venous problems and must put my feet up whenever possible. I suggested we begin by introducing ourselves and describing what we hoped to gain from the marathon experience. That's a useful opening technique for a therapist. The group relaxes somewhat, the therapist learns the names and picks up cues about attitudes. It is important to observe where people have chosen to sit and how they're sitting, whether their bodies are in loose or rigid positions. Body language is as important as they say it is.

Most of the girls spoke of being scared, of being unable to trust anyone, of not being sure they liked being female. One girl with an Afro cut said, "I've never had a good meaningful relationship with anybody really."

When the some thirty girls had finished, I described myself, my three living children, and my most recent miscarriage, my third.

"I wanted six children," I told them, well aware that in this group pregnancies are regarded as calamities. "I guess I have three hundred children in Odyssey House though, in one way or another."

I sat straighter, tucking my feet under my dress. "I'm very interested in the role of women, in our identity, in what we can and can't do, what we are permitted to do and what we are not permitted to do. I have a unique confrontation with this, having a staff of one hundred and ten, most of whom are male."

The first to begin to talk about herself was Serena Hyatt, whose baby was soon to be born. Serena, seventeen, is a classic example of a deprived and illiterate Bridgeport Black, where Blacks are much less integrated into mainstream society than in New York City. She had almost no education because she dropped out of school to help her mother care for her younger brothers and sisters. Her father died in the hospital after being mugged by teen-agers on his way home from working in a bar. Serena has always believed that his life would have been saved by the doctors if he had not been Black. Consequently, she hates all physicians.

We talked in general about having a first baby. Two of the girls were fourteen when they had their first babies, another was fifteen, another said she had two children by the time she was seventeen. I asked what it meant to them and one replied, "When I was pregnant it seemed like everything I had planned for myself was going down the drain. I wanted to get away from the whole thing." There was an understanding murmur in the room.

Julie Ojeda, a Puerto Rican girl of seventeen whose baby was born after she came to Odyssey, sat on her heels on the far side of the mattresses and tried to reassure Serena, who seemed dazed, listless and frightened at the prospect of facing labor and maternity all alone. "I feel the same way you do about the father of my baby," she said in a rushed voice. "I have the same kind of resentment. I know he's still on drugs. But now is the time to express yourself. . . ."

"Julie," I said, "go sit next to Serena and comfort her."

Julie stepped over the sleepy girls scattered on the mattresses and crouched at Serena's feet. She earnestly explained that Serena should let her feelings out, that she, Julie, knew how lonely and frightening it was to be having a baby all by herself. Abruptly, Julie stopped and began to howl with her own grief, rocking and screaming. There was a rush toward her. Laurie Palmer, who was nearest, put her arms around Julie and held her. I crossed the mattress floor and sat near them. Serena was stunned, watching the keening White girl at her feet with frightened eyes.

When Julie was calmer, I moved away out of concern for Serena's resentment of doctors. I did not want to inhibit the process. Serena began to cry softly, stirred by Julie's intense outburst.

"I've been running away all my life," Serena was saying. "People act like they're afraid of me."

"Because you're always so angry," I explained. "You come across so hostile."

"You're really a softie," Julie told her, composed again. "People *like* you. People cried when you wanted to leave Odyssey a little while ago. The *staff* cried when you wanted to leave. We were upset because of your baby, Serena. You can't take your unborn baby back to drugs and the streets."

Serena struggled with this. "A lot of times I have to do things,

324

325   Julie Ojeda and her daughter, Raquel.

typing and such," she said in a weary voice, "but I can't read and I can't spell. People laugh and they make fun of me, and I don't like it."

"We can help you learn," I observed, "but first comes trust. You've got to trust first. We can teach you to spell, we can teach you many things. But first you must let us love you. You've got to show us feelings. That's the first bridge to your getting better. You can share with Julie what Julie shared with you, the feeling of being human and pregnant and female and alone. Then she'll teach you to spell, to read, and to know all the things that hurt you because you don't know them."

There were only two lamps in the cavern of the auditorium, giving us restful semi-darkness. Voices were becoming languid. Some of the girls, feeling the pre-dawn chill, had wrapped blankets around their shoulders and were having trouble staying awake. The Black girls were using picks to part their hair in neat squares, making tight, twisted braids in each square. The clock on the auditorium wall read 3:35.

We had reached Serena. She had promised that she would not be afraid of the doctors. She promised that she would relax and trust them while she was having her baby. I smiled at her.

"Now let me ask you something," I said. "Do you think there's any reason in the world why I might be jealous of you?"

"No," Serena answered at once, decisively.

"Do you think there's *any* reason?" I persisted.

There was a look of comprehension. "You mean you're jealous of me having a baby?" she asked.

"I'd love to be having another," I told her. "I feel just that, envious."

She was pleased. "I can see that," she observed with dignity.

"So can we share this baby?" I asked. Serena grinned at me proudly. "And do you want to congratulate Julie on being a Level IV?"

Julie was ready for the promotion, and it seemed a strategic time to make the announcement, a good mood-breaker to put vitality into the sleepy group. There were screams from some, others clapped; the girls hugged one another and jammed around Julie, pounding her on the back and throwing their arms around her. Julie put her head back ecstatically and said, *"It's beautiful!"*

"You answered the question of a Level III.* You are responsible for people," I told her. "I'm very proud of you."

We had been listening to a description of an abortion. The girl, only sixteen, said she wanted the baby but her mother made arrange-

* See Appendix I for a description of the Levels.

ments with a hospital and forced her to have the abortion. Her morbid mourning was interrupted by a wail from across the room. A girl, crouched on her knees, was crying, "My baaaaaby. Aaaaah, my *baby!*"

I moved to a couch closer by and the girl, Cassandra Jones, a fifteen-year-old, cried out the story of an abortion she had had the year before.

"You were fourteen," I pointed out. "There was no way in the world that you could have cared for that child. Do you think a child could grow up normally with a father who was in jail, a father who beat you up so badly that you needed stitches?"

Cass, still sobbing, agreed weakly.

"No," I said. "Now you have to make the commitment not to repeat that mistake. You will have to do, in a different way, what Serena will do—live your life so that meaning will come out of what happened."

It's something I believe in. The only way people can deal with tragedy is to integrate it positively, to go forward. I had to make meaning out of the birth and death of my mongoloid child by entering the field of psychiatry and making a contribution in the field of mental health.

In an effort to share with the still distraught Cassandra, one after another in the group talked of her abortions. Sheila O'Donohue, a staff member with a beautiful, luminous face, spoke of her agony in deciding on an abortion in order to spare her parents the pain of knowing she wasn't a virgin. She is a devout Roman Catholic, and church-educated, with four years of missionary work. The resultant guilt almost destroyed her. She described the year's penance she gave herself —no relationships with men, not even dating.

Lynn Winfield, a heavy maternal figure in a striped jersey, said haltingly, "I'd like to tell you something that is a little different, Cass. I can't have children at all. I've been to some of the best gynecologists in New York because I don't have periods, and it's been established that I can't have a baby."

Cass cried harder.

"Why are you crying now, Cassandra?" I asked on a sudden intuition that it was not sympathy for Lynn.

"I was told after my abortion that there was a chance I would never have kids," she explained, wiping her face with a tissue.

"My reaction to you is one of anger," I told her hotly. "Severe anger. You're very selfish. Everyone has been pouring out their feelings, and Lynn has now shared something we didn't know. It's a deeper pain than any of the rest of us have. Look at it. *Look at it!* Her pain is deeper than anyone else's in this room."

I felt one with Lynn. When I was nineteen I had kidney surgery and was told by a doctor that I should never risk my health by having children. I had felt panic at the possibility of being barren.

There was a round of indignation directed at Cassandra for failing to console Lynn. I had observed previously that the group had been growing less sympathetic as Cassandra's crying went on. When Julie Ojeda wept, they had moved toward her like filings to a magnet. In contrast, there was a space widening around Cassandra. It always amazes me that the group instinctively knows who is for real. Someone made a derisive comment about men being to blame.

"No," I said sadly. "We do it to ourselves. It isn't the fault of men. We who have low self-esteem do not set the limits. It's not the men who do it to us, it's we who do it to ourselves. Love should contain mutuality, concern, commitment, decency, honor as well as physical possibility or chemistry. Cassandra, and others of you, didn't demand any of the former values."

The group dealt with Cassandra, who was becoming shrilly defensive, while I talked with Lynn. Lynn's first sexual relationship had been at the age of fifteen after she had been told, in clinic after clinic, that she could never have children. None of the doctors she saw cared enough about a ghetto Black girl to treat what Odyssey later discovered was a hormone imbalance, or take the time to understand what it would mean to an adolescent girl to be told that she is condemned to never bear a child. Her symptoms should have been obvious to any concerned doctor. She had a classic adrenogenital syndrome, which in simplest terms means that she was producing too many male hormones.

Given the sentence that she was barren, Lynn felt *What the hell* and became a prostitute. This was a futile attempt to prove that she was a complete woman. As she described her symptoms to me, I was certain that the clinics had been wrong. I promised her a complete gynecological work-up as soon as the marathon ended. It later developed that I was right; she could be helped, and now she is menstruating.

I asked her about her years as a prostitute. Her face miserable, she told me she had done "terrible things." "I still feel dirty," she said. "I don't think I'll ever feel clean."

The room was hushed and listening. I had a sense of desolation. I asked if there was any way she could do penance as Sheila had and, symbolically, receive absolution. Lynn, a Fundamentalist Baptist, looked at her hands, at her long pointed fingernails painted white. All she could suggest was that it might help if she could finish the program.

"You must be cleansed of this feeling of sin before you will be able to move on," I insisted. There was comment from others that Lynn had progressed well when she first came into Odyssey but she had been stagnant for some time fearing to progress into re-entry. Lynn nodded unhappily and said it was true.

"Can you confess to anyone what you did as a prostitute? Is there anyone you could spill it all out to?" I asked.

Lynn considered. "Angela Green is the most like me," she said.

"Then we'll call Angela here to listen to all of it," I responded. "But I will warn her first, so she doesn't smother you with maternal forgiveness and fuck it up. She'll have to be her righteous, fundamentalist Baptist self."

i don't want to do it

        i remember the feelings of the night
                when life first started
but now it is being taken away from me
        on a 3rd floor sterile broadway dormitory
    with my friends near my aorta and the chinese peasant
                getting goofs from his pistol
                    of knock me out
    i cry: RUN AWAY FOR IT ISN'T REAL
                PEPPERING MY INSIDES OUT
        don't describe the pinches and wiggles
            or the dishonesty of crawling to the water
                            fountain
    for i am at the moment a blank
                on the 3rd day he arose; i lost
    should anyone comfort me in my time of selfishness
        i don't want to do it
                        but it is done
            i lost

I dozed lightly, the sound of a wailing schizophrenic in my ears, as she went on, and on, and on, knowing that Sheila could handle it. Trays of hot coffee were brought in, and the kitchen crew cleared away some of the debris. It was fully light outside, and we could hear birds singing in the linden trees behind Odyssey.

I was overwhelmed by the pain of these young girls, most of whom were under seventeen years of age, by the bleakness of their

* Poem written during poetry therapy by an adolescent girl to explain her feelings during an abortion against her wishes but insisted on by her family.

relationships with men and by their self-loathing. I had an urgent need for distance. I sat up. "I'm changing the rules," I informed them. "I see most of you have fallen asleep and the rest are too tired to go on. I think we should all sleep for a while. It's eight-thirty. We'll leave instructions to be wakened at noon."

I left, trailing a blue blanket. Like Fred Cohen, when the pain is too great I withdraw. I curled up in the privacy of my office. The rest sorted out the blankets and pillows and arranged themselves on the mattresses and couches. There were distant sounds of Odyssey House functioning—water running in the old pipes, steps overhead. In a few minutes, there was deep breathing and some snores in the room. No one stirred.

Someone awakened me at noon. The street was hazy with heat. I felt sticky and depressed as I returned to the auditorium, where groggy girls were eating scrambled eggs and bacon.

Angela Green arrived shortly after we started again. I took her into my office and instructed her. I wanted her to be tough with Lynn, to use a stern tone. Lynn didn't want understanding or forgiveness but, rather, someone to share her own self-disapproval while she poured it out. Angela understood the dynamics and collected Lynn. I left them alone in my office. A good therapist knows when to be absent, when others can do a better job.

In my absence, the marathon had continued. They now were dealing with a familiar problem: a middle-class Jewish addict who wanted to be Black. Many Jews become addicted because they don't like their own identity. They seek out Blacks in order to act out against their parents. Doris Silverman was explaining that she wasn't really Jewish, even though three of her four grandparents were Jewish.

"When we tell you you're not Black, you get mad," hissed a Black girl turning to me. She added, "Judi, she don't know what she is."

"She can't be Black!" I exclaimed. "Doris, if Cassandra Jones was sitting here saying, 'I don't like Black people and I want to be White,' what do you think the room would be saying to her?"

"That she's not White, she's Black," Doris said in a husky voice.

"Don't you think the room would feel a little angry with her? Wouldn't they say that she's copping out on her own people, she's rejecting her own people, she doesn't have decent identity concerning her own people?"

"Yeah, sure," Doris agreed.

"You're not a Black person, there's no way in the world you can be," I declared. "As a White, I'm pretty annoyed at you. If I were a Black person in this society with all the problems of a Black person, and some little cookie who was White and had none of these problems came running along saying, 'I'd prefer to be Black,' I'd be very annoyed. I'd interpret it as a kind of rubbing salt in the problems I have."

Doris looked confused and one of the Black girls looked incredulous. "You don't get it!" she exclaimed.

I glared at Doris. "It's a way of making yourself feel less inadequate at their expense. Doris, is it easier or harder to be Black? In this world, is it easier or harder?"

"It's easier to be White," she admitted reluctantly.

"Yes," I nodded. "Don't you think its pretty fucked up to be yelling and screaming that you want a harder road? Don't you think you're gaming with them? And anyway, it's really not one of life's choices open to you. You haven't got a chance in holy hell of waking up tomorrow morning Black. So why do you bother with such nonsense?"

"I just can't accept . . ." Doris began.

"You have no choice," I said flatly. "Just like you have to accept, whether you like it or not, that you were born female. Right? These are some of the things that we can't waste time over. . . . This is a rebellion against your mother. This is the way to sock it to your mother the most, by being an addict and a prostitute and having a Black pimp."

The mood of the room was lazy and warm, a summer-afternoon feeling as I asked Doris: "What have you learned in this part of the marathon?"

She chose her words uneasily. "All this rebelling against my mother . . . I think I was rebelling against . . ."

"Being a Jew," someone suggested softly.

Doris was silent, biting her lip.

"What does it mean to be a Jew?" I asked.

She answered quickly, "It means I'm not Black."

That's what it means to be a Jew?

She amended, "It means . . . that . . . I'm a . . . White . . . Jew. That's what I am, a Jew that hasn't been in a synagogue."

"Whoooooeeee," I cried cheerfully. "Listen to that hostility!" The room laughed and Doris, after a moment, joined them sheepishly. "Okay," she told me resignedly. "I really know I'm Jewish."

We talked about religion for a while, many of the girls describing mixed-religious backgrounds and the confusion they felt. It's something I shared fully. When I attended an Episcopal high school, I was considered Jewish like my Father's family, and when I attended a Jewish summer camp they were aware I was Christian, like my Mother.

I told the girls, "No matter where I was, I was different. It was another part of the extreme alienation I felt then. From my experience, there is nothing worse than not knowing who you are, from what you have come and where you're going to belong."

I was waiting anxiously for Lynn and Angela to return. At last they came in and Lynn, radiant, leaned over and kissed me. The group was delighted at the change in her.

"She looks marvelous! You did a good job," I told Angie. "How are you feeling Lynn?"

Lynn's face was tired but she smiled purely. "You both gave me back the respect I had lost," she said simply.

"You've only been away an hour and a half," I told her fondly. "That's not so bad. From what you indicated, I thought you'd be gone twelve hours."

"I told her all the feeling I had, all the things I did," Lynn said in an exhausted voice. "I had to feel better about myself before I could go higher in the program. What I told Angela I couldn't tell in here. At twenty-two I'm a lot older and I've been through much more than the other girls. I feel better."

I was so pleased.

She grinned at me. "In fact, I feel a *lot* better."

She was sitting on the mattress near me and I reached out with my foot and rubbed her shoulder affectionately. "I love your face now. You're a nice person."

Lynn said, "You're a nice person too, Judi."

Susan Dabney began to speak. She is a proud-faced woman who has completed the Odyssey program and is employed as our records librarian. Her husband and two older sons have lived in California for the past ten years. She is raising her youngest son, Curtis. He is three years old, having been born during her addiction. Her husband had expressed a willingness to have her and the baby join him. I thought it was time that she give her marriage another try.

Pensively, she agreed.

"It's time for us to push you out, in love," I told her. We all were quiet and I looked at her, sitting across the room from me with her graceful hands hanging loosely from her wrists, her forearms on her knees. She looked relieved but sad. I stood up and walked to her, giving her a hug and a kiss.

"You're still an independent Black bitch," I said with tears in my eyes. "Making me walk all the way across the room."

The marathon moved along. We worked next with a big-eyed wan teen-ager who said she had never in her life been happy, then with an angry fifteen-year-old who had shown her rejection of the marathon by sleeping almost constantly. Around six o'clock the kitchen crew came in and cleaned away most of the litter, leaving us dinner. We clustered around a lovely, gifted Black girl raised by aunts who detested their race and told her all her life that Blacks are ugly and stupid. The Blacks in the room were depressed as she talked of early experiences with discrimination.

Cassandra Jones observed, "People are sitting next to you, but I don't feel they are reaching you and giving you comfort." She was right. We were feeling listless again.

It was almost midnight when Monique LaVoie began to cry. The group had been discussing the frequency of their sexual activities. One teen-ager with an innocent child's face said she had begun to have intercourse at the age of eleven. In the three years since, she had slept with thirty men. A sixteen-year-old dragged deeply on a cigarette and commented that thirty wasn't many. Monique, a shy, withdrawn White fifteen-year-old from New Hampshire who resembles my own daughter, murmured in a low voice that she started at the age of twelve. Something in her tone caught my attention.

"Let's hear from Monie," I said quietly, "and then we'll get back to this subject. What about you, Monique?" I had a premonition that it was to be the worst moment of the marathon.

Monique started slowly in a low flat voice. She told of now being a lesbian after having been a prostitute at the age of twelve. She picked up a different man every night by standing on a street corner. Her mother was an alcoholic prostitute who told her every evening to go out and not return until she had money. When she was old enough to hustle in bars, she was grateful because they were warmer than the street. She began to drink heavily herself and several times passed out. Once she awakened to find herself being raped by several men in the back seat of a car parked outside a bar. She was raped and lacerated another time, viciously.

Her voice sounded dead and her eyes stared into empty space. When she described being in the same room while her mother turned tricks, she began to cry. Lynn Winfield, her face shocked, grabbed her and held her tight.

"I feel terrible," Monique sobbed.

I could almost not breathe. "Monie," I said in a comforting tone. "It's all over. Just put it in the past. That's what Odyssey is all about, beginning again. Just cry it out and you can begin again." Monie cried harder. Lynn was rocking her and her face was hidden by her long lank hair. Her body was curled up almost at my feet.

"Let her cry," I advised the others. "The best thing, Monie, is that you're not rationalizing, that you remember and feel it in terms of what happened. Now cry. Just cry." We waited while Monie moaned and wept. Many of the girls had tears on their faces, of which they were unaware. Ten minutes passed slowly.

Then I told Monique to sit up. "We have to do a bit of verbalizing now," I said gently. "Not to be cruel, not to be mean, but to help you get better and to help others not to hurt themselves as you have in this way." Monique straightened up obediently but kept her face hidden.

"No one in this room thinks badly of you," I continued softly. "We feel great sorrow that you went through these experiences at twelve and thirteen, when you were a baby. Exposed to bars and the backs of cars when you were twelve years old.

"Don't blame your mother. It's fruitless. Your mother is such an unhappy person herself." I looked at the averted head. "Come on, Monie. You've got to talk to us . . ."

"I feel so very low," she whispered.

"Your word is low," Lynn observed. "Mine was dirty."

"Should prostitution be legal?" I asked Lynn and Monique when we were all more composed. "Would it be worse or better for girls?"

Lynn reflected. "I personally can't think of anything worse than making it legal." Without expression, she added that she and Angela had calculated that she had sex relations with 3,800 men during her three years as a prostitute addict. She averaged between five and fifteen tricks a night. "I'd do anything to get a bag of dope, *anything!* Every kind of way with a trick, I did it all. I hated the men, and I hated myself more."

If prostitution were legalized, she thought, "it would be like society telling us that it's all right. And it isn't. Not for women."

Monie nodded in sad agreement.

334

A seventeen-year-old was talking about her two illegitimate children when I fell asleep again, totally drained by so much pain. There's such a gap in experience between the life of my daughter Trissa, who is also a teen-ager, and these children. I wonder constantly how they can ever understand one another and work together.

I roused myself and checked the time: two in the morning. Many of the group were sleeping and others had haggard faces. "We all need a break," I announced. "Let's start again at six." The kitchen crew was bringing in a supper of spaghetti as I left, once again dragging a blanket behind me. I had to seek healing by means of solitude. I slept blessedly alone in my office.

Four hours later we began again with housekeeping. The girls folded blankets, emptied ash trays, swept the squeaky wooden floor, piled dishes and cups on the trays. Most of them had brought a change of clothes in shopping bags or small overnight-size luggage. They lined up to use the downstairs shower. Their movements were sluggish and docile, like refugees coming from a disaster. There were some complaints of sore throats and headaches.

Coffee arrived, along with buns and fresh fruit. The girls ate gratefully, saying little. Lynn Winfield was taking Doris Silverman to the Bronx for a court appearance. She would assure the judge that Doris was still in treatment at Odyssey and doing well. Both had changed into fresh dresses for the occasion. Serena Hyatt, heavy with child, was waiting for Julie Ojeda who was taking her to Metropolitan Hospital for what perhaps would be her final pre-natal checkup.

The marathon began without me. I felt a desperate need to refresh myself with a visit to the beauty parlor. It was Dadaesque to go from that scene in the auditorium to Kenneth's. I dropped in on the marathon for an hour and found Cassandra on the point again, still annoying the group with her self-preoccupation.

"They don't even know me!" she was protesting heatedly.

"I didn't know Lynn very well, right?" I said patiently. "A little bit better than I do you, but not very well. In the middle of last night my response to Lynn was 'What a nice person you are.' Right? I didn't say that to you. There are things you *do* that make people move away from you, and there are things Lynn does that make people move toward her. Why is the group angry at you? Did all of us get up this morning and make a secret compact that today we will get Cass?"

"No," she said without enthusiasm.

"You must understand it's what you do, your behavior, your

attitude, that sets into motion other people's reactions," I told her forcefully. "You don't see that you're part of all these relationships. You always blame the other person. Sheila is concerned this morning with being Sheila, not with attacking Cass. Betty is concerned with being Betty. Everybody wakes up with themselves and then they react to other people. You seem to think that everybody wakes up with some reason to go after this sweet innocent thing called Cass! And it's just not true."

Cassandra's hands fluttered. "They keep doing these things to me and I say, 'Oh, they're just doing it, they're just doing it to me.' And I am crying and all this stuff," she sniffed in illustration, "and I am saying, 'Why do they do this to me?'"

"Let me try again," I said. "Suppose you and I are having an argument over something. Can you change me?"

"No."

"Can you change you?"

"Yeah."

"That's the only person you can work with," I told her, hitting my hand on the sofa arm for emphasis. "You keep trying to change everybody else. It's one of the things that therapists see most often—people who keep demanding that others change, rather than look to themselves."

Betty Agabedian, a schizophrenic, hitched herself forward excitedly, her long hair swinging. "You're not looking at the things you do and changing what's coming from you—your ideas, your values, your opinions, things like that. You're just projecting on others. Understand?"

Cass looked baffled and wounded.

"Let me put it another way," I tried. "I can't expect other people to change. The weight is on me to look at the situation, decide if I like the situation as it is, and if I don't, I move. The only person I have control over is *me*. What paralyzes situations is people constantly expecting the world to change. The world never changes. Only one's reactions to the world change. Most of our destiny is within our control, and we tend not to know it."

I sighed. "You've heard candidates-in start the bullshit about how it's not their fault?"

"The needle jumped in their arm and everything," Betty elaborated.

"You put the needle in your own damned arm," Susan Dabney glowered at Cassandra.

Cass showed signs of comprehension. As I left, Sheila O'Donohue was having an inspiration. She was getting everyone to their feet for spirited calisthenics to counteract the bone-deep lethargy. I hoped it would work.

As Fred Cohen drove me to the hairdresser's, I was profoundly depressed. "Have I lived in a fantasy of good fortune all my life?" I asked him. "I have not known the kinds of problems those girls have known. I've never had an unpleasant relationship with a man. Never. I've never had a relationship in which there was not mutuality, caring, tenderness and protection. I've never known the violence and betrayal they have known. Is my life a fantasy?"

"If so," he whispered gently, "so be it."

la deux—seis un guatre un

hello   how come there is nothing for me?
    first thing in the morning. Leather blue skirt and a strawberry lollipop
another equator from comrade but does it mean as much as the captains
        gorilla face full of sunlight
the first touch of the sensitive skin in a dinge 8th avenue under-ground home
the long brown beauty is coming into play walking by the wire fence
    to encounter a sweaty body of bermudas but a tasty kiss
        no matter how strange it seems I LOVE YOU
two flat surfaces, pardon me, two molds of womenhood and the disease
                of manhood
        with an additional obstacle: a reason of motherhood
                enclosed in a 2 by 4
suntie the doors are closed its perfectly ok her womb couldn't possibly
        hold anymore than it has now
comrade; walk with the swiftness of the garment of the '70s with the
                tips of your walking hands bouncing towards the
intersection of 7th Avenue on the street where I live this i see thru the
            bars of the escape which hangs on the street where I
live

AU—REVOIR, MON CHERIE

° Poem written by an adolescent girl about the pain of being a woman.

Judi I

I was born on November 13, 1934, in New York City. My Father, Gustavus Augustus Gerber, also known as Augustus G., was thirty-nine at the time. He was in the process of being admitted to the New York Bar after successfully completing careers as an economist and a chemical engineer.

My Mother, Beatrice Densen, was twenty-eight. She was a practicing attorney as well. My Mother married only once and my Father several times. My Mother was his second marriage. They have been divorced since 1954.

My Mother was an early advocate of women's rights, and she kept her maiden name after marriage. When I was born she had me registered as Judianne Densen-Gerber in order that she be equally represented.

My Grandfathers present a fascinating contrast. My Father's Father, Julius Gerber, was the Executive Secretary of the Socialist Party of the United States and one of the organizers of the American Federation of Labor. He is described in history books as a social anarchist of his time, although his views were to the right of today's liberal Democrats and Republicans. He was the publisher of the New York *Call*, the *New Leader* and founder of the Rand School of Social Sciences, which became the New School for Social Research. Interestingly, many Odyssey graduates are now matriculating there.

He and my paternal Grandmother, Lena, were eastern European immigrants. They met in this country after my Grandmother ran away from her home in Europe at the age of sixteen and crossed the ocean alone because she refused to submit to the Orthodox Jewish custom of head-shaving and wearing a sheital. She was an extremely strong and proud woman who greatly influenced my early childhood.

My Father was the eldest son of eight children. One day when he was sixteen his Father left his Mother alone to raise eight children on fifteen dollars a week; he preferred to dedicate his life to causes. I don't believe she could read or write when it happened, but she taught herself to do both. She pawned his gold watch for $50 which she used as a down payment on her home where she continued to live for fifty-five years. Her life revolved around her children while my Grandfather believed the individual was subordinate to the masses. My Grandmother saw that her children had the best possible education. They became doctors, lawyers and schoolteachers.

When I was small I asked her how she had managed to raise her family on fifteen dollars a week. She shrugged and said, "If you have to, you do, and you work to better yourself."

She was a remarkable woman, warm, motherly and capable. She made another observation which has stayed with me: There is enough to go around. I've never understood competition for a limited amount of resources. I have a naïve idealistic belief that if everyone labors according to his ability there will be enough. We are given a pair of feet, a pair of hands and a good mind, with which we can sustain ourselves in all but extreme crises—at which time we should be able to draw on a community of good friends. Add a little concern, and you've got Odyssey House.

We don't understand waiting lists at Odyssey. When someone comes in we just put down another bedroll and we all work a little harder. Odyssey has had a good deal of criticism from the medical profession and other members of the Establishment because of this policy. When a group turns away someone sick and needing help, it says something about the group.

My Mother's Father, Michael Densen, whose Father was an architect in Utica, New York, left home when he was eight years old to seek his fortune. Characteristically, he was successful by the time he was twenty. He built a paper-box manufacturing empire. One day when he was out walking, he saw my Grandmother working in the fields. She was exceptionally beautiful. He went over to her and teasingly pushed her hat down over her head. He frequently did this in later years. It always annoyed her, but they were married because what Mike wanted, Mike got.

My Grandmother Sarah is in her nineties now. She's continuing to be the person in the whole family to whom I feel closest. I'm like my Grandfather Densen in my determination to achieve a goal and in the wholehearted pleasure I take in having fun, but I am like my Grandmother in my soul. She has an earthy farm-girl quality I share. Once when I was a teen-ager living with her, she described her wedding night. She said my Grandfather was covered with freckles— "and when I say freckles everywhere," she added, "I mean *everywhere*." Like my other Grandmother, she continued to teach herself after she was married. She has never missed reading the morning paper, exercising her vote or watching the eleven o'clock news.

My Grandfather was called "Mike the Red" because of his hot temper. He had the well-known Danish trait of quickness to anger. He was an arch capitalist, a feudal lord. All the family feared him, his children especially. I have a junior Uncle who was secretly married for eight years because he thought his Father would disapprove. The farce ended abruptly one day when my Grandfather said, "She's a nice girl. It's about time you married her."

I've been told that in my Grandfather's house the children were cautioned not to make noise when he was home. Several of his grandchildren were in a panic in his presence.

He never frightened me. He truly loved me and I him. Even when he was annoyed at something I had done, he was playful. He was my major male role model as a child. I delight in the fact that my Husband is also named Michael. My Michael has the same kind of strength as Sarah's Michael.

During the last two years of his life, when he knew he was dying of cancer, my Grandfather began talking to me in existential terms about life and death and the importance of a good name. I was about fifteen when the conversations began, and he dwelt often on what I could accomplish with my life. He had resisted my Mother's ambition to enter the family business because he thought commerce was unseemly for a lady—despite the fact that she had invented new manufacturing procedures and was talented in that direction. She therefore chose law as a substitute career. She has been successful in all her career endeavors. She has a great deal of good practical common sense.

However, by the time I was growing up, he had decided that he would not permit himself, or me, to regard being female as a limitation of any kind. He said that through me the Densen name would be immortal. It would never be forgotten. I should prepare myself, therefore, for a life of great significance. He transferred to me his sense of personal destiny that is sometimes a heavy load.

He wasn't religious, but just before he died he made large donations to Protestant, Catholic and Jewish organizations. He said he didn't know which one was right, and it didn't make any difference anyway, but he might as well make his peace and cover all his bets.

It was important in my development that I was aware from the earliest age that there wasn't only one life style or one set of values to consider. My two sets of Grandparents provided me with distinct alternatives: My Mother's family had many concepts about status and social acceptance and protocol, meeting the responsibility of one's position and doing the *right thing*. They are rigidly Establishment people. My Father's family placed tremendous emphasis on education and being the master of your own fate, molding the environment as you see fit.

While they had a well-developed sense of social responsibility, my Father and his Father had almost no sense of family responsibility. My Mother's people, on the other hand, have a total sense of family—which seldom extends beyond. When anyone in the family is in trouble, the others race to bail him out. It isn't done out of warmth. It is done out of familial responsibility, pride and a concept of orderly behavior. My Mother is always there first whenever there is any difficulty; everyone looks to her for guidance.

My Grandmother Densen was considered eccentric because she used public transportation. She said it was nice to talk to someone you didn't know while traveling. She compromised with the family's sense of propriety by riding the bus only one way, returning with the chauffeur.

When my parents first married they lived in a two-room house in Greenwich Village. It had a bay window in the front. People were always coming in to ask if it was a library because my Father had a collection of more than thirty thousand volumes, some of which could be seen from the street. He has total retention of whatever he reads, a characteristic I'm grateful to share. We even read and clip newspapers the same way and, like him, I'm very verbal and able to think quickly on my feet.

When I was six we had a Densen family tragedy that had a deep effect on me. In December 1940 my Grandmother Sarah and my Aunt Jeanne, her favorite child, were driving to Florida with Aunt Jeanne's Husband and two children. They were involved in an accident. My Aunt, who was driving, was killed, and my Grandmother's back was broken. My Uncle almost died, and their children were badly injured.

My earliest childhood memory is of my Parents standing at the foot of my four-poster, canopied bed, telling me they had to go to Florida. They were both crying. They believed at that time that everyone in the car had been killed. They were so distraught that they gave me no explanation. They just left.

My Father returned a few days later but my Mother was gone two and a half months, pulling her sister's family together. I suffered beyond description. I cried all the time. No one understood or responded. To add to my difficulties, the Nanny I had had from birth, Lucy, had left three months before. I loved her dearly and had been feeling her loss acutely.

I was sent for a while to my Grandmother Lena's house in Brooklyn. I was even more frightened there. I stopped eating. I remember feeling that I had lost everything: I had lost my Mother, my Father, my Nanny, my bed and my panda. My Grandmother wasn't affronted by my rejection. She had the good sense to order my Father to take me home and become responsible for me.

I returned and assorted Densen Aunts and Uncles looked after me. I was positive my Mother was dead. I took down her portrait and hid it. My Aunts and Uncles railed at me. I told them that since my Mother was dead I didn't want to see her picture. They called me an ungrateful child and spanked me. The picture was replaced. The next day when I saw the picture again, I decided to kill myself. I locked myself in the bathroom and swallowed a bottle of iodine. They found me, and I was treated and reprimanded again.

In my child's mind, I could have borne the pain of my Mother's death if I didn't have to look at her picture. I have since learned about myself—that I can handle any pain if I am allowed to deal with it in my own time and way. It is a profound belief of mine that all pain is borne alone. It can be empathized with but not shared.

I emerged from that experience with two convictions. One is that I am different. My inability to be understood by anyone around me during that agony led to a feeling of isolation I have never lost. I seem to have different thoughts, different ways of reacting, a different way of being, than most people around me. Because of it, I am always striving to explain myself in the hope that I'll be finally understood and the isolation will lessen.

It is this sense of alienation that ties me to many in Odyssey—to Jimmy Murphy, John Cox, Clifford Robinson, Fred Cohen and others. It is something I share with them. Like them I have the sense of being orphaned. The soil I grew up on was arid and could give me little nourishment. I was somewhat separate from the rest of my family: alone.

The other powerful consequence of that childhood experience has been that I see a dichotomy between doing and being. My Family, it appeared, cared only about what I did—in the appearance of things. They cared not at all how I felt. As a result, I have learned to be circumspect when the occasion demands it, hiding myself.

Only when I feel very safe do I allow my real feelings to show.

On other levels, such as intellect and accomplishment, I received nothing but encouragement and involvement from my Family, especially my Mother. I was dressed liked a prized Dresden doll. I had speech lessons with the same teacher who instructed Franklin Delano Roosevelt. I had riding lessons, dancing lessons, summer camps, private schools. I had my intelligence tested at nursery school and my Mother was informed that it was so high I would either become maladjusted or a genius, a fact which she promptly shared with me and which made her very cautious about giving me any freedom. It resulted in such strict supervision that we didn't resolve that problem until I became an adult.

A Densen family tradition was followed in my education: The first six years are spent in a public school, learning that all people are the same, and the rest of it in a private school making the proper associations. I was sent, in the seventh grade, to Riverdale School for Girls, an Episcopal school. I was miserable there and totally friendless, which increased my sense of isolation dreadfully. One of my difficulties was that with minimum effort I had the highest marks in the class, which generally is resented; and too, I had a great many dates, which also can be an unlikable attribute in an all-girl school. The most damaging factor, however, was my hopelessness at athletics. The school prided itself on zestful team sports, and I was a liability in every game. I was always the last one picked.

When I went to college, all this changed and I made many women friends. At any one point in time, my life has been characterized by one or two very close friendships, which can be of either sex or of any age, together with many, many dear acquaintanceships. I was always comfortable with men. I never in my life have had an unpleasant personal relationship with a male, never been abused or exploited or hurt, but always protected and comforted. I fondly remember my Father carrying me around and singing to me if I were in pain. I had an abundance of dates, though my social life was complicated slightly by my Father's curious habit of resting on the living-room sofa in his underwear and socks. He would stand up when I brought my young men to meet him, thump his chest and howl like Tarzan.

I was very happy at Bryn Mawr College, meeting for the first time women more intelligent than I. It was my first intellectual competition, and it was good for me. For one thing, I felt less different there. It was the happiest period of my whole education, and I made many warm and deep friendships. It was the first time I had a roommate, and I enjoyed it so much I vowed not to have an only child.

At eighteen I fell in love with a Haverford boy who was a Mormon. We became engaged, though we both knew there were some difficulties in the way of marriage for us. However, his family was exceedingly warm and practiced togetherness. They showed me what family life can be like for the children when there are parents who love and like each other.

I graduated *cum laude* and went on to law school because my Family expected it. My Mother had a firm picture of the two of us being among the first mother-and-daughter firms in the American legal system. My real intention was to become a doctor, but I agreed to be legally trained first as a condition precedent. I found law school amazingly easy. I had no difficulty with it at all. I received a Bachelor of Law degree from Columbia University Law School in 1959 when I was twenty-four. It was changed to a Doctor of Jurisprudence in 1969.

Before I graduated in law I had married Michael Baden. One of his attractions for me was his childhood. I knew my childhood had been unhappy and lonely, but Michael had been through even more. That he had survived with such strength gave me comfort. His parents were separated, with raging bitterness on both sides, when he was very small. Because of the family disruption he was placed, when he was six, in a home for delinquent children. He says that he didn't perceive it as a reformatory. He was sent there after he had been expelled from the first grade in school for being unmanageable.

He skipped grades in Hawthorne, which was the name of the reform school, and became aware of the fact that he was highly intelligent. He was pleased by this because he already had decided he would be a doctor. He made up his mind when he was three and in the hospital with a mastoid operation.

When he left Hawthorne at the age of nine, his Mother was living in a project, a housing development for low-income people. His ambition to be a doctor was considered absurd by everyone except his Mother, who dedicated herself to seeing that this was realized. He entered the College of the City of New York, which is tuition-free, when he was sixteen. He was one of the youngest graduates in his class, as well as being president of the senior class, editor of the college newspaper and class speaker at the graduation of more than two thousand. Also, he had won some medals for tennis and chess.

He went to New York University School of Medicine on a scholarship that included a living stipend. He heard about me from his roommate, Roger Bloom, a law student who told Michael there was a crazy girl in his class who planned to start medical school as soon as

she received her law degree. Michael was intrigued. He preferred intelligent, self-reliant women and, because he was brilliant, Jewish and soon to be a doctor, he was being courted by wealthy Jewish mothers and inundated with their clinging-vine daughters. It's not his style to admire dependency or manipulation in any form.

Michael called me on the telephone and asked me, since I was interested in law and medicine and because it was free, if I would like to meet him in the morgue. It was Memorial Day 1957, and we had our first date in the old Bellevue Mortuary. On our second date, also an inexpensive one, he took me to watch the delivery of a baby. Our third date was to Rye Playland.

After that I went out half the time with Michael and half the time with my fiancé, trying to make up my mind. What decided me was Michael's strength and uncomplicated sureness about himself. He has no existential doubts whatsoever, no wondering about the meaning of life or why he was born. It's all clear-cut with him: You assemble the information, you make a decision, you carry it out. I was still a very confused person and I knew I needed that stability and clarity. I could lean on him.

Michael has never considered me a particularly capable or over-whelming person within our family life. He sees me as someone to protect, not much differently than he sees the children. I love being taken care of. I'm sometimes enraged by the demands he casually makes, paying no attention at all to my schedule, but I'm grateful constantly that he has such confidence in himself that he is uncon-cerned by my achievements. In fact, throughout our marriage he has pushed me forward. In the area of my career, he regards me as wholly competent, with unlimited potential. I wanted to quit many times in medical school and wanted to quit during the "Great Split" of '67, but Michael wouldn't allow it. He feels that I have as much right to a career as he has.

In addition, he's a tender, sentimental man who often brings me flowers. I feel conflict most in the morning because I love to sleep late and he always wakens me at six or seven to say good-by as he is leaving for work. One time when he decided not to disturb me I could hardly get through the day.

He's also oblivious to money, including mine. He seldom carries more than two dollars in his pocket and will write a check for a bellboy's tip. My Family, which is watchful over money matters, requested that he sign an ante-nuptial agreement giving up his share of my fortune. He did so, with complete indifference. I promptly wrote out a will leaving him everything.

He was poor most of his life—he once was hospitalized for

malnutrition because he was dating me with his food money—still he never developed an interest in money.

Our decision to marry was reinforced by the hullabaloo both our families made. My Mother has come to love Michael and once by mistake introduced him as her son and me as her daughter-in-law, but at the time of the engagement she thought him most unsuitable. His Mother was mortified that I wasn't Jewish. She refused to attend the wedding. We thought it over very carefully. We were married on June 14, 1958.

Five days later we departed on a four-month honeymoon trip around the world. During the five-day delay Michael, in his practical fashion, financed the trip by having us appear on a television program "Do You Trust Your Wife?" starring Johnny Carson. Michael, in his protective fashion, didn't trust me enough to allow me to answer any questions. He answered them all and won the money that paid our hotel bill. Michael, in his ambitious fashion, combined the honeymoon with his education and obtained research credit studying medical-examiners' systems in many of the cities we visited.

So, we spent the honeymoon visiting morgues. Everywhere we

went, disaster co-operated. We arrived in India at the height of a cholera epidemic; in Thailand there were a number of political assassinations; in Egypt we saw mummies with smallpox; everywhere we traveled people were dying of diseases we rarely see in the United States. Three weeks after we were married, Michael wanted to spend the night in a leprosarium in Tokyo. I put my foot down. I balanced it by making him visit a women's prison for every morgue he took me to. We presented a problem to our travel agent.

As soon as we got home I became pregnant. Michael and I fought frequently during that pregnancy. It's the only time we've ever considered divorce seriously. I think it was because we both had fears about being parents. We felt we didn't know how, since both of us had had disruptive childhoods. On one level, we desperately needed to establish a family and therefore wanted a baby intensely, but on another level, we were terrified we would be inadequate parents and would hurt the child through loving too much.

I had just finished law school when Trissa was born. There is no blessing greater than having a daughter. We had a daily babysitter but no other help, and in the evenings I was caring for the child, running the house, marketing and studying medicine simultaneously. Michael quickly taught me that he was not going to be a partner in household chores. The first time I sent him to the store with a grocery list containing the item *juice,* as well as milk, cream, eggs, bread, etc., he returned home with a half gallon of clam juice. He said it was irresistible because it cost only nineteen cents.

This was one of the periods when I most wanted to give up. Michael wouldn't tolerate it. Later he had the same attitude about me sitting for the Bar Admission examination. I had missed it many times because of pregnancies and had lost interest, but similar to my Mother, Michael believes that one must finish what one starts. I was in labor when it was time for me to be admitted to the Bar so Judge Bernard Botein granted us the unusual privilege of allowing Michael to stand by my side, as a precaution in case I delivered during the ceremony.

While I was completing Law School, four years at New York University Medical School, an internship at French Hospital and psychiatric residency first at Bellevue and later at Metropolitan Hospital, I was pregnant six times. Two of the pregnancies ended in miscarriages, three of them produced our children, Trissa, Judson and Lindsey, and one of them ended in the birth of a child suffering from Langdon-Downs disease, better known as mongolism. She was my second child, born when I was twenty-six, and she died. We named her Julianne Michael.

Because medical science had made a breakthrough three years before, it was possible for Michael and me to determine whether the mongolism was the inherited or an accidental type. We were tested and assured that the possibility of us having another mongoloid baby was only slightly higher with us than in the normal population.

We spent a year agonizing over whether or not to have another child. Michael was influenced by the misery of a colleague who had an eighteen-year-old retarded son who eventually was institutionalized. This son had been a source of great pain to his family, with a devastating effect on his normal sister. Michael sought counsel from his Chief at Bellevue, Dr. Marvin Kuschner, who advised, "Stop agitating, Michael. Just let things be and love one another."

We decided to have another child because of that wise comment, in part, and also because we felt it was important to demonstrate to our daughter, Trissa, that she should not be afraid to bear children when she became a woman.

It was because of that child, Julie, that I decided to enter psychiatry rather than follow my original plan to teach medical jurisprudence. In order to preserve sanity, I had to make some sense of the tragedy. It is important to me to meet the challenges in my lifetime by integrating them into myself and growing. Otherwise disaster is nothing but meaningless pain.

In order to come to grips with the pain of that experience, I had to stop demanding mothering and attention from my Husband. I had to grow up. It was intolerable to permit the baby's retardation and death to count for nothing but pain. I decided the message I would take from it was that I should devote my life to mental health.

The death of a child is different from any other death because it is out of time.

Much of my life seems to me predestined. I was about sixteen years old when I read Pearl Buck's book about her mongoloid child. I cried terribly and had an absolutely certain premonition that I was going to bear such a child. When I became pregnant with that baby, I knew from the start this would be the one. There was something wrong with the pregnancy from the beginning, and I complained about it bitterly. No one listened to me. It reminded twenty-six-year-old me of the six-year-old me, who also had been unable to communicate her pain and fear to anyone.

Michael was superb after the baby was born. He took the weight. I was weeping uncontrollably and insisting that we should bring the baby home. I would leave school and dedicate my life to her, I said.

Michael was opposed and flatly refused. He said it wasn't fair to Trissa, who was only two.

When the baby died a week later, Mike came home and gathered Trissa in his arms and rocked her back and forth and wept for an hour.

The difference between the way Michael and I face adversity is best illustrated by the fact that I talk about that baby often but I cannot bear to see a retarded child. If I encounter one somewhere, I have to go away and compose myself. Michael, on the other hand, is totally mute about that child. But he is on the Board of Directors of the Rehabilitation and Research Center for Mental Retardation and the Board of Advisors of the Andrew Menchell Infant Survival Foundation.

Despite the normal chromosome tests, I was understandably frightened throughout my next pregnancy, frantic that the baby might not be normal. I have never had an uneventful pregnancy. I bleed throughout and am always afraid of a miscarriage. I have varicose

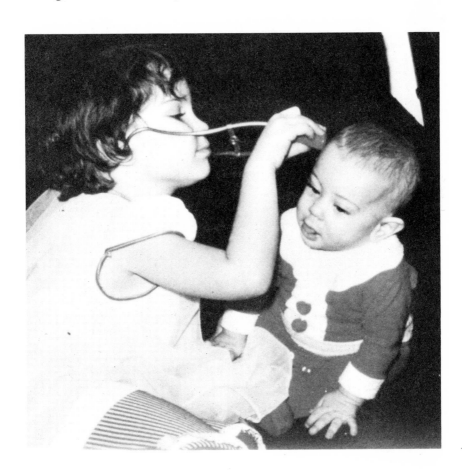

Judson Michael Baden.

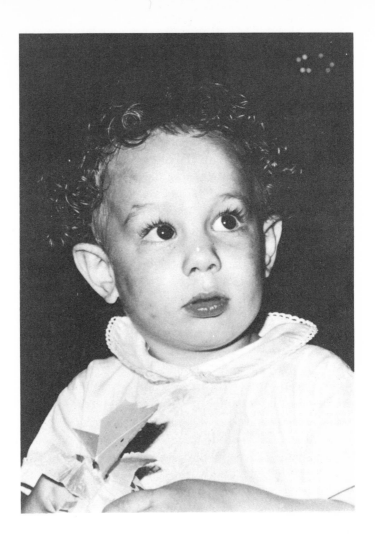

Lindsey Robert Baden.

veins as well. I was in my fourth year of medical school during that pregnancy and wanted to quit, but again Michael wouldn't allow it. He bought me a folding stick chair to take on rounds so I could frequently rest, relieving the pressure. That baby was called Judson, "Son of Judi." His middle name is Michael, after his Father. He is very special to us. We brought him home early from the hospital, when he was only two and a half days old, so he could be a present for Trissa's fourth birthday.

Our next son, Lindsey, has been an endless, marvelous surprise. I carried him through my first year of residency and never missed a day. That was the pregnancy when I was assigned to work with the so-called hopeless drug addicts. I went into labor with Lindsey while standing in a voting booth during John V. Lindsay's mayorality campaign.

I have had sometimes dangerously uncertain health. At five years of age I had viral encephalitis, post German measles, during which I suffered a convulsion and temporary loss of the use of my left side. It is still slightly weak. For about two and a half years I markedly dragged my left foot. Mother used to put my food at the end of the room and make me walk to get it. I'm grateful that she did, grateful that she never let up on saying *Lift your leg!* because now I walk without any dragging.

At nineteen I went into uremic coma, at which time I had major kidney surgery. The doctors advised me that I should never attempt to have children. Because of these and many other illnesses I'm trying to live double the amount so I will have lived long even if I die young. I resent sleep. Mike too is obsessed with the reality of death. He's a pathologist, so he's made death his life.

I see life as ying and yang, good and evil, life and death, paradoxically always traveling together. Death is the final affront to living and forever wins. The only residue that remains on earth is good works. If you have lived a good life, I believe the hereafter will take care of itself.

The most definite message I give is to find out who you are, what you are and where you want to go. For me, the crisis of any lifetime is the solving of identity, and after that you live with acceptance and work out appropriate solutions.

Be yourself; within that is *like yourself.* If you do something wrong, simply accept the consequence and move on. Don't be paralyzed by guilt. Take your lumps and get on with it.

During most of the period this book covers, I was in agony over my identity as a female. It wasn't only that I was asked in Washington to suggest a man to be the first Executive Director of the National Advisory Awareness Council, an agency I myself designed—it was *unthinkable* to the powers that be that a mere woman could run it; or that when Odyssey first presented a proposal to the Department of Defense, it was initially refused because they felt the generals could not work with a woman; or that the most vicious and punishing attacks on Odyssey have come from a highly placed clergyman who detests women. But, it's all of that and much more.

I read a piece in the New York *Times* about Simone de Beauvoir. In it she examined the anti-female propaganda she had been subjected to all her life, starting with the finest compliment her father could imagine to give her, which was that she "thought like a man." It struck home. I'd been hearing that ever since I was a child. It's meant as a compliment when a man, *any man,* tells me that I'm his equal. I am supposed to be grateful.

I have finally realized how patronizing and demeaning that is. I spent the summer of 1971 going through a series of revelations about the role of women. One came to me when I was having lunch at City Hall with John V. Lindsay as my reluctant host after the bus tour of New York City with the Assistant Secretaries of State. I looked at myself and Congresswoman Bella Abzug, the only two women sitting at the table, both of us very heavy, and I thought that the men probably regarded us as non-biological, non-sexual human beings. I resolved at that moment to go on a diet.

There was a troop of handmaidens, slim young things in mini-skirts, who were doing the serving: the secretaries. I was almost immobilized by my acute awareness of what the Black experiences: that his kind are good only to serve the masters.

Black males tell me there is no comparison between the oppression of Blacks and females, but Congresswoman Shirley Chisholm understands. She says that being Black is an asset at times but being female never is. Michael and I gave a dinner party across Party lines for her when she was running for President in the Democratic primaries. That evening, she frustrated several men who asked her to state her platform when she replied, "My platform is that I am Black and that I am a woman. You must recognize the disenfranchised people." The men could not understand that first of all women must gain acceptance and recognition as being *people.* Then we'll give them a platform.

I had an insight during the Women's Marathon that one of the ways women are getting back at men and expressing their rage is the tyranny of the female orgasm. It isn't enough that women enjoy sex: Young women demand that the male bring them to fulfillment. They lie there doing very little, they don't co-operate, they're negative and critical; they're taking revenge, grading him against their other partners.

My opinion that men treat women as objects was reaffirmed during one of the J.E.S. Marathons. A young ex-addict involved in the concept of *machismo* was talking about a dispute with his girl friend. She wanted to go to a movie or something and he wanted to make love. She refused him and he was outraged. She didn't have a right to refuse him, he felt. They fought for a while, he forced himself upon her and then he left the house.

The following day Jimmy Murphy and Fred Cohen told him that he should apologize to her, that a woman had a right to refuse sex. He couldn't see it on any level, but the other males in the agency were so adamant about it that he returned to the girl and offered his idea of an apology, by giving her another opportunity to "take care of business," the addict's euphemism for sexual intercourse. She acquiesced. This was the account that he brought to the marathon, pleased with himself.

Knowing about the incident, I vowed to myself to discuss it in a reasonable way. I talked to him about the need for personal territory, the right to decide for yourself what you do with your body. He was amazed. A woman hasn't the right to refuse her man, he told me, and besides it was all a game. In reality the woman always wants sex and she says no only to tease.

The other males in the group tried to get him to see that women are people. He couldn't accept it. They suggested that he should apologize to me, as a symbol of all women and the girl he had insulted. He said it was impossible, under any circumstances, for a man to apologize to a woman.

Running through my mind at that moment was the fact that I had just come from the hospital where I had been comforting René Casaclang, an Associate Director of Odyssey, whose twin sons had died minutes after being born. In less than an hour after the tragedy, all of Odyssey's Executive Staff were at his side. We were moved by the love and selflessness that René showed for his wife. He thought only of how to comfort her. I thought of my own Husband and dead child.

To return to the J.E.S. Marathon, fresh from that, and listen to a male who unfortunately expressed attitudes shared by about 75 per cent of all males, was more than I could stand. John Cox and Fred Cohen fell asleep, defensively withdrawing from what was coming. There was no one there to protect the patient from my rage. I called him every name in the book. I asked him how manly he was if he always had to be in control of a woman. I said we were sick of being slaves, and on, and on, and on.

It was a rare phenomenon, my expressing such rage to a patient. In all my years of medical practice, I have done it only three times. Afterwards we discussed at follow-up staff meetings whether I had a right to lose my temper. Fred was furious with me. He felt that no therapist has a right to behave that way. I had no defense except to say that I had lost control. Fred correctly confronted me with an issue of proper professional conduct, but my misbehavior occurred because I was in great personal pain over the indignities that women suffer. Fred eventually appreciated that I could not be expected to keep control when I was so wounded and humiliated and there was no one to protect me. Jimmy, Charlie and Fred promised they would stand with me in these affronts in the future, which is all the Blacks can expect from us too.

Of course I could never again be that patient's therapist.

Earlier that year I had been asked to give the keynote speech at the first meeting of the Professional Women's Caucus. I was standing on the platform, being nonchalant but not very slim because I was into my seventh pregnancy; I talked lightly about how we should get along with men. The two sexes must learn to get along, I was saying, because there is the biological need and we can't survive apart.

The audience consisted of about four hundred and fifty women from all over the United States, some of the most accomplished women in the world. Suddenly from somewhere near the back of the crowd, a young braless girl stood up and shouted that I should take a vow against penetration and lead the other women to follow. I looked at her sheepishly and said, "What do you suggest instead?" I told her if she could come up with a viable alternative I would consider it, but at that moment, being pregnant, it would be hypocritical for me to take such a vow.

"You older women have copped out!" she yelled at me. "It's your attitude. *Take a vow against penetration.* If you must, look at it as the female enveloping the male. Penetration is a violation of our person. It's better we envelop and smother. It is our turn to be in charge and to be in control."

I shrugged and said that if it would help us to continue the meeting I would propose a toast to all great envelopes, which I did. It seemed to satisfy her. But a better answer would have been to suggest that we mesh together.

At that time I thought that it was a pity so many women were struggling in the first stages of the identity crisis, particularly in the area of sexuality, while the important work of securing more rights for women needs to be done. Many women's lib groups are talking nonsense. I'm no bluenose, but all this talk about vibrators and the superiority of the lesbian orgasm seems to me to miss the point that we have been divided into he's and she's for good reasons, the predominant one of which is the preservation of the species. The quicker we accept it, the happier we're all going to be. But that has absolutely nothing to do with the way we're paid or promoted.

I couldn't be bothered sifting through the nonsense so I didn't join the movement until the week after I was asked by one Congressman if another had his fly zipped when he talked to me. I had gone to Washington to discuss addiction and the garbage in the streets and it turned out that I was only an object for which one zipped or unzipped one's fly. I was livid. I called the president of NOW, the National Organization for Women and said I was coming out of my professional silk into the burlap of reality. I wanted a membership.

Being a woman is a hell of a trap to be in. And it truly is a trap. No matter how much help she has in her home, for instance, she carries conditioned responsibility for the most mundane chores. She may be head of a business or a government agency, but she has to remember the lamb chops even if it is only to ask her husband to remove them from the freezer.

I am desolated by the plight of women, which is only part of what is wrong in this country. I fear that our beautiful nation is dying, and I don't think the government gives a damn. They don't even care that our children survive. We have no tribal identity as Americans.

I can't understand the difference between a New York child, for instance, and a California child. It is incredible to me that politicians think of children as belonging to one state or another and treat them differently, according to the mood of their local electorate. I can't see that it matters where a child lives or what his color is; he's a child and that's enough.

I'm not very fond of adults. Frankly, adults are often hard to take. Often they care only for children who look like themselves. Or who have the same last name. Or the same religion. Or live in the same part of town.

It is possible that we hate our children. I came to that realization after fighting for treatment for adolescent addicts. I naïvely began with the concept that once I proved the existence of children addicts, people would flock to help. I thought of them as American children, not Republican children or Democratic children. I learned differently. The children don't exist. What matters is making a beneficial deal, looking good, humping the public so that one can get to a higher office.

I see one of two things going to happen to this world. Either we'll blow ourselves up by the leaders setting off the atomic holocaust, or we'll turn over leadership to the howling mobs and a Dark Ages will begin. Civilization will be taken over by very primitive people who have not had an opportunity to appreciate music, art, beauty, flexibility, emotional growth. It has already happened in the ghettos, which have brutalized people. They react with passive aggression and hostility, which as they mount will be met with a fascist, savage back-lash, with the large dogs and all the rest. Those of us who see things differently will not exist. There will be a conformity of mediocrity and all deviation will be stamped out.

The generation coming up will not be able to stop this because it will be saturated with drugs. Schools bear much of the blame. They desensitivize and dehumanize children. They are full of the male competitive need for scientific fact, for infallible computer answers, for absolute truth, rather than the intuitive beauty of sensitivity and values.

We don't teach our children how to learn, we teach them what to know. It's all existence exercises rather than essence. I believe, and it is an Odyssey concept, that if you help the person to know himself or herself, he or she'll be able to handle whatever comes along. Law school to me was learning where to look, not learning facts.

We aren't going to survive. Literary ability isn't going to survive, nor music, nor craftsmanship. How can quality survive if the individual sees only the pay check and not what he has produced? How can you survive if doctors want to work nine to five and regard as a nuisance patients who choose to collapse at six? How can beauty survive in a society that can't even dispose of its own garbage?

Too much of our legislation has been produced by lawyers. With lawyers, life is an ego-adversary contest. Everything is a game; the courtroom is a game and when they get into politics, politics is a game. It's all trade-off, wheeling and dealing, *winning* something.

I once was asked to assist former Justice Arthur Goldberg in his gubernatorial campaign. He wanted to develop an attractive, charismatic attitude. We were sitting under a tree on the rear terrace of the Mother House on Sixth Street and I said, "For a start, Arthur, if you want my vote prove to me that you're not King Solomon."

He was startled to be told that he appeared to me a King Solomon type. I added, "You are, except that you would insist on cutting the baby in half in the service of your highest principle —that of compromise." He was indignant and said how dare I talk like that. I sighed. He walked away.

Six weeks later, one of his aides phoned and asked if the remark about cutting the baby in half was original with me. I said it was. The next day Goldberg used it against Lindsay in the Ansonia, Long Island, Con-Ed fight—without giving credit. It was the New York *Times* "Quote of the Day."

It's a dog-eat-dog world, and people are unlovely. We're supposed to be a herd animal, but it's one herd against another, and we've now reduced the herd to the nuclear family, and the nuclear family to one lonely individual which is what the addict talks about—one lonely individual pitted against another in a cynical jungle.

If we are to stop the slide into hell, and we must work on the assumption that we can, we're going to have to look unafraid at our child-raising techniques. For the most part, they are disastrous. The Odyssey Mothering Program is a good start, as is Child Advocacy and the Treat the Streets project that is gathering dust in the files. We need to spread out parenting, get more flavor and variety and safeguards into the lives of all our children.

While I question the effectiveness of the nuclear family and suggest that we have the extended family in its stead, this isn't to negate the importance of monogamy or early bonding. It cannot be questioned that the human infant requires a secure, affectionate, constant relationship with caretaking adults during his first years.

Looking at the early lives of our residents, we can't draw any conclusions. Addicts come from working mothers and stay-home mothers, from broken homes and from intact homes, from devoutly religious homes and from non-religious homes. The only pattern that emerges is excess: either too much was done for the child or too little. Either there were no rules at all, as in the typical permissive family, or everything the child did was wrong. There is no balance.

With permissiveness or severity, there is no legitimate freedom for the child. In the first instance, there is no mold at all, and the child is confused and resentful. In the second, there is such a rigid mold that the child can't fit without distorting himself.

I've seen homes so ruinously indulgent that the mother goes out to cop dope for her addict child, and I've seen homes where the parents hate the child so much they have tried to kill him.

I dislike the overprotective home more than the openly hostile one, bad as both are. Overprotection is a form of control that expresses anger and dislike of the child as an individual while motivating guilt within him for the resentment he legitimately feels. There are women who regard mothering as a profession. If the woman derives her primary value from raising children, then at least one of her children must remain a baby. Usually it is the youngest one. We have had many youngest children in Odyssey, and several medical papers have been written to point out the high statistical frequency of addiction among the babies of families.

There is also a good deal of addiction found in oldest children, where the dynamic seems to be the parents' fear that the child isn't ready to face the world and should in all ways be protected in his best interests. Sometimes the child becomes the pal of the parents, which is another kind of trap because there is no one to look to for limit-setting. Sometimes a child lives in an authoritarian family where there is continual struggle for control. The child is damned if he does and damned if he doesn't.

Before we can change the way parents raise children we have to change the way they relate to each other. The primary source of many problems is the relationship between husband and wife. There is rarely any respect or partnership or mutuality even in the sex relationship. There's no awareness that they are both responsible for what happens in the bed or out of it. There's no enjoyment of themselves as people first, with the pleasure of the bed something added to it.

They don't talk to one another. In many cases it's because the wife has nothing to talk about. The husband's job doesn't interest her; indeed she often resents it. It may not interest him. They don't read, they rarely go out. Their relationship becomes sterile and non-exciting. Often they relate only through the children. I'm against togetherness of that kind. Husbands and wives should have rich separate lives, coming together to share what they have been doing. They should be good friends, not parasites on each other. Marriage is the expression of the joy they have in their children and in maintaining their home. One of the nicest things Michael ever said to me is that I am his friend. The feeling is returned.

Unfortunately, many parents live through their children, which cripples the children. We should expect nothing from our children except the pleasure of watching them grow up and seeing the child fully actualized on his own terms. Limits should be set in such areas as bedtime, meals, neatness and some of the socializing rules that society observes. But this does not mean control. Control is choosing one of several good alternatives and declaring that only one will be permitted. An easy example that comes to mind is in the area of dress: the child has several outfits that are equally suitable to the occasion, but the parent insists on a certain one. That's stifling control.

The child should have enough sleep; the child should always have the consideration to inform the parents where he is; the child must have regular meals. These are areas where discipline is applicable; but there is no place for discipline over thought, which is where the clash in families often occurs.

Our perceptive son Judson made an observation when he was seven that enchanted me. Michael was lecturing Judson seriously that he didn't take proper care of his younger brother, Lindsey, whom he had just kicked. Judson was protesting that he loved his younger brother dearly. Michael asked him for his definition of love. Judson thought for a minute and said, "Love, Daddy, is secretly stealing somebody else's problems." We must be doing something right.

Jud said this on a day when I was particularly concerned with the preservation of love concepts within Odyssey. With bigness, we seem to have imperiled some of the original ideas of freedom, pulling together and mutual support. The obsessive, compulsive, non-creative, easily threatened, status-seeking middle echelon—the bureaucrats—have a tendency to take over whenever a school or a business or a country or an agency becomes very large.

Both the top and the bottom suffer, and the middle is in control. Jimmy Murphy, Louie Sarra, all of us who started Odyssey, fight a daily battle against the hardness, cruelty and rejection bordering on sadism that flows from the middle echelon. And then they disguise their merciless indifference to those beneath them by describing them as apathetic and cynical.

I wonder if the problems of size can be overcome. There's no question that Odyssey keeps changing—the very name suggests change, and without change there can be no growth. There is a balance to be struck: One must weigh between doing things in one's own style—which results in total control and dominance, frustrating others from developing along their own pathways—and the sometimes distressing consequences of allowing others the freedom to do it their own way.

I have moved from sharing that sheltered warm womb of experience in Odyssey, where I found myself, to attempting to become involved in the massive problems I see in my country. That choice of direction means that, to a large extent, others at Odyssey must take over.

The country depresses me so that I sometimes have a fantasy that I will stop running around and instead I'll stay in Odyssey and perfect this tiny jewel of experience. But I don't know if that would be right.

Michael suggested recently that to eat an elephant you take one bite at a time. I am trying to eat an elephant. I can't permit the enormity of the addiction problem in this country to paralyze me. We must all begin to clear up whatever area we can relate to, assuming that others will be nibbling away in other areas and we'll meet in the near future.

We have to decide first that rehabilitation is mandatory. Society cannot allow addicts to walk around untreated, unable to function, in very deep pain and contagious to others. In some cases, we may have to devise locked environments in which addicts can at least be segregated. They shouldn't exist there in a vacuum, as so often happens in prisons. A method must be developed to treat and return them to society. For some we need sheltered workshops. We can look at it as we do the paraplegic: It is better for him to be in a job where ramps have been built so he can move in his wheel chair. It is society's responsibility to build the ramps, and then it's the paraplegic's responsibility to use them and to work.

Addiction is a contagious disease. Unless we can take the addict off the streets, millions of children will be infected. We should never forget the lesson of the Pied Piper of Hamlin. Because the town officials higgled and haggled over price, the children were marched into the sea and drowned.

I'm appalled by the decision in so many communities to fight heroin addiction with methadone, another addictive narcotic. It doesn't make sense—it's like replacing scotch with bourbon as a treatment of alcoholism. It is believed to be cheaper. There appears to be a great deal of money and political power committed to methadone. It demonstrates the preference for political expediency rather than problem-solving. If we do everything in the short term, eventually there will be no long term.

I become very bitter at times and profoundly depressed on occasion. It is so terrible to watch a generation being thrown away. I'm sustained on my darkest days by my sense of religion. I read the Bible frequently. The story of Job is very meaningful to me, as is the Song of Solomon.

I look to God as a source of inspiration, not as someone who can come down and do me favors. I have been much influenced by the Buddhist belief that there is a universal essence. My concept of Christ is Adoptionist and Unitarian, based on the Gospel of St. Mark, a Jew, that Jesus Christ became one with God and found peace and meaning as a young man because of the existential choices he made. What I take from Christian symbolism is that we must live up to our sense of integrity even at the highest personal sacrifice, and that we must accept all mankind as one.

I pray for guidance. I pray for an understanding of God, for oneness and strength.

The water falls,
As God sighs,
For the sins of man
For which He cries.

For the burden of the cross
Is heavy, you see.
For the measure of weight
Lies in you and me!

—TOMMY MOTT

CURRICULUM VITAE

JUDIANNE DENSEN-GERBER, J.D., M.D.

EXECUTIVE DIRECTOR OF ODYSSEY HOUSE	1967 to present
Bachelor of Arts, Cum Laude, Bryn Mawr College	1956
Bachelor of Law, Columbia University Law School	1959
Doctor of Medicine, New York University Medical School	1963
Doctor of Jurisprudence, Columbia University Law School	1969
Rotating Internship, French Hospital	1963–1964
Psychiatric Residency, Bellevue Hospital	1964–1965
Psychiatric Residency, Metropolitan Hospital	1965–1967
Admitted to New York State Bar	1961 to present
Admitted to practice Medicine and Surgery, New York	1967 to present
Medicine and Surgery, New Jersey	1969 to present
Medicine and Surgery, New Hampshire	1971 to present
Medicine and Surgery, Utah	1971 to present

PROFESSIONAL SOCIETIES:

American Medical Association	1968 to present
New York State Medical Society	1968 to present
New York County Medical Society	1968 to present
Member of Sub-Committee on Drug Abuse	
Member of Sub-Committee on Delivery of Health Care	
American Academy of Forensic Sciences—Member	1969
—Fellow	1972 to present
American Academy of Legal Medicine—Fellow	1971 to present
New York Association of Voluntary Agencies on Narcotics Addiction and Substance Abuse, Inc.	
—Board of Directors	1968 to present
—Legal Consultant	1969–1971

36

American Psychiatric Association—Member	1970 to present
New York Women's Bar Association—Member	1969 to present
Society of Medical Jurisprudence—Member	1967 to present
American Bar Association—Member	1972 to present
American Academy of Psychiatry and the Law—Member	1970 to present

OTHER SOCIETIES:

Women's City Club of New York	1956 to present
All Souls Unitarian Church	1958 to present

BOARD OF DIRECTORS:

President, Odyssey House Board of Directors	1967 to present
Simpson Street Development Association	1969
Hospital Audiences, Inc.	1971 to present
Institute for Child Mental Health—Professional Advisory Committee for the Study of Drug Use Among Children and Adolescents	1972 to present

ADDITIONAL PROFESSIONAL ACTIVITIES:

Research in Forensic Psychiatry at Metropolitan Hospital, creating and developing the program which is embodied at Odyssey House	1966–1967
Taught seminars on drug addiction at New York University Law School	1966–1967
Trainee Core Staff Office of Narcotic Coordinator of the City of New York, Doctor Efren Ramirez	1966–1967
During third year Medical School, did six months special research under the direction of Dr. Morris Herman evaluating Truth Serum, administering over 250 Sodium Amytal interviews	
Vice-President of the Psychiatric Section of the Fourth International Forensic Medicine Conference—Budapest, Hungary	1967
Chairman of the Plenary Session of Drug Abuse—Chicago American Academy of Forensic Sciences	1970
Delegate to the White House Conference on Youth	1971
Member of the National Advisory Commission on Criminal Justice Standards and Goals established by the Law Enforcement Assistance Administration	1971 to present
Member of the Democratic Platform Committee on Crime and Violence	1972

ADVISOR TO:

James Buckley, United States Senator from New York
Seymour Halpern, United States Congressman
Jacob Javits, United States Senator from New York
Edward Koch, United States Congressman
Louis Lefkowitz, Attorney General of New York State
Thomas Mackell, District Attorney of Queens

Thomas McIntyre, United States Senator from New
    Hampshire
Harrison Williams, United States Senator from New
    Jersey

1. Outstanding Young Women of America	1969
2. Who's Who in American Women	1969 to present
3. Dictionary of International Biography	1969 to present
4. National Social Directory	1968 to present
5. Community Leaders of America	1970 to present
6. 2000 Women of Achievement	1969 to present
7. Who's Who in the East	1971 to present

AWARDS:

1. American Association of University Women	1970
2. Myrtle Wreath Award—Hadassah	1970
3. Woman of Achievement Award—B'nai B'rith Women	1971
4. B'nai B'rith Woman of Greatness Award	1971

Born: November 13, 1934
Married to Dr. Michael Baden, Deputy Chief Medical Examiner—New
York City
Mother of three children.

PRESENTED THE FOLLOWING PAPERS:

1. 1967—Budapest, "The Therapeutic Community Treatment of Addiction" at the Fourth International Forensic Medicine Conference.
2. 1969—Palo Alto, California, "The Therapeutic Community Psychiatric Treatment of Addiction Through Professional & Ex-Addict Teamwork" (with James Murphy) at the Committee on Drug Dependency Division of Medical Sciences, National Academy of Sciences, National Research Council.
3. 1969—Toronto, Canada, "The Psychiatric Therapeutic Community Approach Reviewed" (with James Murphy) at the Fifth International Forensic Medicine Conference.
4. 1970—Washington, D.C., "Statistical Analysis of Odyssey House Residents During the Period of July 1, 1968–March 31, 1969" (with Paul Herzich) at the Thirty-Second Meeting of the Committee on Problems of Drug Dependence Division of Medical Sciences, National Academy of Sciences, National Research Council.
5. 1970—Chiago, Illinois, at The American Academy of Forensic Sciences: "Psychiatric Treatment of Addiction,"
    "The Social Impact of the Legal System and Law Enforcement Agencies on the Problem of Drug Addiction" (with Peter Weimer),
    "Education and Prevention of the Addictive Epidemic" (with Paul Herzich),
    "Different Experiences vs. Double Messages" (with James Murphy).
6. 1971—"The Therapeutic Community: The Odyssey House Concept,"

in *Drug Abuse, Proceedings of the International Conferences,* edited by Chris J. D. Zarafonetis, M.D., Philadelphia; published by Lea & Febiger, 1971 (with Charles Rohrs, M.D. and James Murphy).

7. 1970—New York, "The Concept of Para-Medical Bridges" (with Paul Herzich and Alton Johnson) presented at the 28th Annual Convention of the American Society of Group Psychotherapy and Psychodrama.

8. 1970—Lauzanne, Switzerland, "The Changing Face of Addiction—The Adolescent Epidemic" (with James Murphy) presented at The International Council on Alcohol and Addiction.

9. 1971—Washington, D.C., at the Scientific Program of the American Psychiatric Association's Annual Meeting:
   "Bridges and Communications" (with Alton Johnson and Donald Dougherty) (Adult Addiction),
   "An Epidemiological Survey of Adolescent Drug Abuse in the New York Metropolitan Area 1968–1970 Period" (with Charles Rohrs, M.D. and Barbara Muney, M.A.)—(Adolescent Addiction),
   "The Changing Face of Addiction: An Adolescent Confrontation" (with James Murphy).

10. 1971—Phoenix, Arizona, "Treat the Streets" (with Frederick Cohen) at the Academy of Forensic Sciences.

11. 1972—Atlanta, Georgia, at the Annual Meeting of the American Academy of Forensic Sciences:
    "The Phenomenon of Adolescent Addiction" (with Charles Rohr, M.D.; James Murphy; and Bernard Goldsmith, M.S.),
    "Sexual Behavior, Abortion, and Birth Control in Heroin Addicts: Legal and Psychiatric Considerations" (with Malcolm Wiener, J.D., and Rowen Hochstedler, M.D.).

12. 1971 to present—Columnist: New York *Law Journal*
    Manchester *Union Leader*

13. Author:
    Drugs, Sex, Parents and You with daughter Trissa Austin Baden, published by J. B. Lippincott, 1972.
    We Mainline Dreams: The Odyssey House Story with several Odyssey staff members.
    Book on the Woman's Changing Role for Saturday Review Press to be published in 1974.

"Who Else in the World Can Help Us?"
A Sermon delivered at All Souls Church on February 27, 1972
Judianne Densen-Gerber, J.D., M.D.

We are each a product of our past experiences and relationships, and it is extremely difficult for me to imagine on this Thursday morning as I write this sermon on old-fashioned kindergarten yellow-lined paper roughly milled with bits of wood still in it, paper that was donated to Odyssey New Hampshire so that ex-drug addicts could learn their ABC's, what I will be feeling standing on the other side of the pulpit three days hence. In fact, today, this Sunday morning, February 27, 1972.

Memories flood through my mind making it almost impossible for thoughts to come ordered or logical, but sensations and feelings are almost overwhelming and so I have chosen to collect my ideas on childlike kindergarten paper for it brings back the security and familiarity of my early and more manageable learning years.

It is to this church and congregation that Michael and I turned as two frightened but very much in love young people in 1958 to resolve the conflict of different religious life styles in a world which at that time was barely ready to tolerate religious intermarriage, and it is here that we found fellowship and acceptance. Thank you.

It is here that we had the pleasure to introduce three children to the congregation at Christening services: in 1959, Trissa; 1963, Judson; and 1965, Lindsey. And it is from here that in 1961 we buried our daughter Julianne who was born defective and lived but a short time.

It is the last experience which molded my own life. Cut as if pressed swiftly and without warning against a razor's edge, I realized the transient quality of each human life. I was bewildered and I groped; I prayed and I received no answers; I cried and I felt no better; I raged and I was only too exhausted to sleep; I clung to Michael and I became fearful that he too would die without reason, long before his expected time. Finally, I faced myself and the brutal fact of the human condition. Since death is the final affront, then man must begin to live each day to its fullest with meaning and dignity.

What did that mean? To me, it meant that we must look at ourselves as individual people, as an American society, and as the human species. It meant realizing our individual and collective potential for good but also clearly recognizing our instinctive heritage for evil. I have no doubts that there is much validity in the ideas of Robert Ardrey which he has expressed in *African Genesis* and *The Territorial Imperative*. Ardrey writes:

> Man is a wild species, and every baby born is a wild young thing. Advancing age, weakening vitality and a long accumulation of fears and experiences may at last work a general inhibition on certain animal sources of human behavior. But, the dilemma of any society, closed or free, finds its chief place of residence in the birth rate. Every accouchement delivers to society a creature

who somehow must be tamed. Every accouchement—today, tomorrow, and until the end of our species time—presents civilization with an aspiring candidate for the hangman's noose. Yet to truly domesticate him means probably to destroy him . . . Man has survived because he is basically the killer ape with a strong tribal competitive identity which not only excludes other species but which is frequently turned against his own kind. Man alone finds delight in the habit of killing his own and man alone has developed his competitive need for total supremacy to the point where annihilation and subjugation rather than defeat and retreat are the only terms of battle.

However, we can only tolerate our irreverence for life and our thorough disregard of the feelings of those we torture and kill by reinforcing our tribal identities. Therefore, we rationalize our conduct and defend against the possibility that it could happen to us by viewing those we victimize as less than human or not as good as we are. Obviously, these defenses are strongest on racial lines for *they* don't even look like us and *they* do all look alike; but then religious differences work pretty well too for, if *they* have not got the right belief in the true God they are not worthy; and ethnic boundaries are easy to draw for they speak a foreign language and have strange customs. But I have seen this vicious separation drawn between our states. So that, what happens to a New York child is of no concern to New Jersey and New Hampshire could care less about Utah and in Utah, the methadone maintenance program is almost exclusively for Blacks, while Odyssey's drug-free program treats all ethnic groups. The Federal Government stores or burns wheat surplus in Iowa that it has bought to stabilize the farm economy and American children go to bed hungry in Appalachia, New York and Chicago to wake up in the morning brain damaged due to malnutrition. And we do not question the President and we do not impeach him.

In 1969, Odyssey New York treated a fourteen-year-old, tow-headed boy from New Jersey who had been addicted to heroin for two and a half years, whose father is an alcoholic, whose mother is in the boy's words "a whore," and whose eighteen-year-old brother is in jail for armed robbery.

From twelve and a half to thirteen, a period of six months, he lived in Central Park, building a hut of newspapers, sleeping in parked cars or over subway gratings to keep warm on cold winter nights and at times eating pigeons. No one noticed him or his nine-year-old companion whom he describes as even worse off than himself—for the younger child, since the time he was four and a half had

had no home or bed, but lived like "a puppy" going from friend's house to friend's house staying a month or two at each—as long as the family would tolerate him. Finally, the two children met a teen-age drug addict and they began to use heroin.

Our tow-headed youngster paid for his heroin mostly by baby-sitting for a heroin-addicted prostitute mother of three children under five who needed someone at home while she turned her tricks. She often left the boy and her children without money or food for two or three days at a time. This was New York 1967.

By 1971, as had many other children from twenty-six different states, the boy was cured by Odyssey House New York. Yet, we faced the problem of his re-entry to society. We had no family or place to return him. So we decided to be his family until he was 21. We could not send him to school in New York or New Jersey because the class-rooms were too contaminated with drugs. In September 1970, the New York Board of Education admitted that 7 per cent of its students were seriously involved with drugs; this equalled 35,000 high school students. In fact, some home rooms were reporting that twenty-nine out of thirty students were drug users.

We decided to send him to New Hampshire and the New Hampshire Odyssey, but discovered that New Hampshire only educates New Hampshire children of New Hampshire residents. There was no free ninth grade for him to enter. He could go to school only if we paid the eight hundred dollars a year it cost the local community. As a charity with certain by-laws, we were not permitted to do so, hence we returned him to New York where he goes to the special school within our facility for patients in treatment. This is not a normal re-entry situation.

Whatever happened to the right of free education for all our children? When Odyssey first tried to obtain teachers for our children at a time when we had the only beds in the United States for addicted children, teachers were denied to us because we did not have proper lighting, doors that opened the right way, or separate bathrooms for the teachers.

As this congregation well remembers, since Dr. Kring arranged for Mr. Costikyan to be my most able attorney, I was shortly thereafter arrested by the City for keeping children in an overcrowded facility. However, as Mr. Costikyan proved by my acquittal, I was justified in so doing as neither the City nor State at that time provided any treatment alternatives; therefore I had no choice. They were still denying these children existed, but almost immediately the Governor and the State Legislature appropriated $65 million to treat adolescents. We had won and now could begin in this one very small area.

But much remains to be done—and *you* must ask why it is not being done. Each of us lives in a tiny isolated little world from which we do not venture. We do not look around, we do not feel an impetus to inform ourselves or to shatter our secure fantasy of safety. As long as all seems well at home, at the office and with a few friends, we do not question. Why look for trouble? What you don't know won't hurt you is the rule of the day. And yet, this is not true. For heroin addiction, as is the case with other communicable diseases, knows no boundaries, and no one is safe. The white plague spreads with the same rapidity and virulence in the twentieth century that the Black Plague did in the seventeenth—only there is no countryside for the rich to flee to for refuge and as yet no Great Fire of London to burn the pestilence to the ground.

But heroin is only the herald of the holocaust to come. Our society is closely geographically bound together and its people have little respect for each other. There is second-class angry citizenry on all sides. Blacks, women and the young, are only a few of the groups who feel disenfranchised and not in charge of their own destiny. Such a society cannot long endure. As it stands now, rampant, uncontrolled violence is the future for the American Killer Ape.

If we are to survive, we must find answers to relevant questions. To me, they are found here. For we, as Unitarians, believe that we are all made of the same "human stuff" as was Jesus; and those of us who follow the doctrine according to the Gospel of St. Mark believe that Jesus is the symbol of a man who through dedication and sacrifice became one with life and the instinctive rage within us all. He taught us as noted in Mark 9:36–37.

Mark 9:36—"And he took a child, and set him in the midst of them: and when he had taken him in his arms, he said unto them,"

Mark 9:37—"'Whosoever shall receive me, receiveth not me, but him that sent me.'"

I would rephrase the message of love and concern this way for our time: Look back not in anger, look ahead not in fear but look around in awareness. I would like each of you listening to me to pledge today to find one child within our immediate community who has a multitude of problems, who needs a child advocate. It could be a drug-addict child in treatment at Odyssey, or awaiting sentence in a youth house. It could be a child before the Family Court in trouble himself, or one of the 2,000 battered children, or one who is retarded in Willowbrook and subject to the cruelties and forgettings of an indifferent state and its people. It could be a child in utero with one of Odyssey's pregnant addicts. For, as of today, Odyssey has the only beds in the United States for pregnant addicts and the only in-residential aftercare program for mother and child—even though over a thousand babies will be born addicted in New York City alone in 1972. And like the early days of our adolescent-treatment community, this program remains totally unfunded and dependent on private donations.

Much must be done. For instance, a child in utero has no legal rights. He cannot even demand responsible conduct of his mother, and she may, until the moment of his birth, shoot drugs, turn tricks, have venereal diseases and poor nutrition, all of which limit his chances of being normal, and not handicapped.

I believe the only answer is for us to begin caring for *all* our children. As Camus said, "Perhaps we cannot prevent this world from being a world in which children are tortured. But we can reduce the number of tortured children. And if you don't help us, who else in the world can help us do this?"

Odyssey stands ready to work closely with you and this church in developing a meaningful child-advocacy program.

We await your response to our call for action—the children need you. If you learn about one child, you will learn about a multitude of problems. We will together begin our walking-the-walk and not just talking-the-talk about living Christianity and its reverence for life. For Christ came to teach us to leave the isolation of self and walk among our brothers and sisters who now as never before are inextricably bound to our own survival. Truly, we have no choice.

I would like to close with a vignette from our Third Avenue community outreach center. I quote from the report that crossed my desk yesterday written by a twenty-year-old Jewish ex-addict still in treatment. He writes:

> February 11, 1972—At one o'clock, Maria Romanoff came in. She is the lady who has been here about five times asking for publicity. She claims to be the messiah and the granddaughter of the Czar of Russia. She told us that she had no place to go and that she spends all night in a telephone booth. Lyle gave her a sandwich and then tried to talk seriously to her about getting a job or getting on welfare. She finally said she would go to a welfare office. We hope they accept her. It is certainly a shame and a very bad reflection on our society that the messiah has to sleep in a phone booth.

Indeed, if we do not help our people and our children, "who else in the world can help us?"

OUR THANK YOU
Dr J D G

We thAnk you for sAving our lives
we Thank you for Leting us
be ApAet of your thought
we also thank you for giving us
a home away from hell - for
everyone in the odessey really apperiate
it Because there is no more to apperiate
thes is what we want out of Life
and now we finally Got it and she
made it possible for us to Live be normally
people again. a person Like dr J.D.G.
we thank you so much for the
knowloge and mind that you've giving
us. and we will Love to Give you something
in return that you will enjoy Be Proud
of,
       thank you very much

       the odessey house

Discharged Persons Group

AUGUST 18, 1971

Odyssey graduates, called D.P.s—a pun based on their awareness that they are displaced in society—meet with several staff members once a month in my home. It's partly a social time, partly a reaffirmation, and all those who wish to attend are invited. We're more friends than a therapist meeting with patients. On this particular group night, I was preoccupied with Odyssey's new Mothering Program and with news that the six-year-old daughter of LaVerne and Silas Whitfield was showing signs of becoming emotionally disturbed.

As I have said before, I'm not sure that a mother who didn't experience warm mothering herself can ever learn to give warm loving to her children. LaVerne was one of ten illegitimate children born of five different fathers. After her mother died when she was ten years old, the father in the foster home where the city placed her attempted to assault her. She ran away, told her social worker and was placed in a reformatory. She was twelve at the time.

Her life was tragic, but she has done remarkably well in the Odyssey program, which she entered while pregnant for the second time. She came to us to have her baby because she wanted this baby to be born drug-free. One day she determined by sheer will alone that she was going to build a better future for her children than she had known. She entered Odyssey House, where later she met and married Silas. He has assumed the father role for her two children, LaVonne and Matthew—named for Matty Ancona. At the time the group was

374

meeting, that child, Matthew, was slowly dying of a kidney cancer that had metastasized to his brain.

Understandably, the dying child caused problems at home. Rowen Hochstedler had just given me an unsettling report of LaVonne's behavior. It had to be discussed in the group.

Rowen, Louie, Clifford, and René Casaclang were there, sitting on four chairs in my small brick-walled room. Matty, Jimmy and I sat with our backs against the mural, noisily settling ourselves into the beanbags. Charlie, puffing contentedly on a cigar, occupied the other beanbag. Ellis Williams stretched out flat on the floor.

"I think LaVerne should take a leave of absence," Rowen was saying. "At least until LaVonne is reassured and feeling better."

I brooded. "What symptoms is LaVonne showing?"

Rowen answered, "Mainly, she's very clinging. She doesn't want her parents to leave in the morning. And she's scared of her own room and being alone in it. She reported to LaVerne seeing witches."

I was distressed. "She shouldn't see witches at six," I exclaimed.

"Is it pathological at that age?" Rowen inquired.

"Yes, definitely. The normal range is three to five. It's normal to start at three and carry over to six, but to begin seeing witches at six . . ." I shook my head.

"This was apparently the first time it has ever happened," Rowen told me, looking worried as well.

"She must feel very threatened and needs attention," I interpreted.

We discussed the problem for a while. We concluded that many Odyssey residents were sufficiently rigid so that they saw their children as small adults. For instance, Dennis Watkins had reported in group that his two-year-old was "acting out" and "exhibiting sociopathic behavior." Dennis accordingly had decided to reprimand him and require him to make a commitment that he would behave better. On learning of this, I became more depressed.

"Did anyone explain to Dennis that two-year-olds are not twenty-year-olds?"

Charlie grinned at me around his cigar. "Yes, we filled him in."

We all felt that the Odyssey nursery had been a healthy environment for LaVonne Whitfield. However, at the time of the dispute with Angela Green, the Whitfields and Coxes had removed their children from the nursery, claiming it was too expensive.

"The kids are the pawns in this," Charlie sighed.

I recalled several conclusions from Prescott's experiments with monkey mothers and their children which applied to the discussion. While giving their baby monkeys inadequate, indifferent care these mothers were enraged if the babies went to play elsewhere or sought other mothers. "In one instance, the mother actually bit the baby's arm off when he tried to leave her," I informed the group. "The need to be symbiotic with the baby, this unhealthy symbiosis, plays a big part in their behavior. Even when they can't adequately care, they will allow no one to substitute for them. Their needs are more important than their child's. Furthermore, Harlow confirmed that a baby needs holding and touching as much as food."

Charlie informed me that we now had ten mothers and babies in the Odyssey House Mothering Program, with fifteen additional inquiries about the unit. I wondered how we would feed and care for them all, since we had no funding. The latest was a mother admitted with her fourteen-month-old baby; she wouldn't come in for treatment for her heroin addiction unless the baby could accompany her.

"We must find a psychologist to design instruments to study human mothering," I commented. "Nobody's done anything like this, and if we ever want to challenge established beliefs about motherhood, we must have documentation. If we ever announce that we have proved Prescott's monkey experiments are applicable to human beings, they'll probably tar and feather us."

Charlie agreed. "What is probably the truth is going to be damaging and explosive."

"But if it is true, it will have to be said," I declared with conviction. "The real point is that the monkey experiments show that with minimum intervention you can train the infant of the deprived mother to become a normal mother. You *can* intercede. With adequate peer relationships and surrogate mothers, the damage doesn't have to be passed on from one generation to the next. We must break the cycle."

Prescott's experimenters started with twenty monkeys, but they couldn't tolerate the pain the babies were suffering beyond damage to the fourth one. By then they had shown that deprived baby monkeys who played with other monkeys, either peers or adults, clinging to them and having group closeness, could develop into adult monkeys who were adequate mothers.

"It doesn't matter who the surrogate is," I remarked. "It doesn't have to be the natural mother as long as there is skin contact, touching early enough, contact without violence or ambivalence—as long as there is consistency of caring. This also was reaffirmed by Harlow."

Our ex-addict mothers, like the monkeys, were not involved with their babies as persons, we were discovering. They had little interest in holding or touching them. We had another parallel with Prescott's work. He found that young monkeys deprived of mothering exhibited early sexuality, much earlier than in monkeys with normal mothering. "That's what we're seeing in Odyssey," I said. "Children of eleven and twelve who have had no mothering and who fill their need for affection with promiscuous heterosexual contact.

"Many of our girls want only pre-genital sex from their partners," I added. "They want closeness, holding, clinging, and suffer through the penetration of adult sexuality to get it. What I don't understand is why nobody is looking at this. Is it too terrifying? I think it's dangerous. Questioning the nature of mothering is an explosive issue. The authorities may turn against us."

Charlie leaned forward, looking thoughtful. "The danger comes in how its interpreted," he commented. "I hope no one sees it as a class or racial thing . . ."

"The early sexuality we're seeing in New Jersey is White," I reminded him.

"I know it is, but will it be seen that way? To me, the explosive thing is that it may be interpreted as a ghetto problem, belonging to only one class or group. Certainly, there's a wealth of inadequate parents in the affluent suburbs, but they're too well defended, too well protected, to ever allow this type of information to be viewed as applicable to them."

I asked Matty how his first wife—from whom he is divorced—was behaving with his two sons. She had had a sordid situation in her childhood. After a seven-year incestuous relationship with her father, which started before she was ten, she reported him to the police. After he was convicted, served time and was released her mother took him back. She blamed her daughter. Obviously, Matty's wife would have difficulty knowing how to be an adequate mother.

Matty was upset because previously she had kept their two sons in a dark room and recently she had not fed them over a period of a few days. She had done this in order to punish Matty. Since then he had been giving additional food money to an aunt of his who lives in the neighborhood in order to provide for the children.

The courts are wrong to give preference to the mother in awarding custody of children after a divorce. Both mother and father should be evaluated equally; not infrequently, the father is much more responsible. If they are equally responsible, I would award the girl children to the mother and the boys to the father, unless the child has a preference. "I see them cuddling her on occasions," he told me in a despondent tone, "kissing her and stuff like that."

"Does she respond?"

"Fifty-fifty. Sometimes she does and sometimes she doesn't."

There was a troubled silence. There is little Matty can do. In group he often speaks of his despair.

Charlie mentioned a baby in the program who had been in a fine foster home and arrived in Odyssey in marvelous shape. Now that her mother was caring for her, the baby was beginning to droop. One of the residents had asked how Odyssey could submit babies to such misery. I was having a hard time with this myself.

"Everything is structured in the world today to keep the mother and child together," I observed. "The structure is seldom modified by experience. We must study some of these situations."

I ran my fingers through my hair. "We're going to watch that baby, and I tell you I'm going to die. We're going to watch that baby go from being the sweetest, loveliest baby to having nightmares, to being afraid, to start pulling her hair, and all the rest of the symptoms she's going to get."

"Is it necessary that we use this child?" Charlie asked. "I mean, there are institutions filled with children who have no parents."

"That isn't what we're studying," I said urgently. "We are studying the relationship of a child to his natural mother, who is anti-social. The real problem is that the law says the natural mother and child are a healthy biological unit. Top-A quality, no matter what is real. That's what it says, right?"

Charlie was gloomy. "When I am holding that baby I think *I* would create a better mother-child relationship with that infant than her mother has."

"Of course you would," I agreed. "You had a normal mother-child relationship. You can love. But do you think a court would buy it? You go and say you're a more adequate mother, and they'll put you away, Dr. Rohrs."

The courts later proved me wrong. Charlie testified that another mother was homicidal, and the judge granted him custody of the baby.

Silas Whitfield, arriving late, eased himself through the door and found a place beside Matty. He had been visiting his dying young son in the hospital and looked tired and depressed. I cleared my throat and told him we had been talking about mothering.

'What's happening with LaVonne?" I asked. "I hear she's in difficulty."

"She is," he said resignedly. "She doesn't want to go to bed. When I came home Wednesday, she was hollering and screaming that she didn't like the house, she didn't want to stay there, she wanted to go to Margaret's, she wanted to go to my mother's, she wanted to go to my aunt's, any place but our house. I went down to speak to Rowen. He came up and talked to her. I don't really know what's happening."

There was a pause and I said, "Of course you and I and LaVerne have talked about it many times and we know that LaVerne herself

378

was never mothered. She has much to do to learn how to be a mother. Mothering is very threatening to her, and certainly your son Matthew's illness doesn't help her feel more secure."

Charlie and Rowen suggested, without pressing it, that LaVonne had seemed happy in the nursery and that it might be helpful for her to return. Silas listened stolidly, without replying. When I asked him what he was thinking, he blurted out that he thought LaVonne was being manipulative.

"She's not an adult, Si," I assured him. "She's a baby. This is the normal way a six-year-old acts when she's feeling insecure. You can't blame or assess guilt for attention-seeking, not with a six-year-old. There's only action and reaction in a baby, there's no long-range planning. You can't punish the child for seeing witches or being afraid to go to sleep or wanting to flee to one place or another. It's her way of expressing what she's feeling. She's telling you something and it's your responsibility as an adult to say 'What is this child telling me?' and to find a way to understand."

I took a breath. "Take over, Charlie. I'm getting hostile."

"Does that make sense what Judi says," Charlie inquired promptly.

"It makes sense," Silas answered readily.

I was drinking a large glass of buttermilk, pampering my nervous stomach. Jimmy Murphy, after explaining carefully that he was not rejecting the group but had been up all the night before, stretched out on the waterbed beyond the soft light of the one lamp in the room. Clifford Robinson wore an expression of concern as he followed the conversation. Louie was becoming upset, touched by LaVonne's plight.

"I always thought the child acted a little peculiar," Silas was saying.

"Did she have an average six-year-old upbringing?" Louie demanded indignantly.

"No."

"All right then," Louie said, sinking back. "Don't you think she has the right to react a little differently? She's had some pretty tough breaks." Silas nodded, tears slipping down his cheeks.

"LaVonne is a normal child," I told him. "She doesn't have any of the severe mental illnesses that children could have."

I described for Silas the great strain LaVerne was experiencing. "Ye gods and little fishes," I said with compassion, "she's been through a whole lot. It would be hard if she had the most stable upbringing. I had a very hard time coping with it when I had a child who was not right, who was going to die. Michael and I were, in quotes, comparatively stable individuals with years of medical training. You've got a crisis that would try anybody—watching your two-year-old son slowly and painfully die of cancer."

The discussion ended a half hour later with Silas promising to let us know his decision whether LaVonne would return to the Odyssey nursery. I told him it was essential that he not be critical of LaVerne, who had enough on her back.

Ellis seemed to be going to sleep, his eyes closed and his hands folded on his chest. Clifford watched us all, leaning forward with his chin on his fist.

Around midnight I asked, "What's the matter with you, Clifford? On the phone you sounded depressed."

"I'm all right," he replied with a lazy smile. "Everything is fine."

"Oh, good," I commented in the same tone. "We're finished with C.R." We all laughed, but it developed that, as usual, C.R. had said all he intended to say. He was still planning to marry Diane Silver, he expained, "as soon as the economy settles down." We were delighted with his nonsensical rationalizing. We knew we would soon be going to his wedding.

We then discussed a plan I was formulating to give Odyssey graduates some sort of recognition, a pin for being drug-free for five years perhaps or a certificate for finishing the program. On September 21, 1971, Jimmy Murphy would be five years' free of drugs, and I thought it should be a big event—a party, his name on an Honor Roll in the auditorium, a ceremony of some sort.

"We should keep a record," I said, growing more enthused. "We should have names on a plaque. This is the group we'll look at ten years from now to see if any have returned to addiction. This is the group that is the final arbitrator of success. If any one of you returned to addiction then I would have to question everything we've done."

We started remembering names of those who were close to the five-year mark. Richard Alves, Tommy and Ellen Turner, Tony Enriquez, William Rosado . . . Louie had been clean of illicit drugs for almost five years, Ellis was in his fifth year, Matty had almost four years completed, LeRoy Folkes belonged in the original group, and Bob Meyers. . . .

"That's nine people in the first group," I counted. "Nine people that are totally well. You're totally well, godammit."

Judi II—
Past, Present, Future

9/13/71

To Judi

Who are you who holds my soul
and gives me life and hope
to conquer death that tries
to drag me to the bottom
of a vacuum.

Who are you so mighty, so alone
who bears her pain and burden
with a dignity that puts
to shame the little man.

You are she who goes her way
and lights her candles
when the stars refuse
to share their light.

So silent, so alone, a
soul that must not cry
because so few can bear the pain.
Yet where does your soul
search to find solace
for the aching moments?

Can the pace relieve the pain
or only seek to out distance it.
Each moment is a race
with the solitude which
binds us all and
seeks to overcome us
and trap us in the knowledge
of our isolation.

May you win the race
for we cannot all be trapped.

—MARGARET WARD

New York *Times* Editorial   February 2, 1970

WHO CARES ABOUT DRUG ABUSE?

The seriousness of New York City's drug abuse problem and the utter inadequacy of the governmental response to it have been demonstrated by a series of developments within the past several days.

A 17-year-old Barnard College freshman died after inhaling an overdose of heroin over the weekend. A 17-year-old Brooklyn boy, an 18-year-old Bronx girl and a 19-year-old Staten Island boy died from drug abuse last week. Altogether, 224 teen-agers died from drug abuse in the city's five boroughs last year.

Drug abuse has become more pervasive among the city's very young. A deeply addicted 12-year-old girl was found in a narcotics daze last week and returned to her expensive East Side home. An 11-year-old girl was admitted into the privately run Odyssey House rehabilitation program and an 11-year-old boy was arrested with his two companions, ages 13 and 15, on charges of selling heroin.

It is hard to understand why city officials tried for a time to block the release of statistics sketching the vast dimensions of the drug abuse problem, or why they have failed to launch a preventive or rehabilitation program of the scope clearly required. They have, instead, sought to close down the Bronx Odyssey House, the only facility in the country devoted solely to the rehabilitation of teen-age addicts. They summoned Dr. Judianne Densen-Gerber, director of the program, into criminal court on charges of violating a building code provision against overcrowding. She faces a jail term.

Neither the city nor the state has made available presently unused buildings which could be turned into treatment centers to the Odyssey program or to other private organizations trying desperately to fill the void created by official inaction. Such action is urgently needed. The city and state ought also to launch educational programs on drugs to reach youngsters in the lowest school grades. There are probably 100,000 heroin addicts in the city, an estimated one-fourth of them teen-agers. Additional thousands of other youngsters are experimenting with heroin and other dangerous drugs. Preventive programs require immediate launching. Rehabilitation centers need to be opened quickly. The Federal Government should help underwrite city and state efforts in these areas.

Mayor Lindsay has so far remained strangely aloof. He provides for no new rehabilitation centers in his capital budget. Governor Rockefeller recommends further study. For the state to propose the treatment of 150 teen-agers in a pilot project that might get under way in six months, as Assembly Speaker Duryea proposed last week, is for it to continue ignoring the urgency and the dimensions of the problem.

How many youngsters must die before Government becomes alarmed? How many families of all economic and social strata must know heartache? Is there within the remote bureaucracy no one who owns a sense of honest outrage?

Pageant Magazine   August 1970

HERE'S A PLACE THAT MAKES YOU WANT TO COME BACK

Once a monkey is on your back, life becomes a continuous game with death.

And it is the specter of death that 35-year-old Dr. Judianne Densen-Gerber deals with daily.

Dr. Densen-Gerber is a woman whose life is devoted to helping drug addicts—especially adolescent addicts—make it back into the world.

Some people call "Doctor Judy" a saint, a heroine. She is formidable —fantastically emotional . . . sometimes abrasive . . . always honest. She is the founder and the executive director of Odyssey House, private drug-care centers for addicts in New York and New Jersey.

One ex-addict at Odyssey House has commented, "Dr. Densen-Gerber was in on a marathon group session I was in. She would ask just the right questions—and a kid would spill his guts." Said another 17-year-old ex-addict, "I don't trust any other psychiatrists but her. She's like a mother to me. I never saw anybody like her. She knocks me out."

As for Doctor Judy, she doesn't claim to be a saint or a martyr or a heroine or anything else. She was severely ill as an adolescent and says that from that point on, she was determined "to help other people to live." Her illness made her try to "cram two or three lives into one" (she is a lawyer and a psychiatrist and has three children).

Odyssey House is for addicts who want to cure themselves without the help of drugs.

Today, it has 13 permanent centers—several of them specifically for adolescents. According to Dr. Judy, about eight kids a day knock on their doors for help.

Dr. Densen-Gerber seems to be perpetually in motion. Many times, she works an 18-hour day, caring for "the children" and raising money to house and feed them. (She receives some money from the state and federal governments but Odyssey House is financed primarily by private donations.)

The way Odyssey House operates is as a therapeutic treatment community. Psychiatric professionals work with ex-drug addicts in helping patients change themselves. Group therapy and peer-group pressure are the main tools used. In approximately a year and a half to two years, the addict "graduates" into health.

Odyssey House claims to have success with seven out of ten patients. In short, its motto seems to be: Start changing yourself today!

Odyssey House, on 87th Street in New York City, is a four-story tenement which will probably be torn down one day to make way for a super high-rise luxury building. But walk through its doors, and life and hope become apparent. Plants grow in the windows and the walls are painted in bright pastels. On a bulletin board hangs a sign: "Good people and good causes go together."

Some 50 adolescent addicts live at Odyssey House. Fran, Austin, and Billy are among them: they have all mainlined heroin (shot it into their veins) and they are all committed to changing their lives.

Fran, 17, comes from a middle-class Jewish family in Rockaway, Long Island. Her father died when she was 11. "When I started high school," Fran says, "I met kids who smoked pot and took pills. I wanted to see what it was like. Then it became a habit: We'd be sitting around and someone would always say, 'I'm bored. Let's have some fun and turn on.'

"So I tried LSD; it made me feel like my body was in another dimension while I was walking on earth. One time the snow on the ground felt like styrofoam; another time the mud felt like rubber. But when I took acid, I felt grubby, like I had to keep washing myself . . . I could have bad trips on acid. Once I got very paranoid. I saw police cars and ambulances coming to get me and I heard strange noises. All night I heard the constant dripping of water. It almost drove me crazy . . ."

384

Duke Ellington and
Judianne Densen-Gerber.

TWO WED TO M.D.'S GET M.D. DEGREES

Women, two unusual young women, paced the field of graduates when New York University's 6,384 graduates donned caps and gowns yesterday to end their academic trek.

Both are married to doctors.

Both women now have M.D. degrees to call their own.

Johanna Pindyck Steiner, 25, a striking brunette, won almost all the NYU Medical School honors hands down.

Besides placing first in four-year medical academic standings, Mrs. Steiner won four coveted awards for excellence and promise.

She is the wife of Phillip Steiner, M.D. an intern at Bellevue Hospital.

The other young woman is Mrs. Judianne Densen-Gerber Baden, 29. Not only was Mrs. Baden a good medical student, but she is a counselor at law, too.

Since 1959, when she won her L.L.B. at Columbia, she has practiced law in association with her parents, Gustave A. and Beatrice Densen-Gerber.

Classmates held a rather breathless graduation countdown for Mrs. Baden, who is expecting a child in two weeks.

She braved NYU Med School "last day exercises" Tuesday. But yesterday she bowed to superior wisdom and decided not to risk trying to march down the aisle in the commencement ranks.

"I was almost 9 months pregnant this same time four years ago at my law graduation," sighed Mrs. Baden with a smile.

Her child born then is a girl, Trissa Austin Baden.

Dear Mother Mother
Today is Mother's Day
For you to relaxe all day
Today is a special day For you
Not only to be waited on
But also to have some fun

Though today we
Celebrate the things
You've done for us
On all the Other
Days though
We love you all the same

Happy Mothers Day

Love Teri

Judi's Grandmother Densen,
Trissa and Judson.

The Unitarian

Church of All Souls

Founded in 1819

1157 Lexington Avenue (at 80th Street)

WALTER DONALD KRING, D.D., *Minister*

Vol. XVII   SUNDAY, FEBRUARY 27, 1972   No. 9

Dr. Judianne Densen-Gerber
   "WHO ELSE IN THE WORLD CAN HELP US?"

Published weekly (except for 12 weeks between mid-June and mid-September)
(2ND CLASS POSTAGE PAID AT NEW YORK)

DR. DENSEN-GERBER TO PREACH TODAY

The sermon will be delivered by Dr. Judianne Densen-Gerber, who is a member of All Souls and has made a conspicuous mark by her significant community activity. Many of you mayknow her better as Mrs. Michael Baden for her husband is a member of our Board of Trustees. Dr. Densen-Gerber is a Doctor of Medicine trained in psychiatry, and after her medical and psychiatric training she took a degree in Law. She is the founder of Odyssey House for the rehabilitation of drug addicts.

I have invited her to preach because I believe that she is in the All Souls tradition of persons who have worked actively in the community: Henry Bellows who was president of the United States Sanitary Commission during the Civil War, Henry Bergh who founded the Societies for the Prevention of Cruelty to Animals and Cruelty to Children, and Louisa Lee Schuyler who founded the first nursing school at Bellevue and the State Charities Aid Society. Miss Schuyler's sister, Georgina Schuyler, was the first woman elected to the Board of Trustees in 1923, and the Reverend Berjouie Bergler was, I believe, the first woman minister to preach at All Saints. I believe that Dr. Densen-Gerber is the first "laywoman" to preach in our pulpit. We also welcome the Odyssey House Choir who will close our service by singing two hymns.

THE INQUIRING FOTOGRAPHER

THE QUESTION:

Dr. Judianne Densen-Gerber, executive director of Odyssey House, blames the alienation of today's youth on the increasing permissiveness of parents. Do you agree?

(Of the answers, one agreed, four agreed in part, one disagreed.)

New York *Times*   Tuesday, January 11, 1972

ODYSSEY HOUSE DIRECTOR FAVORS COMPULSORY CURING OF ADDICTS

Firmly grasping two opposing horns of one of the many philosophical dilemmas surrounding drugs and addiction, Dr. Judianne Densen-Gerber said yesterday that she personally believed marijuana should be legalized to preserve respect for the law and that heroin addicts should be committed by the state for three to five years of compulsory rehabilitation.

In a wide-roaming, outspoken discussion with editors and reporters of the New York *Times*, the flamboyant executive director of Odyssey House also said she could foresee in four years the creation of three million young addicts, largely as a result of an influx of veterans returning from Vietnam as addicts.

Arguing that the debate over marijuana legalization involved choices among several evils, Dr. Densen-Gerber declared: "The evil that we now have is that kids are learning to break the law—and finding that breaking the law means nothing."

She said that while she personally favored the legislation of marijuana, she felt that the issue should be put to a referendum.

Dr. Densen-Gerber said it was estimated that there were six million alcoholics in the United States—not to mention cases of alcohol-related diseases—and that by leaving alcohol legal while banning marijuana, the older generation was saying to the younger, "We can have our habit, but you can't have yours."

She maintained that the effects of marijuana had not been proved to be worse than those of alcohol—"and alcohol is a terrible poison."

TOUGHER ON HEROIN

Attacking the issue of the treatment of heroin addicts, Dr. Densen-Gerber took a harder stand.

She argued that having heroin in one's bloodstream should be made a crime and that new, airtight laws should commit addicts to three to five years of treatment, which would confront them with the choice of rehabilitation or incarceration.

"The firm hand is the loving hand," she said, when asked whether her proposal might be in conflict with her generally libertarian opinions.

Dr. Densen-Gerber, a psychiatrist who also has a law degree, said that addicts who were referred to Odyssey House's facilities by the courts often responded excellently to its psychotherapeutic program.

But, she added, it is imperative to coerce addicts into a program because "addicts don't volunteer for anything."

"The addict is only a caricature of the problems of society," Dr. Densen-Gerber remarked, getting to the heart of her argument: Addiction is one of the symptoms of society's most serious malady.

Dr. Densen-Gerber asserted that an element of this malady was the inability of government and political leaders to respond to felt needs, which breeds the atmosphere of dismay and alienation in which addiction flourished.

"Are they going to spread the great white plague throughout the country?" she asked rhetorically. She expressed doubts that the country could survive such an epidemic of addiction. There are now about 315,000 heroin addicts in the country.

She argued that teen-agers turned off by their political and familial role models and believing that sex will solve their problems of alienation turned to sex.

But, she said, the teen-age girl, "hung up on the idea of the female orgasm," ends up humiliating her masculinity-obsessed but usually inexperienced and inadequate partner, leaving them both disillusioned with sex and ripe for drugs.

This syndrome, she continued, is a "major route" to youthful drug abuse and addiction.

CALLED CONTAGIOUS

An addict, she said, has a profound need to proselytize and create the company of other addicts, making addiction a powerful contagious disease.

One G.I. addict returning to Menlo Park, California, soon created 50 fellow addicts, she added.

She described as "irresponsible" the Nixon Administration's resistance to long-term confinement and treatment for returning addicted servicemen and predicted that "50,000 or 70,000" ex-soldier addicts would create 3 million addicts by 1975.

Entering further into the psychosociology of addiction, Dr. Densen-Gerber said that there was a low incidence of schizophrenia among black addicts—about 10 per cent of those she has seen—and a higher incidence among non-Puerto-Rican whites—15 to 20 per cent. But there is, she said, a strikingly higher incidence of schizophrenia among Puerto Rican addicts—80 per cent.

This she took to indicate that there was little psychological wrenching involved when a Negro became a heroin addict, given the prevalence of addiction among urban blacks and what she termed the disarray of the black family. But, she said, the intact family life of Puerto Ricans tended to inhibit addiction and make it psychologically more difficult to adopt the lonely life style of an addict.

A firm advocate of a woman's right to pursue her own career, Dr. Densen-Gerber asserted that in the American home it was necessary for children to grow up with a strong father as a role-model.

Dr. Densen-Gerber is married to Dr. Michael Baden, the city's Deputy Chief Medical Examiner; they have two sons and a daughter. Trissa Austin Baden, their 12-year-old daughter, has written a book, "Drugs, Sex, Parents and You," which will be published by J. B. Lippincott & Co. in March.

"I suppose if you asked me what was the one answer," Dr. Densen-Gerber said, "I guess I would say that America has to learn to love its children instead of hating them."

Lawrence, Massachusetts, *Eagle Tribune*　　　　　June 24, 1971

PRESIDENT'S DRUG PLAN ASSAILED

President Nixon's plan for treating Vietnam veteran drug addicts won't work, Odyssey House Director Dr. Judianne Densen-Gerber charged last night at Merrimack College.

The result, she said, could be a million new teenage addicts within two years, as up to 75,000 ex-GI addicts return to cities and towns across the nation and push dope to support drug habits acquired in Vietnam.

Dr. Densen-Gerber, whose 30 Odyssey House drug rehabilitation facilities are among the most successful in the country, spoke at a seminar sponsored by the Greater Lawrence Community Drug Council.

Dr. Densen-Gerber, a woman of ample proportion and informal manner, sat down before the microphone to deliver her talk.

She spoke without notes and without hesitation for a half hour, leaning forward to her audience of several hundred persons. Her hands were clasped in intensity.

The hall was absolutely still during her address. A half dozen waiters and waitresses who had earlier manned the buffet table came from the kitchen and stood against the wall to listen. Light from two spotlights illuminating the stage for Western Electric TV cameras taping her appearance flashed from her glasses as she moved her head back and forth in accent.

"No one has ever looked at the soldier addict," she charged. What basis is there, she asked, for Defense Department plans to release GI drug users after a seven-day detoxification period and just three weeks of aftercare?

She said it was possible that GI's would require a shorter treatment period than other addicts but suggested one year as more realistic than one month.

Moreover, she said that soldiers should be kept in the service until they are cured. If laws need to be changed to do this, she said, then they should be changed.

She said the military services had no right to loose thousands of drug addicts upon the country to sell drugs to children or use techniques of violence learned in Vietnam to commit other crimes to finance their habit.

She cited a recent California study which showed that a single Vietnam veteran addict there had turned 50 children to drugs.

She urged her listeners to write President Nixon.

Dr. Densen-Gerber also blasted those who think the drug problem can be solved by methadone maintenance programs.

The mortality rate for those on methadone maintenance is actually higher than for the heroin addict on the street, she said.

Saying she had found methadone suitable for only a handful of the 5,000 addicts she has treated, Dr. Densen-Gerber charged that in most cases it simply makes a pusher out of the doctor.

"It's the same kind of lying that is really what the addict is protesting about," she said.

Such programs must instead "offer viable alternatives. We must begin to tell the truth."

"If you don't look at the consequences, drug-taking is pleasurable," she said. She compared shooting heroin with "a long-term sexual orgasm," which cuts all anxiety. "Nothing bothers you."

What is lost, she said, are "all interpersonal relationships." Drug addiction leads to a "sterile, isolated life," with absolutely nothing having any value except the next fix.

What young people must be taught to realize, she said, is that drugs interfere with becoming a "full-functioning citizen."

Referring to the idea of inoculating children with a "narcotic antagonist"—an idea mentioned by Dr. Jerome H. Jaffe, President Nixon's new drug program head—she said children should instead be "inoculated with values."

She stressed the need for "one set of rules" for both young people and adults. She critized a private school in New Hampshire which dismisses students caught smoking marijuana but allows teachers to smoke it "at their own discretion."

Dr. Densen-Gerber, herself both a doctor of medicine and jurisprudence, said many addicts are very intelligent people.

She advised therapists to assume the addicts are smarter than they themselves. "They could sell you anything."

This ability to "con" people has led to many problems in drug treatment, she said, because communities are accepting many unqualified and often irresponsible ex-addicts to run their drug programs.

She said that one person who left Odyssey House without permission, after a few months of treatment—and stole a television set to boot—was immediately hired by the courts of New York as a counselor.

Another patient, who had been given a life sentence for his crimes, split from her program before being cured and is now the director of another drug program at a salary of over $20,000. In spite of her efforts, the court has done nothing about putting his jail sentence into effect, she said.

Dr. Densen-Gerber, who has recently been busy setting up the 30th Odyssey House in Hampton, N.H., offered consolation to the Greater Lawrence Community and Reality, Inc., on recent troubles over the firing of the Challenge House director and consequent loss of patients to his new program.

All of the leading drug treatment centers, including Odyssey House, have had similar revolts in their early years, she said.

New York *News*   Sunday, August 2, 1970

ODYSSEY HOUSE OFFERS TO AID CHILDREN

Dr. Judianne Densen-Gerber, executive director of Odyssey House, announced yesterday that she would open the drug rehabilitation centers to children from the city's overcrowded children's shelters—whether or not they are using drugs.

"We would not turn away any child who wanted to enter Odyssey House," she said. "Drug addiction is just a reflection of other problems and any child in one of those shelters would have emotional deprivation.

"I don't think you should be punished (by not being admitted to Odyssey House) for not using drugs. We would accept any child that seemed motivated."

Dr. Densen-Gerber said she was aware of rampant drug use in the city's children's shelters. "I know there are a lot of drugs in those shelters because some of our kids have come from them. In fact, some of them first turned on in the shelters."

WOULD LIKE TO HAVE THEM

"We would like to have groups in the children's shelters," she continued. This means that Odyssey House would send in teams of drug-free ex-addicts to talk with residents of the children's shelters that are using drugs. After a few group sessions, where those residents recognized their drug problem and became motivated to overcome the problem, Odyssey House would be willing to accept them into their program.

"We would want these children to be transferred to us," Dr. Densen-Gerber said, "and we would send reports on them to the courts."

RECEIVES NO AID

Odyssey House, which does not receive any state or city funds, is currently operating its juvenile houses entirely on contributions. "Even though one third of our kids are committed to us by the courts, we pay for everything," Dr. Densen-Gerber said.

She added that if some of the children from the children's shelters were transferred to Odyssey House she "would like" to receive the same amount per child that goes to the children's shelters.

Dr. Densen-Gerber said she "is currently under arrest for keeping children in unsafe and overcrowded buildings."

SHELTERS OVERCROWDED

She added that the children's shelters were overcrowded. "It's terrible if we do it with love, and it's all right if they do it with indifference," she said.

"We admit we're overcrowded due to lack of funds to build new facilities. But there's a difference—our houses are neat and clean because there's pride," she said. The *News* inspected the Yorkville facility on East Eighth Street without notice and found the entire building immaculately clean.

Dr. Charles Rohrs, medical director of Odyssey House, will make the formal offer of the houses' facilities tomorrow to Mayor Lindsay and Welfare Commissioner Jack R. Goldberg.

Boston *Globe*   July 5, 1970

NEW YORK CITY'S DRUG DEATHS RISE IN "YEAR OF THE OSTRICH"
Odysey House tries to prove solutions possible as officials hide heads in
sand

Some say that 1970 will be recalled in New York City as the Year of the Ostrich.

This is the year the medical examiner's office has announced repeatedly that drug abuse has become the city's main public health problem.

Narcotics, chiefly heroin, now are the leading killer of New Yorkers under the age of 35.

Deaths from the epidemic of narcotics abuse are still rising, with 377 fatalities already reported this year. Further investigation following autopsies is expected to increase this statistic.

Among persons 15 to 35 years of age in New York City, preliminary data for 1969 show that the 770 deaths from narcotics exceed those from accidents (570), homicides (525), suicides (345) and cancer (420). At least one fourth of last year's deaths caused directly by drugs occurred among teenagers.

Within recent months, a 17-year-old Barnard College freshman died from an overdose of drugs on a week-end party. A deeply addicted 12-year-old girl was found in a narcotics daze and returned to her expensive East Side home.

And an 11-year-old girl and a 9-year-old boy were admitted to a unit of Odyssey House, a privately run rehabilitation program struggling to prove that solutions are possible to this problem while Federal, state and city authorities hide their heads in the sand.

What bothers Dr. Judianne Densen-Gerber, founder of Odyssey House, about the ostrich attitudes of most people in the community toward the drug problem is their refusal to admit what is happening throughout the social system.

Representatives of a number of suburban Massachusetts communities have become sufficiently aroused to visit Odyssey House this year. Nevertheless, efforts to establish programs based on this model in the suburbs invariably meet with opposition from neighbors.

"Even if it were possible to cure all present addicts today by some miracle, this would be but a finger in the dike," says the 36-year-old psychiatrist. "There will continue to be two new addicts for each one cured if we do not change the attitudes of dependent peoples."

"If our adult society continues to pretend that 25,000 addicted children under 18 do not exist in our midst, our nation will be destroyed from within," adds this militant mother of three.

It was actually through a request for maternity leave that Judi, who is the wife of Dr. Michael M. Baden, New York City's deputy medical examiner, became determined to change the hopeless future of drug addicts.

Instead of leave, the director of psychiatry at Metropolitan Hospital assigned his pregnant resident to the drug addiction service.

"He assured me that leave was not necessary because working on this service would allow me as much time as I wanted," she recollected. "He said addicts never get well, anyway."

Four years ago, his statement was essentially correct. In the city's only official drug treatment program at Metropolitan Hospital, there were eight known cures among 17,000 addicts admitted over a six-year period.

"The trouble seemed to be we were getting two conflicting messages from the staff at Metropolitan," explained Jim Murphy, a former patient and ex-addict, who directs the central Odyssey House program today.

"In group therapy, they were trying to build up your self-esteem. The rest of the time, you lay in bed while a nurse gave you a cyclazocine pill (a maintenance drug) every day which enhanced the idea you were a sick and dependent person. It now costs the city $120 a day for each addict lying in bed."

"One of the reasons there is so much addiction today is the popular belief there is a magic pill for everything," said Jim.

One day in August, 1966, 17 patients on Dr. Densen-Gerber's services requested the right to live without drugs. The senior staff told them they could leave.

Their refusal to take cyclazocine caused a conflict with the hospital administration because funding was for research in maintenance drugs and not for psychotherapy or drug abstinence.

With support only from their young woman doctor, the Odyssey of the first patient began. They spent a week cleaning up an old house belonging to Daytop Village, another drug treatment program. They lived in a log cabin in Bridgewater, Conn. for a while, next in an old frame house in East Harlem belonging to a couple Judi had in marital therapy, which didn't work.

In May of 1967, a building which would accommodate 70 residents was found on East Sixth Street in the heart of the East Village. Friends of Odyssey had two weeks to raise $40,000, half the total price.

"We call this the Mother House in honor of Judi," Murphy explained. "We see our Odyssey structure as a pyramid with Judi at the top. Mike (Dr. Baden)—he's the top of the top."

To the addicts and workers of the Odyssey movement, which now operates six residential treatment centers and some drop-in store fronts in New York and New Jersey, Dr. Judianne Densen-Gerber is part mother and part myth.

After a long hot day as guests of the Odyssey family in East Village recently, teachers from an Institute on Youth and Drugs at Northeastern University half expected a friendly Mrs. Darling to come in and kiss all 70 Wendy and Michaels in her charge good night.

Instead of a Never-Never-Never land orientation, however, Judi conveys total reality when she arrives after a day exhorting legislators and newsmen to "do something" about children and drugs.

She tore into the teachers with their innocent questions as if they were a group of newly arrived junkies.

"Until you learn how to talk up and relate to authority yourselves, you will never be able to deal with your students," she told the group sponsored by the National Association of Independent Schools.

"Many of you copped out on your own group sessions today," she chided the teachers who instruct the upper class cream of the crop. "You can teach all there is to know about drugs in an hour, but you may not be able to teach respect for human beings and for honest labor in a lifetime."

Odyssey House has the distinction of being the first program in the country for treatment and rehabilitation of narcotics which combines supervision by professionals and ex-addicts working together.

It is psychiatrically oriented and medically oriented, in contrast to self-help groups directed by ex-addicts alone.

It also has the distinction of operating the only adolescent treatment unit exclusively for rehabilitation of teenage addicts in the nation. The house for youngsters is in the Bronx. It is totally inadequate to meet the needs of the 55 youngsters now living there.

"Everything about the children's house is illegal," said Herbert Goldberg, veteran public school math and graphic arts teacher, who is director. "It's an old fire trap and the bathrooms back up, but they can't close us up. There is no place in the whole city to take these kids."

Gaining admission to the Odyssey House program for the "Raw" addict is comparatively easy, whether adult or child. Children under 16 may be admitted any time of the day or night. They need only a consent form signed by a parent or legal guardian.

Adults seeking induction may come in off the streets or on referral from a parole officer, welfare agency or the courts. Adults are told to report to a group session the day after admission. They must turn up in reasonably coherent condition.

The first phase of treatment after admission is known as the "pressure cooker" period. Induction includes learning the rules; no drugs, no stealing, no physical violence and no sexual activity. Breaking the rules leads to immediate expulsion.

Emphasis at the start is on participation in jobs within the house and participation in group sessions. Following the induction period, an addict can be asked to leave if any member of his group votes against him. If he wants to return badly enough after a negative "probe," as this session is called, he may gain readmission.

"The door is open 24 hours a day, but if you want to help yourself, you don't leave," explained Ted Tann.

For the first nine months of treatment, the addict may not leave the building alone. Even then, visits to old friends and family must be limited to saying "hi and 'bye," explained a woman addict who now runs the central office and has progressed to visits with her own children.

Children are not allowed visits from their parents until well advanced in treatment, she explained. Often the parents themselves are involved in the drug scene.

The concept of earning position and emotional growth through positive social interaction is deeply engrained in the program. Patients are rated bi-weekly by each other and monthly by the staff, and it is partially on the basis of these evaluations that residents move from one level to another.

Daily urine-testing for the presence of drugs is an integral part of the program, and continues twice weekly after graduation.

Oddly enough, for a psychiatrically-oriented program, the urine-testing procedure is seen by the addicts as a "contribution to the community."

Unlike some of the self-help communities of addicts, the Odyssey House program is not intended to last forever. Following discharge after 12 to 15 months of treatment, the addict is helped to return to school, to work, and is put in touch with other treatment resources. Some join the staff of Odyssey House or other drug rehabilitation programs, but others are encouraged to enter occupations unrelated to their drug-oriented past.

The original Odyssey House core group of 17 addicts estimate that their "golden arms" were worth $1.2 million in illegal cost to society.

From 100,000 to 200,000 addicts are now estimated to be continuing their habits among the 9 million residents of New York City.

Judi's motherly message of concern comes through to officials with the abrasive warmth of sandpaper on stone.

The Year of the Ostrich continues.

DR. JUDIANNE
DENSEN-GERBER

"Addicted adolescents are not a legal problem, only a medical one"

Dr. Judianne Densen-Gerber, the founder and executive director of the fifteen Odyssey Houses for the prevention and treatment of drug addiction by psychiatric means, is a pretty woman of thirty-five who makes up her eyes but forgets her lipstick, who drives an orange-coloured car, and who can not be fazed or intimidated. The mother of three children, the wife of Dr. Michael Baden, Deputy Chief Medical Examiner of New York City, the mistress of a town house, and the possessor of a bachelor of arts degree, *cum laude*, from Bryn Mawr, 1956, she is both a Doctor of Jurisprudence from the Columbia University Law School, and a Doctor of Medicine from the New York University Medical School. Her detractors call her hysterical, some of them summoning her to court because the houses she has had to use for addicts are old and rotten. While the newspapers chronicle the deaths of children from overdoses of heroin, her enemies say that she pays children to act as addicts. Nonsense. For Dr. Densen-Gerber, psychiatrist and lawyer, is a flexible woman, using the funds she can raise, the housing she can get. Her ego is not tied up in being right. At Odyssey Houses, there are addicts but no guards. Each house is a therapeutic community in which half are addicts and half are staff, with the staff busy with guidance and therapy. At an Odyssey House the past is never used to excuse current behaviour. To avoid present responsibility for oneself is discouraged. The addict must lead a structured life, highly organized, for the patient and his way of life were sick. Odyssey House is never a loving, permissive parent. It is a way to a new life without conning, gaming, manipulation. Nothing is done for the patients that they can do for themselves. After treatment in residence, a former addict works out his reentry into the non-addictive world by getting a high school equivalency diploma if the patient is not a high school graduate, by holding a job, and then by approval of his peers and the professional staff for discharge. Balancing this intricate program is Dr. Densen-Gerber, a laughing woman with a taste for the bizarre.

VOGUE, June, 1970   JACK ROBINSON

ONE MORNING

Mommy —
    I love you
very much   I miss

you and need you
I will be back soon
to bring unambivalent,
non-coded concerned,
healthy _joy_ to you—
                    Daddy

Dear Judi,

And what can one give back to you
who has given so much —

Every Thing seems so insignificant
before all you are.

And yet I say thank you
because I can say that

Thank you for being you
and helping me to be me.

                    — Margaret
                    Christmas 1971

COLUMBIA UNIVERSITY
School of Public Health and Administrative Medicine

October 7, 8, and 9, 1968

FACULTY

✳ MICHAEL BADEN, M.D., Associate Medical Examiner, Office of the Chief Medical Examiner, New York City; Assistant Professor, Pathology, New York University Medical School; Director, Laboratory of Addictive Drugs, New York City

HENRY BRILL, M.D., Director, Pilgrim State Hospital, West Brentwood, New York

CHARLES E. CHERUBIN, M.D., Assistant Professor, Epidemiology, Columbia University School of Public Health and Administrative Medicine; Hospital Epidemiologist, Harlem Hospital Center

✳ JUDIANNE DENSEN-GERBER, M.D., Clinical Director, Odyssey House, New York City

VINCENT P. DOLE, M.D., Professor and Senior Physician, Rockefeller University, New York City

ROBERT DOLINS, Assistant Commissioner, Narcotic Education, New York State Narcotic Addiction Control Commission

✳ MAX FINK, M.D., Professor, Psychiatry, New York Medical College

FRANCES R. GEARING, M.D., Assistant Professor, Epidemiology, Columbia University School of Public Health and Administrative Medicine; Director, Evaluation Project, Methadone Maintenance Treatment Program

FACULTY (continued)

FLORENCE KAVALER, M.D., Deputy Executive Director, Bureau of Health Care Services Medical Assistance Program (Medicaid), New York City Department of Health

SHERMAN KIEFFER, M.D., Associate Director, Patient Care, National Institute of Mental Health, Bethesda, Maryland

MARTIN KOTLER, Deputy Commissioner, Bureau of Prevention, Addiction Services Agency, Human Resources Administration, New York City

HAROLD MEISELAS, M.D., Associate Commissioner, Treatment and Rehabilitation, New York State Narcotic Addiction Control Commission

✳ JAMES MURPHY, Associate Director, Odyssey House, New York City

MARIE NYSWANDER, M.D., Guest Investigator, Rockefeller University, New York City

✳ MITCHELL S. ROSENTHAL, M.D., Deputy Commissioner, Addiction Services Agency, Human Resources Administration, New York City

RAY E. TRUSSELL, M.D., Director and Joseph R. DeLamar Professor of Administrative Medicine, Columbia University School of Public Health and Administrative Medicine

REVEREND DONALD WILKERSON, Director, Teen Challenge, Inc.; Ordained Minister of the Assemblies of God Church

MELVIN WILLIAMS, Director, Harlem Odyssey, New York City

Notice the interesting combination of faculty.

Check stub for appearances on the continuing dramatic series "One Life to Live." I played myself interviewing and treating the young heroine, Cathy, in two performances.
Odyssey House played a part in the series for three months.

PLEASE DETACH AND RETAIN THIS PAY STATEMENT
CREATIVE HORIZONS, INC.

"ONE LIFE TO LIVE"

DATE	GROSS COMPENSATION		DEDUCTIONS						OTHER PAYMENTS
	SALARY	OTHER	F. I. C. A.	FEDERAL WITHHOLDING TAX	N. Y. S. WITHHOLDING TAX	N.Y.S. DIS.	N. Y. C. WITHHOLDING TAX		
JUL 13									1,000.00

$1.95

DRUGS, SEX, PARENTS, AND YOU

BY JUDIANNE DENSEN-GERBER, J.D., M.D.
& HER DAUGHTER TRISSA AUSTIN BADEN

WITH A SPECIAL INTRODUCTION FOR PARENTS
BY JUDIANNE DENSEN-GERBER, J.D., M.D.

To my favorite Therapist From me — etc. J.P.M.

Flowers sent by James Paul Murphy to me when I was down in the dumps

New York Law Journal

OFFICIAL DAILY LAW NEWSPAPER DESIGNATED PURSUANT TO THE JUDICIARY LAW

NEW YORK, WEDNESDAY, OCTOBER 27, 1971   ©1971 New York Law Publishing Co.

Narcotics Problems

Marijuana:

Issues Defined

———— By Judianne Densen-Gerber ————

This column inaugurates a weekly feature by Judianne Densen-Gerber, founder and executive director of Odyssey House, one of the largest therapeutic communities in the country for the treatment of narcotics addiction. The column will be published on Wednesdays. Dr. Densen-Gerber is a member of the New York Bar and a physician. The purpose of the column is to keep the legal profession informed of issues relating to drug abuse and other social problems. Comments from readers are invited.

MANCHESTER  UNION LEADER

"There is nothing so powerful as truth"
—DANIEL WEBSTER

©1972, by Union Leader Corporation

NEW HAMPSHIRE'S LARGEST DAILY NEWSPAPER

———— Beginning Saturday ————

Doctor Will Write
Weekly Drug Series

Dr. Judianne Densen-Gerber, noted drug addiction specialist and founder-director of the Odyssey House drug treatment program, will write a weekly column for the Manchester Union Leader. Her first column will appear in this newspaper on Saturday.

Dr. Densen-Gerber will discuss drug-related subjects of concern to all. She hopes to spur interest and involvement on the part of readers so that they will write in their problems. All letters from readers will be answered personally or in the column. Writers of letters which are published will be identified only by initials and hometown.

Dr. Densen-Gerber's articles will deal with the methods of drug treatment and how parents can handle the problems they face bringing up children in the confusion of a permissive society.

COLUMN   Page 13

DR. DENSEN-GERBER

MEMORANDUM FROM

OLIVER PILAT

ASSISTANT TO THE MAYOR

6/22/67

Mike:

This will confirm that you are down again as
Night Mayor for Tuesday, July 4.

Look and see if the Night Owl you presented
the Mayor is still there. I've never been
sure which one it was. Did the Mayor ever
accept your invitation to swim? You are
so inventive as well as constructive that I
hope the ban on preliminary tours is lifted
by the time you serve.

Special memos on the Night Owl room wall will
tell you to whom to call in case of neighborhood disturbance and how to reach the Mayor
from hour to hour during the night.

Everything else I think you know. Best &
to Judi, the only woman so far as I know, to
accompany her husband on the night trick!

Ollie

Note change from 1970 card where only individual facilities were named. The 1971 Christmas card shows Odyssey House in four states. Since then, three more states—Michigan, Connecticut and Nevada—have been added.

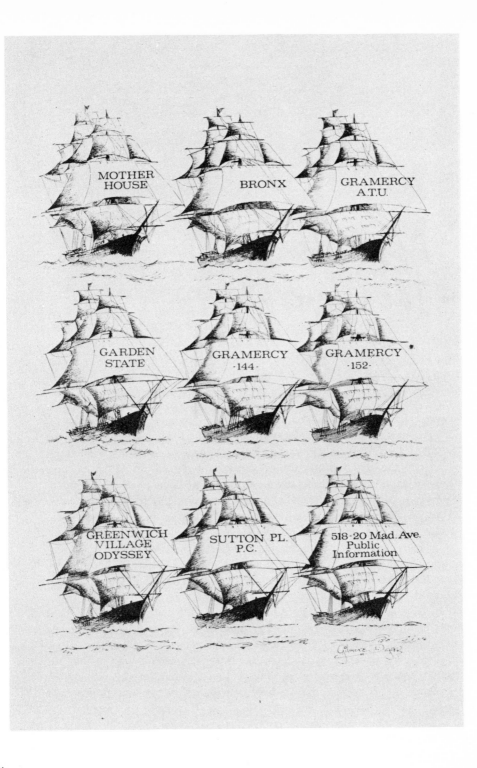

MOTHER HOUSE

BRONX

GRAMERCY A.T.U.

GARDEN STATE

GRAMERCY ·144·

GRAMERCY ·152·

GREENWICH VILLAGE ODYSSEY

SUTTON PL. P.C.

518-20 Mad. Ave. Public Information

Appendix I:
The Concept

O D Y S S E Y   H O U S E ,   I N C .
A Therapeutic Community
G E N E R A L   S T A T E M E N T   O F   T H E   O D Y S S E Y   H O U S E   M E T H O D

Odyssey House, Inc. is a voluntary non-profit agency that began as a pilot research program at Metropolitan Hospital in January 1966. At this time, Dr. A. Ronald Sorvino was assigned the task of evaluating the use of the maintenance drug, cyclazocine. Based on his prior unsuccessful experience with methadone drug maintenance alone, Dr. Sorvino asked the resident psychiatrist assigned to the ward, Dr. Judianne Densen-Gerber, to develop a long-term psychotherapeutic setting in which the narcotic addict might be more responsive to psychiatric intervention.

In early January 1966 Dr. Densen-Gerber visited with Dr. Efren Ramirez in Puerto Rico. Impressed with his work, she agreed to try to adopt his method to the New York City milieu. Odyssey House is the successful outgrowth of that project.

In August 1966 the patients influenced the doctors in charge of the program to conclude that continuance of the maintenance drug cyclazocine was no longer necessary. In reality, the maintenance concept gave the anti-therapeutic message that the patients were crippled and unable to function normally without drugs. The patients requested discontinuance of cyclazocine. However, a drug-free project, no matter the promise it showed, was incompatible with Metropolitan Hospital's commitment to drug testing. Therefore, the patients were discharged from the hospital in October 1966.

Seventeen of them elected to continue the work of the therapeutic community. Their dedication to the belief that they can function without

406

drugs, that they can be successfully treated by psychiatric intervention, and that they have a responsibility to prevent, through education and example, the spreading and continuation of addiction, rallied many members of the community to aid and assist them. Three psychiatrists volunteered their services free of charge in the initial interim period. At the same time, a small seven-room building was loaned to them. Until June 1967 the group was self-sustaining, supported minimally by donations.

In March 1967 Odyssey House was incorporated. It received tax exemption from the Internal Revenue Service. Its strong belief in the therapeutic-community method in the treatment of addictive diseases, based on the statistics of the Rio Piedras Experience and its own high success rate, committed Odyssey House to the expansion of its program to meet the compelling needs of the community. A voluntary agency has the important ability of being sufficiently flexible to develop, test, and modify its ideas and methods. The small professional staff is dedicated to the observation, recording and analyzing of the treatment data accumulated. Every session in the community is recorded for future research evaluation.

In order to expand, in May 1967, Odyssey House rented a building at 309–311 East Sixth Street in Manhattan. These quarters have facilities for approximately sixty persons, forty males and twenty females, plus eight resident ex-addict staff. Odyssey House occupied these premises in early June 1967.

Within the next year Odyssey House grew quickly, responding to the desire of more and more drug addicts to enter treatment. A "pressure cooker" was opened in Harlem at 1982 Lexington Avenue, and a "re-entry house" was leased to Odyssey by the Roman Catholic Church for $1 per year. This building was at 955 Bruckner Boulevard in the Bronx.

By March 1969 Odyssey House had facilities for 130 residents and was continuously overcrowded. One of the causes for the overcrowding was the great number of teen-agers seeking admission to the program. It was at this time that Dr. Densen-Gerber spearheaded the public outcry against the rising number of teen-agers becoming addicted to heroin in New York City. Her husband, Dr. Michael Baden, Deputy Chief Medical Examiner of the City of New York, grimly confirmed this trend as he reported almost one teen-age death daily in New York City from heroin.

Reluctantly, government officials decided to recognize the problem. But not before Odyssey House took the initiative and opened an adolescent treatment unit totally dependent on private funds. Technically this was illegal, since Odyssey House did not possess an appropriate Certificate of Occupancy and the Odyssey House Charter did not allow for treatment of patients under sixteen.

Consequently, the city administration, under Mayor Lindsay, decided to have Dr. Densen-Gerber summoned to court as having irresponsibly broken the law. She was later acquitted by the courts. In the meantime, because of her actions the State of New York recognized the need to fund adolescent programs. The state and city provided Odyssey House with funds to continue the same program for which she had to answer in court.

Almost one year after the Adolescent Unit was opened, it was officially funded, with new quarters at 208–210 East 18th Street. Shortly thereafter, a young adult facility was also added to the Odyssey complex. New York Odyssey now has 180 funded beds and 100 beds supported by private contributions. In October 1969 the first out-of-state facility was opened with 60 beds in Newark, New Jersey. This is half federally funded and half supported by private donations.

As of July 1971 Odyssey House also has a residential facility for young girls and pregnant women, a Spanish house for drug addicts who have difficulty expressing themselves in English, a Junior Executive Staff residential facility in midtown Manhattan for residents with superior I.Q. and exceptional talents, and a second out-of-state facility in New Hampshire for 60 residents; plus outreach centers called Community Involvement Centers in New York, New Jersey, New Hampshire, and Utah.

Odyssey House has facilities for four hundred residents and an open-admissions policy. A new vocational rehabilitation program includes a thrift shop, art gallery, newspaper, graphic arts department and a factory in New Jersey, which presently operates an automobile repair shop.

The adolescent program is recognized as Public School 203, all adult residents are required to obtain their high school equivalency, and Odyssey House now has a scholarship program for graduates to enter preparatory school or college.

In spite of rather phenomenal growth, Odyssey House has been able to maintain high standards of excellence in therapy. This is because the Odyssey House concept is unchanged from the program begun by Dr. Densen-Gerber and the original core group.

The rehabilitation service program is divided into three phases: 1) pretreatment of induction, 2) intensive residential treatment and 3) post-treatment or re-entry. Induction is divided into two stages; first, the motivation of the street addict to enter treatment accomplished while he remains in the community; and second, the first in-residence challenge, the candidacy-in, to determine the sincerity of his motivation.

The treatment phase is divided into three Levels to be discussed more fully subsequently. The post-treatment or re-entry phase is divided into three stages: the in-residence one of Level IV, during which time the patient begins resocialization; second, that of candidacy-out, accomplished in the community with patient's return for aftercare only; and last, that of discharged person when the patient has completed all Odyssey has to offer.

The initial presenting problem for the raw street addict is his tenacious hold on street values called the code of the streets. It represents to him the only remaining code for survival to follow. This hold not only supports him in his rebellion against organized society, but also strangles any effort of his to seek and benefit from conventional treatment. He is unable to interact in a patient-doctor relationship, even if his initial indifference, skepticism and negativism can be overcome.

The pretreatment phase is designed to motivate the street addict to enter into a meaningful therapeutic endeavor. Its primary function is to pave the way for the future doctor-patient relationship. The extreme importance of this is obvious to any professional who has been the object of the reactive contempt the addict initially shows toward the non-addict world, because of his own psychopathology of isolation, loneliness and low self-esteem. However, within most addicts is the faint, but real, desire to return to functioning in a positive manner. Therefore, the first constructive therapeutic relationship is, by necessity, that of an ex-addict group leader to a raw street addict.

Through the Community Involvement Centers, trained ex-addicts conduct several group sessions with raw addicts each week. Presently these take place in areas where the incidence of drug abuse is high, as in Central Harlem, South Bronx and Central Ward of Newark. In addition, these centers are located in midtown Manhattan; Great Neck on the North Shore of Long Island; Portsmouth, New Hampshire; and Salt Lake City, Utah.

Paid professionals assist the ex-addict supervisors of these "storefronts." Hopefully, the confrontation of the street addict in the storefront will result in his wanting to enter the Odyssey House program. Many referrals to the rehabilitation service program are made through the Community Involvement Centers. These outreach centers see approximately 6,000 raw addicts and 4,000 non-users a year. Approximately 25 per cent of all admissions are referred through the storefronts.

The raw addict may come on his own initiative or be sent from another referring agency, either private or public, such as Motivational Guidance, Inc., the Department of Welfare and the Vera Institute of Justice. The Induction Supervisor screens and accepts for admission addicts who are in prison, on the request of their counsel, or by court order, or through the parole division of the Department of Correction. He has secured special permission to enter the facilities of the Department of Correction. The source of referral is unimportant as long as the raw addict is exposed to the first motivational phase. However, the Induction Supervisor reserves the right to refuse admission to any applicant. The overwhelming majority of drug addicts are not psychotic. They are legally and psychiatrically responsible for the consequences of their actions and should be held accountable. Experience has shown that those addicts who are incarcerated by the law, or who feel incarcerated, or who are unwilling to accept treatment voluntarily, will be amenable to treatment when a proper pretreatment phase is instituted.

The youthful addict or drug abuser under the age of sixteen is accepted immediately into the program at any time, regardless of whether he has used drugs within the past few hours. The older addict must show sufficient (although quite minimal) motivation before he will be allowed to enter treatment. This is achieved by displaying a co-operative attitude, appearing on time for induction, and decreasing his addiction to a point where he can enter the residence without requiring detoxification. No addictive substances are permitted or prescribed within the residences.

Detoxification has not been found to be necessary. Severe withdrawal is a rarity; all residents spend their first seventy-two hours in the program with a "buddy" and are closely watched by physicians and registered nurses as well as trained ex-addict supervisors.

When the raw addict is considered by the ex-addict team ready for admission to the community for the second stage of induction, the candidacy-in, he is sponsored by the Level IV coleader to the ex-addict and medical-treatment supervisors of the intensive-treatment unit. Either one can refuse admission, returning the applicant to the beginning groups for further motivational work.

In addition, the previously described method of admission is therapeutic for the Level IV residents. It exposes them to the confrontation of the street and its values, beyond which they have now grown. This confrontation or challenge occurs at the beginning of their own resocialization and re-entry into the general community. It is the initial weaning from the protective isolation of the residence. The Induction Supervisor is continuing not only his confrontation with the addicts in the street, but also he is assuming the responsibility of training others, the Level IV residents, to undertake responsibility. He is increasing his sphere of authority. His staff is responsible for summarizing all the contacts with the patients during the first stage and beginning the resident's individual chart.

Within twenty-four hours of admission to Odyssey House, the second phase of induction is begun, the "candidacy-in." This is initiated by an "inquiry-in," which is conducted by the House Co-ordinator in conjunction with representatives from the entire community. The functions of this meeting are to familiarize and acquaint the resident-patients with the proposed new member, to take a complete history and to afford him a constructive sense of belonging. An additional purpose is to identify, as quickly as possible, any major problem areas which later may complicate the interpersonal in-residence relationships.

The inquiry-in is for the benefit of both the patient himself and the community; not only to enable the group to function better therapeutically, but also to be protected from and to cope with the inevitable gaming and testing behavior which has a unique flavor with each resident. The inquiry-in openly confronts the patient with the expectations and demands of the community upon him as regards his behavior, and the consequences that will ensue from negative behavior. That such consequences must ensue

410

without the possibility of mitigation is essential to the growth of these patients. The breaking of any of four cardinal rules means immediate expulsion from the residence.

These are the use of contraband, stealing, a threat or act of physical violence and any sexual acting out, whether hetero- or homosexual in nature. The latter three rules are enforced by the senior patients and staff. The first is not left to the clinical evaluation of the other patients and staff. In order to ascertain with certainty that the residents and staff are drug-free, their urines are analyzed on a daily basis and certified to be free of all substances such as opiates, barbiturates, hypnotics and amphetamines, by the Office of Chief Medical Examiner of the City of New York.

The inquiry-in constitutes the first formal community challenge to the addict. It tests sincerity and motivational drive. It is a clear demonstration of the positive construction functioning of the therapeutic community. The patient is shown dramatically that the community means business. A copy of the inquiry-in, plus comments from the resident-patients present, are appended to the chart. The patient is now a candidate-in.

The candidate-in is responsible for the major manual work within the community. He is supervised by a Level III resident. The candidate-in has four and one-half hours a week of group work with a therapist and a senior Level III in his facility. The candidate-in has no voting rights or voice in the running of the community.

The candidate-in is given a complete medical work-up within twenty-four hours, including not only a routine history and physical but also complete blood and serological testing, urinalysis, chest X-ray, TB skin testing and an EKG. All female residents are given a PAP test. There is a licensed physician and a registered nurse assigned to each facility. All medical problems are worked up under the direction of the full-time Medical Director. The Medical Director also sees that each resident receives a complete psychiatric evaluation by a qualified psychiatrist within seventy-two hours of admission. A complete medical and psychiatric report is appended to each resident's chart.

The "probe" constitutes the next formal challenge to the candidate-in. When suitable progress has been made by the candidate-in, he may be sponsored by the treatment staff to become a full participating resident. The sponsorship must have the endorsement of the group leaders in charge of the proposed patient. The probe usually occurs three to six weeks after the inquiry-in. A candidate-in is entitled to one probe a week after his initial week within the community, or a single probe by default at the end of six weeks if he has not been sponsored. The probe is conducted by a member of the treatment staff and is attended by selected representatives from each higher in-residence Level as well.

The function of the probe is for the candidate-in to prove to residents as well as the professional staff, by both word and deed, that he has a usable understanding of the concept of the house and a commitment to live by it while in residential therapy. In reality, this means that the patient accepts the doctor-patient relationship, that he is willing to look into him-

411

self for the answers to his problems, that he will accept responsibility for himself and his actions, and finally, that he will submit to the authority and discipline of the community.

If he passes the probe, the candidate-in moves to Level I. If there is one negative vote, in a sponsored probe, he remains a candidate-in. If the probe is by default, he is returned to the street-addict groups for additional motivational work and future application for readmission to the House.

It is important that the program have value to the patients participating and to those considering admission. It must be preserved as an entity above and beyond any individual member. Therefore, there are times when a resident must be excluded from the community. It has been repeatedly demonstrated that confrontation and actualization of discharge have rededicated the majority of the persons affected, causing subsequent improved functioning on readmission.

If the candidate-in passes the probe, he is accepted as a full participating member. He now begins the intensive treatment phase per se. A copy of the probe, including comments by all those participating, is appended to the patient's chart.

TREATMENT PHASE

Now the addict begins in earnest the process of personality reorientation, or reconstruction. He comes relatively quickly to the realization that he is not a chronically sick person in need of drug maintenance, but rather that his way of life, or orientation toward functioning, is sick or distorted. It becomes very evident to him that his behavior is a result of free choice. No matter how deviant the past behavior of an addict has been, he has the innate capacity to function positively when properly challenged. The energies which before were destructive in nature are directed constructively in accord with those of society.

Acceptance by peers constitutes the prime force available in beginning therapy to the professional and ex-addict coleader treating a group of sociopaths. Once deviant behavior is no longer rewarded by his group but has become grounds for exclusion, the speed with which new members are oriented to and accept positive, affirmative attitudes toward treatment, and adopt the senior members' judgment as to the therapist's qualifications is amazing. The therapist is an expert participant-guide in therapy meetings, but the patient participants are considered primarily responsible for the success or failure of any single endeavor. It is their work that counts, only they who stand to benefit from treatment, or to lose if they game.

From its inception, the Odyssey House program is designed to create receptive peer-group relations, thereby permitting residents to relate to each other and the staff without fear of reprisal. There is no contraband in the house, no threat or actualization of physical violence and "no contracts of silence" or "defending each other" in group therapy. The residents have assumed sole responsibility for the enforcement of the rules they have instituted. This permits the treatment staff to devote full time to therapy rather than enforcing police or security methods. Thus, they are maximally able to utilize their training with minimum waste of effort, talent or money. This prevents much of the frustration and depression often seen in professionals who treat addicts.

The emphasis in therapy is on present behavior, interpersonal relationships and attitudes. The use of the past to excuse current behavior or to avoid present responsibility is discouraged. The past for many of these patients is one of extreme deprivation, cruelty and loneliness at best. Much cannot be analyzed into acceptance through understanding and interpretation. It is explored and evaluated when of clear relevance, such as in homosexual patterning or unresolved Oedipal conflicts. Stressed is resignation to the unchangeable reality of the patient's early life, a "so what, now what" posture, coupled with an examination of what resources are present in the patient which he can tap to cope effectively in the here and now. The patient is challenged to begin today!

Excuses for poor functioning are not tolerated. The therapist is forcefully judgmental in his attitudes. To consider the patient, rather than his way of life, sick, serves to reinforce the pathological defense of dependency on the part of the addict and the need of the professional to mother him.

The original Odyssey House core group of seventeen addicts had "golden arms" worth $1,200,000 in illegal cost to society. This supported their actual yearly use of $400,000. It is obvious, upon reflection, that they had the capacity to find room and board, to make and keep telephone appointments and hoodwink the most well-meaning, attuned professional.

The inevitable conning, gaming and manipulation is combated by permitting group work only, and refusing all demands. This insistence on group work exclusively subjects each resident to the constant scrutiny of, and open confrontation by, his peers. No single resident can play one staff member against another or against the community or vice-versa. This forces openness in therapy and prevents informing and gossip gathering. The only demands met by the staff are those of guidance and therapy. The professional is no longer a symbol of authority, police or pill givers. There is a constant refusal to "do for," such as find jobs, education or homes, but only to help them find themselves and group identity.

Thus, many of the basic pathologic features in the addict—his loneliness, isolation, dependency and low self-esteem—are overcome. To recapitulate, the two cardinal prohibitions for the professional are no individual work and no demand meeting. It cannot be too greatly emphasized how little help the ex-addicts require. They take great pride and "grow behind" doing for themselves. Whatever is accomplished has much more meaning and value to the patient under these circumstances and affords him the necessary stimulus for the required maturational growth.

The Odyssey House techniques, though effective, have been difficult for many professionals to accept. They necessitate a relinquishing to the senior-patient population authority and responsibility, as well as according them respect. For it is respect for themselves and others that they must develop. This can be accomplished only through supervised, structured practice. The goal is positive, full-functioning independent people. It is difficult for many professionals to survive in the therapeutic community environment, because acceptance and status are accorded by the patients to a professional on the basis of his functioning as a real, warm, capable person, and not, on title per se. No one can—either patient or worker—demand respect, but each must earn it. Odyssey House, Inc., has an active program in the training and education of interested professionals.

Odyssey House is an integral part of the community medicine program at several New York City medical schools, such as New York University College of Physicians and Surgeons, Mount Sinai School of Medicine and the Albert Einstein School of Medicine. In Newark, Odyssey participates in programs at the New Jersey College of Medicine and Dentistry. Several senior medical students have taken their clerkships or elective time at Odyssey House.

In addition, various workers in the field of addiction, as well as related fields, frequently visit the House to take part in the activities. To date, four senior law students have written their final dissertations on the Odyssey House Method, as has one candidate for a degree in Social Work at the New School for Social Research. With the facilities of the Mother House, particularly the three-hundred-seat auditorium, Odyssey House is able to reach and influence many professionals and mental-health workers through formal lectures, symposia, small groups and actual participation in the work of the program.

The concept of earning position and emotional growth through positive social interaction is deeply engrained in all the work. The residents are continually evaluated and re-evaluated by each other and the staff. The patients are rated bi-weekly by each other and monthly by the staff. It is partially on the basis of these evaluations that a resident will move from one Level to another. Tuesday, the day of evaluation and phasing, is one of the most significant days of the week. This minute subdividing or hierarchy creates additional incentive for positive growth, in accordance with the socially acceptable norms. The desire of an individual resident to win the approval of his peers and favorable recognition from an authority figure is clearly demonstrable.

The residential day is structured from waking in the morning until bedtime. Little opportunity for leisure time is afforded. Between three to six hours a day is allotted to group meetings. Psychological testing is part of the general psychiatric evaluation.

Due to the severity of the psychopathology of drug addiction with its attendant social disruption to the lives of the addicts, it is felt that an in-residence setting is a prerequisite for successful treatment and that psychiatric intervention be intensive. All activities in the House are considered to be part of the therapy which is directed to returning the addict to normal living patterns. The residents are responsible for all the maintenance, laundry, cooking, office work, etc., which living demands of the rest of society. Nothing is done for them that they can do for themselves.

This serves three purposes: one, it teaches them that they can do it for themselves; two, it gives them future job training such as typing, switchboard operation, bookkeeping, printing, etc.; and last, but not least, it greatly reduces the cost of running a project for sixty persons.

In the past few years several new group forms have been developed, as well as the expansion and alteration of already existing methods. There has been liberal borrowing from Synanon, Daytop, Ramirez, Maslow, Berne, and others. The attitude has been to test anything that seemed to offer promise, to discard nothing without a trial, to alter as deemed necessary and to accept on an empirical basis, if positive changes occurred. There is a tacit commitment to being open, inventive and willing to learn from professional, ex-addict and resident alike.

Meeting forms that have evolved are as follows: business and general administrative meetings; concepts either visual or verbal; special visitors meetings, including the negative reinforcement one given by the Office of the Chief Medical Examiner, during which slides depicting data illustrating narcoticism and death are shown; regular group-therapy sessions with a psychiatrist and alternates without; supervision of ex-addict coleaders; encounters general, special, or marathon; orientation sessions for candidates-in, inquiries and probes; and phasing and evaluation with "feedback," to list only a few. It is impossible within the confines of this paper to describe the above in detail, but a representative from Odyssey House, if requested, would be glad to discuss any aspect of the program.

The transition from the protection of the resident unit, with its sixteen hours a day therapeutic structured environment, to functioning within the community at large, is accomplished in supportive stages. It is begun by a Level IV resident. This usually occurs after the resident has lived within the house for a period of ten months to a year, and he is deemed by the staff and his peers to have experienced sufficient behavioral change and growth to cope with the demands of the street. Within the Odyssey House Method, one can see a slow developmental process unfold with increasing responsibilities and privileges. The candidate-in does most of the physical work and has only motivational therapy. He must affirmatively answer the questions: "Do I accept myself as a person needing help?" In Level I, the number of therapy hours is doubled, with voting rights and a voice in the community afforded. He must learn the therapeutic techniques to help himself. He accepts that change will occur. In Level II, the shift from predominantly physical labor to office work is made with the development of certain vocational skills. He learns self-discipline by successfully completing tasks assigned to him. He is responsible for things. Supervised family visits are permitted. In Level III, authority and leadership toward other residents is undertaken. He is permitted to travel alone on house business and receive unopened mail, he has earned trust when within the confines of the house. He attends therapy not only as a participant but at times begins to assume coleadership. He can head a small department. He learns to accept authority by being an authority figure. He is responsible for people.

Re-entry is divided into three stages. The first is that of Level IV, then candidacy-out, and the last is discharge to outpatient status.

Level IV begins the exodus out or re-entry. A Level IV spends increasingly more time out of the house, meeting with the public, both formally at speaking engagements and informally whenever representing the house. He accompanies the Induction Supervisor in confronting and motivating the raw street addict in prisons, storefronts or hospital settings. He assists the Treatment Supervisors in the running of the house by supervising general departments, and by coleading candidate-in groups. He may with permission leave the house for personal reasons or business, and may occasionally spend an evening out. He has begun to assume authority not only over others within the house, but the even more difficult task over self in the world at large. After he is observed to be functioning at a mature level, he may be sponsored for the candidacy-out or the second stage of re-entry. He must affirmatively answer the question: "Will I leave the protective shelter of Odyssey House for the community at large?"

The inquiry-out is a meeting before his own peer group, the one above and the staff. Here, the proposed candidate-out discusses his future plans, presents a reintegration program and is questioned in detail as to the realities of the outside world in relation to himself. He must consider and choose alternatives in the social and work areas. If the plan is considered complete and realistic, he is voted a candidate-out. At this Level he may begin to put it into effect.

In the period of the candidacy-out, the resident acts upon and effects his reintegration plan. He may start school or formal vocational training. He must have obtained a high school equivalency diploma as a Level IV if he is not a high school graduate. He must hold employment outside of the field of Drug Addiction. He spends increasing time with his family, spending overnights or weekends with them. He may marry or divorce during this period. He must answer the question: "Will I succeed?" in the affirmative.

The candidate-out lives outside the program as an independent, functioning, useful citizen. He is salaried and a taxpayer. If he is employed at Odyssey House, his involvement with the program becomes more intense and demanding. If he works in other fields, his contact with Odyssey House is limited to weekly candidate-out groups in the evening which are geared by a physician or a Director of the Program. He continues to give up urine on a regular (but unscheduled) basis.

The last challenge to the candidate-out is the "probe-out," which constitutes discharge to outpatient status.

This is the most important evaluation in the program because once the candidate-out becomes an outpatient, he is considered independent of the program except for the five-year follow-up studies and occasional urinalysis. The only therapy requirement will be a monthly group session, led by the Executive Director, for approximately two to three years after discharge.

416

In about 30 per cent of the residents, problems of a neurotic nature are unmasked when the sociopathic-behavior patterns are lifted. Just prior to or at the time of re-entry, if one of these patients requests, he will be referred to individual therapy, but this must be in addition to the continuing group work. Individual work is permissible and desirable at this time. These patients now have the prerequisite anxiety to make them amenable to therapy, they can form the necessary transference relationships and they can control their behavior sufficiently to keep appointments. Once salaried, they will independently negotiate on a fee-for-service basis with the treating psychiatrist.

The last phase needs no further discussion as the participant, except for the reservations listed above, functions as any other member of society. He has become a full-functioning, independent, constructive member of society. Most have chosen lives independent of their past drug usage; others have chosen employment within the field of drug addiction and prevention. He may now be employed by Odyssey House.

The concept under which the community flourishes has been expressed in the following ways by its residents:

1. Positive growth occurs in the soil of self-knowledge which is best seen in the mirror of peer-group interaction.
2. We see ourselves best in the eye of a brother. Therefore, the brother must open his eyes and speak honestly about what he sees.
3. The basic concept of our program is continual open confrontation with the reality of ourselves, our peers and our environment.
4. By open confrontation, and the experience of the concern of others for me, for the first time in my life I have learned first to trust and then to cope positively. First I coped a little, now big.
5. And finally, it is the rule of three. By first doing, I proved that it can be done. The second doing followed with ease, and the third slipped unnoticed. I had a habit of living.

JUDIANNE DENSEN-GERBER, J.D., M.D.
EXECUTIVE DIRECTOR

Appendix II

H. R. ✳ 14676

To Establish National, Regional, and Local Awareness Advisory Councils in order to facilitate communication between the President and the people of the United States, and for other purposes.

Be it enacted by the Senate and House of Representatives of the United States of America in Congress assembled,
That this Act may be cited as the "Awareness Advisory Councils Act of 1972."

NATIONAL AWARENESS ADVISORY COUNCIL ESTABLISHED

Sec. 2. (a) In order to facilitate communication between the President and the people of the United States with respect to the programs and policies of the Federal Government, there is hereby established the National Awareness Advisory Council, composed of the National Council selected in accordance with the provisions of section 5 and the Executive Director.

(b) There shall be an Executive Director of the National Council who shall be appointed by the President, by and with the advice and consent of the Senate, for a term of six years. In making such appointment, subsequent to the initial appointment, the President is requested to give due consideration to recommendations submitted to him by the Regional Councils established pursuant to section 4. The Executive Director shall be the chief executive officer of the National Council and shall carry out the programs of the National Counil subject to the supervision and direction of the members of the National Council.

(c) There shall be a Deputy Executive Director of the National Council who shall be appointed by the President, by and with the advice and consent of the Senate, for a term of six years. In making such appointment, subsequent to the initial appointment, the President is requested to give due consideration to recommendations submitted to him by the Regional

418

Councils established pursuant to section 4. The Deputy Director shall perform such functions as the Executive Director, with the approval of the National Council, may prescribe, and be acting Executive Director during the absence or disability of the Executive Director or in the event of a vacancy in the office of Executive Director.

ESTABLISHMENT OF LOCAL AWARENESS COUNCILS

Sec. 3. (a) Any group of from four hundred to six hundred people eighteen years of age or older may form a Local Awareness Council by delivering a petition with their names inscribed to the Executive Director. No one shall be a member of more than one Local Awareness Council. The Executive Director of the National Council shall take whatever action he deems necessary and appropriate to encourage the establishment of Local Councils.

(b) Each Local Awareness Council may elect one of their number as a Regional Awareness Council. Election of a delegate shall require the affirmative vote of 75 per centum of the members of the Local Council. No member of a Local Council shall be eligible to vote who has not attended 75 per centum of the meetings of the Local Council. No delegate shall serve for longer than one year unless he is re-elected in like manner. No delegate shall serve for more than four consecutive terms.

REGIONAL AWARENESS ADVISORY COUNCILS ESTABLISHED

Sec. 4. (a) The Executive Director shall assist in the formation of Regional Councils consisting of one hundred duly elected delegates of Local Councils. Each delegate to a Regional Council shall spend not less than one quarter of his time at the Local Council level.

(b) It shall be the function of the Regional Council to discuss and select the problems, needs and desires of citizens of the constituent Local Councils which are of great concern and to prepare a report containing an agenda of matters of concern to that region for presentation to the National Awareness Advisory Council meeting.

SELECTION OF THE NATIONAL AWARENESS ADVISORY COUNCIL

Sec. 5. (a) Under such regulations as the Executive Director shall prescribe, once in each year each Regional Council shall by democratic procedures select one member to represent it on the National Council. The National Council shall in turn select from among its membership not more than forty individuals to serve on the National Awareness Advisory Council. Each member of the National Awareness Advisory Council and the National Council shall spend not less than one quarter of his time at the Local Council level.

(b) It shall be the function of the National Awareness Advisory Council to report to the President on matters raised by the Regional Councils, and prepare an agenda of matters which the President has furnished to the Council to be submitted for discussion to the National Council, Regional Councils and Local Councils.

(c) No member of the National Council or the National Awareness Advisory Council may serve for a period in excess of four consecutive years.

Sec. 6. (a) In order to carry out the objectives of this Act, the Executive Director is authorized to—

(1) prescribe such regulations as he deems necessary governing the manner in which his functions shall be carried out;

(2) receive money and other property donated, bequeathed, or devised, without condition or restriction other than that it be used for the purposes of this Act; and to use, sell, or otherwise dispose of such property for the purpose of carrying out the provisions of this Act;

(3) receive (and use, sell, or otherwise dispose of, in accordance with paragraph (2)) money and other property donated, bequeathed, or devised to the National Council with a condition or restriction, including a condition that the Executive Director use other funds of the National Council for the purposes of the gift;

(4) appoint and fix the compensation of such personnel as may be necessary to carry out the provisions of the Act without regard to the provisions of title 5, United States Code, governing appointments in the competitive service, and without regard to the provisions of chapter 51 and subchapter III of chapter 53 of such title relating to classification and General Schedule pay rates, but no individual so appointed shall receive compensation in excess of the rate prescribed for GS-18 in the General Schedule under section 5332 of title 5, United States Code;

(5) obtain the services of experts and consultants in accordance with the provisions of section 3109 of title 5, United States Code, at rates for individuals not to exceed $125 per diem;

(6) accept and utilize the services of voluntary and non-compensated personnel and reimburse them for travel expenses, including per diem, as authorized by section 5703 of title 5, United States Code;

(7) enter into contracts, grants or other arrangements, or modifications thereof to carry out the provisions of this Act;

(8) make advances, progress, and other payments which he deems necessary under this Act without regard to the provisions of section 3648 of the Revised Statutes, as amended (31 U.S.C. 529);

(9) rent office space in the District of Columbia; and

(10) make other necessary expenditures.

(b) The Executive Director shall prepare and submit to the President, for transmittal to the Congress, each year a report of the operations of the National, Regional, and Local Councils established pursuant to this Act, which report shall include such recommendations as he deems appropriate.

DEFINITIONS

Sec. 7. As used in this Act, the term—

(1) "Executive Director" means the Executive Director of the National Awareness Advisory Council;

(2) "Local Council" means a local awareness advisory council established pursuant to section 3;

(3) "Regional Council" means a regional awareness advisory council established pursuant to section 4;

(4) "National Council" means the national council established pursuant to sections 2 and 5;

(5) "National Awareness Advisory Council" means not more than forty members of the National Council established pursuant to sections 2 and 5.

COMPENSATIONS

Sec. 8. (a) Section 5313 of title 5, United States Code, is amended by adding at the end thereof the following new paragraph:

"(21) Executive Director, National Awareness Advisory Council."

(b) Section 5314 of title 5, United States Code, is amended by adding at the end thereof the following new paragraph:

"(58) Deputy Executive Director, National Awareness Advisory Council."

APPROPRIATIONS AUTHORIZED

Sec. 9. There are authorized to be appropriated such sums as may be necessary to carry out the provisions of this Act.

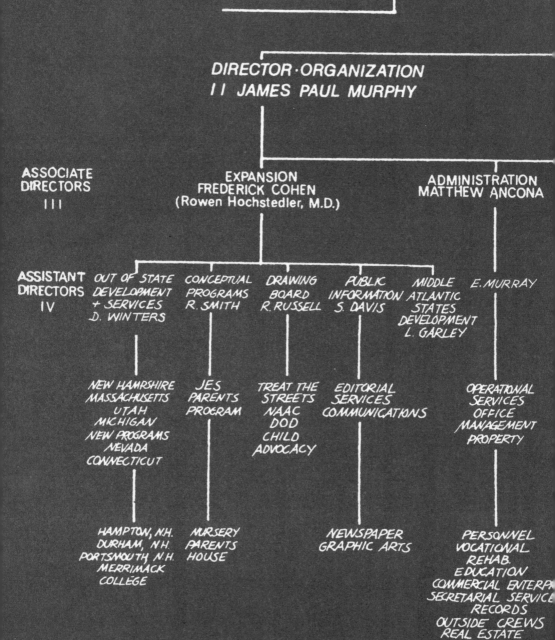

BOARD
CHAIRMAN · R

GENERAL COUNSEL
III MALCOLM WIENER

EXECUTIVE ASSISTANT
V MARGE BOLLEN

EXECUT
I DR. JUDIAN

DIRECTOR · ORGANIZATION
II JAMES PAUL MURPHY

ASSOCIATE
DIRECTORS
III

EXPANSION
FREDERICK COHEN
(Rowen Hochstedler, M.D.)

ADMINISTRATION
MATTHEW ANCONA

ASSISTANT
DIRECTORS
IV

OUT OF STATE
DEVELOPMENT
+ SERVICES
D. WINTERS

CONCEPTUAL
PROGRAMS
R. SMITH

DRAWING
BOARD
R. RUSSELL

PUBLIC
INFORMATION
S. DAVIS

MIDDLE
ATLANTIC
STATES
DEVELOPMENT
L. GARLEY

E. MURRAY

NEW HAMPSHIRE
MASSACHUSETTS
UTAH
MICHIGAN
NEW PROGRAMS
NEVADA
CONNECTICUT

JES
PARENTS
PROGRAM

TREAT THE
STREETS
NAAC
DOD
CHILD
ADVOCACY

EDITORIAL
SERVICES
COMMUNICATIONS

OPERATIONAL
SERVICES
OFFICE
MANAGEMENT
PROPERTY

HAMPTON, N.H.
DURHAM, N.H.
PORTSMOUTH N.H.
MERRIMACK
COLLEGE

NURSERY
PARENTS
HOUSE

NEWSPAPER
GRAPHIC ARTS

PERSONNEL
VOCATIONAL
REHAB.
EDUCATION
COMMERCIAL ENTERPI
SECRETARIAL SERVICE
RECORDS
OUTSIDE CREWS
REAL ESTATE